Neuro-Education:
A Translation From Theory to Practice

A brain-based teaching guide for the remediation of language literacy, behavior support, mental health, and academic challenges

Art by Alina Bugochuk

Edited by

CHRIS MERIDETH
University of Portland

ELLYN LUCAS ARWOOD
University of Portland

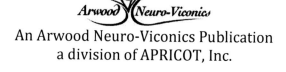

An Arwood Neuro-Viconics Publication
a division of APRICOT, Inc.

Formatting and Production
ALYSE ROSTAMIZADEH

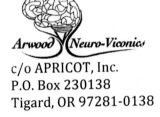

c/o APRICOT, Inc.
P.O. Box 230138
Tigard, OR 97281-0138

www.apricotclinic.com

Arwood, Ellyn Lucas.

Neuro-Education: A Translation from Theory to Practice/Ellyn Lucas Arwood, Chris Merideth. – 1st ed. – Tigard, Oregon: Arwood Neuro-Viconics © 2017

ISBN: 978-0-9679720-2-2

Sold and distributed by **APRICOT, Inc.**

Printed in the United States of America.

Print on Demand through Lightning Source, Inc.

Table of Contents

Acknowledgments

Chris would like to acknowledge his family and friends who helped proofread and view the content of this book in a new and fresh light. In particular, he would like to thank Tiffany for her many hours of assistance in fine-tuning the language of this anthology and helping to sharpen the intended communication. In addition, Ben and Emily provided valuable summaries of the methods used in each chapter. A hearty thank you to Alyse for tackling the formatting, to Michelle for providing excellent cartooning examples, and to Mabel for handling the production and distribution of the book. Lastly, Chris would like to send sincere appreciation to Ellyn for developing the theories and methods used in this book that have helped countless individuals learn, as well as for the opportunity to cultivate and edit this work. This book is dedicated to all readers who wish to expand their horizons about how we think about education and re-conceptualize how it is that children learn best.

Ellyn would like to thank all of you who have contributed to this compilation of work - authors of chapters, neuroeducation students who added content, students of the contributors, their friends and family members. A special thank you goes to Chris Merideth for his expertise and to Alyse Rostamizadeh for her production. And, thank you to those who continue to support a change in the educational paradigm to allow for our children and youth to learn to think deeply.

Introduction

There is an old adage that states that fish, being the aquatic and branchiate creatures that they are, cannot truly perceive the water that envelops the world around them, unless of course they were removed from this liquid medium and forced to survive without it. Only then, by being thrust out of water and onto land, for example, could they truly be able to see the building blocks of reality that made up their formerly aqueous environment. The journey that the authors in this collection share of learning how to incorporate neuroeducation theory into educational practice can be thought of as an awakening parallel to the metaphorical fish being thrust out of water. The transformation of each author's thinking, from learning to recognize the possibilities and limitations of our current educational system in the United States, to understanding how brain-based theory informs how children learn best, is no less than a paradigm shift in how we view the educator's role in the classroom.

This book provides a starting point for educators to learn the theories that make up neuroeducation and use these principles to transform their teaching practice. What exactly is neuroeducation, one might ask? The contemporary version of neuroeducation accepted across many academic institutions (sometimes referred to as Mind, Brain, Education Science) draws from the fields of neuroscience and cognitive psychology and aims to translate the research of these disciplines into cutting edge educational practices. This book is not a comprehensive view of the field, though it does draw from the successes achieved in brain-based learning. Readers who are curious about a complete history of the discipline can view either Tokuhama-Espinosa's 2011 book *Mind, Brain, and Education Science*, or Doris Brevoort's 2012 manual *A Guide to Neuroeducation for Teachers*. These resources will provide a more complete overview of the achievements made by numerous experts in the field. This new brain-based approach of dissecting learning from a scientific perspective is enthusiastically applauded by the main authors of this book; however, these authors lament the nearly complete absence of the study of language as a third theoretical discipline into the field of neuroeducation. Thus, it has not been factored in to any brain-based model of learning currently in the field today.

Why is the inclusion of language as a theoretical lens so important? The answer is so simple it is almost always overlooked. Language names our thinking, meaning that the language we use represents the underlying semantic thought processes happening in our minds. Language is the ultimate developmental product, unique only to humans, that represents both the biology of the brain and the workings of ephemeral cognition. It is only by viewing how language functions for an individual that we may truly know how they best acquire concepts and how their mind operates. This book, as of publication date, is the only known collection to include all three disciplines – neuroscience, psychology, and language – into one cohesive model of neuroeducation. The authors in this collection hope to convey just how transformational this third branch of knowledge – language – is to viewing the whole of education as greater than the sum of its parts.

As each contributing author comes from a background of education, this book makes fellow educators as its primary intended audience, though practitioners in other fields may certainly find the knowledge collected here insightful. Moreover, it is clear that readers from different backgrounds, neuroscientists, psychologists, counselors, parents, etc., may each interpret differently the academic theories underlying the methods proposed in this book. This is because we all bring with us our own schemas and assumptions about what learning is, and how we can best promote critical thinking in children. Having differing vantage points is healthy and leads to true interprofessional collaboration.

It is indisputable, however, that by using the Viconic Language Methods[1] proposed by Arwood's Neuro-Education Model, the authors collected here have unlocked levels of academic achievement not previously seen before in their struggling students. Therefore, regardless of any possible skepticism one may use to interpret the findings presented here, the results that these authors achieved speak for themselves. Throughout this collection of academic essays, case study examinations, and analyses of current educational practices, each author chronicles their own odyssey of understanding why using status quo pedagogy has not worked to promote student learning, and how the theories and methods proposed by Dr. Ellyn Arwood's Neuro-semantic Language Learning Theory[2] achieve results that frequently exceed expectations.

The authors' work compiled here represents a wide range of educational experience, from Pre-K to high school, from special needs to "neurotypical" populations, and includes diverse professional roles such as teachers, speech and language pathologists, and behavioral specialists. As a result, each author brings with them a rich background from their respective fields and illustrates the diversified populations to which neuroeducation principles may be applied. Efforts have been made to clarify terminology that may not be familiar to an educator outside of these fields. Nonetheless, it should be noted that the theories and methods presented in this anthology may be applied to working with any child, not just those who have special needs or those who struggle to learn.

Unit 1 begins with an introductory chapter exploring the history of the field of neuroeducation and dissecting the differences between Arwood's Neuro-Education Model and other brain-based learning theories currently used today. This unit introduces the rationale behind using neuroeducation theory to inform the educational methods that will be explored in units 2-4. In addition, Unit 1 contains a review of literature of brain-based learning undertaken by a recent doctoral graduate in neuroeducation studies. The author provides evidence from numerous primary source research studies in the fields of neuroscience, cognitive psychology, and language that support and substantiate each tenet of Arwood's Neuro-Education Model.

The three chapters in Unit 2 provide accounts of educators reversing the conventional wisdom of how children learn that has entrenched U.S. school systems for the past fifty years. On their journey toward the paradigm shift proposed by this book, each author shifts their own practice from teacher-directed pedagogy to learner-centered metacognitive strategies. In addition, these authors show how the teaching methods proposed by this work can provide a model of inclusion that can incorporate even the most diverse learners into a nonrestrictive classroom environment. As Dr. Bonnie Robb, a chapter contributor to this anthology says, "Children who know how to learn rarely exhibit social-emotional and behavioral problems in school."

The authors in Unit 3 delve into four case studies that document the successes of using neuroeducation inspired methodology with students who have previously languished in school. These chapters illustrate the tenet that true learning knows no boundaries. A smattering of insights from this unit includes: increasing a pupil's thinking also raises their social-emotional awareness; children do not need to learn how to read using sound-based methods; a child's behavior can become more pro-social if they can see in their mind's eye how their actions affect others; and the movement of the hand is a seldom explored method of entering raw information into the brain. These are just a few of the discoveries presented in this unit and represent the far-reaching potential of the ideas presented in this book.

Unit 4 zooms out to take a more "macro" view of some of the limitations of our current educational system including assumptions of how literacy must be taught, why students refuse

---

[1, 2] Arwood, 2011; See Unit 1 preface for more information

to use organizational tools that do not match the way that their mind operates, and how the system of phonics, as a whole, has disenfranchised countless students who do not learn to read using sound-to-letter correspondence. Possible next steps for this new, emerging, and exciting field are also explored here.

It should be noted that each chapter concludes with a brief summary section written collectively between the main authors of this book, as well as two post-graduate students studying neuroeducation at the University of Portland. These summary sections aim to help the contributing authors support their thinking with research terminology culled from the field of neuroeducation as well as viewing their findings from an academic perspective.

The purpose of these summary sections is twofold. Firstly, the practitioners presented here represent different proficiencies in understanding educational theory. They all use successful brain-based learning strategies in their teaching practice and achieve great results. It is important to summarize why these methods worked the way that they did so that future practitioners may feel less inhibited to try something new. Secondly, expounding on the theoretical tenets underpinning their analysis provides preciseness to their claims so that researchers and educators alike can further investigate these assertions if they would like to learn more.

A final concluding chapter is included to encapsulate many of the assertions of Arwood's Neuro-Education Model as well as explain "how" and "why" the students presented in this collection made the tremendous progress that they did. It should be noted briefly that each author received permission to catalog the student work included in this book and that all efforts have been made to erase identifying information of any of the learners portrayed here.

Finally, due to the relative newness of the academic theories presented in this anthology, the main authors would like to acknowledge that currently only a few publications exist today that reference Arwood's Neuro-Education Model as a primary source. The authors collected here document theories and use methods that have not yet been widely disseminated out into the fields of neuroscience, psychology, or education. Because of this, some scholars may question the origination and validity of the models and research contained within. The main authors of this anthology would respond that the power of a theory lies in the ability of its claims to be replicated in multiple settings and populations. In addition to the ten authors chronicled here, dozens and dozens of other practitioners have found success using these methods, though they may not have written up a formal case study, and therefore their results have not been included in this anthology.

Because these methods are new, they had not been previously used with students. Neuroeducation methodology, therefore, functions in this anthology as the newly introduced dependent variable when working with children. All of the educators who submitted chapters witnessed a wide variety of enduring growth in their students by exposing them to these methods. Because of the consistency of the findings, this book makes a strong case that the success these teachers found using these methods can indeed be replicated in a wide variety of educational settings and with a diverse set of student populations.

Having presented the research of the theories of neuroeducation at numerous conferences around the United States, including events geared specifically to neuroscientists and psychologists, the first two questions professionals pose are often: 1) "Why isn't this material published more widely?" and 2) "Where can I learn more about this particular model of Neuro-Education?" This book aims to provide a scholarly response to both inquiries. Accordingly, the publication of this anthology not only affords a cause for celebration, but also helps to challenge the research assumptions currently held in contemporary brain-based models of learning.

In the interim, before more publications in this field are finished, curious readers can learn more information about Arwood's Neuro-Education Model by browsing the references section at the end of the book. In particular, readers will be rewarded by referring to the dissertations of doctoral students[3] at the University of Portland who have recently graduated with an emphasis in neuroeducation studies. Many of these students spent three years finding primary research studies in neuroscience and cognitive psychology that validate the theories examined in this book. Furthermore, readers will also benefit from reviewing the tenets of the Neuro-semantic Language Learning Theory (NsLLT) as proposed in Arwood's seminal book *Language Function* (2011). Much of the methodology and educational rationale explored in this collection stems directly from the tenets of this theory.

Our hope is that this book will inspire teachers, counselors, parents, paraeducators, and anyone else working directly with children to start thinking from the perspective of their pupils to understand what it is that *they* need in order to learn best. Making the full paradigm shift can be arduous and can take time. Climbing out of the metaphorical water of our current educational practice is the first brave step.

Chris Merideth, M.Ed.
Co-author, Editor, and Chapter Contributor
March 2017

---

[3] See: Robb (2016); Green-Mitchell (2016); Xiang-Lam (2016)

Unit 1: Developing and Explicating Arwood's Neuro-Education Theory

Preface

Unit 1 begins with a chapter explaining the uniqueness of Arwood's Neuro-Education Theory and how it differs from other models in the field of Mind, Brain, and Education science. This first chapter is written by one of the main authors of this book and namesake of the corresponding theory, Dr. Ellyn Arwood, a professor at the University of Portland, Oregon and a speech and language pathologist with over forty-five years of experience working with learners from a wide variety of backgrounds. Over the course of her career, Dr. Arwood has cultivated an understanding of the study of language as an educational discipline that is unmatched in the field today.

This deep apperception of language has culminated in creating the Neuro-semantic Language Learning Theory (NsLLT, Arwood, 2011), a model of learning that provides a pivotal cornerstone of neuroeducation methodology and that significantly differs from the conventional wisdom presented by the specialties of neuroscience and cognitive psychology. Some readers may be familiar with the similar idea of *linguistic relativity* (often incorrectly referred to as the "Sapir-Whorf Hypothesis"). In its strongest iteration, linguistic relativity states that the language one uses determines one's thinking (Hickman, 2000). Others, however, argue that language is independent of thinking, and that one's ability to think precedes our ability to communicate (Pinker, 1994). In essence, the NsLLT states that both ideas may in fact be correct. Language is indeed separate from thought, but it *represents* the thoughts that we conjure. And, language *determines* our thinking because what enters into the brain *changes* the brain. In this sense, the NsLLT is neither a refutation nor a substantiation of the most well known ways of looking at language. It is an entirely new theory that describes language as the mediating factor (or glue) that ties together child maturation, social development, behavior, communication, and human thinking (Arwood, 2011).

Because all of the contributing authors of this anthology utilize pedagogy directly inspired by the NsLLT, a brief overview of its significance is presented here. The Neuro-semantic Language Learning Theory posits that we are not born with an innate knowledge of how to use language; rather, we must acquire the ability to use language through a series of small, incremental steps that are part of a developmentally complex process that starts at birth and progresses throughout the rest of our lives (Arwood, 2011). Once acquired, our language functions to connect us to our world through our thinking. In essence, we think utilizing the meaningful patterns and concepts that we have learned throughout our language acquisition. As our ability to synthesize more and more complex language increases, so too does our ability to think at higher and more complicated levels of cognition (Arwood, 2011).

The Neuro-semantic Language Learning Theory argues, "language is learned as a set of neuro-semantic steps" (Arwood, 2011, p. 36) that initially starts with the input of new information into our being. The only known method for us to receive such new information is through our sensory receptors (Arwood, 2011). The eyes and the ears capture sensory information that will allow us to acquire language. After all, we predominantly communicate with others using auditory and visual language structures.

Beginning at birth, our brain connects us to our sensory receptors and establishes a feedback system that continuously processes raw inputted information (Arwood, 2011). As we begin to experience certain sensory input over and over again, our brain starts to recognize patterns and begins to organize these patterns into clusters of semantic meaning (Arwood, 2011). These meaningful patterns overlap, and as new information adds itself to already established older chunks of meaning, our brain begins to form larger structures or circuits of images known as concepts. It is by attaching new information to older recognizable patterns that we acquire conceptual meaning to new information to layers of overlapped patterns.

Therefore, learning in the brain is defined in the Neuro-semantic Language Learning Theory as following a unique four-tier model that progresses through a series of discernable acquisition stages. The first two tiers of this model have already been explained: raw sensory data (light waves, sound waves) input into our sensory perception systems and overlap to form meaningful patterns. Examples of these patterns in children would be committing new vocabulary words to memory, memorizing how to write one's name, imitating the dance moves of the hokey pokey, and reciting the pledge of allegiance, just to name a few. Once these patterns have been acquired in the brain, children can use them in our oral conversations, in their writing, and in their actions.

From the perspective of much literature in neuroscience and cognitive psychology, learning has fulfilled its course in the brain during these first two tiers (Anderson, 2010; Baars & Gage, 2010; Tallal, Merzenich, Miller, & Jenkins, 1998). The patterns have been stored in different categories of long-term memory and can therefore be pulled back up by the mind at any time for our use. This two-tier model is called "input-output," and for many scientists, this is sufficient evidence of learning. After all, neuroscientists define learning as a permanent change in cellular structure (Baars & Gage, 2010). Because a permanent change has taken place in the brain's cellular structures, they assert, learning must have occurred.

Many teachers in the field of education use methods that are inspired by this two-tier model without even knowing it. When a teacher asks students to fill-in-the-blanks on a worksheet, complete a multiple choice test, call and respond to spelling rules, or recite multiplication tables, they are often seeking a correct "output" answer from their pupils. A correct answer may in fact be evidence of true learning. But, just as likely, the student may have pulled stored facts from memory without analyzing them. Often, students simply borrow and repeat the language a teacher has given them because they know getting the right answer will lead to positive reinforcement. However, if a student does not use their own language to explain their thinking, we cannot truly know if they understand the material or are just imitating correct responses (Arwood, 2016; Brown, 2012; Robb, 2016).

To allow students to develop such higher order thinking abilities, we must allow their brains to develop the third and fourth tiers of the NsLLT: concepts and language. Concepts form in the brain when patterns connect to other patterns and cluster together creating circuits of access to those connected patterns. Neurobiologically, we can see fiber tracts of vast connected neurons (called circuits) that wire together in the brain (Hebb, 1949; Linden, 2007). When enough of these circuit clusters form even more dense fiber connections with other circuits, they form complex networks of interconnected cells in the brain. Researchers can now follow electrochemical impulses as they cascade all around the regions of grey and white matter in the brain (Pulvermüller et. al., 2006). Beautiful and fascinating images are emerging from laboratories of networks of neurons that are color-coded by how frequently these cells fire together. Neuroscientists are starting to develop intriguing anatomical representations of what it might look like for the brain to "think" (Pulvermüller, 2013).[4]

So, researchers are discovering exciting new evidence of biological circuits and networks; but, they are struggling to understand how these circuits and networks fit into the default two-tier model explained above. This newer neuroscientific evidence suggests that the brain does not operate solely in an input-output fashion, but few theories exist that can account for these intricate developments, outside of Arwood's NsLLT, which uses a third and fourth tier of learning to explain such phenomena. As a result, the significance of many findings in cognitive psychology and neuroscience are constrained. That is, scientists continue to struggle to find a theory that incorporates and explicates evidence of circuits and networks in a meaningful way.

When viewing the scope of such evidence, it is this author's opinion that Arwood's Neuro-semantic Language Learning Theory provides a much more plausible explanation for how the brain processes information. Only the NsLLT connects the evidence of circuits and networks to the idea that language is the mediator that drives this neurobiological development. Language names our thinking, and the language one uses to function represents the brain's underlying semantic processing. As a result, language acquisition parallels brain development in the same discernible, developmental stages explored in this book.

Therefore, language represents the brain's acquisition of the connected semantic circuits and networks to think and communicate. According to Arwood, language represents the "underlying development of concepts" (2011, p. 53). The more developed concepts become, the more language abilities evolve. Additionally, the richer and more complex language becomes, the more advanced thinking becomes. Arwood connects language and thinking abilities by saying, "because language represents cognition, then language function represents how well a person thinks and therefore acts" (2011, p. 54). When a learner's level of thinking increases, then language function allows the learner to use that thinking in more complex ways.

Over her forty-five years of experience working with struggling students, Dr. Arwood has also developed a methodology that aims to translate the brain-based theories of neuroeducation into a series of teaching practices. These strategies are called *Viconic Language Methods* (VLMs) and can be used with any child or adult who thinks with a visual learning system (such as making pictures in his/her head, retrieving a photographic memory, etc.) In addition to studying neuroeducation theory, all ten authors compiled here have received training in how to incorporate VLMs into different educational settings, such as classrooms, counseling sessions, speech and language therapy, and schools for the Deaf/Hard of Hearing populations. This book provides numerous examples of how educators have incorporated VLMs in their work and attempts to walk the reader through how they could apply these strategies into their own practice.

Unit 1 continues with Chapter 2, which is a review of literature and a case study written by a recent graduate of the University of Portland with a doctorate in neuroeducation studies. The author, Carol Xiang-Lam, examines each claim of the Neuro-semantic Language Learning Theory in detail and provides numerous primary source research studies in the fields of neuroscience, cognitive psychology, linguistics, and education that validate these claims. Because the field of neuroeducation encompasses such a wide swath of knowledge in each of the connected disciplines, it can be daunting for a layperson to comb through the literature themselves. Moreover, in order to read articles in each of these subject areas a person must understand a series of complex terminology and suppositions that are often only understood by practitioners in that field. Therefore, the work of authors such as Xiang-Lam provides a dual

---

[4] For examples, see National Geographic (2014) – *Secrets of the Brain*

purpose: 1) it can point researchers to the scientific evidence used to substantiate a theory used in education, and 2) it can explain that evidence to individuals who may not be scientists themselves.

This work illuminates the point that many experts (e.g. Brevoort, 2012) in the field of neuroeducation/Mind, Brain, Education science argue is the biggest strength of this discipline: its ability to translate scientific evidence from obtuse language to a concrete vocabulary that makes sense to educators – most of whom are not scientists. The second most important strength of approaching the study of neuroeducation as an educator is that we are the ones who have spent the most amount of time working directly with students and therefore know what will be most relevant to them as a consumer of knowledge. Through witnessing countless hours of how students behave in a wide variety of learning situations, we are best able to discern whether certain brain-based methods and recommendations are worthy of trying, or are merely hype produced in an attempt to convince us to buy a product.

In sum, the scope of knowledge that this anthology aims to translate is limited to understanding the principles of the brain and mind that inform us how children learn best and how they can become pro-social members of society. However, it is also true that this scope is vastly complex in its aim, as human thinking and behavior are arguably the most complicated processes created by the eons of evolution. Somewhere within the colossal interconnectedness of the estimated 100 billion neurons of the human brain lies the key to understanding how our cognition works. But, it may be many more decades before neuroscientists have cataloged every cell in the human brain and deciphered their nexus and function. Until then, as informed practitioners we must rely on the best hypothesis of how human thinking occurs to inform the methods we use in the classroom. The authors of this collection believe that the Neuro-semantic Language Learning Theory provides the most conceivable explanation of learning that exists today. Ultimately, however, readers must look at all of the evidence and decide for themselves. After all, the fields of science and education are not so different, as the study of both requires the learner to be an active participant and continue to refine their own thinking through the language that they acquire.

Chris Merideth

Chapter 1

Why Use Neuroscience to Inform Educational Practice?

Ellyn Lucas Arwood, Ed.D., CCC-SLP

Abstract

In this chapter, the author introduces Arwood's Neuro-Education Model as a theory of learning that draws from the fields of neuroscience, cognitive psychology, and language. This theory is contrasted against different iterations of brain-based learning models used at other universities, institutions, and publications. In particular, the inclusion of language as a lens through which to view primary research in the sciences is recognized as a unique hallmark of this model and provides the impetus for the author to upend much of the conventional wisdom about learning that has been shared throughout decades of inquiry in the fields of neuroscience, psychology, and education. In Arwood's Neuro-Education Model, language names human thinking; that is, the language one uses to communicate represents the deep semantic ideas that their mind is processing. In addition, all human language can be separated into auditory and visual properties. English consists mainly of auditory features while other languages such as ASL and Mandarin rely heavily on visual components to facilitate communication. The author cites decades of research that illustrates that visual thinkers who make pictures in their heads can often struggle with the sound-based nature of English. In this chapter, the author proposes a manner of translating the auditory properties of English into visual characteristics that the minds of visual thinking students can more easily acquire.

About the Author

Ellyn Lucas Arwood has been a speech-language pathologist, educator, and special educator for over forty-five years and is currently a professor at the University of Portland in the School of Education. The author of eight textbooks including *Language Function: An Introduction to Pragmatic Assessment and Intervention for Higher Order Thinking*, numerous articles, chapters, and monographs, Arwood is well respected and a prolific presenter in the area of learning and language. Her development of assessment methods and instructional strategies for children and adults has positively influenced the lives of thousands of individuals, both nationally and internationally.

Introduction

Congress declared the 1990s as the decade of the brain (e.g. Cacioppo & Berntson, 1992). With this declaration, micro- and macro-investigations began in neuroscience, particularly in the application of neuroscience in cognitive psychology, the socio-cultural effects of neuroscience, and policy aimed at brain research. Since the 1950s, the reductionist approach

10

(breaking down the whole into parts) was used as the basic scientific model of research, which in neuroscience meant examining the minutest detail of the brain's anatomy with the hope of understanding the brain function as a whole. For instance, whole teams of researchers would dissect and analyze one region of the brain, perhaps the cingulate gyrus, and hypothesize what purpose this structure played in overall cognition. These minute details are then sometimes applied directly to education resulting in misconceptions or neuromyths about the brain. As an example, neuroscientists inspired by the principles of behaviorism believe that all learning can be defined within an input-output model, where a student shows true "learning" when they repeat back an answer exactly in the same manner in which the educator modeled. In education, reductionism is used to teach students an idea that has been broken into small parts because this is felt to be the best way to ensure learning. This tenet of behaviorism is still practiced in classrooms across the United States. Although reductionist methods are pervasive in the current educational culture, there are researchers who question the efficacy of reductionism for teaching and learning (Foster, 2013; McLeod, 2008; Newkirk, 2009; Poplin, 1988; Robb, 2016). These researchers believe more than an input-output model of neuroeducation is needed to translate brain research into effective educational practices.

Historical Context to Neuroeducation

This reductionist method of breaking down the brain into minute regions opened up basic science discoveries starting at the smallest level of function, though often in non-human models. In fact, most of our understanding of neuroscience comes from studies of animal populations. For example, the genetic mapping of the drosophila (fruit fly) in the 1990s provided a solid description of specific gene functions applicable to understanding gene mechanisms in humans. However, such details about a drosophila did not seem directly applicable to an educator's practice of teaching content or skills to children or adults.

There also emerged just as many macro-applications, where basic neuroscience discoveries were widely, and almost directly, applied to education. These macro-applications of neuroscience concepts were translated into education, which opened the door for many neuromyths to develop. For example, neuroscientists who explored brain neuroanatomy attempted to define the functions of human brain regions. An early discovery showed differences in function between the left and right hemispheres of the human brain. When educators applied this knowledge of functional differences between the two hemispheres to educational practices, educators treated students as if they had two brains, a right brain interested in the arts and a left brain interested in analytical language like the law. Such a macro-application of neuroscience to education resulted in "right-brained" and "left-brained" activities and lessons. This application suggested that there existed two independent hemispheres; even though the brain functions more holistically. The resulting application of this macro-analysis of neuroscience was a basic neuromyth. In fact, humans use both hemispheres of their brain in a synergistic manner, meaning that information travels rapidly back and forth between the hemispheres during cognitive processing. Interconnected, synergistic brains operate efficiently because the whole of the brain is greater than the sum of its individual parts (Arwood, 2014; Brevoort, 2012, Gallistel & Matzel, 2013, Levine, 2000).

More often, these macro-analyses would end up in the educator's "must do" toolbox. So, the educator would attend workshops, professional development sessions, and read numerous articles and books about how to apply such research regarding the "left brain" and "right brain" findings towards student education. Even forms of assessment such as inventories to determine who was "left-brained" or "right-brained" were developed in order to set up data collection for educational lessons.

Eventually, this neuromyth, like most neuromyth-based educational translations, would not result in more effective practices; consequently, the educators would default back to their typical assumptions of pedagogy for a particular grade and age. Such new applications of brain research to educational practice stirred up a great deal of hype but did little to change the thinking of the educators. In other words, the neuroscience discovered about the brain and then translated directly into the pedagogy or art of teaching did little to help educators actually master the science of learning. The work that the neuroscience community provided during this time did not change the underlying assumptions of how humans think, and thus the educational translations they provided about how humans learn continued to be insufficient.

By the end of the 1990s, brain research piqued educators' interests. There was a Mind, Brain, Education (MBE) movement in several locations credited to the Harvard Graduate School of Education, the Tokyo Initiative in Neuroscience and Education, and the Organization for Economic Cooperation and Development (OECD) in Paris. In 2004, the International Mind, Brain, and Education Society (IMBES) was founded to join biology, cognitive neuroscience, and education together into a translational field. The authors of the first article of the IMBES journal asked the question "Why Mind, Brain, and Education?" (Fischer, Daniel, Immordino-Yang, Stern, Bator, & Koizumi; 2007). In their summary, they suggested that perhaps the best of what we know about learning and development may not just come from science research, but may also come from examining educational practices. They concluded, "Research in practice settings is essential for the field of Mind, Brain, and Education, in the same way that research in medical settings is essential for knowledge about medical practice (p. 1)." In other words, educators must research the applications in practice in their field just as rigorously as scientists do in their own profession.

At the same time these organizations were developing, educational leaders were demanding an understanding of how the brain absorbs information in education. James Comer, Founder of the Yale Child Study Center School Development Program, and Robert Pianta, Curry School of Education at the University of Virginia, posted a statement published in the Boston Globe (October 5, 2010) that teachers do not know how children "really learn." They called for more knowledge about how the brain operates to be disseminated to educational professionals. These developmental specialists also cited a growing body of research that they believe educators tend to ignore in their practices. One of these growing bodies of research is in the neuroscience of how children actually learn. They felt that teacher preparation programs focused too heavily on developing pedagogical practices and not enough on how children acquire information through their own cognitive processes.

Comer and Pianta concluded their editorial with the concept that if educators' mission is really to help students learn, then educators should know the neuroscience of how the brain actually learns on a neurobiological level. This call to arms marked a shift in the emerging field of neuroeducation from relying on the hype of neuromyths to concentrating on the neuroscience research that informs us about brain circuitry and function.

Language Adds a Third Lens to Neuroeducation Studies

The historically ineffective translation of the minute details of non-human science into macro-applications that resulted in neuromyths, along with the need for educators to understand something about how the brain learns, suggests a need for integration between the fields of neuroscience and cognitive psychology. Moreover, it is time for educators to begin looking at teaching and learning through a lens that considers the assumptions underlying both these fields, namely, the brain science and the resulting mind applications. This new lens, this new translational tool to bridge the gaps between neuroscience and cognitive psychology, is the study of language.

Language is necessary for research scientists to explain their data. And, language is necessary for the learner to understand how the science pertains to human functions of the mind such as listening, speaking, reading, writing, viewing, thinking, and calculating. Without a thorough understanding of language – what it is and isn't, how language is acquired, and what the relationship is between language and other forms of human learning – the translation of neuroscience and cognitive psychology is restricted to the interpreter's thinking about the scientist's data. In other words, a researcher's claims will only be as profound as the theoretical background they bring with them to interpret their data.

As previously expressed, the default lens of interpretation has been to translate findings from neuroscience directly to educational practice, and this has produced mixed results at best. However, an educator who understands language function, along with cognitive psychology research about learning and how the brain learns, is more likely to create effective methods that consider the variables involved in learning. Some of these variables pose intriguing questions, such as "Does the learner turn input directly into thinking?" or "Is conceptual thinking different for all learners." The research on language provides the connection that has historically been missing between the analysis of the mind and the study of the brain. In this way, using a language lens helps educators understand how language mediates a child's academic and social development.

There is a plethora of literature about learning and language available to the educator. Likewise, there is a huge need for educators to improve student learning. Connecting the available literature about learning to the need to improve student learning through a lens that considers the learners' levels of language, their levels of learning, their specific needs for input to create learning, and how to maximize the learners' abilities to learn, requires a model that incorporates these learning variables: language, cognitive psychology, neuroscience, and education. Historical models of Mind, Brain, Education (M.B.E.) have struggled to remain relevant in educational practice today because they have not utilized the study of language to guide the interpretation of their research findings. Indeed, many educational practitioners studying the brain under the M.B.E lens have often been left with more questions than answers when interpreting research findings (Tokuhama-Espinosa, 2011).

Even with a decade of the Mind-Brain initiative, there still exists the question of what theoretical model to use to interpret and translate literature between multiple fields of study. Put another way, many researchers wonder what the standards for neuroeducation are, who sets these standards, and how are they determined, as well as what are the biases and the underlying current assumptions of this new area of study. Clarity of the efficacy of this field's research is sought by many organizations such as IMBES, across many programs such as the Transformational Classroom project, and across international partners.

The authors of the chapters in this book have in fact learned something about how the brain learns and have also learned about the role of language in different types of learning activities. In the process of connecting micro-data (such as how we process input through the senses into concepts) with macro-interpretations about application across all forms of literacy and the teaching of content, each chapter contributor has applied the theory of one specific neuroeducation model into their educational practice, collected artifacts of student learning under this model, and analyzed these artifacts to show growth as a professional in the field. Specifically, the model of neuroeducation used in this book looks at neuroscience and cognitive psychology research through a language lens. Each contributor provides the reader with self-evident practices of "what works" when an effective model of neuroeducation is applied to the contributor's setting or situation.

Overall, the purpose of this book is twofold: 1) to propose an effective model of neuroeducation for better translation of mind-brain research into practice; and 2) to help close the aforementioned translational gap that occurs between theory stemming from science, and practice stemming from "what works," or more poignantly, what hasn't worked.

Why do we need a Neuroeducation Model for Improved Student Learning?

Any translation of research assumes basic biases or premises in constructing the research and in interpreting the findings. Thus, a neuroeducation model must account for these biases when translating the research into practice. For example, if a neuroscientist and a cognitive psychologist were to study struggling readers, they might assume that the ability to connect sounds and letters into oral fluency is what defines reading. This might be true for a phonological or sound-based approach to oral reading, but most readers don't use sounds and letters for understanding concepts (Arwood, 2011). Furthermore, there are those people who are deaf and read well without ever hearing the sounds (Arwood, Ormson, Kaulitz, & Brown, 2013).

Such initial beliefs or assumptions spring from an introspection methodology, where an adult thinks about what parts need to be added together to teach a task such as reading. A reader needs to be able to connect sounds and letters in order to recognize the written words on a page. This introspection or use of one's mind (Theory of Mind; ToM) results in biases and assumptions that may not be semantically accurate with research from other bodies of literature. Put another way, an adult's mind functions very differently from that of a child. This is because an adult has already acquired language to name their thinking about an idea, whereas a child is learning that same language slowly through a multitude of examples and experiences. Because adults think in a functionally different manner than children, we cannot rely solely on the adults' minds to introspect what a child needs.

Therefore, finding a model or a set of standards in neuroeducation continues to be of significance to those studying the field. This search for an effective model resulted in a project, the Delphi survey by Tokuhama-Espinosa in 2008, which used 20 international experts from six different countries to look at a typical neuroeducation model. These authors embarked on this research for the purpose of creating a model that would translate neuroscience directly into educational practice. From the Delphi work, where the authors reviewed publications, training textbooks, and online resources, came the notion that neuroeducation should use the standards of the parent fields of neuroscience, psychology, and education. Furthermore, the Delphi study culminated in a series of goals and tenets (Tokuhama-Espinosa, 2010) for the academic discipline of Mind, Brain, and Education science.

Interestingly, these goals followed the same underlying assumptions about teaching and learning that are found in education. Much current research (e.g.: Robb, 2016; Green-Mitchell, 2016; Poulson, 2017) illustrates that educators typically utilize the behaviorist model of the 1950s to guide their practice even to this day. For example, the majority of the focus of teacher preparation programs is to provide teachers with teaching strategies that will allow their students to complete a variety of academic material. However, what is not overtly expressed is that many of these teaching strategies fall under the input-output model of learning such as fill-in-the-blank worksheets, multiple choice tests, imitation of patterns, memorization, etc. Educators use these practices because they have been deemed "evidenced-based." But, do these practices provide evidence of bona fide long-term learning in children? This author would question such claims.

In sum, many teachers still continue to use behaviorist methods (direct instruction, positive reinforcement, etc.) without knowing the underlying theory that guides their practice. This is an example of a macro-analysis approach: the assumption is that all teaching directly results in learning. The teacher teaches, therefore the students learn. This is a simple input-output model. If this is the assumption, then what is the neuroscience that supports this model? More must be done to bring these assumptions to light, so that teachers can understand the underlying biases about learning that their practices contain.

This author argues that translational applications are most effective when they pull literature from several disciplines into an effective and accurate interpretation of the brain research. However, as previously mentioned, the majority of the findings presented by the Mind, Brain, Education movement have attempted to translate directly from one science to education. This has often resulted in making theoretical claims about human learning that are scantly supported by evidence of actual humans.

For example, much of the body of research in the field of neuroscience is gathered from non-human sources such as fruit flies, rodents, and apes. The basic neuroscience model of defining learning comes from these species. Neuroscience research on non-human models suggests that sensory input forms perceptual patterns (sensory integration) in a direct response to a stimulus. When interpreting this research in terms of educational findings to humans, neuroscientists default to an input-output model of learning, in that the teacher provides a stimulus, the student provides a response, because this is easy to demonstrate scientifically. Therefore, there is a parallel model between the education assumption about pedagogy (input-output teaching) and basic neuroscience (input-output learning). This input-output model is a simple teaching model. The question remains, however, does it explain learning in humans? If teaching and learning are not the same, could there be other brain levels of learning, above and beyond the sensory integration levels? In other words, are there other levels of structures and functions within the human brain besides those we see in animal models?

The answer is yes. There are structures of the brain unique to humans that function beyond the sensory integration levels of cellular messages relayed and interconnected at the lower levels of the central nervous system (CNS). These structures include pathways and circuits as well as networks. So, why not use these other higher brain levels to create a model of human learning that is different than that of other animals? Could human learning actually be more complicated than a two-tier input-output model?

Neuroscientists are working to determine the functions of these higher, more synergistic, levels of the CNS. The most cutting edge research that uses imaging technology to capture the brain as it learns in real-time shows great promise to revolutionize our conception of how human learning is unique. However, the theories neuroscientists use to explain human thinking have not kept up with the advancements of their technology (Baars, 2010). As a result, findings in this field are often interpreted using outdated models of cognition. This often results in scientists making conclusions about educational practice that are too far-reaching or neglect to factor in processes such as human metacognition (Anderson, 2010). More on this phenomenon will be explored in the conclusion to this book.

In the meantime, is there anything in the field of cognitive psychology that would allow a window into understanding about what these brain structures do? Since research in cognitive psychology considers human behavior as a product of the mind, then what are the human functions that reflect the mind that can be examined? The most complex behavior of the mind is language. Human language is different than any other animal's communication system. For example, apes communicate and use tools in their lives, but it does not compare to human's capacity for language. Primates have been known to memorize up to 2,000 written words and 1,000 signed words (Fischer, 1999). As a result, they may be able to have primitive "conversations" with adult caregivers, including multiple back and forth exchanges. However, the brains of apes have evolved with an evolutionary linguistic ceiling, so to speak, of never progressing past highly restricted communication (Eysenck, 2000). Apes do not demonstrate sophisticated planning for the future, for example, nor do they use tools in continuously sophisticated ways that match human's abilities (Wallman, 1992). Because of these limitations, their brains will not evolve over time to produce thinking that rivals human cognition (Arwood, 2014).

If a chimpanzee sees bananas in a tree, the chimp will find a stick and pull down the bananas, eat the bananas, leave the stick, and move on. If another bunch of bananas is needed, the chimp finds a new stick. But, a human's communication system is much more involved. The human will use the stick, repurpose the stick, refine the stick for easier use, keep the stick, create a case for it, etc. The function of the human's learning system has evolved into a refined system of symbolizing experiences into artifacts, such as speaking, reading, writing, art, music, and dance. In addition, we have improved the quality of our lives through transportation, tools, housing shelters, clothing options, etc. These artifacts of the human experience have been made possible by millions of years of the brain changing due to human ingenuity and innovation. The brain changes based off of what is inputted into the brain (Anderson, 2010; Arwood, 2014; Baars & Gage, 2010). Moreover, all of these higher order human acts involve the development of language as that symbolizing product of human brain learning.

Surface vs. Deep Structures of Language

Language on the surface level is viewed as a set of structures, such as words, parts of speech, and grammar. These are specific to the conventions of a particular language; so, an English speaker uses the structures commonly found in English. However, it is well documented in the literature that these structures are only the surface forms of language (e.g. Bruner, 1975; Carroll, 1964; etc.). They do not represent the underlying semantics or deep structures of language. The deep structures, such as learning to be literate and self-aware, are acquired through the child's neurobiological learning system (Arwood, 1983; Chomsky, 1968; Clark, 1977). So, what are the acquisition processes for these deep structures of language?

The acquisition of language (deep structures) is different than the study of the developed products of the surface structures. Studying the surface structures provides the knowledge of the language. More importantly, understanding how a child acquires the deep semantics onto which the surface structures map is central to understanding all levels of learning. In other words, understanding language acquisition provides the window into how the human neurobiological learning system functions. This acquisition process is well researched from understanding the relationship between and among signs and their symbols (e.g. Peirce, 1800s); to understanding the way meaning is acquired through social functions (e.g. Bruner, 2006; Dewey, 1910; Vygotsky, 1962) to understanding the semantics that underlie language (McCawley, 1976).

Furthermore, neuroscience has well defined the properties of the human neurobiological system. For example, neuroscience has gone beyond the original mapping of regions and their functions to understand how cellular structures interconnect to form circuits and networks. Connecting this neurobiological data with what language does for the human mind assists in developing a translational model: the new model of neuroeducation explored in this book. Neuroscience provides the understanding of what the neurological system forms and learns; language function research connects the neurobiological system to what the human is capable of learning; and cognitive psychology literature helps define what the mind learns. The findings of these three disciplines inform one another and triangulate to form a new branch of study, neuroeducation, that specializes in analyzing scientific truisms to determine how children learn best.

Understanding that humans use their brains to learn to think and become literate, coupled with the notion that the mind is the brain's product, helps create a model of learning that shifts the biases and assumptions from a reductionist input-output model to one that is much more dynamic and considers the human potential to learn. This proposed model of learning is not a direct translation of neuroscience research into educational practice. Instead, it uses an intersection of brain research (neuroscience) with research about the mind (cognitive psychology) and knowledge about language function. The proposed model used by the chapter contributors in this book is referred to as Arwood's Neuro-Education Model.

Arwood's Neuro-Education Model

The neuroeducation model used in this book by the contributors was designed out of Arwood's 45 years of practice. Arwood, a speech-language pathologist, received formal education in cognitive psychology, neuro-anatomy/physiology, and language. In 1981, an editor for a medical publishing company asked her to write about the methods she used with students who struggled with language acquisition. Many of these students had developmental disorders, such as autism, ADHD, learning disabilities, intellectual disabilities, syndromes, or other developmental delays.

When Arwood published her first book, *Semantic and Pragmatic Language Disorders,* readers wanted to know the theory that she used to support her educational methods working with these populations. So, in 1983, she published another book, *Pragmaticism: Theory and Application* about her philosophical beliefs related to the theory behind learning language. Pragmaticism, a term coined by Charles S. Peirce, refers to the "whole is greater than the parts." In this way, Arwood suggested that the whole brain functions synergistically, and its function is greater than the addition of parts. This principle has been verified by modern brain research (e.g. Pulvermüller, 2005). In other words, knowing the neuro-anatomy of the brain and its cells is important; but, how all of the parts work together is important for understanding human learning.

This Pragmaticism philosophy was further supported by Arwood's research with practitioners and clients. In fact, Arwood often worked with clients that had not found success under conventional instruction; however, after utilizing her practices, these learners were able to make great progress using methods that considered the intersectionality of how a learner thinks coupled with the learner's level of language provided effective, inclusive, literacy methods (Arwood, 1991).

During the late 1980s and 1990s, Arwood gave many five day, all day, workshops on Pragmaticism Methodology, a set of methods based on these beliefs and supported by client evidence. With the 1990s, the decade of the brain, it became apparent that the neuroscience about the brain supported Arwood's ideas about the relationship among development, learning, and language. A human learned and therefore developed, and language was the product of such deep learning. By 1991, Arwood published another book, *Semantic and Pragmatic Language Disorders (2nd Ed.),* which summarized her translation of the science research behind the senses and their perceived patterns that resulted in specific ways that human learners are able to create concepts named by language. In this book, like her other books, her methods, beliefs, and theoretical principles were supported by evidence collected on the many patients, clients, and consulting relationships that she experienced over the years, across populations and across the United States and Canada. Arwood's integration between learning and development resulted in translating the neuroscience into a theory: The Neuro-semantic Language Learning Theory (NsLLT).[5]

This model of learning was easily supported by the decade of the brain's neuroscience. In fact, Arwood was able to support many of her existing theories about language development

---

[5]   For a literature review of Arwood's Neuro-semantic Language Learning Theory, see Chapter 2

by re-interpreting neuroscientific data into the NsLLT. For example, Arwood was able to propose that, as opposed to beliefs held even to this day (e.g. two-tier input-output), human learning follows a four-tier model of brain scaffolding and mental development. At the first level of learning, the Central Nervous System (brain and spinal cord) acquires sensory input. Eventually, with enough overlap of this sensory input, patterns will form. Integration of sensory patterns represents the second level of learning. As these sensory patterns overlap, they create pathways of circuits or images. These circuits represent the third level of the NsLLT. When these circuits are assigned the patterns of language, a human is able to name the images or concepts. This is the fourth tier of human cognition. More on the NsLLT will be explained in the preface to Unit 2.

This four tier NsLLT model (sensory input, perceptual organization, conceptual images, and language function) integrates the findings of cognitive psychology, neuroscience, and language to explain how a human learns, how they think, and how they become literate. The NsLLT sits at the intersection of Arwood's Neuro-Education Model (See Figure 1.1).

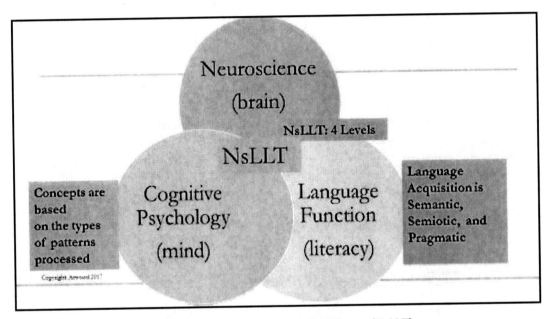

Figure 1.1: Arwood's Neuro-semantic Language Learning Theory (NsLLT)

Why does Arwood's Neuro-Education Model Include Language Function?

Up to the 1990s, the mind seemed to include the brain. Psychology was the study of the mind. The biological basis of the mind was the brain; but, consciousness was thought of as solely consisting of the mind. With the 1990s research about the brain, there seemed to be a much more distinct separation of the brain and mind – more of a duality. Each, the brain and the mind, could exist separately. In one supporting example for duality, researchers discovered that the brain existed after death when a person's consciousness disappeared (Pallis, 1983). However, a healthy, living brain seemed to create its own consciousness in a manner that is still not fully known today.

The debate between duality (brain and mind exist separately) and monality (brain and mind exist together) has continued. There is one factor that has been thus far ignored in this

18

debate and must now be considered: language function. In order to discuss the coexistence of the mind and brain, a person must have language. To translate the brain research into applications of the mind (literacy, attention, focus, motivation, engagement, etc.), a scholar must use language to describe the neurobiological phenomena that they observe.

Not only does the use of language influence the researchers' perceptions of what they are seeing, it also provides a backstory of experience that is unique to that individual. Therefore, all researchers may interpret the same results in a slightly different manner. For example, to examine an animal's intentionality of behavior, a researcher must use language to describe its actions. In addition, anytime a human analyzes animals in a study, they must ask themselves critical questions such as, "Can we really know what the intentions are behind an animal's behavior? Can we know if an animal is experiencing feeling or emotions? What does a correlation actually mean between the behavior of an animal and the corresponding regions that light up in their brain during fMRI scans? Does an animal feel emotions akin to humans?" As previously expressed, using human language to interpret animal research has not been without its complications.

One classic example from the field of neuroscience that attempts to translate animal behavior to applications of the human mind is the Morris water task. This water task consists of a barrel of water with hidden platforms that can be raised, lowered, and/or moved around within the barrel. The mouse is put in the barrel and electrodes are placed on the mouse's brain to interpret its movements. To the layperson, this research seems pretty scientific. However, the scholar uses human language for any interpretation of the mouse's behavior, despite the fact that researchers cannot possibly know what a mouse is

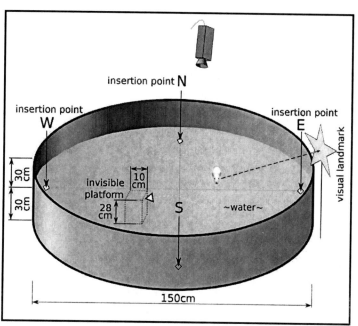

Figure 1.2: Morris Water Maze Experiment
Image Credit: Samuel John, Creative Commons

thinking. For example, if the scientist says the mouse "seeks out" and "finds" the platform, then the researcher is assigning human properties to the mouse. These words imply that the mouse has direct intentionality to its actions, which would mean that the mouse can scan their environment, analyze variables, and problem solve to find a solution. This anthropomorphism (human traits assigned to animals) complicates the science. See Figure 1.2 for an example of this task.

Can a mouse really analyze and problem solve sufficiently to "find" the platform as the researchers claim? Or, do the animal's sensory-perceptual systems simply move the mouse out of the water as it tries not to drown? This author would argue that the humans interpreting the mouse's behavior over-exaggerate the profundity of the mouse's actions. The mouse does not use deliberate intentionality to methodically plan out its actions; this interpretation would be over-reaching into areas of the mouse's mind that we cannot truly determine. In the water, the mouse cannot rest, eat, sleep – basic biological functions. Therefore, the mouse does not think about how to find the platform, which is the researcher's own interpretation. Physically, all we can distinctly determine is that the mouse is equipped to survive out of the water, is not equipped to survive in water, will drown if it keeps swimming, and will stay alive if its legs land on the platform. Any interpretations of the mouse's intentions or hypotheses about the mouse's thoughts are simply conjectures from a human perspective.

Sometimes, human emotions and other language functions are attributed to animals. For example, mice in these experiments are often interpreted as being "scared," so they swim really hard in circles to find a platform. Emotions are language-based, and mice do not have language. Mice can communicate, but they do not have a grammatical language. Language represents human thinking and has only developed in humankind because humans have evolved out of a need to communicate increasingly sophisticated thoughts in order to survive (Mead, 1934). Since the mouse has no language, then the mouse does not have the higher levels of thinking with a formal level of cause and effect. He does not use problem-solving to deduce a way out. Instead, he simply swims in circles until he bumps into the platform. Obviously, there is sensory input from the mouse's environment that results in the mouse using a specific form of movement; but, the mouse does not have the capacity for the type of logic or language that neuroscientists often purport. The logic and language belong to the researcher.

Two Tier vs. Four Tier Levels of Learning

Currently, study of the brain and the mind neglects to acknowledge the role of language in human cognition. Remember that no other theoretical model in the field of Mind, Brain, and Education science (except Arwood's Neuro-Education Model) includes the study of language as a lens to interpret primary study research in the fields of neuroscience and cognitive psychology. Recognizing what language is, what language does, and how language mediates any interpretation of scientific research helps scholars separate the mind from the brain. This separation allows for better interpretation of the science, especially in regards to the study of human thinking.

In fact, when a human is raising a child, they spend a great deal of time trying to distinguish what that child is communicating. For example, the child says, "dirt bike" and the adult interprets this utterance as, "Oh, you want to go dirt bike riding!" knowing that the child's oral language represents the child's thinking, then the interpretation may or may not be accurate. Interpreting the child's utterance is "mind reading" and may not be semantically accurate. The child's brain on the other hand is able to give meaning to only what the brain can produce at that time. In other words, the child "knows" only what the child produces, not necessarily how their words will be interpreted.

Over time, the child may acquire more meaning. If the child does, then the child is able to semantically expand on "dirt bike" to say, "go dirt bike riding." Eventually, with enough added meaning, the child says, "I went dirt bike riding last Saturday with my cousins and my aunt. My aunt took us up to the mountain where we all spent the day riding our dirt bikes. We also got to have a picnic for lunch. At the end of the day, my aunt brought me and my cousins home. It was the best dirt bike day ever." The child's language abilities develop in tandem with their ability to process more advanced levels of cognition.

This child's capacity to expand ideas and to add extra meaning to create more complicated utterances is a result of the brain learning relationships and making connections about acquired concepts. Such learning represents language function. Without the understanding of the intersectionality of concepts and language, the study of learning and the translation of neuroscience to education research focuses only on the lower levels of learning, such as input-output (first two levels of the NsLLT). Primitive animals are capable of lower-level, input-output learning: dogs can be trained to follow commands to precise specificity.

This is not to say that the first two levels of the NsLLT (sensory input and perceptual patterns) are not important. In fact, they are indeed necessary precursors for all human learning to take place. The problem arises when researchers attempt to interpret research intended for humans by using a model of learning that only considers these first two levels. As stated, humans think at levels that are infinitely more complicated than animals. Stopping at level 2 of the NsLLT only paints half of the picture of what is happening inside the human mind. Figure 1.3 shows the four levels of learning within the NsLLT.

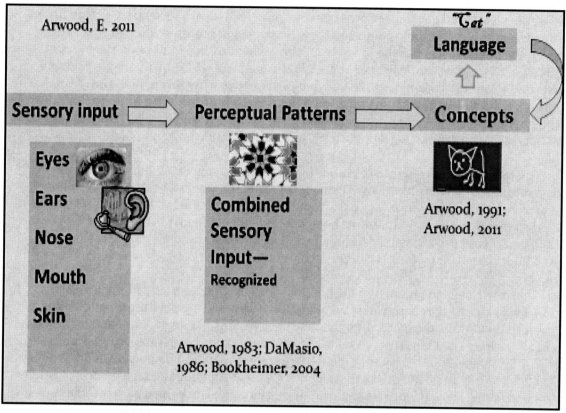

Figure 1.3: Diagram of Arwood's Neuro-semantic Language Learning Theory

Because the NsLLT utilizes all brain levels of activity, not just the lower levels of sensory input and integration for skills, the NsLLT allows researchers and practitioners to consider the whole brain, as well as the interpretations of research that utilizes language assumptions. Furthermore, the NsLLT also allows a model to examine higher order learning and thinking. The higher order learning needed for deep conceptual learning comes from the higher functions of the brain. These higher functions of the brain allow for the deep levels of thinking called language function.

Language function develops from the neurobiological acquisition of meaning. Such meaning or semantics is neural in nature (neuro-semantic) and is unique to each learner's experiences (language learning). The child, who expressed the more complicated concepts related to his dirt bike riding day, learned the meaning of those relationships he expressed over time. He did not imitate the structures and practice them until they were habituated and generalized for expression. His language was naturally representative of what he had neuro-semantically learned through his biological system. The Neuro-semantic Language Learning Theory supports such natural and representative language that reflects the underlying acquisition of concepts, not just patterns and imitated structures.

Language Function Parallels Brain Function

There are some basic principles or similarities that define the human brain. The specific neuroeducation model one uses must consider the similarities of human brain function, not the differences. For example, a meta-analysis of neuroscience literature about human brains supports some basic brain similarities regardless of context or aggregate group (Socioeconomic status, disability, etc.). These brain similarities include the following: 1) Human brains learn at multiple levels (e.g. NsLLT); 2) Human brains are able to use patterns in flexible ways; 3) Human brains learn to create higher order circuits parallel to concepts; and 4) Human brains develop networks with multiple points of access for language representation of concepts. Moreover, the human brain has the capacity to learn, which results in development (e.g. Linden, 2007; Mascolo & Fischer, 2003; Posner et al., 2001; Smilkstein, 2002). This simple example suggests that the human brain has a high degree of neuroplasticity throughout the lifespan. This neuroplasticity can be defined as the function of the search for the human brain to find meaningful input. Again, the literature about language echoes the neuroscience about how the brain seeks meaning, connecting new patterns to consolidate meaning into higher forms of thinking.

The Delphi survey, referred to earlier in this chapter, supported this connection between meaning and neuroplasticity. The panel of experts in the field concluded, "Human brains seek patterns upon which they predict outcomes, and neural systems form responses to repeated patterns of activation (patterns being individually defined)." This means that neurobiological patterns form in the brain when new information connects to previously acquired information. Therefore, the brain is continuously rewiring itself to accommodate this new input.

This rewiring of the brain is made possible because of its capacity for neuroplasticity. In addition, the brain changes based off of what input it receives. The more meaningful input one receives into their brain, the more potential they have to consolidate memory and higher order thinking processes. The Delphi researchers supported this belief with research literature (e.g. Fisher, 2005; Japikse, 2002; Norman, Pollen, Detre & Haxby, 2006; Thompson, Giedd, Woods, MacDonald, Evans & Toga, 2000; Yan & Fischer, 2007). This understanding of neural plasticity in learning takes learning beyond a simple input-output model described earlier (when sensory input is thought to lead directly to perceptual motor output). The human brain's potential for neuroplasticity makes it possible for simple inputs (such as light, sound, movement, etc.) to eventually layer over time and create elaborate learning circuits and networks.

Today, neuroscientists are researching how these higher order neural systems might be organized and how they might function to produce human thinking (Gallistel & Matzel, 2013; Göetzmann & Schwegler, 2010; Pulvermüller, 2003, 2005, 2012). So far, scientists have concluded that these sophisticated neural networks can in fact be activated through multiple points of access. For example, some sensory input takes the form of light bouncing off the edges of objects and hitting the photoreceptors in the eyes. Other input enters the brain through the auditory pathways as these mechanisms process raw sound waves, while the movement of the hand can provide motor input that activates both the motor and visual cortices (Sadato, 1996). Put another way, various inputs can access circuits and networks of learning in a variety of ways depending on the way the way the neural systems utilize the input. In other words, these neural systems depend on the input from the sensory systems (eyes, ears, hands) in multiple ways to form higher capacity circuits and networks. As the language literature shows, such refinement of cognition requires scaffolding a learner's thinking through language used by others who assign novel meaning within a context (Arwood, 2011; Lam, 2016; Piaget, 1959; Robb, 2016; Vygotsky, 1962). The refinement process between a learner (thinker) and others parallels the importance of feedback externally and internally. In other words, the input one processes in his/her mind comes not only from others but also from internal language. This means that it is just as important for children to spend time mulling over ideas in their own heads as it is for them receive input from a knowledgeable adult. Children will only learn to advance their own thinking if they have a balance between time spent with an adult helping them clarify their thinking and time alone to semantically refine their own creativity. And, as previously mentioned, this internal refinement is only possible through the use of language. Language names our thinking and represents the underlying neurobiological acquisition process of deep structure cognition (Arwood, 2011).

The theories and principles presented in this anthology clearly indicate that the process of education must form a reciprocal relationship between adult teaching and student learning. Thus, an effective model of neuroeducation must consider how exactly humans learn information, and how this differs from other sciences. Arwood's Neuro-Education Model stands alone from all other versions currently in the field because it considers all of the processes that make up the human mind, including: internal neurobiological development, external assignment of meaning, different neural levels, and the importance of language in mediating one's thinking. By using the unique vision, purpose, and methodology of this model, the authors chronicled in this anthology have had success working with students who had previously struggled in school. For many of these children, the intervention these authors provided was the first time they had ever been connected to school in a meaningful way.

The NsLLT Provides the Missing Link Between Brain and Mind Science

As previously mentioned, unlike any models currently used in the fields of neuroscience and cognitive psychology, the Neuro-semantic Language Learning Theory (NsLLT) provides a unique interpretation of how children learn to think. The key variable is that a person "learns" to think. A baby is not born able to see objects or hear language. Their eyes and ears as well as their auditory and visual pathways have not been developed sufficiently in order to make sense of the stimuli in their environment. In fact, a baby's view of the world around them can actually be described as blurry blotches of light and indiscriminate noise (Anderson, 2010). They have not yet acquired the language to interpret what these blotches might represent.

Neuroscience provides the detailed account of how the baby learns to see. First, babies see the reflection of light along the edges of objects as features, and they hear the sound differences in patterns of speech. These sensory inputs provide the learner with much overlapping input of the features of light and sound. Light bouncing off the edges of shapes creates images of shape (beginning of concepts or thinking), and the sounds of speech provide the time and tonal properties of meaning associated with the auditory pathways. Such integration of both the sight and sound pathways create a mental image of a person's own acoustic voice or auditory thinking (Arwood, 2011). This auditory thinking is used by individuals as a mental sketchpad of sorts where acoustic images are stored and manipulated in the mind (Anderson, 2010). Moreover, what children are asked to do with this mental sketchpad often depends on how adults assign meaning to children's behavior.

For example, learners in the dominant North American cultures are expected to hear what another person says as meaningful interpretations of what a person sees. An example would be how a mother or father uses words to describe a child's actions such as, "Look at you wiggling your toes." Over time, a child learns that an adult uses language to assign meaning to their actions. After years of being exposed to multiple layers of examples, it becomes clear to the child that a word, or oral sound tag, represents a person, object, or idea in reality.

Not all babies are born with neurotypical brains that allow them to process sound sufficiently enough to convert it to a corresponding mental image. The neurological ability to integrate sound and sight requires a learner to have auditory pathways that function to pass along meaningful sensory input into higher order regions in the brain, such as the visual and auditory cortices, the parietal lobe, and the pre-frontal cortex (Baars & Gage, 2010). If these visual and auditory pathways are indeed working, then sensory input will in fact create mental auditory images, or the sound of one's own voice. These auditory mental images are created by simultaneously integrating what others say with what one sees. Effectively, if a child can process the sound of someone's voice and make meaning from this sound, they will be well-equipped to function in the dominant culture of North American society.

Because English is an "auditory" language, this means that the vast majority of individuals who learn English do most of their communication through oral speech or through written text. Moreover, learners who attend school in English speaking countries are required to be proficient in both of these mediums. This is because English is a language that has the alphabetic component that comes from the sound integration of how people name the letters of what they see in print. In other words, spoken English is based off of an ever-evolving set of rules of how to pronounce written words. Therefore, if a student wishes to fit in to school culture, they must be able to use the auditory capacities of their brain to "take sound off the page."

For a child to be successful in school, their auditory pathways must be able to interpret the sound parameters of the acoustic wave that reaches the ear. Sound waves include the time of when a wave starts and when it finishes. Children born with neurotypical brains are able to internally process these time-based properties. In this respect, English is also considered a time-based language because the brain picks up and records the properties of the sound waves used in oral speech, such as loudness, pitch, and duration. Interestingly, English writing was once considered a one-to-one correspondence between the sound of the spoken English and the written word. This meant that each letter of the word "walked," for instance, would be pronounced like /wᵃlkêd/. Over the last many hundreds of years, the oral pronunciation of English words has evolved and changed at a faster rate than their written counterparts found in dictionaries. Many individuals learning English as a second language find it challenging to memorize these pronunciation rules as many connections found today such as sound-to-letter correspondence are based off of outdated modalities.

It should be noted that not all languages are alphabetic in nature, and therefore do require learners to be able to intuit sound properties in order to acquire a full language grammar. For example, many indigenous languages like Chamorro spoken by the people of the Mariana Islands, languages that are based on contextual ideas like Mandarin Chinese, and languages that are spatial in aspect, like American Sign Language (ASL), do not need a sound component to represent the ideas being expressed (the underlying deep semantics.) For a child learning these languages, the ability to use sound is not a requirement. This is because the languages contain an internal architecture that is solely visual in nature. This means that the surface structures of the language (words, characters, shapes, movements of the hands, etc.) map on to visually overlapped patterns or visual concepts (ideas, expressions, etc.). The visual + visual formula to these languages results in a completely different set of surface conventions that learners must pay attention to in order to become fluent. Such conventions might include visual properties such as *aspect*, or the ability to differentiate between nearly identical visual shapes based on their proximity to other visual components[6].

For example, in Figure 1.4, the reader can observe that the visual language properties of ASL requires a learner to apperceive and mentally catalog the position, placement, movement, and directionality of the hands and fingers in relationship to the signer, as well as that signer's facial expressions and gaze (Bellugi & Fischer, 1972). When the eye processes this visual input,

---

[6] More information on visual components of Mandarin will be explored in Chapter 2; the concept of visual aspect will be examined in Chapters 7 and 9.

it relays the electrochemical signals through the visual pathways, into the visual cortex, and then to other processing stations in the brain such as the hippocampus, parietal lobe, and pre-frontal cortex (Baars, 2010; Sadato, 1996). For obvious reasons, ASL has evolved as a full grammar language completely independent from one's ability to use auditory pathways to process sound. As a result of sound being missing from this form of communication, other elements of the visual language must take the place of the sound-based components, such as tone, pitch, inflection, pauses, and pronunciation (Bellugi & Fischer, 1972). Notice that English does not use these forms of visual discrimination as a necessary building block for communication.

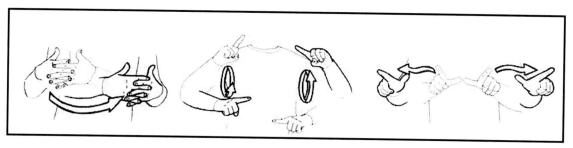

Figure 1.4: Example of Visual Properties of American Sign Language
Image Credit: Clayton Valli, Gallaudet University, Public Domain

This knowledge about other languages coupled with knowledge of the NsLLT provides educators with a tremendous depth of understanding about how we learn to think. To review, humans can learn auditory languages based on the capacity to use patterns of sound or sight in different ways; but, humans can learn visual languages by attuning to the overlap of visual properties inherent in the framework of that language. Poignantly, this author worked for over four decades with children who are born in an auditory culture but who struggle to use sound to make meaning out of the English language. These children who struggle may or may not have been born with neurotypical brains or have been identified as having special needs. The struggle of children to attune to the auditory properties of English cuts across all ages and disabilities. Therefore, the methods proposed in this book offer alternative ways to teach literacy skills, such as reading and writing, that are not based on a learner's ability to process sound. These methods have success because they match the visual manner in which the majority of children think.

Visual Learning Systems and Visual Language Methods

Over the past forty years, this author has conducted a variety of formal and informal studies (Arwood, 1981, 1983, 1991, 2000, 2011, etc.) that substantiate the claim that upwards of 95% of individuals think with a visual learning system.[7] This means that, for these students, their minds best process the world around them by making pictures, images, and movies in their head. These individuals can be called "visual thinkers." Some of these "visual thinkers" are able to easily convert sound (oral speech, etc.) into corresponding mental images, while some cannot. Those who were born with brains who cannot intuitively translate from auditory to visual information often lag behind their peers in terms of grades, knowledge retention, and rates of literacy acquisition (Arwood, 2011; Green-Mitchell, 2016; Lam, 2016; Robb, 2016). Through no fault of their own, the minds of these children have great difficulty using auditory language to refine their own thinking.

---

[7]   Please see (TemPro; Arwood & Beggs, 1989) for a review of these methods

The experience of working with children who struggle to process sound properties has spurred this author to propose a longstanding axiom to offer assistance. The principles of this idea, the bulk of which is contained in the Neuro-semantic Language Learning Theory, posit that individuals who struggle to make meaning out of sound-based instruction can in fact learn English by using Viconic Language Methods (VLMs) as the primary method of acquisition. This means that these children who struggle can become literate in English by sidestepping its sound-based rules and instead attuning only to its visual properties (Arwood, 2011).

Effectively, throughout the past four decades, this author has developed a learning methodology that completely re-conceptualizes English as a visual language that is more akin to Mandarin or ASL[8]. Arwood has devised dozens of teaching and learning strategies that aim to present learning by overlapping visual modes of input, such as bubbling the shape of a word to anchor it as one single idea, drawing out multiple images next to an idea to provide visual examples of what this idea might look like in different contexts, and drawing/writing hand-over-hand with a student to activate their visual and motor cortices. Units 2-4 of this anthology chronicle these Viconic Language Methods (VLMs) in explicit detail and explain how they can be used both in classroom instruction and one-on-one remediation. To this author's knowledge, this viconic language method approach to becoming literate in English is completely unique, and to this date remains the only model of neuroeducation that uses the function of visual language to reach individuals who think with a visual symbolizing system.

Indeed, much of the current literature about learning does not acknowledge the possibility of overlapping visual information to provide such alternative methods from the assumed auditory method of sensory input entering into the brain. As stated, language can in fact be created with visual perception that results in a visual metacognition - this means that literacy does not have to control for sound. Furthermore, language is more about the communicator's environmental needs to communicate (semiosis or purpose of language), the assignment of meaning to what is communicated (semantics), and the cultural effects of the assigned meaning (pragmatics) than it is about the surface structures.

Brain Principles Contained in Arwood's Neuro-Education Model

Using this knowledge about how language is a mirror to the mind (cognitive psychology) and the interpretation of the neurobiological system (neuroscience), educators can begin to triangulate findings in the literature to discover effective maxims about learning. Some of these principles contained in Arwood's Neuro-Education Model are: 1) Children learn language through the way the neurobiological system works; 2) language learning requires semiosis, semantics, and pragmatics; 3) the human brain has neuroplasticity, where the function of the brain is parallel to the function of the learner using his or her own neurobiological system to assign meaning; 4) if languages do not need the sound components to communicate human concepts, then the brain is capable of learning complex language functions in ways that parallel the neurobiological system's cross-modal system of either acoustic and visual or visual and visual acquisition; 5) literacy education can follow the properties of the languages that parallel the neurobiology of the brain's function; 6) most children in North America think with a visual metacognition, meaning their language represents their visual thinking; and 7) if most children in North America use a visual metacognition, then the properties of non-sound based languages can be inserted onto literacy lessons to create a better learning environment for most children today.

---

[8] For a complete review of this methodology, please see Arwood's 2011 book *Language Function*.

Such application of the aforementioned seven concepts, coupled with knowledge of the NsLLT, results in an approach for helping children learn and acquire literacy in English that is more effective than current educational practices. Therefore, several individuals within the author's local region who have all studied under this author's tutelage offered to write about their experiences applying Arwood's Neuro-Education Model, where the NsLLT is central to the triangulation of the literature. The following chapters of this anthology chronicle these authors' journeys through incorporating the seven tenets of Arwood's Neuro-Education Model presented above into their own educational practices and discusses in detail the positive results their pupils achieved while immersed in an environment conducive to promoting neuro-semantic learning experiences. The contributors of the chapters in this book are using the Arwood Neuro-Education Model while designing the research from their professional applications. These contributions provide an initial foundation to a paradigm shift needed in education at all levels: research, adult, and child learning. These works begin to show a shift in a paradigm from the assumptions of an input-output model to a dynamic model that explains more of the synergy of how the human brain functions.

Conclusion

The NsLLT at the center of Arwood's Neuro-Education Model provides the foundation for an educational paradigm shift. Among other principles, this shift includes the following: an emphasis on learning neurobiological processes rather than the surface developmental products, a focus on brain functions rather than focusing on language-based assumptions of the mind, emphasizing higher use of the brain (language complexities at the cortical level) rather than teaching the patterns of the lower portions of the brain, and a shift from the input-output model to the higher order thinking, conceptually-based language model.

Chapter 2

A Literature Review of Neuro-Education

Carol Xiang Lam, Ed.D.

Adapted by Chris Merideth, M.Ed.

Abstract

In its design to translate scientific findings into educational settings, the Neuro-semantic Language Learning Theory (NsLLT) places language at the core of learning, which emphasizes the learner's abilities to acquire higher-level concepts. This chapter expounds and provides support for the theoretical model of the NsLLT proposed by Arwood (2011) by analyzing its fundamental principles as well as some applications of this theory to classroom pedagogy. The review of literature presented in this chapter was drawn from the three disciplines that make up Arwood's Neuro-Education Model including neuroscience, psychology, and language theory. The scientific findings in these areas consistently provide reinforcement to the model and the tenets of NsLLT. Lastly, this author summarizes a research study aimed at increasing fluency among individuals learning Mandarin as a second language. In this study, the author explored the impact of the NsLLT and the related literature in neural and psychological sciences to investigate adolescent American students who used semantic-imagery strategies to learn Chinese characters. She found that NsLLT can not only stand as the theoretical framework supporting visual language learning, it can also provide methods for the analysis of the learner's cognitive processes in language learning and thinking. This chapter uses the NsLLT model as a method of analysis to explain the cognitive process of the participants in the language learning study.

About the Author

Dr. Carol Lam is a former ESL teacher with a background in linguistics and psychology who has taught college students in China and the United States. After earning her Doctorate in Education with an emphasis in neuroeducation studies at the University of Portland, she now teaches in a Chinese Immersion Program at Portland Public Schools. In this program, Dr. Lam incorporates Arwood's Neuro-Education Model of teaching and learning to help American students learn the Chinese history, culture, and language based on their visual cognitive strengths. Dr. Lam is an advocate of incorporating teaching methods that aim to help learners to holistically make use of their visual and language systems for conceptual understanding and creation. Based on Dr. Arwood's Neuro-semantic Language Learning Theory (NsLLT), she developed *Vimage Learning Methods* to be used in project-based multidisciplinary teaching on elementary school students in China. Most recently, Dr. Lam has presented the research results at several neuroscience and education conferences and is currently working on subsequent publications of her research.

Introduction to the NsLLT and the Viconic Language Methods

Since the 1990s, neural imaging studies on humans' language abilities have drawn the interest of many researchers and educators in the fields of language acquisition and special education. These research results have been transferred into classroom applications and educational theories, which seek to resolve problems and facilitate learning in students who have struggled in school. The Neuro-semantic Language Learning Theory (NsLLT) integrates theories with scientific evidence and affords a four-tier model of how a learner acquires language (Arwood, 2011; Arwood, Kaulitz, & Brown, 2009). The NsLLT suggests ways to consider the metacognitive thinking of an individual in the acquisition of concepts. A learner's mind can be classified as an *auditory* thinker, meaning they think only in the sound of their own voice in their head, or a *visual* thinker, meaning that in addition to thinking verbal mental thoughts, they also make pictures/movies in their head and use phonographic abilities to replay in their mind words that have been spoken by others (Arwood, 2011). These phonographic abilities are like a tape recorder that internally simulates the playing back of audio in the mind (speech, music, etc.) that a person has heard in real life. Neuro-semantic language learning, as defined in the NsLLT, is the acquisition of language across the neurobiological hierarchy of the human learning system: sensory, perceptual, conceptual circuits, and language (i.e. neuro-semantic networks; Arwood, 2011).

The NsLLT contrasts against the more traditional *structural* approach of language learning that claims that learning can be broken down into a series of incremental structures (Gardner, Cihon, Morrison, & Paul, 2013). Instead, the NsLLT emphasizes learning the function of language, which represents conceptual thinking. By function, Arwood indicates the way in which the learning system acquires the cognition needed for social development as a human being (2011). Each stage posited in the NsLLT depends on scaffolding from previous stages with the goal of arriving at healthy cognitive development for a child. The four stages show interfaces between the learner's brain and the environment (Arwood & Kaulitz, 2014). Specifically, the four neuro-semantic stages are listed below.

a) Sensory receptors across the body receive inputs according to the input's properties, e.g. light waves and acoustic sounds;

b) As sensory inputs overlap in multiple forms to create patterns, the cellular structures, mostly at the subcortical level, start to recognize these patterns;

c) As various patterns continue to bundle and integrate to form large patterns, the firing of cells moves the patterns along cerebral circuits, where old and new patterns connect to create layers of images, i.e. the creation of conceptual meanings;

d) Concepts or neural circuits of meaning continue to layer deep within cortex across hemispheres to develop patterns of meaning for language function.

The important notion in this theory is that concepts are created through layers of images within cerebral circuits and then across networks. Auditory concepts can form from acoustic patterns overlapping with visual patterns within auditory pathways (Arwood, 2011; Arwood & Kaulitz, 2014; Campbell, 2008; Stevenson, VanDerKlok, Pisoni, & James, 2011). An example of an acoustic pattern would be the brain incorporating sensory data from the eyes and the ears simultaneously, such as watching a cat's mouth open, hearing a "meow" sound come out, and associating the production of this sound with the opening of the animals' mouth. Individuals with neurotypical brains, regardless of if they are an auditory or visual thinker, can acquire acoustic patterns with varying degrees of ease, depending on how well the wiring of these sensory information streams integrate in the brain.

However, individuals can also form visual conceptualization by overlapping visual patterns with other visual patterns. An example of this would be when both the eyes and the head move to scan a room and notice what is inside. Though we think we see three-dimensional objects, our eyes actually only process two-dimensional points of light. It is our brain that actually "sees," meaning it is our brain that assembles raw sensory information into our perception of reality (Eagleman, 2015).

When sensory patterns are integrated into images (i.e. concepts), they provide the learner's functional use of language, thinking, and creation. Arwood believes that for the learner to acquire language, functions should come before structural patterns, paralleling the principle "whole is greater than sum of parts" (See the following section for more detail on this idea) (1983). In other words, when the learner's semantic meanings increase, the structures that represent the underlying meanings also improve.

Survey studies showed that about 95% of the general child and adult population in the English culture think with a visual system where the visual inputs form visual images or patterns, rather than thinking with the auditory system (Arwood & Kaakinen, 2008; Arwood, 2011). Since the NsLLT proposes utilizing learners' strengths to design a strength-based approach, learning concepts necessitates learning the language by accessing the visual pathway for conceptualization for most learners.

Based on the NsLLT, various visual methods have been applied to ordinary classrooms for both neuro-typical and neuro-atypical learners to enhance their conceptual understanding. Some of the practice-proved methods, named the Viconic Language Methods (VLMs), are incorporated as part of the NsLLT. VLMs help the learner to utilize visual properties of language to facilitate visual language processes of thinking. In addition, they help learners translate visual cognition into auditory English and vice versa.

Some examples of VLMs include cartooning, the use of oral viconic or relational language, hand-over-hand shaping of words, picture dictionaries, context creation by "I" Stories, adjustment of materials to create more visual context, and drawing concepts in real time (See Arwood, 2011 for details). As mentioned above, these methods take advantage of the students' visual learning systems to create images in their brain. By connecting the images with contextual information to create larger images, the learner develops higher order thinking represented by improved language (Arwood, 2011).

Though the Neuro-semantic Language Learning Theory is a unique way of conceptualizing how learning takes place in the brain, its findings also resonate with many notable academic theories of today. In particular, the scientific findings of numerous psychological and neuroimaging studies of language acquisition lend support to the core tenets of the NsLLT. The next section of this chapter briefly reviews this literature and provides primary, secondary, and tertiary sources that validate the claims explored in this anthology.

Review of Language Literature

Linguistic studies in the 20th century generally dichotomize language analysis into the study of semantics (i.e. meaning) and structure (i.e. sound or orthographic form). In general, linguistics considers the structures of language to be the products that humans create to communicate, and refer to semantics as being the thought processes underlying this communication. For example, Ferdinand de Saussure (1959) defines these concepts as *signified* and *signifier*, where Noam Chomsky (1972, 2013) refers to theoretical constructs as either being *deep structures* or *surface structures*. The terms these philosophers use here correspond to the meaning and structure of language respectively.

As to the relationship of meaning and structure, Saussure emphasized the arbitrariness of the two planes, meaning that the language structures humans create do not often emulate or imitate the ideas they correspond to. In other words, the association between the structures and semantics of a particular language comes only through conventions and uses and evolves spontaneously by one's need to communicate. In Saussure's view, a linguistic structure does not make sense on its own. It must be connected in a meaningful relationship with other structures in order for a string of ideas to make sense (Chandler, 2007; Saussure, 1983).

Different from Saussure's arbitrariness principle, Chomsky (and later his followers) argued that generative transformational grammar can transform the deep structures of language into surface structures such as words and phrases (Lakoff, 1969). Chomsky claims that the deep structure of a language represents our underlying thinking. In addition, these deep structures preexist their corresponding surface forms. This would mean that mankind's ability to think precedes their ability to use language. In addition, he argues that every human is born with an inherent underlying guide for how to transpose their thoughts into an organized language by following logical rules. These logical rules help translate the deep structure of the mind to the surface structure of grammar and syntax. Chomsky states that these rules apply to all humans because we are all born with an innate sense of universal grammar.

Another influential thinker who aimed to analyze the purpose of human languages was Charles Sanders Peirce, a pragmatist philosopher and logician. He proposed a triadic model of a sign system that evolves within three components: a *representamen* (i.e. structure), an *object* (i.e. referent meaning), and an *interpretant* (i.e. interpretation) (Peirce, 1931-58). Peirce noted that the meaning of a sign arises in its interpretation (Chandler, 2007). According to him, the interpretant relates to and mediates between the meaning and structure; as such, the structure represents the meaning through interpretation. Essentially, this means that the signs we use to represent language (such as words) are themselves meaningless. But, when we assign meaning to the sign, they transform into it a critical element that represents an idea. By continually assigning meaning to a sign, the sign takes on a set of values and logical purpose as the interpretant interrelates and participates with other signs (Merrell, 2001). Figure 2.1 shows a diagram of how the meaning of a sign can be forever evolving.

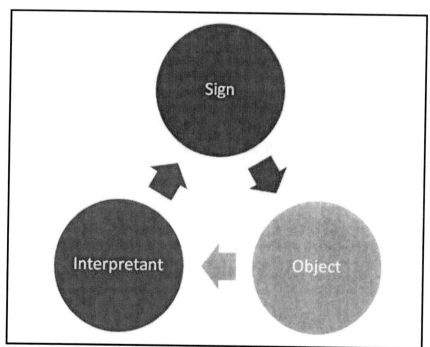

Figure 2.1: The meaning of an object is continually being refined.
Image Public Domain

As the interpretation of a sign continues throughout time, the sign develops some new features that might continue to refine its interpretation. This idea explains why the meanings we attach to words are always changing, such as how centuries ago the word "clue" meant a ball of yarn but today means a hint or piece of information (Curzan, 2014). In other words, it is the learner who interprets signs and creates the meanings of a sign, which can be further refined in meaning and structure. With these thoughts, Peirce helped to take apart the building blocks of language and pave the way for modern linguistic analysis. In addition, the fundamental tenets in Peirce's theory of signs and symbolizers are consistent with the NsLLT's developmental model of language acquisition and the principle that function determines structure. More on this will be explored in the next section.

Neuroscientific Evidence Supports Arwood's Neuro-Education Model

Researchers have long wondered about how information is inputted into the mind and brain and then recalled for use in human thinking, communication, and behavior. Many recent neuropsychological and neuroimaging studies on the nature of semanticity have found substantial evidence in how meaning is established and represented in the brain. These studies provide insights in how language is acquired in humans. Modern research shows that semantic knowledge or memory is embodied and mapped within the sensory-motor systems, which are multimodal in nature (Gallese & Lakoff, 2005). This means that our sensory receptors (eyes, ears, hands, etc.) perceive the world around us, and then our brain compiles this data to create our experience of the world.

Another way to put this is that semantic knowledge or memory is grounded in all the primary and secondary sensory systems including sight, hearing, touch, motor actions and so on (Ghazanfar & Schroeder, 2006; Klemen & Chambers, 2012; Pulvermüller, 2013). Within the sensorimotor systems, semantic meanings may be processed in either higher-level multisensory integration regions or lower-level sensory cortexes (Ghazanfar & Schroeder, 2006). In other words, the knowledge of how to do some habituated tasks such as walking or driving can be stored in subcortical regions of a person's brain because they have practiced these tasks until they become rote. However, other types of activities such as learning a new language require all regions of the cortex to work in sync because this knowledge is new to the learner and demands full mental faculties (Baars & Gage, 2010).

It is posited that perceptual activities in the early visual cortex are followed by the visual properties of objects, which tend to converge, forming the multimodal representations of concepts. In the NsLLT, this multimodal input is referred to as forming a visual pattern, meaning that two or more visual layers (such as light or movement) have overlapped in the visual cortex. But, this electrochemical flow of visual information does not stop at just one region of the brain. It continues to connect to many other regions of the brain such as the anterior areas in the temporal cortex and prefrontal cortex, among others (Gainotti, Ciaraffa, Silveri, & Marra, 2009). Neuroscientists can study this electrochemical flow using Functional Magnetic Resonance Imaging (fMRI). In essence, the fMRI machine works to see where oxygenated blood flows in the brain. It is widely known that more blood flows to cortical areas when the neurons of those regions are activated; on an fMRI machine, these areas would "light up" on the scan when showing activation (Baars & Gage, 2010). Figure 2.2 shows a sample image of looking at fMRI scans of the brain from a side and top view. The bright blob-like areas represent brain activity during the scan.

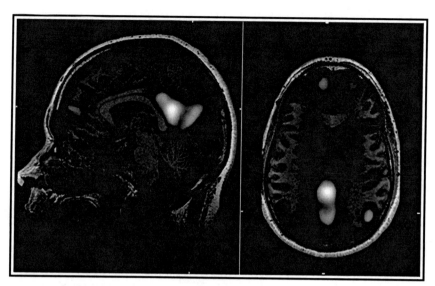

Figure 2.2: fMRI Scan
Image Credit John Graner, Public Domain

By using this technology, neuroscientists are able to determine when the neurons in certain regions of the brain tend to fire together. A scientist could ask a participant hooked up to an fMRI machine to engage in a task and then look for areas of the brain that light up in use together during that task. This allows researchers to diagram areas of the brain by presumed *functional connectivity*, meaning that these multiple areas might need to work together in order for the participant to be able to operate.

For example, Clarke and Tyler conducted an fMRI study examining brain activations by having individuals look at similar and dissimilar objects (2014). They wanted to see what areas of the visual perirhinal cortex lit up when engaged in semantically similar tasks such as looking at images of a mushroom, onion, and pumpkin.

They found that when the brain processes items that are similar in category, it tends to group these neuron connections in close physical proximity to one another. So, the brain tends to cluster together the visual processing of animals to the lateral occipital cortex, and the processing of faces in the ventral temporal cortex (Clarke & Tyler, 2014). Moreover, these results support the idea of a "progressive" processing pathway in the ventral vision channel. This means that even simple visual stimuli such as images can trigger many regions of the brain to fire together in concert, presumably to recognize what the object is and how it relates to the person viewing it.

These findings all parallel the NsLLT's four-tier learning model as it suggests a differentiation of learning at different semantic levels. In other words, the NsLLT states that learning progresses in four stages, starting with sensory input and eventually leading to concepts and language. The study presented here, among numerous others, supports the notion that visual concepts layer over time by increasing in semantic complexity in the brain (Arwood, 2011).

As stated, the brain processes visual input at lower levels (subcortical), middle levels (visual cortex) and at higher order levels (prefrontal cortex). At higher-level integration stations, multisensory integration is believed to be the norm (Gallese & Lakoff, 2005). Put another way, the higher one gets into the brain, eventually arriving at the prefrontal cortex, the more connections one will see to other brain regions. In addition, neuroimaging studies have revealed that different types of integrations (e.g. auditory with visual messages) may enhance message binding and perceptual certainty (Klemen & Chambers, 2012). This means that the brain acquires information best when it is presented in multiple ways using multiple sensory modalities. Notice that this evidence supports the tenet of the NsLLT that visual concepts (such as a word) will only form if enough visual patterns are overlapped (such as multiple drawn depictions of that word). This suggests that the creation of pathways or circuits that include multimodal inputs may well provide the most meaning, especially for visual thinkers (Arwood, 2011).

In the prefrontal areas, research has found that the brain responds to both visual and auditory signals; activities can be cross-modulated by the two signals, depending on the congruency of the two signals, also known as *synchrony* (Fuster et al., 2000; Ghazanfar & Schroeder, 2006). These findings may indicate that the integration of the visual and auditory components in the prefrontal areas (e.g. the left inferior prefrontal area) may be the underlying mechanism for fine-grained decision-making on lexical meanings associated with auditory sounds (Poldrack, Wagner, Prull, Desmond, Glover, & Gabrieli, 1999). Arwood (2011) defines such cross-modal integration as acoustic input pairing with visual input to form an acoustic pattern. Similarly, visual input pairing with visual input will form a visual pattern. Figure 2.3 shows a diagram of how visual input travels from the eyes and crosses

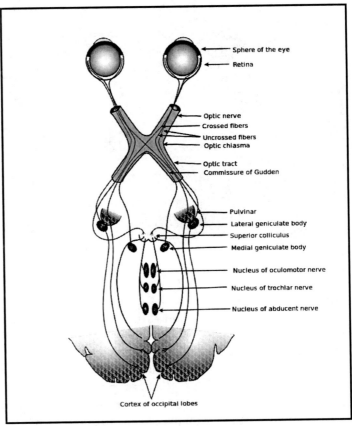

Figure 2.3: Visual input as it travels to occipital lobe
Image Credit K.D. Schroeder, Public Domain

numerous times as it progresses into the occipital lobe. Remember that the eyes can process light (one visual input) but also movement (second visual input, such as scanning a room). When light and movement overlap, for example, this will form a visual pattern (Arwood, 2011).

In order for the brain to integrate acoustic + visual or visual + visual inputs, these processing channels must not only function *upstream*, meaning electrochemicals must travel to the prefrontal cortex, but also must function *downstream* in the form of feedback along these same channels. In fact, for every piece of input the brain receives up these channels, it cascades feedback at a rate of ten times that down these same channels (Blakeslee, 2003). This fact is supportive of a semantic system that is not just structurally hierarchical but depends on cross-modal congruency or synchrony among inputs. In other words, one input into the brain will provide a great deal of meaningful sensory feedback; however, multiple inputs will increase this feedback exponentially. The more feedback the regions of the brain receive, the more synchronously they will operate (Arwood, 2011; Baars & Gage, 2010). Therefore, using semantic-based or meaningful materials for learning provides an external form of congruency with the strengths of the learners' neurobiological conceptual learning. Providing students with a wide variety of multisensory inputs will increase the activity in their brain, and therefore increase the probability that the information will enter into long-term memory (Arwood, 2011; Gallistel & Matzel, 2013; Robb, 2016).

Diving deeper into this process of learning, neuroscientists have confirmed that for successful integration of stimuli to take place in the brain, electrochemical messages must follow a bidirectional route of bottom-up feedforward (upstream) and top-down feedback (downstream) projections. Although forwarding new inputs to higher-level processing areas is necessary in the learning process (such as in the visual perception process), large scale multisensory integration can only be possible via feedback from the higher order integration sites, especially for higher-level conceptual understanding and cognitive tasks. Figure 2.4 shows a diagram comparing the signal flow of neurons in the brain involved in eye movement and processing of visual information. The left image illustrates the path of sensory information as it inputs into the retina, travels through the thalamus and visual cortex, and eventually integrates into muscles that cause the eyes to move in response to that stimulus. The right image shows the vastly more complex process of generating images in the mind's eye. Notice that more brain regions are involved in this internal processing and more feedback is spread throughout the brain (indicated by bi-directional arrows). This means that when the brain provides itself visual feedback, it activates numerous semantic circuits and networks and therefore makes more meaningful connections.

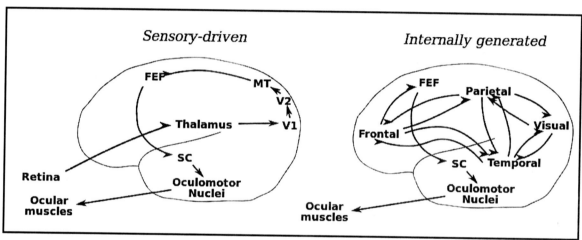

Figure 2.4: Brain networks involved in "seeing" vs. internally generating mental images
Image Credit L. Looie, Public Domain

Moreover, the brain uses visual knowledge differently, based off of whether it has simply memorized the information or whether it has internalized that information to be used spontaneously. The brain will dump meaningless patterns after approximately six weeks (Arwood, 2011). But, if these patterns are integrated into existing information in the brain through meaningful functional connectivity, they will eventually form concepts and language, according to the NsLLT (Arwood, 2011).

In one example to illustrate the difference between short-term and long-term memory acquisition, a man recently memorized an entire French dictionary in nine weeks and then proceeded to win a Scrabble tournament in that language. The man memorized the definitions of all of the words in the French dictionary, but he could not use them to form sentences or communicate his ideas (Willsher, 2015). In order to complete this large processing feat, his brain must have been extremely adept at storing cross visual modal information, or what some would call using a "photographic memory." But, it is doubtful that these stored mental pictures would stick into his long-term memory because he was not mentally manipulating these images such as including them in language. In other words, the brain tends not to store information if it will not be used in the future. In this sense, visual input can be processed at all levels in the brain (low, middle, high), but unless the brain cements these ideas using its natural feedback process, these ideas may fade away (Arwood, 2011).

Evidence can be found in recent neuroimaging studies that early visual areas are activated in imagery tasks (e.g. making mental images from memory), indicating feedback projections from higher-level cognitive areas (Falchier et al., 2002; Kosslyn, 1994). This phenomenon explains how and why humans are able to "see" pictures in their heads – sometimes as vividly as if they were looking at the real object. Notice that Arwood postulates that 95% of individuals are able to make pictures and movies in their head; this tenet provides one of the cornerstones of the NsLLT (2011).

In one extreme example of the mind providing visual feedback for itself, a prisoner who had been put into solitary confinement for many months began to hallucinate so lucidly that he no longer saw the darkness of the walls that surrounded him. Because his visual processing system had a complete absence of input (i.e.: light bouncing off of objects), it is hypothesized that his brain reallocated its resources entirely to providing visual feedback in the form of visual and auditory hallucinations (Eagleman, 2015). Presumably, because his mind was completely clear of stimulus, it needed its own metacognition to provide a purpose to continue existing. Over time, this prisoner began to have complete back-and-forth (fabricated) conversations with a variety of real individuals from his life, such as his family and friends. When asked to recount these conversations years later, he expressed the sentiment that these memories were as real to him as any other memory he had acquired in his life.

This idea that the brain provides its own critical feedback is substantiated by Klemen and Chambers, who estimate that there exists a greater abundance of backward rather than forward connections in the brain (2012). That is to say, neural feedback may play a more crucial role in higher-level cognitive functions for integrating new inputs with previously integrated sensory or perceptual units. This provides support in creating meaningful education based on a learner's own use of concepts from their past experiences so as to provide such feedback to the learner's system. Ghazanfar and Schroeder have introduced an expectation of a new education paradigm that emphasizes the multisensory and interactive connection model between the lower and higher brain regions and networks (2006).

In sum, the work of many neuroscientists and cognitive psychologists explored in this chapter provide evidence from primary research studies that substantiate many tenets of the Neuro-semantic Language Learning Theory. Many researchers would agree that evidence of tiers one and two of the NsLLT (sensory input forming patterns) has been accepted: scientists define this process as input-output or a permanent change in cellular structure (Baars & Gage, 2010). Furthermore, this literature review also provides evidence for the idea that human thinking might actually be more complex than two tiers. Specifically, evidence exists that sensory input may indeed get bundled together at higher order regions of the brain (circuits, level three) and eventually be represented as mental language (networks, level four). In fact, scientists may be looking right now at evidence of a four-tier model, but not know how to articulate what they are looking at. This is where Arwood's Neuro-Education Model can fill in many theoretical gaps that are currently stumping researchers.

In particular, neuroscientists are starting to be able to track how visual stimuli get recorded in upstream data processing channels in the brain; and, they are able to track how simple visual input can result in a cascade of information back downstream as it connects to multiple other regions. Arwood defines this reciprocal relationship between input and feedback in the brain as a human being able to refine their own thinking through metacognition (2011). In fact, by following oxygenated blood in the fMRI machine along its intricate pathways as it forges a myriad of connections, scientists may actually be looking at a physical manifestation of how the brain actually "thinks". Because 95% of the population thinks with visual mental imagery, viewing this densely interconnected architecture of electrochemical impulses may represent what it looks like for the brain to create mental pictures that the mind can then "see." As time goes on, more evidence is collected of the brain refining itself through metacognition. This idea fits hand in glove with the idea that the language we use names our thinking; and, that what we put into the brain (language) permanently changes the capacity of the brain to process information more effectively (Arwood, 2011).

Cognitive Psychology and the NsLLT

Thus far, this review of literature has focused primarily on how many findings in neuroscience support the scientific principles proposed by the NsLLT. In addition, because language acts as a key mediating factor for cognition in this theory, understanding how integrated messages are encoded into existing circuits and networks for later accesses (NsLLT Level 3 and 4) should be critical. Levels three and four represent the mind engaged in metacognition or using stored brain messages to think. Cognitive psychologists have long been fascinated with these abilities of the mind and have wondered how humans are able to store so much information and manipulate it in real time to form new ideas (Anderson, 2010). Taking a moment to review the literature in this field provides key insights into how the mind and brain interconnect.

Psychologists have attempted to categorize the knowledge that is stored in the mind into semantic networks or maps (Quillian, 1966). These maps diagram how it might be that we encode conceptual knowledge into *schemas* or shorthand representations of complex ideas.

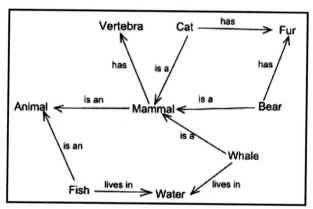

Figure 2.5 shows a semantic network for the concept of "mammal." Each arrow represents a semantic relationship that connects two linked ideas together. It is hypothesized that the mind clumps ideas together based off of how closely they are semantically related. Notice that this idea of clustering together similar semantic concepts to one another matches the aforementioned evidence that neuroscientists have found about the brain grouping neurons together physically based off of the need to process similar categories of information.

Figure 2.5: Semantic network for "mammal"

Though many iterations exist of how to carve up the knowledge in one's mind into groupings with interconnected relationships, psychologists are not in agreement as to how this knowledge becomes stored in the brain in the first place (Anderson, 2010). In particular, psychological studies on semantic memory have generated theories and established empirical results on the issue of memory and feature encoding. Two theoretical accounts have gained prominence, i.e. *feature structure differences* and *semantic contextual relationships*.

The theory of feature structure differences emphasizes that feature structure of a concept or category (e.g. red roses typically represent flowers) is important to semantic memory (Woollams, 2012). Empirical studies on feature listing revealed that words that generate more features produce faster naming, semantic decision, categorization, and recall (Hargreaves, Pexman, Johnson, & Zdrazilova, 2012; Yap, Pexman, Wellsby, Hargreaves, & Huff, 2012). Put another way, learners have a greater chance of encoding ideas when they are given language in instruction that evokes a visceral, multi-faceted response. Scientifically, as semantic features increase in quantity, the encoding of semantic memory is also enhanced. This supports the findings of the second and third tiers of the NsLLT that a multitude of multi-sensory patterns must overlap in order for the brain to form a concept.

Among all the sensory modalities, it was found that the visual systems are the most dominant sensory channel for acquiring semantic features, especially for natural objects (McRae & Cree, 2002; Tranel, Logan, Frank, & Damasio, 1997). When a meaningful visual input is perceived, it is identified at a conceptual level very quickly. This is surprising given the number of brain regions that must work in concert for this input to be identified. Moreover, when visual input is meaningful to the brain, then this related information is easier to be activated for elaborate processing (Potter, 2012). In other words, it can be more easily integrated and retrieved for later use. According to *differential weighting hypothesis*, semantic features differ in the weighting (Gainotti et al., 2009; Kiefer & Pulvermüller, 2012); that is, the higher the weighting is (e.g. more visual features), the easier the activation of the concept in the category can be.

For example, it is hypothesized that the human brain provides a higher "weight" or importance to living beings rather than objects (Warrington & Shalice, 1984). Presumably, this would mean that the human brain is more attuned to process the visual stimulus that a human provides rather than an item. Arwood explains this phenomenon as visual thinkers preferring to watch the visual shapes that a speaker's mouth makes rather than just listening to an audio voice without a head (2011). Her research has indicated that young visual thinkers will "tune out" the sound of someone's voice after approximately five to ten minutes if they cannot see that person's face (Arwood, 1983).

Visual features contain many different types of data, including color, shape, type of motion, texture, and size. In the NsLLT, when these visual features layer upon one another in meaningful ways, they stick in the learner's mind. This may be the reason why in studies memories invoked by visual conceptions are consistently reported to have better effect than other formats (e.g. auditory). This is probably due to the richness of the visual features that lead to higher weighting effects in the brain. The weighting of the features may also depend on relevance of the features to a given context; that is, the degree of semantic relationships among features and concepts. Semantic knowledge that does not directly enter through our senses (e.g. roses have a hundred species) depends more heavily on contextual information (Yee, Chrysikou, & Thompon-Schill, 2014). The mind must gain more higher order thinking abilities to be able to make these connections that are more complex in nature.

When these complex connections integrate into the brain, they wire together based off of geographical location in the brain. From the current flexibility standpoint of neural activities, nearby neurons flexibly cluster with each other and are connected in circuits across modalities under the influence of specific contexts (or congruency) (Baars & Gage, 2010). So, when new information relevant to the contextual meaning is recruited to existing neural circuits or conceptual networks, the existing knowledge of the concept may carry over to the new features and encode them together into the semantic memory system, a relatively long-term memory system (Squire, 1987). Arwood describes this phenomenon as meaningful new information connecting to meaningful old information in an infinite spiral model, where learning is never finished (2011). This is why Arwood's Neuro-Education Model advocates for instructional strategies that activate a learner's prior knowledge of the subject at hand.[9]

Furthermore, this explains why providing multiple visual inputs simultaneously (i.e. hand-over-hand drawing, visual shapes + visual movement, etc.) can help rewire existing neuronal connections to accommodate a "deepening" of a concept. Notice that this multi-sensory experience differs sharply from much narrower pedagogy used in education today,

---

[9]   These strategies will be explored in chapter 3.

such as direct instruction or Applied Behavioral Analysis. These methods aim to restrict the input to one's brain to only one input at a time. In contrast, research in psychology indicates that the brain actually learns best by attaching new ideas to a bevy of previously acquired ideas. Also, because every brain is different, acquisition of a new concept can only be achieved when a learner is able to input a variety of material that is meaningful, specifically to them.

Summary of Literature Review

In summary, the literature reviewed here provides support to the NsLLT model of language acquisition from three angles or disciplines. In particular, NsLLT aligns with language theories pertaining to a learning process from the complex language function to the structure based on the learner's semantic system. The neuroscience findings corroborate this principle on the sensory-motor view of semantic representation and the revealed neurobiological hierarchy of semantic processing in the brain, giving evidence to the differentiated learning stages proposed by NsLLT. Psychological studies on semantic knowledge and memory also offer explanations in the way messages are integrated and bond to become larger units or concepts (i.e. images in NsLLT) encoded in the circuits or networks for further access. Also, the empirical studies about semantic features provide further support for the use of visual features and images that are recognized by the learner to help increase meaning.

Much more research and scientific work is needed to find further evidence to support the model of human learning proposed by the Neuro-semantic Language Learning Theory. In particular, neuroscientists and psychologists could attempt to study the brain in laboratory settings as human participants engaged in real-time learning activities, such as drawing and writing about a concept. The information obtained about how the brain functioned during these experiments (such as flow of oxygenated blood, electrical flow, etc.) could be cross-referenced against a participant attempting to learn this same concept through auditory instructional methods, such as listening. Certainly, different brain regions would light up, as these tasks require different resources for attention and perception. However, it would be curious to see if the input of visual instructional methods into the brain did indeed provide a larger cascade of meaningful feedback along the downstream channels that was then able to forge connections to a wider variety of regions (as opposed to auditory methods). Currently, this hypothesis is one of the cornerstones of the NsLLT and should be explored directly.

In addition, future experiments could attempt to incorporate the language products that humans produce as valuable evidence to aid in the interpretation of results. For example, many psychological experiments ask humans to orally share what they are thinking. But, visual thinkers might provide more useful evidence of their own metacognition if they drew and wrote about their thoughts. In addition, it would be valuable to continue to study how the brains of these visual learners developed over a long period of time when given instructional methods that matched the way in which they think. Presumably, such treatment methods may even prove as effective as reducing the number of students being labeled for special education services or receiving ongoing medication. More research is needed that compares the functioning of the brain with the inner workings of the mind while using language as a third lens to mediate and interpret the first two.

Results of Research Study Using the NsLLT for Chinese Language Instruction

As an example of how the NsLLT model of learning can be utilized to analyze empirical-based language learning research, the following section will demonstrate direct use of this model as this author instructs high school students learning Chinese as a second language. Many of these students have struggled over the years to retain knowledge of this language that is fundamentally very different from their own. As the core of her dissertation, this author proposed a study that was aimed to find a more effective method for English-speaking adolescent Chinese learners to better integrate new Chinese characters (i.e. structures) into their semantic systems for retention recall. The author proposed using the Viconic Language Methods (VLM's) contained within the NsLLT to teach Chinese and see if these methods would be effective.

Reading and writing data was compared among three commonly used teaching methods in a computer-based study. Thirty new characters were equally presented in either an English translation, pictorial illustration, or verbal-visual interpretation method (i.e. storytelling in VLMs)[10]. The English translation method matches how many foreign languages are taught in the United States, where a student is provided a definition to memorize. The pictorial method involved showing the orthographic representation of the Chinese character and pairing this with the equivalent English word. The verbal-visual method involved informing students not only *how* certain Chinese characters looked and *what* they meant, but also *why* the characters looked a certain way. These characters each have a rich history that often relates back thousands of years and connects the present to elements of the past. This provided many opportunities to explore these characters in more dimensions than just definitions and visual representations.

The results of this study showed that the verbal-visual method had a significantly better effect on character retention than the other two methods, and the effect lasted for three weeks. One interesting discovery was that the pictorial method produced highest immediate recalls of the characters, but the retention rates dropped dramatically to the lowest in the two follow-up tests. The English translation method consistently produced lower performance in the immediate and follow-up tests.

To understand the cognitive processes underlying the performance, the researcher drew upon the literature from the three disciplines reviewed above: the language theories, neuroscience, and psychological findings and theories. Thus, a Neuro-Educational model (See

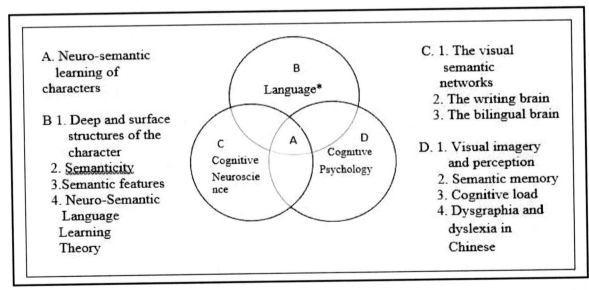

Figure 2.6: A Neuro-Educational model for the study of Chinese character acquisition.

---

[10]   For an example of this visual-language storytelling method, see chapter 3

Figure 2.6) in triangulation of the literature was developed for studying the current problem. Discussions of the results were carried out under the NsLLT framework as it aligns with scientific findings about language acquisition and semantic interpretation.

Under the NsLLT framework, the results revealed that the more meanings matched the learner's semantic system, the better performances were found in the recall of the characters. The visual-verbal method, by verbally telling stories about the meanings behind each character, offered three units of meanings, including the English concept, the semantic components, and the relational or spatial relationships of the components to form the concept. It may be that these meaningful features created a contextual network, which invoked images (as reported by the participants) overlapping to form a "story" of the character meaning. Therefore, the characters and their components may be more easily encoded as the parts of the whole entity into the learners' semantic systems. With more access points in the contextual networks, the retrieval of the characters or components with the images of the entire story would also be easier. On the NsLLT meaning equation, character learning using the verbal method may be the closest to the 3rd level, the level of conceptual meanings.

In comparison, the English method did not offer sufficient information to access the learner's semantic system (or less contextual information); thereby, invoking less mental images of the character meanings and hence less character recall rates. As for the pictorial method, the NsLLT points out a meaning discrepancy between the creators of the pictures and the learners who interpreted the pictures (Arwood, Kaulitz, & Brown, 2009). Although the participants reported "seeing" the images of meaning and character in the immediate recall, the perceived images were not the images or the concepts integrated in the participants' semantic systems.

In other words, though the students were seeing images in their mind's eyes in the English method, these images were simply borrowed from the instructor, akin to storing a photograph in memory. The students had not assigned their own meaning to these images, such as drawing visual depictions of the character or using the character in a sentence or story of their creation. In essence, the students had *memorized* the character and its meaning but had not *internalized* the character using their own visual-verbal language function. Their brains had not made the meaningful connections needed between new information and old information in order to cement this concept into long-term memory (Arwood, 2011).

In the English method, these perceptual images could last for a while in the working memory, but could not be encoded into the long-term memory unless overlaps of the images were available to reach the conceptual level (from Level 2 to 3 in NsLLT). Moreover, using the same pictures to recall the characters via the perceptual images could be heavily interrupted by excessive information in the pictures. This may explain why the pictorial method resulted in the least retention recalls. The limited picture effects in the immediate recall were also reported in another research study (Wang & Thomas, 1992). Therefore, character learning in the English and pictorial methods in this study most likely stayed at the 2nd level, the level of perceptual meanings or patterns, which requires more meaning overlapping to reach the 3rd conceptual level to successfully memorize and recall characters.

In conclusion, in this study character learning was closely linked to the levels of meaning the participants had for the meanings of the characters. The NsLLT has provided a framework for testing and interpreting a teaching method in the way to enhance the learner's conceptual understanding and use of the language. In the study, using the "story-telling" method was proved to be the best method compared to two other methods, because it helped to increase access points to the contextual networks and encode new messages into long-term semantic systems.

Implications

Beyond implications in the Chinese classroom, this study was mainly addressed to those educators or researchers who are interested in the field of language learning and education. Traditional language teaching and learning studies resort to students' behavior or teaching outcomes to find answers to solve a problem, like simply testing a word meaning in English. This behavior-oriented study model stays on the surface of the problem but does not dive deep enough to plant the language into long-term memory. The current research revealed that the learner's semantic abilities to interpret characters are the main reason for acquisition. Future studies in language learning or perhaps learning in general should shift to the learner-centered model, which examines their cognitive abilities and processes. The emerging neuroscience and cognitive psychology have paved the way to provide increasing findings toward cognitive analysis of classroom applications, so educators and researchers can develop better learner-centered curriculum in hopes of ensuring true learning of the material presented.

Unit 2: Incorporating Arwood's Neuro-Education Theory into Classroom Methodology

Preface

As a university instructor who supervises student teachers while they learn how to hone their teaching craft, one of the most common questions this author receives is, "What should I tell my struggling students in order to help them complete the assignments for my class?" New teachers tend to be especially optimistic in their attitude and open to feedback, which can make the supervising role quite rewarding. With the best of intentions, pre-service professionals regularly ask for input from veteran educators about how they can change their practice to meet the needs of the widest range of students.

Though their goals are honorable and well-meaning, their line of questioning often misses the point (or at least the most important focus) of how they can increase student learning. That is, in order to improve their practice many of these teachers ask what *they* can do or say differently. Implicit in their questioning is a desire for instructional tips and strategies that will serve as a sort of "magic bullet" to allow their material to "click" in the minds of their pupils. Such thinking is not surprising to this author, as many accounts of teaching in our society and our media inspire many to believe that quality instruction boils down to a series of battle-tested, motivational tricks of the trade. In other words, teachers are taught to use pedagogy, the art of teaching.

Few beginning teachers, however, stop to think about the validity and effectiveness of the methods and materials that other teachers at their school have encouraged them to use. "If the curriculum comes from evidence-based practices," they wonder, "how could it be ineffective?" After all, their reasoning would make sense in many other fields such as medicine, where best practices can clearly be shown to lead to a recovery from illness or an avoidance of death. When applied to education, however, this line of logic can often break down, as the vast majority of curriculum published in the United States is created by a handful of small corporations (Jobrack, 2011). How well these products are validated with scientific evidence can vary widely from company to company and lead to a glut of unsubstantiated claims about product effectiveness. More on this topic will be explored in Unit 3.

Since most beginning teachers ask what *they* should be doing differently in their practice, this means that they are not asking what *students* should be doing differently to improve their own learning. The fact that teachers are not asking about student learning means that they are less likely to view their classroom through the eyes of their students. Because they are so focused on their own craft of teaching, educators forget that *learning* can only happen in the minds of their children. Because each brain is wired in a unique way, each child will need to germinate the seeds of knowledge via their own learning systems. By viewing education from this reverse direction ("learner-centered"), we can structure our classroom, curriculum, focus, and methodology on maximizing opportunities for our students to learn in their own way. In other words, instead of *teaching*, we can *facilitate learning* in our pupils (Brown, 2012). This process matches the way that the brain acquires meaning and therefore optimizes chances for student success (Arwood, 2011).

Such a transformation from teaching to learning takes dedicated time and effort. The three contributing authors presented in this unit document their journeys toward making such a paradigm shift in their classroom instructional methods. In each chapter, the author provides a backstory of the types of learning challenges they faced before deciding to change their teaching practices. These struggles are relatable to most professionals working with children and include such diverse student concerns as: a difficulty learning to read and write using conventional sound-based methods, an inability to build a foundation of math knowledge in order to problem-solve new and unfamiliar questions, a lack of flexibility when navigating the social etiquette of school, and the vexing task of trying to distinguish between a learning disability and a developmental delay in English Language Learners. These authors walk the reader through their journeys, setbacks and all, to help inspire ideas of how these methods could be used in a wide variety of educational settings.

In particular, the authors introduce a few key concepts that are critical to understanding why neuroeducation methodology works to promote learning differently than traditional methods. To help prepare the reader, a brief primer is presented here:

Reductionist thinking / discrete trials – Though the ideas of behaviorism were created nearly 100 years ago, their grasp on the field of education persists to this day, and is even making a resurgence through such methods as Applied Behavioral Analysis (Arwood, 2011; Matson et. al., 2011). *Reductionist* thinking, a component of behaviorism, breaks down the act of learning a task into small subparts (Bandura, 1965). The goal is that if students show they can master all of the "necessary" subparts that make up the task, then they have demonstrated that they have "learned" this lesson. To work with a student who cannot master a task, the teacher must use *discrete trials*, or a series of repetitive practice strategies designed to imprint a pattern into memory.

Concepts, however, cannot be taught by a teacher; they must be acquired by the learner (Arwood, 2011). Therefore, much of what is called "direct instruction" in the field does not form deep enough connections for a child to learn to think at a higher level. From a neuroscience perspective, the methods proposed by behaviorism only reach the *sub-cortical*, or "lower level thinking," regions of the brain (Arwood, 2011; Baars & Gage, 2010). To acquire higher order thinking abilities, students must be given the opportunity to design their own learning.

Process vs. products – Much of the literature in the field of education today suggests that in order for students to progress in their learning, they must create artifacts that indicate they have amassed sufficient knowledge to master the "standards" of their grade level. Therefore, emphasis is placed on students to create *products* that show correct answers (i.e. multiple choice, fill-in-the-blank, multiplication tables, etc.). The assumption here is that the brain learns by adding to its memory bank in a predictable, additive method.

Instead, as mentioned, learning in the brain actually mirrors a spiral: new pieces of information constantly intermingle with old pieces until an entirely novel concept is born that is greater than the sum of these parts (Arwood, 2011). Therefore, because learning is never completed, it is not the finished *product* that matters, it is the *process* undertaken to make this product that counts. By asking students to explain their thinking *processes*, for example, we can more accurately assess for how deeply they understand a concept.

All behavior is a form of communication – Many educators use the term "behavior" with a negative connotation to describe anti-social actions. In addition, psychologists often interpret these actions as being intentionally mean or hurtful on behalf of the child (Mash & Wolfe, 2012). Therefore, when most adults see a child "hitting" another student, they assume that this child is purposefully causing damage to another human. And, this child will only learn to correct their ways if they receive negative reinforcing consequences, such as punishment.

Arwood (2015), however, describes behavior merely as a collection of acts that a child does to interact with their environment. Moreover, every one of these acts may be interpreted by an adult as a form of communication. In the example of the child "hitting" another peer, Arwood would simply describe the physical actions of this movement, such as, "the first boy lifted his arm, his hand moved through space, and this hand made contact with the arm of the second boy who was standing next to him." Notice that the use of this language to describe the event is without any judgment to the mental state of either child. This is because, as adults, we cannot truly know the intentions of a child unless we ask that child to explain and/or draw out their intentions. By doing so, we may discover that the child did not in fact set out to hurt others. Or, they may not know that their peers could perceive their "behavior" as anti-social or undesirable. Instead of punishing the child, a subsequent conversation about their "behavior" could lead to future growth in socio-cognitive thinking. Any of these interpretations by the learner would necessitate a great deal of language function on behalf of the child.

Learning systems vs. learning styles – These authors talk about how learning systems, the neuro-semantic way of learning to think and use language, are based on how the patterns are organized in unique circuits for thinking. Therefore, the methods must match the way that learners create their thinking concepts. Learning styles are preferences, which students are often educating into having. Such styles may or may not match the learner's system. Whenever the term "learning" is used in this anthology it refers to the learning system, not styles.

In Unit 2, examples of the implementation of Arwood's Neuro-Education theory are detailed as they are used in a variety of educational settings. These case studies illustrate the complexities of working with a variety of students with different learning systems. They show how difficult it can be for some students to navigate the current educational climate in the United States. This unit also highlights the concerns educators have with their own craft and their abilities to assist struggling learners. By using Arwood's Neuro-Education theory, students and teachers alike can overcome many of the adversities they face in the classroom.

Chris Merideth

Chapter 3

Seeing the Journey: One Path to a Paradigm Shift

Bonnie Robb, Ed.D.

Abstract

This chapter documents the journey of one educator along the path towards discovering and utilizing brain-based Viconic Language Methods in an elementary school classroom. The author makes a strongly supported case for teachers to analyze the level of language function in their student populations in order to uncover how their students think, feel, and behave. Data is collected over a five year period that shows a noteworthy increase in student achievement scores as measured by the Developmental Reading Assessment (DRA) after the author began utilizing pedagogy inspired by Arwood's Neuro-Education Model. Students' scores on the DRA are taken upon entering this teacher's classroom in September and then again upon exiting in June. All students' reading and literacy scores increased a minimum of one grade level, with 50% of students making two years or more of growth as measured by the district mandated assessment. 90% or more of students achieved proficiency on district level benchmarks each year, a markedly higher number than students in other classrooms in the same school. During the time of data collection, the school had a student body with a range of 75-85% of students on free and reduced lunch with approximately 30% of the student population designated as English Language Learners. This chapter explains all of the facets of schooling that Neuro-Education methodology can enhance including: student engagement, pro-social relationships, and increasing the complexity of academic thinking.

About the Author

Dr. Bonnie Robb is an award-winning elementary school teacher who has been working in the field of Education for 20 years. For much of this time, Dr. Robb has taught a diverse mix of students including individuals learning English as a second language, native speakers, children with special needs, and individuals who identify as neuro-typical. Dr. Robb utilizes a student-centered teaching philosophy in her classroom that aims to reach all learners, regardless of ability. She has been widely recognized for her success using visual-language strategies. Dr. Robb recently completed her Doctorate of Education at the University of Portland with an emphasis in neuroeducation studies. During research for her dissertation, she investigated numerous primary source studies in neuroscience and cognitive psychology that substantiate many of the theoretical claims presented in this work.

Background

Most people have traveled, so it is no wonder that we often hear our lives compared to a journey or a road we are on as we are always moving forward toward our next destination. The difference between people is often the perception of the journey; there are those who believe the purpose of the journey is to reach the destination, and there are those who believe that the destination is only part of the journey.

I have reached what many consider the "halfway" point of my journey as an educator, as I have been teaching for 18 years. When I begin to reflect on my experiences thus far, I see parallels between the metaphor of a road or journey and my own experiences. There have been some moments of worldly success along the way; beautiful destinations worth remembering. However, these destinations did not just happen; a journey took place to reach each one, and the journey was a process worth remembering. Through the process of reaching each destination, professional growth and refinement occurred, and day by day, mile by mile, I hope children were able to learn.

My goal for this chapter is to take you along on my journey so you can see that real change takes time, it's a cross-country trip, not a run to the store, and that learning is a process that never ends for both students and teachers. We should all try to improve a little each day, to add to our learning, and to understand the learning process so that we can help one more child reach their full potential.

My journey as an educator began in 1995 as a graduate at the University of Portland with a BA in Education and the enthusiasm that only a 22-year-old can have; ready to change the world, one student at a time. Then reality sunk in; the Portland, Oregon area was facing a job shortage due to a radical change in state education funding that was unprecedented. Teachers that were retiring were not being replaced and there were few jobs available, so I resigned myself to substituting and working at summer school.

I had many regular and long-term jobs as a substitute, and I used bribes, rewards, and contests to keep students, with whom I had no relationship, under control. For three years, this was my view of teaching; swooping in for a day or two, maintaining control, trying to teach a little. This part of my journey lacked little refinement or growth as an educator, and although I was highly in demand as a substitute teacher, I was not becoming a better educator of children. However, I was able to see many different schools in many different parts of the city. I observed many different classrooms, lesson plans, and classroom atmospheres. I do not consider this a wasted journey because the experience I gained during these years helped me define what I believed an educator should look like.

In 1998, I was offered a job as a half-time second grade teacher in a job-share situation, which I readily accepted because it was a permanent position within my local school district. This portion of my journey was very bumpy because a job-share can be tricky even when the two teachers are great communicators and thoughtful educators. I was still a very new teacher at the time, and I had hoped that the job would allow me to collaborate with and gain wisdom from my more mature and experienced colleague. This was not the case so I faced my first year of regular teaching with little guidance or encouragement.

I remember that year as being very perplexing. I had a great deal of experience working with a wide range of students over the previous three years; however, I was having constant difficulties with behavior in this classroom. For example, we had a chart with three colored cards; green meant that you were doing well, yellow was a warning, and red meant that you were in trouble and would lose your recess. I had learned that this was a standard behavior plan for elementary classrooms and since I had read about it and been taught about it in my college classroom management courses, I assumed this method would be effective for helping students "see" their behavior choices and make changes. I even had a prize box where on Friday a student could choose a fun prize if they did not receive any red cards all week. What I found, while keeping track of the red cards and green cards, was that the same students always received a prize while another group of students never did. It became obvious after a while that the cards and prizes were not "motivating" certain students to change their behavior. At the time, I was at a loss to understand what to do with the students who did not follow my oral instructions. This system of rewards and punishments was the only model I knew, which was not surprising since it was the only strategy I had experienced in the school setting.

Instructionally, I taught the students what I had been given to teach them, which consisted of reading worksheets, decodable texts, and math textbooks where the students practiced equations, and writing what they copied from the overhead. I tried some science "units," such as learning how photosynthesis works, but these were also mostly worksheets and reading. Most of the students showed little improvement academically during that school year, and once again I wondered what I was doing wrong. I had given the students all of the information they needed to learn for second grade using the materials I had been given by the school district, so why had they not learned it? This year was so demoralizing that I considered leaving the teaching profession.

This part of my journey was full of questions without answers, knowing that there had to be a better way to help children learn. In search of those answers, and with the hope to find renewed purpose, I decided to apply for the Master of Education program at University of Portland in the fall of 1999. At the same time, I was transferred to a position as a half-time reading teacher at another school because the job-share teacher came back to the classroom full time. I wanted to complete an endorsement in Reading as part of my degree, so my job and course work aligned perfectly. In the course of my job I used a phonics-based program with fourth grade students to help them reach state benchmarks in reading. Learning how to read with phonics is the status quo method out in the field today. Teachers, specialists, and parents alike all believe that in order to read a student must be able to connect the letters on a page with the sounds that those letters make. Eventually with enough of this sound to letter correspondence, students would be able to "read" the words on the page, and purportedly understand what they had read.

Using this phonics system, the students did make progress that year in their oral fluency skills, but still did not meet grade level expectations in reading comprehension. Nevertheless, the phonics teaching methodology aligned with what I was learning in my M.Ed. program, so I ended the school year feeling more successful professionally, but still wondering if there was a way to help students achieve more growth during the year. This was another segment of my journey that left me with more questions than answers - questions *still* unanswered by the coursework I was completing as part of my master's program.

Before the second year of the program began I interviewed for another reading support position closer to my home and was hired for the job. I was working nearly full time, primarily with students in first through fifth grade who did not have an Individual Education Plan (IEP) but who were identified as struggling in literacy skills. I felt confident beginning this year with the knowledge I had gained about the reading process from my college coursework. I continued to teach the sounds of letters and ways to sound out words to read as I had been informed to do in my numerous years of schooling. The younger students did not show very much growth, and the older students seemed discouraged and frustrated during our time together.

That fall, there was a small problem with my M.Ed. program because I had already taken many of the classes required for the reading endorsement as an undergraduate. This left me with credits that would normally have been filled with reading classes needing to be filled with electives. Another student in my cohort suggested that I take a language course by a professor named Dr. Arwood because she had interesting strategies for helping struggling students. That sounded good to me since I was always looking for new ideas. I had been traveling along, doing what I knew, teaching how I had been taught without question. This was all about to change. In that first class, the first time I met Dr. Arwood, I could see my road starting to take a new direction.

Introduction

The first impression I had of Dr. Arwood, the creator of this anthology, was that she had a very different way of looking at learning. At first, I had a hard time wrapping my head around what she was saying. This began as soon as I talked about the manner in which I taught reading - she said that was not the best way. She told us that sounds were getting in the way of the students' reading, not helping it. Instead, I should be concentrating on helping students make meaning, not reading words. I had never heard this before, but since I was on a journey, I thought a small detour to see something new couldn't hurt. I wanted my students to make growth and enjoy reading as much as I do, so I decided to try something different with the students. I asked a few questions about possible strategies, and the next day at work, I gave one of them a try.

Dr. Arwood shared that 90% or more of students think with a visual system. This means that they see pictures in their heads, and that these pictures represent their conceptual understanding of the world. Dr. Arwood proposed strategies that would capitalize on a student's visual thinking system. The first strategy I tried in my small groups was with the first graders. While they read aloud to me and they came upon a word they struggled with, instead of sounding out the word, I told them the word. The student then wrote the word down and drew a picture to represent the meaning in a picture dictionary, which is a group of words organized by story, or topic, instead of alphabetically as with every other dictionary I had used. After the students wrote the word, drew a picture, and then read the word again, I had them continue with their reading. For an example of a picture dictionary filled out by a student, see Figure 3.1.

Figure 3.1: Picture Dictionary to Learn New Vocabulary Words

The educational rationale I was given by Dr. Arwood for this methodology was that the brain does not use words as its unit of analysis (Arwood, 2011). What we think of as "words" are actually concepts that must be acquired in the brain through multiple visual scaffolding examples. Students can increase their vocabulary best not by the sounds that the word contains, but rather by learning the shape that the words make and assigning layers of meaning to these visual concepts. Students with a visual thinking system learn best by seeing the whole word as an idea or set of possible ideas (Arwood, 2011). By including multiple visual depictions of each concept in the picture dictionary, students were moving past simply "memorizing" words and were using their own language (drawing and writing) to help anchor the idea to existing information in the brain (Arwood, 2011).

A commonplace strategy I was already using at the time to help students read was to have them reread a book a second time to improve their "fluency," but before using the picture dictionaries, students would more often than not misread the same word over and over. Many reading specialists suggest this strategy, but students were not improving in their comprehension of the material. The first time the students used the picture dictionaries, they could read the word in the book and they did not misread it again in other books. I was astounded! This was the first time I used a strategy that worked so quickly and I was excited to be teaching in a way I had not been doing for the past five years. On my journey to help students learn, this was a road worth taking and I was going to see how far it went.

Visual Language Interventions

The next strategy suggested by Dr. Arwood that I tried was intended for the fifth grade students. These older students were reading two years or more below grade level material and they were having a hard time understanding what they had read when asked to repeat the ideas orally. I asked them to read silently, instead of out loud. I now knew that the sound of their own oral fluency was getting in the way of their understanding in their mind's eye. Sound was distracting, not helping their visual cognition.

After their silent reading time, and before they said anything, I asked them to draw a quick sketch of what they had just read. After they sketched their idea, they answered questions about the story, and this time, the answers were correct. Drawing their ideas had allowed them to "pull out" the concepts of the reading from their mind's eye. Without this step, students were not given the time, nor were they prompted, to make a picture in their heads of the material we had just gone over. Doing so increased reading comprehension, yes; but most importantly, I saw them smile, feel pride in their own thinking, and ask to read more.

As I continued to use this visual language strategy, this group of students began bounding into the room everyday, excited to be at school. Their teachers commented on how they were more confident in class, and on that year's state tests, they showed marked growth, much more than they had shown in past years. Once again, I was amazed at how something so simple and effortless could make such a difference in a student's learning.

Dr. Arwood also introduced a new dimension to how drawing could be used to address problem behavior in my classroom. She suggested that for students who had difficulty following directions, we could draw how we wanted them to look and explain why we wanted them to look that way. We could "cartoon" out the behavior that we wanted to see in our classrooms. I had never tried this strategy before, but was intrigued, so when a first grade teacher mentioned that she had a student who would not hang up her coat and backpack and get to work each morning, I offered to spend some time with the student to see if I could help.

The student and I sat down together, and I drew a cartoon, in boxes, left to right, showing each step needed to take care of the morning job expectations. The student was enthralled and insisted on taking the paper and taping it to her desk. The next day at lunch the classroom teacher came to me completely amazed because for the first time all year the student had done exactly what was expected and was ready before anyone else. She wanted to know what I had done, and if it might work with other students. Figure 3.2 shows a sample cartoon (drawn in real-time with a student) that visually depicts what it looks like to follow morning routines in a classroom.

Notice that in Figure 3.2, the cartooned students have thought bubbles that show what it

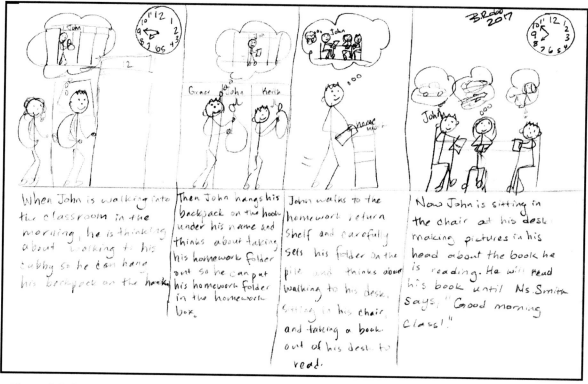

Figure 3.2: Cartoon of Expectations for Classroom Morning Routine

is that they should be thinking about as they progress from step to step. In addition, there is an analog clock in the upper right-hand corner of two of the panels. This allows individuals to orient themselves to the shape that the clock hands make and to make sure they are looking like the drawn individuals at that point in time. Lastly, the writing used to describe each drawing matches closely to what is visually depicted. This allows students to begin to make an important mental association between written and visual instructions (Arwood, 2011).

Cartooning with a student was a turning point for me on my journey because whenever I tried a viconic language strategy with a student, I saw immediate change, either in academics or behavior. This was what I had been waiting for during the five years I had been teaching; a way to really help students learn, grow, and change for the better. I had entered the teaching profession so I could help students feel excited and proud about their own learning, and now I was starting to see results.

Other teachers were really wondering what I had been doing and wanted to know more, so I suggested that Dr. Arwood might present theory and strategies at the next staff meeting. I continued to use her strategies and the students I worked with continued to make growth. I ended the school year on a very positive note and was looking forward to beginning another school year in the fall.

A Visual Language Classroom

As the school year came to a close, I arrived at one destination when I graduated with my M.Ed. with a Reading Endorsement in the summer of 2001. My journey was certainly not finished because in late summer I noticed a full-time job opening for a first grade teacher at an elementary school in my district. This school had a free and reduced lunch rate of 78%, and 20% of the students spoke a language other than English at home. I applied for the job, had an interview, and for the first time, had a job offer for a full time classroom position.

This was a pivotal moment in my journey because I was very happy being a reading specialist. I was at a school very near to my home, the students I worked with showed great success, and I was comfortable. This new job was across town, at a high-needs school, and I would only have two days to get my classroom ready. I was wavering on the decision until a kind colleague told me that this was my chance to really help children, to make a difference, and have some real control over my teaching. Her advice (and that of others) was correct, and with the support of my family, I took this new road on my way to a new destination.

After the whirlwind of setting up a classroom from scratch in two days, I began my first full-time classroom job in the fall of 2001. At the time I felt as though I had plenty of experience and strategies for helping children, but the students still struggled. I tried drawing, but it didn't seem to work as well with a large group of students. We read many books, used hands-on science kits, and used a math curriculum with many games and visuals, but I still did not witness the change and excitement on the scale I had seen before.

By mid-year, I was frustrated so I signed up to attend a Saturday Neuro-Education seminar with Dr. Arwood. There, I learned about the Neuro-semantic Language Learning Theory (NsLLT) and how it could help promote learning for those who had previously struggled. I didn't really know what I needed, but I knew that the students were not changing and growing the way I had hoped. I remember in the seminar when Dr. Arwood had everyone introduce themselves to the group. She asked us to tell our name, what we taught, and why we were there. My answer to the final question was that I wanted to help children learn, and if I could not do that, I might as well quit.

This pivotal seminar was full of ideas that confused me, but also provided my teaching with some answers and a renewed purpose. I contacted Dr. Arwood again and asked if she could visit my room and give me some more strategies for helping students and she graciously agreed to help when she could. However, we did not find time to meet that year. I finished out the school year using the few Viconic Language Methods I knew: picture dictionaries, drawing out ideas, cartooning behavioral expectations, and a few others. Despite my best efforts, my students showed little growth on reading assessments, so I was disappointed for them and determined to make whatever changes needed to be made to help more children the next year.

There was an opportunity to apply for a small grant used for professional development from a local foundation, so I asked Dr. Arwood if she would work with me and some other teachers on a book study using her book, "The Language of RESPECT" along with classroom visitations to refine practice. She agreed and the grant was approved. I was very excited to begin my second year of classroom teaching.

In 2002, I began the year with observations and suggestions made by Dr. Arwood and a colleague Mabel Brown, who graciously volunteered to help with students in my classroom. Mabel brought with her a depth of experience working with students who have language differences in a one-on-one, clinical setting. Mabel also became a valuable learning resource on my journey, spending many volunteer hours in my classroom, sometimes helping with whole class strategies and sometimes with students one-on-one.

The first strategy we tried became very important in the classroom, and required me to give up long held assumptions I had about the reading process. In my teaching endorsement programs I had only been taught that the way we learn to read is to connect the letters to sounds, then put the sounds together to form words. However, my data from the previous year confirmed that this methodology was not effective for all students. The students needed a way to read words without breaking up the sounds and letters into their individual parts. Even though this was a new way to approach reading instruction, I wanted to give it a try for two reasons. First, many of my students were English Language Learners (ELL) and/or had a Speech Individual Education Plan (IEP), so they had difficulty even producing the sounds of the individual letters within words.

Second, when I really took apart what I had previously been taught about the process of reading, I remembered that there are three cuing systems that we can use to make meaning from print; semantic (meaning of words), syntax (English grammar rules), and graphophonic (sound/visual correspondence). Two of these three systems are language based, not sound based, and the graphophonic system does not require that we break words into individual sounds to say the word.

With all these ideas in mind, the students began using picture dictionaries in all aspects of the classroom including writing, math, and science, not just reading. Whenever a student did not know how to read or spell a word in any subject area, I wrote it on a sticky note then they wrote it into their picture dictionary. I let go of the notion of "guess and go" spelling, and worked to deemphasize sounds as a primary strategy for reading and writing. Students regularly drew multiple visual representations of all unknown vocabulary words into their picture dictionaries. When students needed the word again, they were directed to find it in their picture dictionaries.

At the same time, we worked to refine the meaning of our writing by asking and answering the question "why." This forced children to use the word "because" and really use their own language to explain their ideas. For example, if a child drew/wrote, "I went to the park," I would ask them why and help them expand their idea to: "I went to the park because I wanted to play." This process refines and develops language, and increases the complexity of writing as much as two grade levels. Language names our thinking (Arwood, 2011). Therefore, when a student uses more complex language, this represents a more refined semantic understanding in the mind and in the brain. By increasing the sophistication of a child's language, we are increasing their ability to think, problem solve, and understand the world around them (Arwood, 2011).

If reading and writing ability are primarily based upon our ability to use language, the process of using a child's visual-cognitive strengths should produce results. During my first year of classroom instruction I made a conscious effort to help students use brain-based strategies to read and write.

Preliminary Results

I was pleasantly surprised at the end of my full year of classroom teaching when the reading scores of my students progressed from 59% meeting or exceeding on the Developmental Reading Assessment (DRA) to 83% meeting or exceeding the same standard. The DRA is a district-mandated assessment that measures reading fluency and comprehension skills. Even more exciting was that the ELL students in my classroom jumped from 29% meeting to 75% meeting reading benchmarks that June. This was a great improvement, but I wondered... was it a fluke? Were the students just "easier" that year? Would it be possible to have even more children read at grade level or above as measured by the DRA?

Dr. Arwood and I decided to continue our collaboration and add more strategies to the classroom the following year. This process of adding and refining understanding is an important part of learning for teachers and students. The results of the students' hard work was proof to me that what we had worked on together was helping them learn, so I was eager to add more layers to my understanding to be more effective at helping students the next year.

Refinement of Visual Language Strategies

As my third year of classroom teaching began, I focused more on the concept of language development. When I recorded unassisted oral language samples where the students were asked to tell a story using an event-based picture, I found that most of my first grade students had language function similar to three year olds. It became clear that until their language improved to that of a typical six or seven year old, it would be difficult for students to show their understanding of six or seven year old concepts. Language development became the focus of the year, which was a shift in my teaching practice because I began to move away from skill development into concept and language development. Figure 3.3 shows an example of a simple event-based picture that I drew out for the whole class.

In this example, I have put myself in the picture, as I am the one relating the story. I include agents (people), doing actions (swinging and sliding) on objects (parts of the playground). By drawing out these basic semantic relationships in front of the class, I now know that the pictures in the heads of my students will follow what is visually depicted on my sketchpad. Now, we can label all of the agents, actions, and objects in the drawing. Doing so helps individuals make mental connections between the words we use in language and what these words look like in real life. Modeling and practicing these language strategies will help raise the level of cognition for visual thinkers over time (Arwood, 2011).

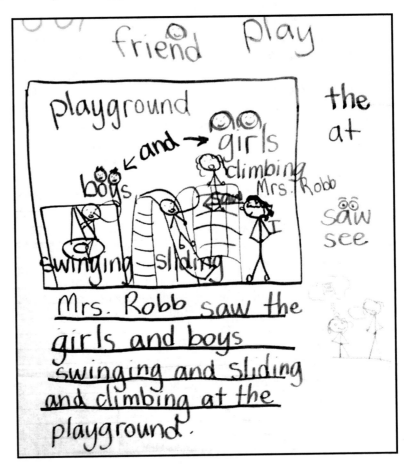

Figure 3.3: Drawing out Event-Based Picture During Whole Class Instruction

One of the ways the students and I worked together on functional language was to understand our place and purpose in the classroom and the school. By this time it was clear to me through my studies with Dr. Arwood, as well as by assessing my own students, that most of the children in my classroom (95% or more) thought with pictures in their heads. They were using a visual learning system to make meaning, so it followed that meaningful visuals were needed to help them gain language about how to work with others. I practiced cartooning and began to draw expectations and relationships in real time in front of students. I drew students in many situations throughout the school day, particularly showing the "because" of situations with a thinking bubble above the head of the student.

For example, in order to help students understand why they should be quiet in the hall, I drew students walking without touching or talking. Then I drew a talking bubble reaching into another classroom where the noise from the talking bubble "popped" the thinking bubble, which was full of pictures of another student. When the children saw this, they were shocked that their actions could stop somebody from thinking. For the rest of the year, their hallway behavior was much improved. By helping the children understand how their actions could affect others, the change in their outward behavior occurred quickly and was long lasting. We drew together, illustrating the rules of the school and the classroom in a relational way. As their social concept language grew, it helped their academic language grow. Figure 3.4 shows an example of this cartoon to work on classroom behavior.

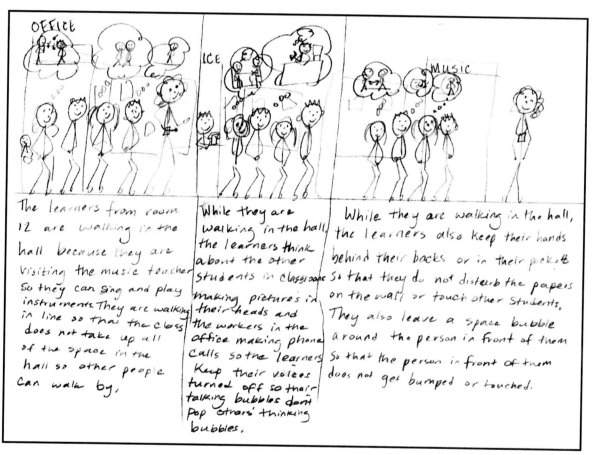

Figure 3.4: Cartoon to Illustrate Classroom Behavior Expectations

Academically, I shifted the focus of learning from individual skills to broad concepts. We did not take apart language to study nouns, verbs, and letter sounds. Instead, we were entomologists investigating insects by asking and answering questions such as, "What is an insect?" "Where do they live?" "Why are there so many different kinds?" "Who is affected by insects?" and "Why do we need them?" We would read, write, calculate, observe, speak, and draw about insects to increase our conceptual understanding of insects. Throughout the year we were also geologists, nutritionists, and literary critics. I observed that as the conceptual language of the students grew more complex through our investigations, they were able to apply that language to other academic areas such as reading, writing, and math. Increasing the students' language abilities seemed to be increasing their ability to think critically as well, and not just in the subjects we were studying.

Many students seemed excited about school and they seemed reluctant to leave, showing pride in their work and learning. These are the intangibles that cannot be tested, but that I had always hoped would exist in a classroom of learners. What I had glimpsed years before while working in small groups with struggling readers was finally happening daily in a classroom full of students.

Visual-Motor Strategies

This third year things were feeling good, but I wondered if the results of the end-of-year testing would reflect the language development I had witnessed during the school year. The DRA results showed 90% of students at or above grade level, and 45% far exceeded expectations, scoring at end-of-year standards in reading for second grade. This was a validation of the work we had been doing together in the classroom, but since the 10% of students who did not meet the standards were ELL, I knew we could do better. I consulted with Dr. Arwood again to refine my understanding of the learning process in order to decide if there were more visual language strategies that could be used in the classroom. I also started coursework to add an English Speakers of Other Languages (ESOL) endorsement in order to learn more about language acquisition and development in conjunction with the seminars given by Dr. Arwood. This part of my journey was crucial because as I added to my conceptual understanding of the visual learning system, I hoped to have enough strategies available to help just one more student in the classroom.

In the fall of 2004, I began my fourth year using Visual Language Strategies in the classroom, working to refine the strategies used in previous years while I added more. My studies with Dr. Arwood increased my understanding of the visual learning system to include students who were only able to put concepts into long-term memory by using a motor access. What this means is that I had to help students by placing my hand over theirs during the drawing and writing process so they could feel the shape of a word in order to create a concept from the shape. Students with a visual symbolizing system require many overlapping visual layers of input. For students whose biological sensory systems do not connect as efficiently, they can benefit from adding layers of movement which can provide much-needed meaning to the brain's visual and motor cortices (Arwood, 2011; Gallese & Lakoff, 2005; Gross, Hayne, & Drury, 2009).

Working hand-over-hand, we completely removed all language relating to the sounds of letters and words for understanding, focusing only on the shape and feel of the words as a whole. Often this process included multiple opportunities to use a concept (word) in the context of a story. First we would draw a story, then we would label the "who, what, where, when, and why" of the picture with words. Then we would write and draw those words into a picture dictionary. Finally, we would write the words from the dictionary onto lines in a sentence, adding pictures over the words if needed to read the ideas. For many students in the classroom, this process of scaffolding meaning through visual means is absolutely necessary to put any concepts into long-term memory and increase language function.

Figure 3.5: Picture Dictionary Completed by Student With Hand-Over-Hand Assistance from Adult

Figure 3.5 shows an example of a picture dictionary filled out by a student, and Figure 3.6 is a drawing made by that same student that tells a story using the new vocabulary words from the picture dictionary. In Figure 3.6, the student has included the "who, what, where, when, and why" of the story. As previously mentioned, expanding upon these basic semantic relationships provides multiple examples of how language can be used to paint a complete picture in the student's mind. The more opportunities a student has to transfer their mental pictures onto the page through drawing and writing, the more chances an adult has to help refine their thinking.

Working one-on-one with students in a class of 24-26 first graders is not always easy, especially working hand-over-hand with my most struggling learners. To address this, I utilized as many volunteers as I could to work with other students in the classroom, including accepting student teachers from local colleges when they needed a placement. I also had students with high functional language be my "helpers" when another student needed help with spelling by giving them a small pack of sticky notes and letting them help others. I found that when students helped each other, they showed ownership of their learning and pride in their role in the classroom. All students see an example of how very capable they can be, and that Mrs. Robb is not the only person in the room that has answers. This "positive pride" surrounding a child's contribution to all learning, and the kind compassion they demonstrate towards other students, was exactly the kind of pro-social atmosphere I always hoped would happen for students at school.

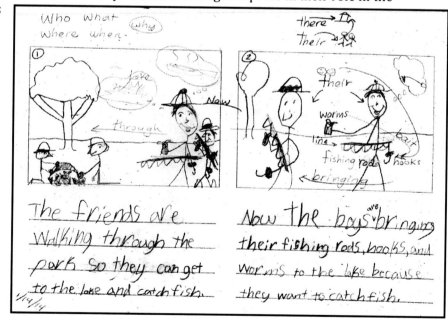

Figure 3.6: Adult and Student Creating Story from Picture Dictionary

Developmental Levels of Language

Another strategy I used that year was based upon my understanding of how language develops. Learners begin all new concepts from a preoperational level, meaning we relate any new information to known information. This attaching of new information to old information can be seen in the brain structures themselves: as the brain processes new information, neurons rewire and reconfigure to other neurons to form perceptual patterns (Arwood, 2011; Baars & Gage, 2010; Levine, 2000). As patterns overlap, they eventually form concepts. This phenomenon of rewiring is called *brain plasticity*, and it represents the nearly limitless potential of the brain to re-engineer itself. Quite literally, the brain can reorganize itself to operate more efficiently – but only if it is given input that is meaningful (Baars & Gage, 2010; Bassett et al., 2011; Frith, 2007).

My goal in the classroom was to incorporate what we know about the brain to help children increase their understanding. Students grow in cognitive development when they can progress from the immediate "here and now," such as with tactile objects, to concepts that are more *displaced*, such as understanding that there are some ideas that we can't see such as "respect" or "forgiveness." When we can understand another's viewpoint, for example, we understand it at a concrete level. When multiple concrete layers are conceptualized, we understand ideas at a formal level.

In the classroom, the process of layering new ideas from scratch often begins with an "I" story. For example, when we began to investigate ideas about insects, I would tell and draw a story about a time I saw a huge beetle crossing the path in front of my house and how that beetle was so big it made me jump a little! Then the beetle skittered off into the grass, and I never saw it again. This is my preoperational story, but when students see and hear a story about insects that is not their own, they are moving to a concrete understanding of what insects are.

Soon, after many students have layered their preoperational stories, they begin to understand that there are insects they have never seen, but that still exist. After they hear and see my story, they draw or write their own story about an insect (preoperational). Then, the students share those stories with each other (concrete). Using storytelling to introduce formal concepts (such as insects) in this way allows all students to be successful as they see a real event that they can relate their own experiences to.

After these first stories we continued moving our learning to higher developmental levels as we asked and answered questions about insects such as: *Where do insects live? Why do they live in different places? What do insects eat? What eats insects? Why are insects here? Why are they important? Who studies insects?* etc. Through relating our experiences we answered these questions and we learned about insects, but we also developed our ability to be literate: read, write, observe, speak, and calculate. When new concepts are acquired through content, they are learned in context, which allows for greater long-term memory storage and retrieval through the semantic networks created for the concept of "insects." Neuroscientists refer to this phenomenon as the brain becoming more *efficient*; meaning, the brain exerts less effort to recode and retrieve information when it is run through the learner's own cognitive system (Baars & Gage, 2010; Pulvermüller, 2003).

Oral Language as Visual Language

By the end of the fourth year, the only students who did not meet grade level expectations for reading, writing, and math were students with a pre-existing IEP, although they did show much growth. In addition, 100% of ELL made benchmarks this year! At this point, Dr. Arwood, Mabel Brown and I decided to collaborate in writing a teaching manual to help others try these strategies in the classroom. This was a great learning experience for me as I began to articulate and write how and why developmental learning was happening in my classroom.

As I entered my fifth year teaching first grade, I continued to use and refine the strategies from previous years; I made a conscious effort to add one more. Since most students think in pictures, I would try to make my oral language create clearer, more detailed pictures. For example, instead of saying, "Let's get ready for P.E.," I would say, "Boys and girls, please put away your books, pencils and other tools you were using where they belong because Mr. Smith is waiting for us in the gym. He is waiting for us because he wants to help you get some exercise and learn a new game, so please put away all of your learning tools so we can line up and walk to the gym to see Mr. Smith." This language proved to be very effective with students and, when combined with drawing, reduced non-learning behavior significantly.

Using all of the Visual Language Strategies described with refinement and "tweaking" here and there for individual students, the end-of-year results continued to be positive. Overall, 95% of students made grade level benchmarks, including two who were on an IEP. Once again, 100% of ELLs ended the year at grade level or above. After three years of such positive results, I felt like I was on the right track. In the spring of 2006, I also completed my ESOL endorsement, which meant that for the foreseeable future, I would be able to keep the ELLs in the classroom with me all day. This seemed to have a positive effect because during the years I was able to provide their instruction solely in the classroom, the ELLs in my class often out-performed their English-only peers.

True Learning Knows No Bounds

From that point on, I continued to use as many strategies as I could and attended as many seminars as I could to keep learning more because learning is never "done." I have found that as soon as I think I really understand something, I realize just how much more there is to know! I did, however, notice another intangible in the classroom. This was a time when classroom minutes were being "prescribed," for example: spend 60 minutes teaching math, or 45 minutes teaching writing, two hours teaching reading. This practice still continues to this day, and in my district, such minutes are being audited by principals and kept on record in case our state education department requests the information.

While the children certainly spend a majority of the day engaged in rigorous, more traditionally defined academic learning, I have always made time for art lessons, joyful picture-book read aloud times, independent choice reading, recess, and choice time where students could create, negotiate, share, and grow as social human beings. Even with time away from the kind of "direct instruction" taking place in other classrooms and schools, the students continued to make excellent growth.

Upon reflection, I now understand that learning that makes sense to students, learning that creates language, as well as learning that changes a student, is efficient and occurs exponentially. This is much different than the skill practice that is often prescribed by current curricula, which requires hours of work to keep skill patterns relevant to the brain. Patterns such as sounds and isolated words in the form of whole group lessons and endless worksheets need constant practice to be maintained in the memory systems of the brain because they are the lowest level of sensory input the brain processes. Unless the patterns are overlapped with concepts, which then overlap to form language, the brain will not keep the patterns (Arwood, 2011; Lenneberg, 1962). If instruction is always at a pattern level, large time requirements are needed, so other valuable classroom learning is pushed aside.

My work through the years has proven to me that there is time for all learning when the acquisition of knowledge is based upon the learning system of the student. The student's individual learning system is the most efficient system for making meaning (great for the student!) and a product of the students creating meaning is raised test scores (good for the school). Undoubtedly, this is why principals give teachers like me a measure of freedom in instructional choices; my students consistently score well on grade level assessments as a natural outcome of their own learning process.

A Paradigm Shift Results in Accolades

During the 2007 school year, I had a three-credit class available to me through the University of Portland because I had mentored a student teacher, so I decided to take another course on language development from Dr. Arwood. We talked about the courses available and Dr. Arwood suggested that we develop a one-on-one course together with the final outcome being a written article that we could submit to a magazine. We decided to highlight the success that incorporating Viconic Language Methods had upon the English Language Learners in my classroom. In January 2008, *ESL Magazine* accepted our submission and we were subsequently published. This was an exciting rest stop on my journey, but I only arrived there through a complete change in my understanding of student learning, and a willingness to change my practice to match what my students needed to learn.

In the fall of 2008, some kind colleagues nominated me for Oregon Teacher of the Year. In December of the same year, I was awarded the Milken Family Foundation Oregon Teacher of the Year, a very exclusive honor for which you cannot be nominated. The foundation, working with state education departments, seeks out those candidates that they wish to honor. It was an amazing stop on my journey, but it was simply a secondary result that represented many years of a continual learning process. It also happened because, as Dr. Arwood (speaking about me) pointed out, "She won it for the right reasons...she won it for what she does with kids."

New School, New Challenges

A year after receiving this honor, I made the decision to leave the classroom and join a team of teachers at the district level to help introduce a new K-5 math curriculum. It was hard to leave the classroom and kids, to leave the school where I had taught for nine years, and to leave a principal and colleagues that I admired and cared about. I hoped to help other teachers on a greater scale to use some of the strategies that had helped so many of my students. During the two years I spent as a Teacher on Special Assignment, I learned many things about how the district operates, the differences between schools across a large district, and about the math curriculum and standards we ask teachers to use.

However, I was not able to affect much change helping others use Visual Language Strategies because I was not a continual resource for any teacher. I would pop into a building, lead a professional development session about how to use Neuro-Education methodology for greater success in the classroom, then leave. However, it dawned on me that it had taken me years to develop my practice using these new methods. For a teacher to understand how students use their own learning system to acquire language takes much more than a "fly-by," it takes an on-going partnership with observations, suggestions for change, and refinement. This left me disappointed because I really wanted to show teachers how they could help their students in a meaningful way.

When budget cuts required me to return to the classroom, it was a good change and a big one since I had gotten used to my office job! I applied throughout the district, found a wonderful principal who saw what I could offer to her school, and was hired to teach second grade. This school had a completely different demographic than I had ever worked with before.

When I left my last school, 85% of the students received free or reduced lunch, 75% were students of color, and 30% of first graders were ELL representing up to eight different languages in the classroom. My new school had less than 15% of students on free or reduced lunch, was 85% Caucasian, and had less than ten ELLs in a school with over 400 students.

One might assume that the demographic profile of the first school would be more of a challenge than the second. I certainly assumed that "the grass was greener on the other side of the fence." I had assumed that children with two highly educated, involved parents (often one who stayed home), and who spoke English would enter school with grade level academic and social language abilities, or at least a higher level of language function than my previous school. I was given this impression when looking at the staffing of the school since the only support teachers were one full time Special Education teacher and a half-time speech/language pathologist; there were no counselors, educational assistants, or reading support specialists. I was even given the impression by other teachers in the building that the children were so well behaved that teachers just taught with no worries about anti-social classroom behavior. My assumptions were about to be proved very wrong.

I began the fall of 2012 at the new school with a new staff, a grade I had not taught for years, and whole new curricula/standards/expectations. I was prepared to use many of the visual strategies I had used before, but I was a little out of practice. Perhaps I took some shortcuts or did not use enough rich "because" language, but whatever the reason, the year began with a drastic change in my assumptions. As I looked over portfolios of students, I saw that 5 of my 24 students, or 20%, were entering second grade reading at a late kindergarten level and only one of those five had an IEP. I found that shocking, but since I was used to helping students to read who knew much less, I was not concerned.

What became apparent after the first few days of school however, was the low overall functional language of the students in the classroom. When I took oral language samples and asked students to tell me a story about a picture, none were able to do so, and none used the word "because" in their sample. In other words, the students were able to explain the "what" of the situation, but not the "why." More distressing to me was that when I transcribed the samples, at least half of the students did not connect the relationships of the people in their stories. They mentioned each person acting separately from the other, which did not bode well for social development. In one example a student said, "There are kids. And a lady shopping. There is a mad man."

| Student 1: "Well the car is flying by and there is a puddle and it is splashing the people and they don't like that...and the guy is holding a stop sign...and I don't think he is stopping...the kids don't like getting splashed by the water...it's a wet day" |
| Student 2: "Well, it looks like the car drive through a pretty big puddle and splashed the kids...maybe the stopper guy tried to tell him to stop but he didn't do it." |
| Student 3: "Well, I guess a car is coming up when the person wants them to stop so the kids can go by and instead they just splashed the kids and they splashed the guy who is holding the stop sign." |

Figure 3.7: Oral Language Samples in Response to Event-Based-Picture

Figure 3.7 shows some sample oral language responses taken from students in my class. These students were shown an event-based-picture of a family driving in a car through a puddle and splashing other people on the road alongside of them. The students were asked to explain the "who, what, where, when, why, and how" of the event. In other words, students were asked, "Who is in the picture? What are they doing? How might the people be related? Where is the scene taking place?" etc. Sample responses were recorded and analyzed. Results showed that students struggled to semantically connect the agents, actions, and objects of the story in a meaningful manner.

This lack of relational, social language was evident in the classroom behavior of at least eight of the students. They did not see anyone in their pictures, and they acted as though they were the only people that mattered. So, they talked when they wanted to, played around with others whenever they felt "bored," and blamed others for their actions. In Piaget's developmental psychology terms, this behavior is "preoperational," meaning typical for children between the ages of three and seven. By taking the language samples I had, I realized my students were socially delayed.

In terms of one of my students diagnosed with autism, his preoperational behavior ("me, myself, and I") was evident; but, there was another student with no official diagnosis who refused most requests I made, loudly yelling "NO" for example, when asked to move to another seat OR draw a picture OR even attempt to read a book. His behavior was much like that of a two to three year old toddler. None of the students had ever drawn before writing (and many had been told that drawing was for babies), so I had to try to convince them that it would help their thinking. At times, it was a challenge.

I knew that the 20% of students who were far below grade level and the student with autism all had a motor access learning system and needed hand-over-hand work, but I received no support to give them this one-on-one time. It was difficult to give one student my attention academically, because so many others who were deemed "Talented and Gifted" (TAG) had anti-social behavior themselves. They would exhibit this behavior as long as they thought they would not get "caught." I quickly realized that we needed to start seeing each other in the classroom as people, with pictures and ideas that mattered; I had become startled to see such anti-social behavior.

Visual Language Increases Pro-Social Behavior

After making the decision to improve the social relations in my classroom, I quickly started to layer in all of the Neuro-Education viconic language strategies I had used before: cartooning behavior with thinking bubbles to represent choices; having students draw themselves using pro-social behavior to reflect the attitudes I wanted to see in the classroom; speaking with rich oral language and including the "why" behind our actions; telling "I" stories to start off a new unit of study; drawing hand-over-hand for those who needed movement access into the brain; drawing out ideas before writing; and always using "because" language to help increase positive relationships between people. My goal was for students to start to understand that their actions could affect others in a positive or negative way, and that they got to choose which path to take.

I asked Dr. Arwood to visit my room to help me understand at a deeper level what was needed to help more students become pro-social; she made many notes on how to refine my strategies. It is not always easy to have a master educator watch you teaching and your students learning in your classroom because we have been conditioned to believe that any suggestion for change is a "judgment" of our performance. Dr. Arwood always focuses on what the students need to learn, not on how I teach. This valuable input left me feeling energized to try another way to help a student learn, and I found myself referring to her notes over and over again.

Academically, it became clear to me that if the students did not have input in the process of their learning, they tuned out and their anti-social behavior worsened. One contributing factor to the social challenges might have been that one-third of the students were identified as Talented and Gifted; these students could read and calculate far above grade level expectations. In effect, the group was a multi-age classroom spanning three grade levels of language and skills, so "one size fits all" was not going to be effective. By the second half of the year, I began to think about how I could help the students manage more event-based project work. I had to remember an important concept; that the *process* of thinking, explaining, and creating was more important than pumping out *products* such as worksheets.

The class then started a unit on ecology. With the idea of process vs. product in mind, I proposed to the students that they could choose and create their own project to represent their understanding of habitats and biomes of the world. We worked through the process of naming the ways we learned new information, and ways to show others what we had learned, with a few guidelines: there had to be writing, and you had to be able to explain your project.

When the students were given this freedom of choice to use their own language, the classroom changed. The anti-social behaviors decreased dramatically as students who could more successfully read and write helped those who could not and those who could represent their ideas through drawing were in "high demand" for self-selected group projects. Many students began to see a world outside of their neighborhood. The child with autism heard another student talking about the huge ball of plastic in the ocean, and went to his neighbors over the next few days collecting as many plastic bags as he could. He brought the big pile of bags to school with a note that said, "Please keep plastic out of the ocean so animals can live." Later his dad told me that this was the first time he had witnessed his son thinking about a situation other than his own.

Another group of girls were worried about wetlands pollution. I helped them complete a bit of research on the computer and we found that there was a wetlands conservancy group here in Oregon because there are no laws to protect Oregon wetlands. We worked through the process of how to collect money from the school classrooms including bringing clean milk jugs for coin collection, writing a speech to explain to the other students why they were raising money, counting the money after it was collected, and writing a letter to the conservancy letting them know who they were and why they raised the money. The Oregon Wetlands conservancy was so touched that they printed the girls' letter in their quarterly report.

This is just a sample of the ideas the students came up with: posters with diagrams and labels, videos of information, games with game boards and rules (for example, prairie dogs evading predators to reach their dens), reports and books. The projects were much more unique than anything I could have dreamed up and being their ideas, the students were more invested in the process and proud of their products. We shared our projects with each other and on our class webpage.

By the end of the year, I witnessed much social growth. The visiting district autism specialist and parents of the child with autism said it was the most successful year of school so far for the student. By the end of the year, four of the five children who came to second grade one year behind in reading made two years worth of growth and left school in June meeting grade level standards. Even my student who still had some unresolved social-emotional issues made over a year's worth of growth in reading. Overall, they seemed calmer and kinder to each other.

We had all made it through the year together, and I am grateful to the students for reminding me of the importance of process over product. They helped me to remember that it is *never* too late to make a change or try a new strategy to help a child learn. They also taught me that all children need strategies based upon their neurobiological learning system, no matter what their skin color, first language or ZIP code. For nearly all of the students, this was the first time they had been taught in the way that their minds work. Using brain-based viconic language strategies had been highly successful in promoting pro-social behavior in the classroom.

Conclusion

On my journey as a teacher, I had momentarily forgotten how important the process of learning was for students. As I began to observe the social and academic growth of the students when their natural learning process was acknowledged, I realized that I was just the facilitator of their schooling, just one guide on *their* journey. It is important for me to *always* remember that what takes place in the classroom is not about my needs as a person, or what my principal wants to see, or the cute projects on the wall, or what the curriculum "tells" me to do. What happens in the classroom should be based upon the individual neurobiological learning systems of the students. Since 90% or more of students think with a visual system (Arwood, 2011), they tend to find most success with the viconic language strategies inspired by Neuro-Education methodology. I am just there to help each student in the classroom use their own learning system to make meaning, both academically and socially.

Every mile on the road of this 18-year journey has given me another strategy to help a child find success and pride in their own education. I am grateful for every mistake I've made because it has helped refine my learning and, hopefully, has allowed me to help just one more child learn.

See you at the next milepost!

Summary of Neuro-Education Methods

The author uses a variety of techniques and strategies to truly access her students' neurobiological learning systems. Neurobiologically, she taught in a way that accessed higher, more evolved regions of the human brain. The complexity of the human cortex is what differentiates human brains from other species. By teaching in a visual, conceptual manner (as opposed to rote memorization, fact drilling, or using reductionist teaching methods like phonics) the author was able to get out of the lower, "older" regions of the brain and into the higher functions of the cortex. In other words, she is not "training" her students (what animal/mammal brains are capable of); she is helping them acquire concepts (what human brains are capable of). With the brain functioning in this more efficient manner, acquired concepts have multiple access points (neuronal connections) and the physical structure of the brain changes to support long-term retention. The next teacher will not need to re-teach these concepts again in the fall.

Socially, the author approaches her students with respect and the deep-seated belief that cognition isn't fixed – the brain has *plasticity*, and therefore may continue to change! Since the author views her students with the mindset that they are capable of cognitive improvement (once their learning systems have been accessed), she has higher expectations for her class and thus she is setting them up for success. She does not simply dismiss her students by saying, "They are not capable of achieving *blank*, so I might as well not attempt to teach it." Instead she says, "I know they will understand *blank* if I can figure out how their brain best receives and processes input."

With this positive, pro-social attitude, the author is helping her students develop a greater sense of self, or agency. With more agency comes higher levels of cognition and vice versa. Furthermore, the author has developed a curriculum and classroom culture rich with conceptual, "because" language. This helps children fill in perceptual gaps and make complete pictures in their heads. "Because" language, picture dictionaries, and drawing out concepts for unknown words are all ways to add additional layers of input for students to help them build more and better quality neuronal connections that go into long-term memory. By helping children create their own concepts for the shapes and meanings of words, the author is facilitating long-term acquisition of whole language and there is no need to teach sound patterns or traditional spelling.

Over time, this author has honed her teaching practice into a balance of theory and achievement. By understanding all of the concepts of how the brain truly learns in a synergistic and systemic way (meaning brain regions do not work in isolation from each other), she has truly served children and helped them to become lifelong and holistic learners.

Chapter 4

My Brain Feels like a Tossed Fruit Salad: Stories from a High School Math Classroom

Amy Klennert, M.Ed.

Abstract

The author of this chapter chronicles the steps along her educational path towards incorporating brain-based visual language methods in a high school math class. The author set out to ask the question: would the Viconic Language Methods inspired by the Neuro-semantic Language Learning Theory work in developing math concepts in the 15-18 year old adolescent brain? Student achievement data is collected over a two-year period in the form of pre-tests when entering the course and post-tests concluding the academic year. The results of these assessments found that Viconic Language Methods did work to promote learning for older age adolescent students, especially those who had struggled with math literacy over their schooling career. Surveys were also given to students at the end of the year asking them to rate their level of self-confidence in terms of their math abilities. Nearly all participants who received instruction using Viconic Language Methods expressed having higher self-esteem as a result of being able to "see" math concepts more easily than they had in previous courses.

About the Author

Amy Klennert teaches math to students at a Title I high school with high poverty and many learning challenges. After Amy graduated with a master's degree in neuroeducation studies from the University of Portland, she began incorporating brain-based visual language methodology into her classroom and finding successful results. Amy serves as more than a teacher for many of her students who struggle with difficult home lives. She has been able to re-engage her most struggling students with a positive attitude towards school, to the amazement and pleasant surprise of many of her colleagues.

Background

My journey into the field of neuroeducation is fueled by a desire to figure out how to reach all students, especially those who struggle. As a former home-school parent, my first paid teaching gig was as a chess coach in a parent-partnered program. I continually saw my feet placed on the path towards trying new approaches to enrich my practice. After spending eight years teaching chess and math without a certificate, this paraprofessional entered the

University of Portland (UP) at the tender age of 44 to attain a teaching certificate in Advanced Mathematics.

I first met Dr. Ellyn Arwood at UP in 2005 as a graduate student in her special education class. I can still see in my mind the stick figures she would draw on the board to represent each disability, and can still remember the first lesson she gave on how exactly our eyes "see" and our ears "hear." One time I stood before Dr. Arwood attempting to explain how this was the first time I had ever forgotten an assignment at home. After telling me I could turn the paper in the next class period, she proceeded to gently suggest that I attempt to color code my notebooks to have a different color for each of my university classes. For example, my Monday, Wednesday, Friday classes would be certain colors, and my Tuesday-Thursday classes would be other colors. My visual learning system would then organize the week by the colors needed each day. I promptly and incorrectly responded that I had an auditory learning system and that this mishap was simply due to stress. I realize now that it was she who was correct.

Nowadays, when attending her courses, she likes me to describe a beach to the rest of the class using my visual learning system. I am always amazed at the gasps and smiles received from my fellow classmates. Their mind's pictures were nothing like the movie going on in my head. Life experiences dictate the pictures in our minds; thus, each student in my classroom develops their own unique mental picture of a concept I am teaching. This fact should be the first lesson planning objective: bringing up students' prior knowledge is key to neurologically connecting brain circuits that enable them to remember content (Arwood, 2011). Understanding brain-based theory is a necessary first step towards promoting effective teaching.

Introduction

I have taught at a Title I high school for the last seven years. My students have challenging issues and are affected by poverty. The first few years I tried different classroom management strategies and continually persevered in learning new ways to connect mathematical concepts. I would blend remedial work and grade level work with higher level questioning and tasks to develop higher-level thinking. In Algebra 1, I felt I made a lot of progress towards building concepts, until I delved into the minds of my Precalculus students. Their ability to move from one mathematical representation to another was near absent, and the rote responses they gave just showed me they had only learned math patterns, not the underlying concepts. My priority changed from sending every Precalculus student on to Calculus the next year, to working towards helping every college bound senior get into a 100 level college math class. I was not satisfied because I could not find the key to unlock the ability to create meaning in my students' learning.

I attended a neuroscience and education lecture at the University of Portland about what drugs and alcohol do to the brain, and immediately began to share what I had learned with my students. They were amazed. I now use PowerPoint presentations by Oregon Health Science University (OHSU) neuroscientists to teach students about how their brain works and how it learns. I knew I wanted to learn more about the brain and how learning actually happens in children, so the next thing I knew I was signed up for the Master's in Neuroscience and Education program at UP. During the first summer class I learned about Dr. Arwood's Neuro-semantic Learning Language Theory (NsLLT). Then I spent the fall developing strategies and began to make a paradigm shift in my teaching of Precalculus. The research presented in my courses showed that the NsLLT worked to promote cognitive growth in younger students, but I wondered... would it work in developing math concepts in the 15-18 year old adolescent brain?

Neuro-semantic Language

The Neuro-semantic Learning Language Theory (NsLLT) is a four-step process that allows a teacher to understand how students learn from a neurobiological perspective. The sensory input of the lesson, mostly in auditory and visual forms, causes neurons to fire in the student's brain. When enough of these neurons fire together, they wire together to form perceptual patterns (Hebb, 1949). The teacher's role is to provide more sensory input using literacy-based strategies (such as helping the students think, view, listen, see, and calculate) to help neurons fire creating layers of patterns (Arwood, 2011). The teacher then provides feedback opportunities using literacy to create circuits in the brain (Baars & Gage, 2010). When enough perceptual patterns overlap, they become circuits of neurobiological meaning. At this point, the students can acquire the concept by attaching their own language to the concept (drawing and writing), which then places it into semantic memory.

The first strategy based on the NsLLT I tried was what I call "Arwoodese" - Dr. Arwood would call it "oral cartooning" or using "because" language. The first time I thought to give it a try was in a middle school math classroom where I had a student who constantly blurted out his thoughts. I knew he couldn't see how his actions were affecting others. I said, "Because you let your pictures fall out of your mouth, your words take up space in the room and you make my pictures go away, and when my pictures go away, I can't teach, so no one will learn." I needed him to keep his words in his mouth and raise his hand to speak. Doing so would allow his classmates to keep their pictures in their heads. As a result of him not blurting out, I could teach and the class could learn.

Visual Literacy Promotes Math Competency

The NsLLT was providing great results thus far, so I decided to incorporate more of its principles into my instruction. Throughout that first school year teaching Precalculus, I implemented two strategies aimed to help visual language learners: Flow-Chart Notes and All–or-Nothing assignments. The rationale behind these strategies was based in brain research. I would help my students connect new ideas to previously acquired neural patterns and circuits, and then add multiple layers of meaning through sensory input to those neural pathways. I created a type of Flow-Chart Note strategy that drew out the prior knowledge of my students and created a give-and-take response between teacher and students. When students realized that they could answer using math examples, hand gestures, have others help them to create meaning of words, or by creating a picture with a term, suddenly all students could participate and wanted to explain their thinking. Figure 4.1 is an example of the Flow-Chart Note strategy.

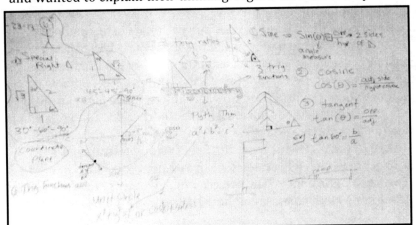

This flowchart has a learner in the top left corner thinking about all of the concepts that he will learn today on the topic of Trigonometry. By including a learner in the overall picture, students will see themselves on the page and will know that they too need to start thinking about all of the ideas presented on the board. Visual and written diagrams are

Figure 4.1: Conceptual Flowchart

connected with arrows to show significant semantic relationships. Students are encouraged to create their own flowcharts, as this represents their own thinking, not the thinking of the teacher.

To model a conceptual flowchart for the class, I put the standard we are learning in the middle of a white board, bubble it, and use pictographs and arrows to attach all the knowledge and meaning in the conversation. Bubbling a concept helps students to see the shape of the word; neurologically our eyes see whole shapes better than isolated parts (Anderson, 2010). The pictographs give students a visual cue to help tag the concept into memory. Arrows help to tie ideas together. I also use multiple mathematical representations to describe the concept using graphs, tables, numbers, and symbols. One time, we created a web of intricate notes all over the white board. Students often remark that if a principal walked into the classroom he would not understand the notes. They are right. The flowchart becomes our notes, our understanding of the concepts, and our creation.

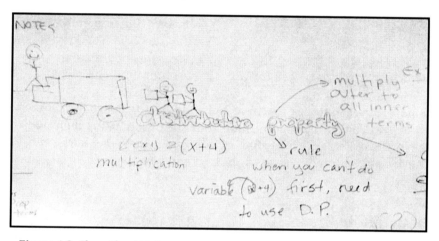

Figure 4.2: Flow-Chart Notes

In Precalculus, during the trigonometry semester, we completed an NsLLT unit in class. As we were beginning a new unit, a student complained about continuing the viconic language strategies. I asked her if it helped her learning, she said yes and never complained again. I continue to use Flow-Chart Notes in all of my classes, even AP Calculus. I have gotten better at bubbling words to see the shape and also at coming up with pictographs to put in the math ideas. Interestingly, the Algebra 1 students are better about wanting and designing pictographs to attach to the bubbled standard, which interprets the concept than the older Precalculus students. Another example of Flow-Chart Notes is in Figure 4.2.

The Algebra 1 students also use the Flow-Chart Notes strategy in their own note taking. They might border their thoughts, put a stick figure of themselves on the paper, or put personal notes to remind themselves what they were thinking at the time. One student uses 4 by 6 index cards for each new concept. He definitely embraced the idea of grounding himself by placing a stick figure of himself in his note taking and bordering all of his work, thus providing multiple visual representations of an idea. He even did this when sharing how to do a problem in front of the class. He confidently states he now can do math after failing and getting low grades in the prior year. I once worked with him on a problem and we were bubbling numbers and symbols. Once we had talked and corrected his work, he looked at me and said, "Is that all it is? I have learned more in two weeks of school then in the entire year last year." His example notes are in Figure 4.3.

The next school year in Algebra 1, I added Dr. Arwood's picture dictionaries to my classroom strategies calling it Concept Cartoons. Instead of writing a verbal definition of an idea, students would draw out multiple visual representations in order to provide enough meaningful patterns to form a concept. Visual concepts stick in the minds of visual learners, while auditory concepts often never form.

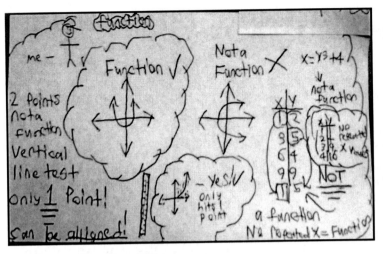

Figure 4.3: Visual Note-Taking

I also gave students an opportunity to write down lingering questions on a half sheet of paper, and I gave feedback to those questions in writing to the student or as part of the lesson the next day. This allows shyer students to participate in the discussion, and the teacher can formatively assess student knowledge. Literacy became this math teacher's friend. I constantly was asking my students to write about their thinking, rank their learning, and to form questions. This caused students to put ideas in their own language, which is a necessary step for concepts to enter into long-term memory (Arwood, 2011).

Each year I introduce more literacy into my teaching and assignments in order to assess more accurately how and what my students are thinking about a math concept using their own communication skills. I can tell by the language level a student uses and by how much negativity is used in their writing how much a student understands a concept and what amount of stress they feel.

Teaching Students About Their Brain

My students enjoy learning how it is that we actually learn new information. I use neuroscientists' PowerPoint presentations to teach my students about how their brain works, and I draw out how their eyes and ears process sensory input. I include neuronal connections, the hippocampus, the amygdala, the prefrontal cortex, and the reward pathway in the limbic system. I show how learning strengthens the connections among all of these brain regions and how the language we use names our thinking in the brain (Arwood, 2011). This helps students understand how learning happens in their brains and how drugs and alcohol affect them. Adolescents need to partner in their learning; this creates engagement. In order for the NsLLT strategies to work, I need my students to buy in to the process.

Teaching about the brain creates ownership in the students' learning. By doing so, we begin to create a culture where students refer to their thinking as the pictures in their heads. This gives a teacher access into students' thinking and gives students a way to communicate their thinking by allowing them to describe the pictures they see in their minds. When students feel that they can participate in a class, they feel like a part of the classroom culture.

One example comes to mind of a student learning how to access the pictures in their head. A calculus student was graphing and defining mathematical concepts. She attempted to try conventional note-taking methods by writing the definitions first and then graphing an example. Frustrated, she responded with, "I can't do this!" I suggested she draw the graphs first, which she *could* do, and then attach her language, her own words and drawings, to the visual representation. She tried this and immediately her stress level reduced and she was able to work through the assignment. Later, she and I discussed her visual learning system and how she could apply this strategy to other subjects. The positive response was wonderful. A girl sitting by her boyfriend said to him, "You sitting next to me is making my amygdala get all worked up!"

Mostly, girls tell me how for the first time they feel good about their ability to do math, and that their confidence continues to improve. Boys earn better grades. However, the journey towards getting students to "buy in" to use methods inspired by the NsLLT is not always easy. One student repeatedly became frustrated when asked to draw and write, and she would exclaim, "I just want you to show me how to do the steps! You are making my brain feel like a tossed fruit salad! Why can't you teach like my teacher did last year! I don't understand!" I met her frustration by renewing my desire to have her remember the math concepts. The strategies used in my classroom helped her neurons to form layers of understanding in her brain so she will remember the math. Just being taught how to do the steps is a pattern, not a concept. Good students will study the patterns before a test and then, after taking the test, their brain will dump the patterns because there is no meaning attached and they will forget the math patterns. I told her that if she wanted to remember the math concepts, she would need to write about them, draw about them, talk about them etc. In other words, if she wanted the material to stick, she needed to use her *own* language.

I learned that from a neuroeducation perspective, the language we use represents the concepts we have acquired in the brain. We can see how a student explains their thinking to see if they only understand the idea at a pattern level (meaning they have memorized a math rule without being able to apply it elsewhere). A student who is forced to expound upon their ideas to explain the *why* behind their answer has truly learned a concept. Language causes all of the brain processes to work together in an efficient manner. The brain will dump patterns that are meaningless, but retain original thinking (Doidge, 2007). This understanding of the brain is how we should be promoting math literacy strategies in school.

Moving Past "Reductionist" Teaching Models

Part of my quest to connect the conceptual dots for students led me to analyze teaching as a holistic endeavor versus an additive building block approach. Year after year, my colleagues teach functions in the building block approach. They do so without really thinking about it, as this is the status quo pedagogy in the field today. For instance: a teacher needs to teach students how to graph a line. Students practice finding the y-intercept and the slope from an equation and then practice graphing using the slope and the y-intercept. They practice countless problems that are nearly identical to each other. Then, they are assessed on each subset of skills to see if they have "learned" (memorized) them.

Next, students will graph lines using tables, a numerical representation. They practice plugging in independent values into an equation to get out the dependent value of the line and they place the values in a table. Using the values in the table, students graph the line. All of these steps so far can be completed at a pattern level. A student doesn't really need to know *why* graphing a line is important, just *how* to do it.

Finally, students are expected to use formulas and other algebra skills to find the slope and solve for the y-intercept and then graph the line using the slope and y-intercept. Each skill is assessed separately. There is no meaning attached to the concept of linear functions. A student might be able to graph a line using the equation, yet flounder at the idea of graphing a line using a table. This is because the pattern of using a table is different from the pattern of graphing using an equation. In education, we expect students to make the connections necessary to bridge the gaps between these two skills. And yet, we rarely stop to analyze whether we are providing them opportunities to do so.

Breaking down skills into subsets of skills and then attempting to build them back up again is called *reductionist* design, and it comes from the study of behaviorism. behaviorists look at teaching from an adult perspective: "Now that I know the whole concept (e.g.: graphing a line), what parts would *I* need to learn if I were taking apart this concept?" As adults, we think we know how the brain puts together information, but really, we are basing this assumption off of our own introspection, not off of science (Arwood, 2011). You cannot teach a concept, and yet teachers try and try. Concepts must be acquired by the learner though their own thinking (Arwood, 2011). As I teacher, I should be focused on providing opportunities for my students to practice putting the pieces together in their own way, not just imitating what I am doing. This is the essence of incorporating neuroeducation theory into classroom practice.

As a result of these discoveries, I have changed my teaching to holistically show students all the different functions they will learn in the next couple of years. I tell them that they will be expected to be able to analyze each function through multiple representations including graphing, both numerically, and analytically. The emphasis will be spent on making sure students will be able to graph *any* function. When they understand they can identify the independent and dependent variable, which together are a point on the graph, they can solve any mathematical representation.

Tagging Pictures with Language

One student in particular who I worked with affirmed for me that the brain-based visual language strategies I was using were working to promote true learning in my students. This student, Sam, is in ninth grade, and is a very quiet individual. She draws beautiful drawings and works diligently to become better by carefully checking a picture on her phone with the picture she is creating. After I had taught the class about the adolescent brain, Sam responded to a written question about her feelings towards math by saying all she sees is numbers and symbols. She did not know how to turn the numbers and symbols into meaning.

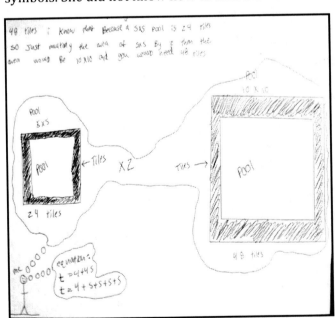

Figure 4.4: Student Putting Themselves in the Picture

I knew that Sam was a visual thinker, so I needed to start accessing her visual learning system. As I bubbled standards, used pictographs, and drew stick figures into concepts, Sam tried all of these Viconic Language Methods. She not only bubbled new words, but began to bubble the math problems and variable terms too. Bubbling the shape of a word and adding multiple visual representations around it finally allowed Sam to "see" that concept because she was finally tapping in to her visual thinking system. For once, Sam was able to create meaning for math concepts using her own learning system. The strategies put her in the driver's seat of her learning.

Dr. Arwood suggested that I ask Sam to tag her pictures with language. Tagging a picture simply means adding your own words to explain something you have already drawn. I modeled how to do this in a picture dictionary or cartoon concept to the entire Algebra 1 class. I looked directly at Sam when I told the class to start tagging pictures with language or words. When we tag our learning with language, it elevates the idea from an isolated pattern into a formal concept unique to that learner. The name of the concept will now draw the student's understanding from their semantic memory. An example of Sam's work is in Figure 4.4.

As we were working on math practice problems using the Distributive Property, Sam actually spoke up in class! She typically does not talk in class; she does not talk to me unless I sit next to her. After receiving the math concepts in a mode in which her visual learning system could finally process the information, Sam was now giving correct answers to the problems in front of the class. She finally understood the math. Moreover, she now felt she could contribute to the class culture. Her brain had finally become activated and engaged. In three months, Sam blossomed socially, making friends and offering to help other students with their math. Many students, not just Sam, now put a border around their notes and their work done in class. This helps students see their own ideas more clearly.

"All or Nothing" Assignments

Another strategy I use in Precalculus is a feedback strategy. In one of my classes with Dr. Arwood at the University of Portland, I read several neuroscience studies about mice and rats. In this class we read multiple case studies about how learning and memory in rats might work. Feedback relays to and from the hippocampus were a common theme in all of the papers tied to learning, which made sense because the hippocampus plays an important role in retaining long-term memory. Learning about this brain connection began to make me wonder about how I could create feedback relays in my students' brains. I figured it out. These neuronal circuits could become stronger by wiring together when sensory input is meaningful.

As a result, I have transformed my thinking about how I portray new information. Now, my goal is to increase neuronal feedback relays in my students. To do this, I layer my instructional meaning, creating enough overlapping visual examples for students to put the concept into their own semantic memory. The strategy I use is called "All or Nothing" assignments and it works very well in Precalculus.

Here's how it works: practice math problems are given after a lesson. Any problems a student does not finish need to be done as homework. The next day, I hand out a colored piece of paper to any student who did not finish the homework assignment. This creates accountability for homework being completed, but also allows students to participate by finishing, or adding to the problem set as we talk about a problem they did not complete. The students are then asked to find any mistakes made in their work by drawing an arrow to the error and then correcting the mistake with different color ink. I ask them to write in their own words what the mistake was and how they fixed it. Each student is also asked to rate his learning on each standard the problem set covered on a scale from 1-5 with a five being mastery. This process also works very well in correcting assessments.

From a neuroeducation perspective, asking students to correct their own mistakes and then explain *why* their answer was a mistake, and *how* they could fix it increases the points of access in the brain to deepen the concept (Arwood, 2011). This reminded me of how Dr. Arwood would say that "learning is not a stair step model; learning is a spiral." What this means is that getting an answer wrong is just as important as getting it right. The most important part of learning is not the finished product, but the process of the mind traveling along the spiral, attaching new information to old ideas, strengthening neuronal connections for related concepts in the brain, and using language to name our thinking and tie the whole operation of learning together (Arwood, 2011).

A student who completes their own feedback strengthens his understanding of the many concepts used in the math problem. Tagging the problem by writing out his thought process helps to complete the conceptual neuronal circuit in the brain. The strategy helps students put what they have learned into semantic memory, not to be forgotten when the concepts are needed on a different problem. It also develops flexibility to use the concepts learned for future problem-solving. Figure 4.5 shows what the strategy of correcting one's own errors might look like when a student is finished.

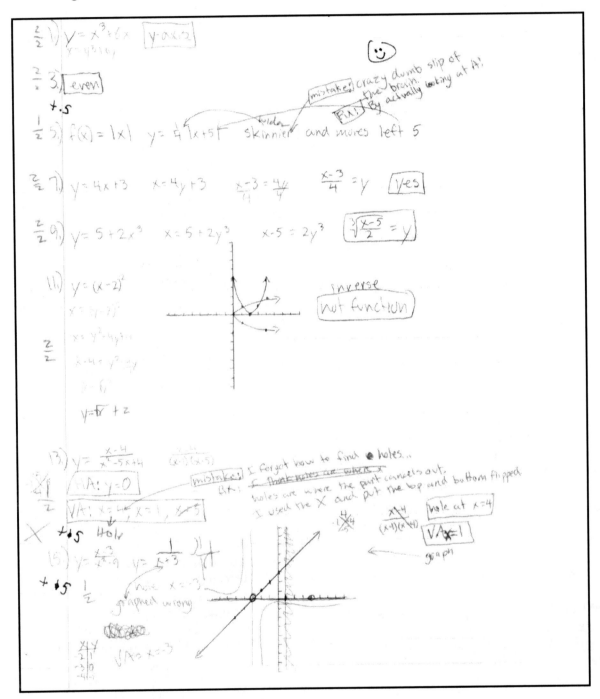

Figure 4.5: Self-Correcting Errors

I attempted to use the strategy in an Algebra 1 class. It did not transfer well because students had not yet acquired a full math grammar needed to explain their answers. Students need to be shown and taught how to find the mistakes in their work, and must first understand basic concepts like order-of-operations in order to take apart their thought process.

I also was confronted with the realization that students can repeat pneumonic tricks, but have no idea how to use the concept. Most can tell me what the acronym PEMDAS is, but they cannot apply it to their math. Numerous researchers in the field of neuroscience have studied this phenomenon. In particular, Varma et al. (2008) discovered that the brains of students who become more efficient and more literate with math do not rely merely on a storage bank of memory and attention resources. The brains of students who were more adept at a wide variety of math problems did not show one area of the brain being strengthened through repetition or "drilling" of problems. Rather, their brains became more efficient as neural functioning shifted from the prefrontal cortex to other regions such as visual and verbal areas. When the brain uses a wider variety of regions to solve a problem, this means that it is less strained and more efficient (Varma et al. 2008). When a student uses his or her own visual language to solve a problem, this information will be acquired by the mind, not just memorized. This means that activating a learner's visual strengths will result in more long-term problem-solving abilities.

When I ask most Algebra students what they remember about lines, most will say "y = mx + b," but they cannot explain their thinking or the meaning for each variable and how to use it. Instead of asking them to memorize formulas or pneumonic devices, I give them four problems at the start of class. When finished, I give them the answers and then give one-on-one attention to scaffold the idea of finding mistakes in their thinking. I can individually discuss with a student their thinking about a problem while developing mathematical communication and formatively assessing what a student understands.

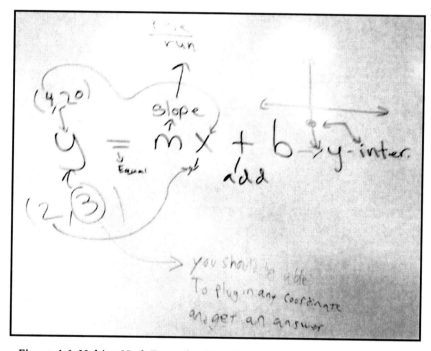

Figure 4.6: Making Math Formulas Visual

I have also started to write formulas on the whiteboard and have students come to the board and write their understanding of each variable; an example of this is in Figure 4.6 using the slope-intercept form of a linear equation. Notice how students attached actual points to the x and y variable and how a graph was drawn to show that b is the y-intercept. I hope to create meaning by refining their thinking and by listening to the thinking of their classmates. I also ask them to use these strategies in their notes.

Concept Cartoons

I also use picture dictionaries but I call them Cartoon Concepts. On the first two days of school, the entire school does community-building activities. The first day is about how to live in the community. In my classes, I modeled cartooning by showing my meaning of the concept of "responsibility." For example, I am responsible when I am required to be at work, but also responsible in my commitments to family, and professionally responsible in being prepared each day to teach. After my demonstration, each student drew a pictograph using three ideas about responsibility. The idea the students write in the middle of the Cartoon Concept is the pattern; the pictographs are the visual concepts. Taken together, these will form language for visual thinkers (Arwood, 2011).

Students can use Cartoon Concepts for any idea, not just math. The second day of school, for example, we cartooned "respect." Picture dictionaries lower the cognitive challenge for visual thinkers to learn a new concept. Neurologically, picture dictionaries are two-dimensional which is how our eyes take in visual information (Baars & Gage, 2010).

"Telling Time" or "Navigating Through Space"

At the beginning of the year, half of my first period Algebra 1 students were coming to class late. One morning I asked them what time school started. Not one student in twenty-seven could tell me. I asked them when I was supposed to be at school and they all chimed in with, "You are supposed to be here at 7:15, but most mornings you are here before 7:15." These were in fact ideas from my responsibility cartoon I modeled for them. After I drew out the details of my day, they were able to see me move through time in a way that they couldn't do for themselves.

We assume that all children, especially high school students, can look at any clock and figure out what time it is. Yes, they can read a clock, but do they know what it means to be "on time" to school? Are their parents regularly "on time," and do they instruct them how to plan "ahead of time" to arrive where they need to be on schedule? From a neuroeducation perspective, children with a visual learning system may not automatically acquire these concepts – they need to be scaffolded for them over many opportunities (Arwood, 2011). In fact, children who think with pictures in their heads actually "tell time" by seeing how much space their actions take up.

To address this issue, I cartooned for them that they needed to have their bottoms in their chair ready to learn at 7:45. I began to draw a picture of an analog clock on the white board with the starting time for class in all my classes. I no longer have a mass tardy problem because drawing out cartoons of the students moving through time allowed their visual learning systems to see time and see themselves move through it. Today, I keep a large analog clock on the front wall so students can watch the second hand tick off time. Now, visual learners can watch themselves move through time.

"Movement Access" Learners

With my Algebra students, I figured I could move from cartooning behaviors, such as learning to tell time, to asking students to cartoon math concepts, but I was wrong. My older Precalculus students had found success drawing and writing, possibly due to more maturity and due to having already acquired many of the fundamental math skills that younger students lacked. Nevertheless, in my Algebra 1 and Geometry classes, I moved outside my comfort zone, and cartooned under the document camera, being careful that the students could watch my hand move.

This was a technique I had learned from Dr. Arwood to reach our students who not only had a visual learning system, but whose brains needed extra layers of visual input in order to begin to "see" ideas in their minds. The movement of the hand on the screen provides a visual-motor layer that the motor cortex of the brain will actually process. Similarly, the movement that a teacher's mouth makes can create visual shapes as well. For my more struggling visual learners, I needed to engage not only their eyes and their ears, but also the movement areas of their brains. Providing more points of access in the brain (i.e. layers of instruction, increases a student's chance for being able to "pick up" on what I am saying) (Arwood, 2011).

Our "kinesthetic" students need movement, but educators miss the boat because we think any kind of movement or tactile sensory input will do. Actually, students need to see the movement of the hand and mouth creating shapes in order to form pictures in their minds. It is the way our eyes work neurologically; there needs to be meaningful context to the movement.

Students need these brain-based visual language strategies daily. Without them, they often flounder. For example, there was a death in my family so I spent a long weekend with them, missing three days of school. I had chosen a substitute who had a reputation of being flexible with students and who spent a lot of time subbing at our school. A lot of classes at my high school are loud and have the students have issues with defiance. When I returned the substitute came before school to tell me about the defiance issues he had had in my Algebra class. For one student, he wrote a referral. I was worried that I had lost all the classroom management gains made from the beginning of the year. When class began, I gave them all picture dictionary templates and sat before them and began to draw math concepts under the

Figure 4.7: Example of Cartoon Concept

document camera. I used the document camera so my students could see my hand movement. I asked them, "What do I need to start my picture dictionary?" and they said chorally, "I need to put myself in the picture." When I asked them why I was bubbling word they said, "So we can see the shape of the words." When I asked them why I was drawing a border around my thoughts, they said, "So my thoughts don't fall off the paper." Two-thirds of the way through the class, I wanted to cry. All the students were giving me ideas and were starting to draw on their own. With the addition of these methods, they became engaged and respectful. It made a tremendous difference in promoting learning. It was wonderful.

The picture dictionaries bring learning down to a preoperational language level within the Neuro-semantic Language Learning Theory. The cartoons, being two dimensional, are easy on the eyes, and the movement of my hand under the document camera reduces the stress level of my students because they can finally "see" what it is I am trying to teach. Drawing a border around concepts helps students contain these ideas together and see the content on the page. For one student, after putting y = mx + b on the white board, I asked him if he could see what it was. He said no. I underlined the formula and asked if that helped him. He said yes and began to do the task I asked the class to do with the formula. Figure 4.7 is an example of Cartoon Concepts from a student in the Algebra class. He has drawn himself on the page, ready to learn.

I am getting better at realizing when I have not created enough neuronal layers for a concept. If a student cannot name the concept or explain how to do a problem, but can draw a picture or use non-mathematical language to describe his thinking, I know that the student still does not formally know the concept. I have students use their own thinking to describe the concept, question the concept, and practice the concept they have learned. They respond by also communicating their needs and frustrations, which lets me know what I need to do next.

Research Data Proves Viconic Language Methods are Effective

Initially, I had set out to ask the question: would the Viconic Language Methods inspired by the Neuro-semantic Language Learning Theory work in developing math concepts in the 15-18 year old adolescent brain? The results found that NsLLT did work for older age adolescent students, but more dramatically for those students who had by in with the methods. For two years, I collected and analyzed data of the pretests my students took upon entering the school year and the posttests my students took on mathematical standards upon leaving in June. The results were inspiring. In both the Precalculus classes and the Algebra 1 class, there was a significant increase in learning after taking my class. Two-tail normal distribution was used to analyze the data. In addition, at the end of the year students also attested to feeling more confidence in their math ability and less anxiety towards the subject and in test taking. An exploration of the research follows.

	n	Mean	SD
Pretest	20	3.50	2.93
Posttest	20	9.15	3.67

$p < 0.001$

Table 1: Pretest and Post Test Mean and Standard Deviation for Algebra Unit 2 and Unit 3 Using NLLT Strategies in the Classroom

A total of 20 students were involved in the Algebra 1 study. All 20 students took the pretest and posttest. Table 1 shows the mean, standard deviation, and group size for the group using NsLLT cognitive strategies with the curriculum and assessment designed using CCSS. A two-tailed normal distribution t-test indicated significant increase in scores ($p<0.01$).

I found that a majority of my Algebra students were able to complete a standard numerically, using tables, and graphically, but struggled with the standard analytically, using formulas. For example, students showed they could find the slope of a line from a table and from a graph, but had trouble using the slope formula. Nevertheless, the benefit of using Viconic Language Methods in my classroom was clear by looking at these results.

My Precalculus class had even better outcomes, possibly due to having already acquired some of the basic math literacy needed to expand upon their thinking. In my Precalculus classes, students frequently collaborate about how to do math and share their thinking until the concept is understood by all. I use Flow-Chart Notes and All-or-Nothing assignments throughout the semester of Trigonometry. One semester, I gave a pretest and an iteration of the pretest as a posttest. I tracked five standards throughout the semester: four aligned to Common Core and one from the text. 79% of the seventy-three students mastered the standards on the final exam. It was the first year I did not have to curve the final. I also had more students who passed college entrance exams then in any year prior. Table 2 analyzes the data from the pretest and posttest. A two-tailed normal distribution was used and there was a significant increase in learning from pretest to posttest (p<.001).

	n	Mean	SD
Pretest	73	0.64	0.70
Post test	73	3.9	1.53

$p < .001$

Table 2: Pretest and Post Test Mean and Standard Deviation for Trigonometry Unit Using NSLLT Strategies in the Classroom

These results answered the question I had sought out to investigate: whether incorporating Viconic Language Methods, inspired by brain-based neuroeducation theory, had a significant impact on student achievement. When I matched my instruction to the manner in which we know visual symbolizing students best acquire information, students were finally able to "see" the math concepts that had eluded them for years. The implementation, from theory to practice, was a success.

Conclusion

In my Algebra class, I have two 10th graders failing every other class except mine. One proudly says he stands on principle; he chooses to work for the teachers where there is mutual respect. A Latino student named Ray with ELL support, who I suspect does not have a grade-level of language function in English, does nothing for any other teacher. He is very quiet in my class, but talkative in the halls with his friends. However, he has buy in to using the Viconic Language Methods in my class. They work for him, where the methods of other classes do not. He diligently keeps his picture dictionaries in my class. When a new student began attending my Algebra class, she sat next to Ray. I asked him if he would help her. He immediately suggested that I give her our picture dictionaries to copy.

I have begun asking some of the students with F's in other classes how I can help them talk with their other teachers. 9th grade Physics is a struggle for a lot of my students. I emailed all of the physics teachers and asked if they could send work for the students so that I could help them in tutorial. One teacher, in honest frustration (an emotion I used to feel before I started working to educate visual learning systems) complained about my students not knowing their multiplication facts, and said they needed to use her method of dimensional analysis. The physics class uses units of measure such as Newtons for which our 9th grade students have no prior life experience. In order for students to learn, educators need to start by finding out what life experiences students have, what pictures they have in their minds.

In fact, researchers in the field of neuroscience have confirmed that these methods of visualizing mathematical calculations are indeed effective. For example, Dehaene et al (2003) discovered that the act of subtracting uses areas of the brain more commonly associated with visual and spatial processing such as the bilateral parietal lobes. They hypothesize that these brain regions correspond with an internally visualized number line in the mind. These regions "light up" on brain scans when individuals are asked to do calculations that are not automatic such as times tables. This suggests that the mind's eye mentally constructs visuals of operations and draws from other previously acquired concepts in order to solve challenging problems.

Flow-Chart Notes are a great visual way to allow students to communicate their prior knowledge of a concept; this allows me to formatively assess what type of experience I need to give them in order to talk about the concept. Hopefully I can trigger a memory in students that will activate a circuit or pattern in their brains so that I can add to it by giving them meaningful sensory input. The end goal is to create a circuit in which the student can name with the mathematical vocabulary, thus putting it into semantic memory.

For example, I have all of my students measure the school's trophy case in US Standard and Metric systems because they have a lot of reference to those measuring units. Still, when we did a word problem about how long it would take a person to pick strawberries on a rectangular plot of land, the students needed to measure and move classroom tables so that they could see the measurement. The tables were a foot too long, so the students created a line of notebook paper along the table end to show a better measurement of the strawberry plot. The students then very realistically talked about how long it would take a person to pick the strawberries. Teachers assume their students understand so much prior school knowledge and create work sheets full of words which visual learning systems have trouble processing without using appropriate visual language strategies. The frustration between students and teacher erodes any possibility for academic success.

The Neuro-Education viconic language strategies work best for adolescents who choose to try the strategies, and through success, they will take ownership of the strategies and begin to use them on their own. My next goal is to give students the ability to use the principles of the Neuro-semantic Language Learning Theory in all of their classes. I talk to ELL students about using their first language to learn English vocabulary through tagging with words and pictures. Sometimes it is still a challenge to get some high school students to buy in to creating their own picture dictionaries. At the high school level their confidence is so low; they believe they can't be successful in school. I have never had a class full of students with no behavior issues, yet my Algebra 1 class is constantly interrupted by security calling and asking me to send my angels to them because of infractions in other classes. This reminds me that students who know how to learn rarely have behavioral issues (Arwood, 2011).

A teacher teaches and stays in the profession because they want to help their students. Title I teachers also have the stresses of dealing with students who have sad and tragic home lives. In one day I went to a meeting to discuss a student's possible drug addiction, had a student tell me his 15 year old cousin died of alcohol poisoning, listened to a 10th grader tell of the disappointment of not being able to see his father because his mother was mad at him, and another one tell me he his grades were slipping because his parents are getting divorced. I walked away ironically thinking that I am here to teach them math, but learning math will be the last thing on their minds. Yes, they need emotional support and advocacy. If students have stressful circumstances in their lives, then learning will be hampered because they are worrying about life situations. However, my classroom can be a bright spot for their education. I can be the one room in school in which they feel successful. I can engage their natural desire to learn.

Summary of Neuro-Education Methods

This chapter discusses three different Neuro-Education based strategies that support student learning. From a neuroscience lens, the Flow-Chart Notes, All-or-Nothing assignments, and Arwood's picture dictionaries work because they access the students' visual learning system and support the cortical layering of concepts. Teachers drawing in real time allow the students to pick up on the shape and movement of the drawing itself to access the visual learning system. Multiple drawings, and in some cases the movement of the hand, can provide multiple access points in the brain for the student. These multiple access points create the layering and scaffolding of ideas that support formal concepts.

From a cognitive psychology lens, the layering of overlapping preoperational and concrete concepts forms formal concepts. An example from this chapter is the picture dictionary about responsibility. First, the teacher shared her I-story about responsibilities that included work and family. By sharing an example, the teacher lowered responsibility from a formal concept to a concrete concept for the students to be able to access. The teacher further increased accessibility to all students by encouraging them to share their own I-story about responsibility, which lowered the concept to a preoperational level. As students shared their stories, the learning interlaced the preoperational and the concrete, mirroring the process of learning being like a spiral.

From the lens of language function, this teacher describes the use of oral cartooning explaining to students why it is important that they not interrupt while the teacher is talking. Oral cartooning or using "because" language uses rich language that informs the student of the "who, what, where, when, why, and how" of a situation. Students need to be able to explain all of these language functions in their own words to truly master a concept. Compare this to restricted language that might be used more typically in a classroom, "don't interrupt," and one sees the difference between rich and restricted language as it is used in the classroom.

Chapter 5

Walking Lines and Shaping Words: Navigating an Auditory World as a Visual Learner

Willow Grossen, MAT

Abstract

In this chapter, the author explains the process of how to sample a student's natural language in order to tell how that student thinks and behaves, as well as how they use their own language to function in the world around them. The path of two students receiving special education services for communication disorders is explored from their initial struggles of trying to fit in a school environment, to their eventual educational success upon receiving instruction that matches their visual thinking systems. In addition, the author examines the unique challenges of English Language Learners who demonstrate scant vocabulary growth despite receiving specialized instruction. In particular, the author parses the difference between a child having a "globalized" intellectual disability versus a child having a cognitive delay due to a temporary inability to acquire auditory concepts.

About the Author

Willow Grossen is a learning specialist serving special education students in kindergarten through sixth grade. She coordinates regularly with general education teachers, speech and language pathologists, and reading specialists to track the progress her students make while in school. After studying the Neuro-semantic Language Learning Theory in her classes at the University of Portland, Willow began incorporating Viconic Language Methods in her instruction and finding remarkable results. As her colleagues have seen the gains she has made with students who had previously languished, they have now started coming to her for help and advice for their most challenging learners.

Introduction

I work as a special education learning specialist for students ranging from kindergarten to sixth grade. One might look at my job title and assume that on a day-to-day basis I mostly run groups supporting students acquiring skills to help them better read, write, and do math. According to my schedule on paper, this is accurate. But in the last three to four years of my seven years as a special educator, I have seen a shift in the way students enter school. I find myself supporting more and more students who fall on the autism spectrum or who qualify for services with communication disorders. These students, but also students with other diagnoses, greatly struggle with just being in school. Most of my days are spent helping to "manage" behaviors because our students are underprepared to cope with the expectations of being in a general education setting: loud, crowded classrooms with quick transitions and instruction that is mostly oral in nature.

My school has done quite well in the last five years. We have managed to pull ourselves up by our bootstraps and become a model school for our district, which is located in North Central Oregon in the Willamette Valley. Our district is the fourth largest in the state and has embraced the progressive nature of the education system. This means that my school often volunteers to be one of the pilot schools for many of these progressive ventures. For example, in the last six years since I have worked there, we have piloted a Response to Intervention program, embraced a new literacy program designed to support English Language Learners and students with learning disabilities alike, and have recently become a Spanish-English dual language school. These have all greatly benefited our 46% ELL population and our 95% economically disadvantaged students. But, even with all these great things happening, I continued to notice my years as a teacher getting more and more difficult.

Until recently, I relied on the programs I was told to use: programs that focused on direct instruction of phonics and phonemic awareness, grammatical structures, and drilling for fluency in reading. I used the systems that were given to me by our behavioral specialists and speech language pathologists, designed to help students navigate their school day. What I learned is that no matter how many times students were given these methods, they still could not "see their day" or see themselves move through time. I was becoming frustrated, as were my students, with the way they seemed to crash through the day, mostly from not being able to organize their learning. And when I say crash, boy, do I mean crash.

In this chapter, I share with you two stories of students with very different needs, one from a behavioral perspective and one from a literacy approach. In my practice, I have applied multiple Viconic Language Methods inspired by the Neuro-Education methodology proposed by Dr. Ellyn Arwood. Over time, she has researched and seen amazing things – things that have changed the way I teach and the way I help form programs for all students, whether or not they are identified for special education services.

Elio – A Student Clinging to Rules

> *Two sneakered shoes tapped the carpet, while the blue sensory pod swiveled back and forth, matching the tick-tick-tick of the clock. For many weeks in a row he had disintegrated into tears, hyperventilating and rocking, before we could coax him into the safety of the blue egg-shaped "sensory pod." What had triggered this meltdown, as we had come to call them? It was seemingly simple: he didn't get to walk first in line. With only two children walking the short jaunt down the hallway, it was too much of a change to be second.*

Elio was a kindergarten student who came to me from an early intervention program, identified as a student with a communication disorder. On his first day of school, his teacher, who had worked for many years in her mother's autism classroom, came to me and said he reminded her of her former students. This teacher had a background in doing *discrete trials*, or what one might call "drill and kill" methods. This practice stems from the theory of behaviorism, which says that learning can be reduced to terms of input and output. If a teacher desires a certain output from her student, whether that be an answer on a test or a particular behavior, she will practice that skill over and over again using different methods of input. In this sense, educational instruction can be viewed as simply trying to find the correct input that will lead to a desired output (Arwood, 2011).

This teacher took Elio under her wing and worked tirelessly with him using techniques culled from her many years in her mother's behaviorist classroom to help him learn. This meant practicing desired behavior over and over again until Elio could imitate what the teacher wanted of him. Elio became comfortable learning how to imitate his way through school. By the time he reached first grade, he no longer cried the whole day and had stopped crawling all over people and furniture.

His first grade teacher was very orderly and structured and spent a lot of time explaining the rules, transitions, and work expectations to Elio. These explanations were an improvement because they provided Elio with more information about how he was expected to be a participant in her class. Elio especially clung to his understanding of the rules, and did not like to deviate from them. He no longer cried daily, and would sometimes finish the whole week without tears. We saw his *echolalic* responses almost fade away, meaning he didn't just yell and scream out for seemingly no reason. After some time he even *almost* managed to have typical peer interactions.

Second grade was a huge transition year for many of our students, especially Elio. During this school year, our district faced a huge budget cut which significantly increased our class sizes. Elio no longer had the comforts of a small class to help ease his anxiety. Instead, he found himself in a class with upwards of thirty children. My staff and I instantly noticed a change in Elio's behavior, as did his parents. While he had always been rigid in his understanding of rules, he had recently become so "black and white" that we were seeing him get stuck in all areas of his day.

His reading teacher once came to me and explained that phonics instruction seemed to be frustrating him more than usual because, as many of us know, the written words of English do not always match one to one with their spoken counterparts. For example, we do not pronounce the "k" in "know," but we do in "kick." The pronunciation of English is filled with more exceptions than rules. Unfortunately, Elio, being the rigid thinker that he was, could not move past these variations and was now having crying spells under the table, especially when it came to our definition of sight words ("have" was of particular frustration).

In another part of his day, his homeroom teacher was trying to teach an addition concept building off of the idea of doubles in math facts. When the teacher explained the neighboring concept of adding one to an existing number to increase that number, Elio started yelling "no!" and reciting the rule of doubles. If the teacher tried to interject and explain, Elio would hide under his desk and cry. While Elio picked up the original patterns quickly, he latched onto them and could not accept the fact that they could change or that we could build off of them. Elio was clinging to rules that he had learned as a younger child, and his academic and social progress was not keeping up with his peers.

Sadly for him, this rigidity also began to affect his day-to-day behavior. Our staff began to see a decline in the progress he had made over the first two years of school. Simple observations became disconcerting to us and we spoke more often with our autism specialist. Elio, who had never really displayed some of the more common traits of autism, began toe walking, hand flapping, and touching the walls when he walked. In some cases Elio leaned on the person next to him as he slid down the hall. He became a second grade Gumby and could no longer sit in his chair. It seemed like the floor was his best friend, as he would slide out of his chair, off couches, and even off the lunch table to lie down on the ground. Unless he could lie on the table top of whatever object he sat at, we noticed him melting away, despite our efforts to coax him into second grade behavior.

I had learned from neuroeducation theory that when a student's brain does not have enough meaningful input, it can effectively "shut down," or drop a few levels of development (Bookheimer, 2002). However, the brain can never be fully at rest, unless a person is dead or comatose. Therefore, a student might start flapping their hands in order to try to give the brain something – anything – to take away previous input that was stressing the neurobiological system (Arwood, 2011). I also learned about Elio's toe walking and "slinking" along the walls in a hallway. From a cognitive psychology perspective, this occurs because a student is not developmentally "grounded;" meaning, they cannot orient themselves safely to their environment (Arwood, 2011). Piaget (1959), a developmental psychologist, informs us that a seven or eight year old student in second grade should be able to see themselves as an *agent*, meaning, they can navigate the world around them. I knew that Elio was in trouble developmentally because he was not flexible enough in his thinking to be able to safely get through a school day without exploding.

Social stories didn't work. Short, choppy phrases demanding the desired behavior fell on deaf ears, and positive behavior incentives only seemed to irritate him. The eventual threat of calling mom would only incite tears while he lay on the floor. We were at a loss. Thankfully, though, the most difficult part of his day soon became the catalyst for change.

Rules are Patterns, Not Concepts

A large chunk of my morning was spent in Elio's class helping him and Wilson, another student with similar needs navigate the general education math program. Once their class finished math we would clean up and head to lunch. For months, the school counselor and I had seen this become the time when Elio and Wilson both had their largest and longest meltdowns. We had begun the year by having Elio walk with the whole class down to the cafeteria, at the front of the line, holding the teacher's hand. This worked for a few weeks until Wilson's behavior necessitated him being near the front of the line. Elio was no longer the leader, but being second and still holding the teacher's hand proved to be acceptable. In November Elio's school pattern was shaken to the core. The multiple school holidays were seemingly unpredictable and walking to lunch with the class, first or second in line, was impossible. He refused to sit at the lunch table with his peers and would sometimes hide in the hallway, having what his mother termed a "panic attack." If we were able to, Elio would come with our counselor or myself and eat in the sensory pod, sobbing quietly and reciting the rules for lunch and hallway behavior.

What was going on with Elio? Studying neuroeducation theory had informed me that by clinging so tightly to following the "rules" of school, Elio was preventing his brain from developing, or moving past a pattern level of understanding. Input into Elio's brain was not reaching any regions associated with higher order thinking such as the prefrontal cortex (Anderson, 2010). Because Elio had been taught using behaviorist methods (learning and behavior follow strict provisions, input directly leads to output, etc.), he had essentially been set up to fail in school. Even though Elio was a seven-year-old boy, he was developmentally "stuck" at a three-year-old level of social functioning (Arwood, 2011). Elio loved to repeat rules, but he didn't really understand them, or rather, he only understood one dimension of them. Elio needed to see that his thinking could become more flexible and that this would actually reduce his anxiety and the stress of those around him.

Eventually, after Thanksgiving break, the staff proposed the idea to walk Elio and Wilson separately from the class, and I was placed in charge of walking them down to lunch a few minutes early. This seemed like a genius idea and worked for three days. Of course on these three days Wilson happened to be absent, so Elio got to be "first in line". On the fourth day, it was a race to see who could be in line first. This is how it went for several weeks, despite my attempts to record a schedule and the counselor occasionally walking one and I the other. It seemed like no matter what our attempts were to preface the change, if Elio was second; he repeated his "panic attack" in the hallway and recited the rules of hallway behavior and who should walk first.

Social Drawing Provides a Visual Referent

By the end of the month, the teacher, our counselor and I were at our wits' end. In a desperate attempt to regain sanity I used a visual language strategy I had learned in one of Dr. Arwood's classes. I drew a cartoon of our line at school, showing me, Elio, and Wilson. Before we transitioned one day, I sat down with Elio and Wilson and cartooned out what it should look like for the three of us to walk down the hallway. It was Wilson's day to walk first so I figured what better day to test this theory?

I started by drawing Elio walking down the hallway and then drew myself behind him. Finally, I depicted Wilson walking in front of him. After I drew the three of us, I drew three thought bubbles coming from Elio. The first one I explained, was him picturing us walking yesterday, and drew the order of us walking, when Elio had walked first. I then drew another bubble, which became the middle bubble, where Elio was walking second, explaining that this was him "picturing" today. In the last bubble I said this would be what he pictured for tomorrow and drew Elio at the front of the line again. For an example of the behavior cartoon, see Figure 5.1.

Figure 5.1: One Panel Behavior Cartoon

I explained that as we walked, Elio should be thinking through the progressions of the days and when he would get to go first. This would allow Elio to see that rules can have multiple dimensions depending on the day of the week. Lastly, I added my descriptions in writing below the drawings so Elio could associate the written patterns with the conceptual pictures I had cartooned. Once I was finished, he asked if he could add his teacher's door and the flag, showing directionality, since it was behind me in the picture. As soon as he asked this question, I could tell that he was starting to see himself as an agent and see his peers as actual people in his mental pictures. Up until this point, his behavior had exhibited that he was functioning at a preoperational level of social development: me, myself, and I only (Arwood, 2011). With one simple drawing, Elio was starting to make the journey to concrete development, or acknowledging the "we" of multiple equals.

After we drew out our cartoon, Elio was very excited, and when we got up to walk to lunch, he told me exactly what I had written: "Wilson walks first in line, Elio comes second in line, and Mrs. Grossen will be last," to which he laughed, and then happily bobbed down the hall, second in line and panic attack free.

For Elio, cartooning opened up a level of language that had not existed for him before. Up until that point, Elio had been given only auditory instructional methods in his schooling. These had been in the form of memorizing rules, imitating teacher behavior, and receiving oral praise or punishment. Studying neuroscience had informed me that the brains of some neuro-typical students could actually process these auditory methods, even if they were indeed visual thinkers (Arwood, 2011). These students were lucky enough to have brain connections that could in effect "translate" the words that teachers use into meaningful pictures and movies in their heads. These students rarely had behavioral issues in school because they could indeed learn in the auditory culture of the American educational system.

Elio on the other hand, had not been born so lucky. His brain was constantly searching for meaning it could process, and when it didn't find such input, his behavior would reflect this in the form of hand flapping, screaming/yelling, and rolling on the floor in panic attacks (Brown, 2012). It is quite possible that my drawing was one of the first times that Elio's brain had received enough visual layers of instruction in order for him to actually "see" himself as a human being that has choices.

I knew the drawing and writing was working, so I kept it up. From then on, Elio would regularly ask me to "draw" him in situations that might be new for him or cause him to have what we would see as anxious behaviors. To learn how to do this effectively, I studied the Viconic Language Methods that more experienced teachers had used to work with similar children. Using these methods, these teachers had seen great results in improving the pro-social behavior of their students. An example of a cartoon to help a student "see" how their actions are perceived by others and how these actions can result in consequences can be seen in Figure 5.2.

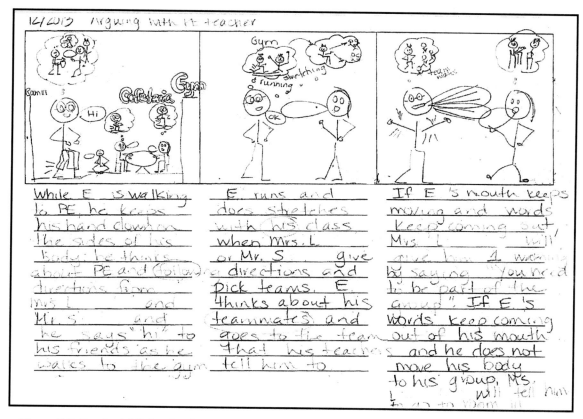

Figure 5.2: Pro-Social Behavior Cartoon
Image © 2017 M. Poulson, used with permission

Though the primary use for cartooning with Elio was to learn about social and behavioral expectations, he asked to use it while in math to help understand word problems. I noticed immense growth in his ability to pull out information in story problems to help me cartoon, which he could not previously have done. If Elio could have processed the sound-based instruction of behaviorism, he

87

would have… but he didn't. I knew I needed to keep adding visual layers because they were the only methods that were working for him.

Changing Oral Language into Visual Language

As part of our cartooning, the staff that worked with Elio began using more visually rich language when giving Elio directions or explanations. Before, we would simply state one or two word directions, such as "sit" or "calm down," but to no avail. As teachers, we are told that we need to "take command" of our classroom and get the "respect" of our students. But really, by uttering demands we are not providing students with enough meaningful words.

While incorporating more rich visual language, we would use more descriptive instructions with our expectations and reasons such as: "Elio, you need to sit with your bottom in the chair, your body facing forward, and your feet on the floor so the teacher can see that you are safe with your body and are ready to learn." We soon found out that Elio could indeed follow oral directions, but only if they were given in a way that would allow him to make pictures in his head of what it is he was supposed to do. When learning new information, Elio still needed to draw and write about it. However, for simple reminders in class like the example above, we could add visual layers to auditory methods and find success. Elio responded very well to these strategies and increased his ability to follow our directions. Our oral directions actually were visual methods.

Elio moved at the end of his second grade year to a neighboring school. His mother had a baby, a little brother for Elio, over the summer. Our counselor and I went to Elio's new school to share this new information with their staff, and I explained how I had hoped to use our new found knowledge of Elio's visual learning system to help him in more than just his behavior and social skills, but also in reading. My hope was that by expanding into all academic areas we would see Elio make growth.

Language Provides a Window to the Mind

Since then, I have taken what I used with Elio and have applied it to a student with similar challenges, Gerald, who was also a second grader. Gerald also came to us from early intervention as a student with a communication disorder, though many teachers and other special educators had expressed concerns that he may have an intellectual disability as well. However, by this point, I had learned that because the educational system often does not know the needs of visual language learners who struggle to follow social norms, they often label these children as having a "communication disorder." This term has become a bit of a catchall classification for many receiving special education services (Arwood, 2011).

Gerald is an English Language Learner and his family speaks largely his native language in the home, with the exception of his older sister, who occasionally helps him with his English homework. In the fall of his second grade year, we held his annual Individualized Education Plan meeting. After hearing what his mother had to say about him at home, I realized that Gerald was born with a visual learning system. In addition, Gerald was most likely severely delayed in his language function. By noticing his lack of communication in both English, as well as his native language, I determined that he was stuck at a pre-language stage, or a level of development typically associated with children zero to two years of age (Arwood, 2011).

In English, Gerald is very difficult to understand and requires a lot of clarification on the listener's part to interpret what he is saying or asking. He generally speaks in one or two word utterances, which indeed could be common for English Language Learners, but Gerald showed other troubling signs. After testing his understanding of cause and effect, we realized he showed signs of restricted *displacement* in his thinking. This meant that he does not use words indicating time correctly. For example, he overuses past tense words and uses them incorrectly such as, "him runned" when pointing at a boy running. Gerald also had trouble ordering the events of a story.

From studying neuroeducation theory of how language functions in the brain to name our thinking and represent the mind's underlying concepts (Arwood, 2011), I knew that Gerald was struggling to make meaning of the world around him. Auditory English is a time-based language meaning that words have high and low pitch, as well as short or fast duration (Arwood, 2011). Some students' auditory pathways in the brain can make sufficient meaning from this acoustic-based input from birth, regardless of the language used by their parents. This means that over the years of childhood, these neuro-typical children will develop at least a rudimentary understanding of time and cause and effect, including concepts such as "before," "during," and "after." We know that for students like Gerald who have not acquired these ideas by the age of eight, their brains will not process auditory input (oral speech, verbal instructions, reading out loud, etc.) well enough to function at grade level (Wolf et al. 2008).

Gerald's use of language provided other clues that he was restricted in his thinking. His multiple explanations were often very redundant, meaning he circled around an idea over and over without answering it accurately. He also displayed limited use of agent, action, and object, meaning he had trouble indicating *who* did *what* in a story. When writing, Gerald would often leave out vowels and only spell with consonants, sometimes even just using the initial sound. Gerald was also slow to respond to questions or prompts, despite what his teachers describe as "tons of thinking time."

His mother reported that he exhibited similar traits in his home language. She said he was very hard to understand and sometimes she just nodded because he got so frustrated with her not understanding what he was saying. She said he misused verb tenses in his home language, as well as gender identifiers. She also shared that sometimes she thought he did not understand her or hear her when she gave directions because he needed to be told so many times before he either did it or she gave up asking. Sometimes she would have his older sister ask in English to see if that helped, but the sister got the same response. I now knew that using sound alone to communicate with Gerald would not provide enough meaning for him to be able to understand social interactions sufficiently.

In contrast, both Gerald's mother and Gerald's general education teacher noticed that Gerald's understanding when pictures were involved was significantly higher. Gerald did better in math than in other areas, especially if he was able to draw shapes and amounts, or see pictures or manipulatives. This improvement in understanding occurred because the input, while definitely not perfect, at least allowed him to begin to see pictures in his head of the intended ideas.

Gerald was struggling to learn language patterns and create concepts in English. I began supporting Gerald in literacy and pulled him from his more traditional reading group that was focusing on phonics based reading. A few weeks prior to coming to me Gerald was in a small group with one of our assistants working with another boy in a reading intervention program. The reading program focused more on the language structure of English and learning through an auditory system, including phonics instruction and fluency drilling, whereas Gerald needed to focus on the function of language and learning through his visual learning system. After all, auditory-based methods such as pairing sounds to letters had not worked for Gerald thus far. Providing him more of the same was doing him no service.

Re-envisioning English as a second language

Alphabetic principles and concepts of print are the basis for many of our programs, especially our intervention programs for English Language Learners. After having the success of working with Elio and other students using methods inspired by the principles of Neuro-Education, I now knew our traditional sound-based methods would not work for many of my students, including Gerald, who rely on visuals to access and learn language.

I had thus far only glimpsed at Gerald's use of functional language from our limited interactions. Once Gerald and I began working together more fully, my first task was to gather a functional language sample from him. I used a storybook called "Snow Friends," by M. Christina Butler, and chose a picture that had an agent, action, and object. I shared a "Once Upon a Time" story with Gerald and then had him tell me a "Once Upon a Time" story, as well. Gerald again conveyed ideas that were very restricted. I was able to use his oral language sample to determine, as I had thought, that he was in the pre-language stage of learning.

After I had gathered the oral language sample, Gerald and I began working on creating our own event-based stories based on the picture we had used for the language sample. My goal in having Gerald create an event-based story was so that he could start being able to distinguish between the "who, what, where, when, why, and how" of the plot. These are the basic building blocks of all social interaction and cognition; however, many students struggle to understand what these ideas mean because they represent a formal level of cognition (Arwood, 2011). Figure 5.3 shows a visual way of representing these ideas with multiple semantic drawings (Brown, 2012). Both adult and student can refer to each box by pointing and drawing when they wish to refine an idea or dig deeper into a concept.

Figure 5.3: Visualizing Formal-Level Question Words
Image © 2017 APRICOT INC, used with permission

If I wanted to raise Gerald's thinking from a pre-language level, I needed to help him refine his understanding of these components of communication. After getting a baseline story from Gerald, he and I created a picture dictionary of many of the words that he had used in his story and picture. I modeled our picture dictionary based off of the examples I had seen presented at a Neuro-Education workshop. For example, Figure 5.4 provides a sample of a picture dictionary that helps a student "see" what certain events in their day look like and how these events are connected. Notice that all of the ideas (words) in the boxes are bubbled; each box has multiple drawings to visual represent that idea, and arrows connect the drawn ideas to show that a semantic relationship exists between multiple concepts.

Using these viconic language strategies certainly helped to promote Gerald's thinking. However, Gerald still had trouble "seeing" the basic units of language needed for social interaction, so over the next few days, we worked with his picture dictionary and worked on conceptually refining his story. I helped him to semantically re-tag some of his agents, actions, and objects by giving them names and drawing the meaningful connections between them. For example, was the older lady in the story the main boy's mother, aunt, sister? Who was making decisions for the group? Where were they going? etc. Adding in these layers of visual language helped us to extend, expand, and modulate the story.

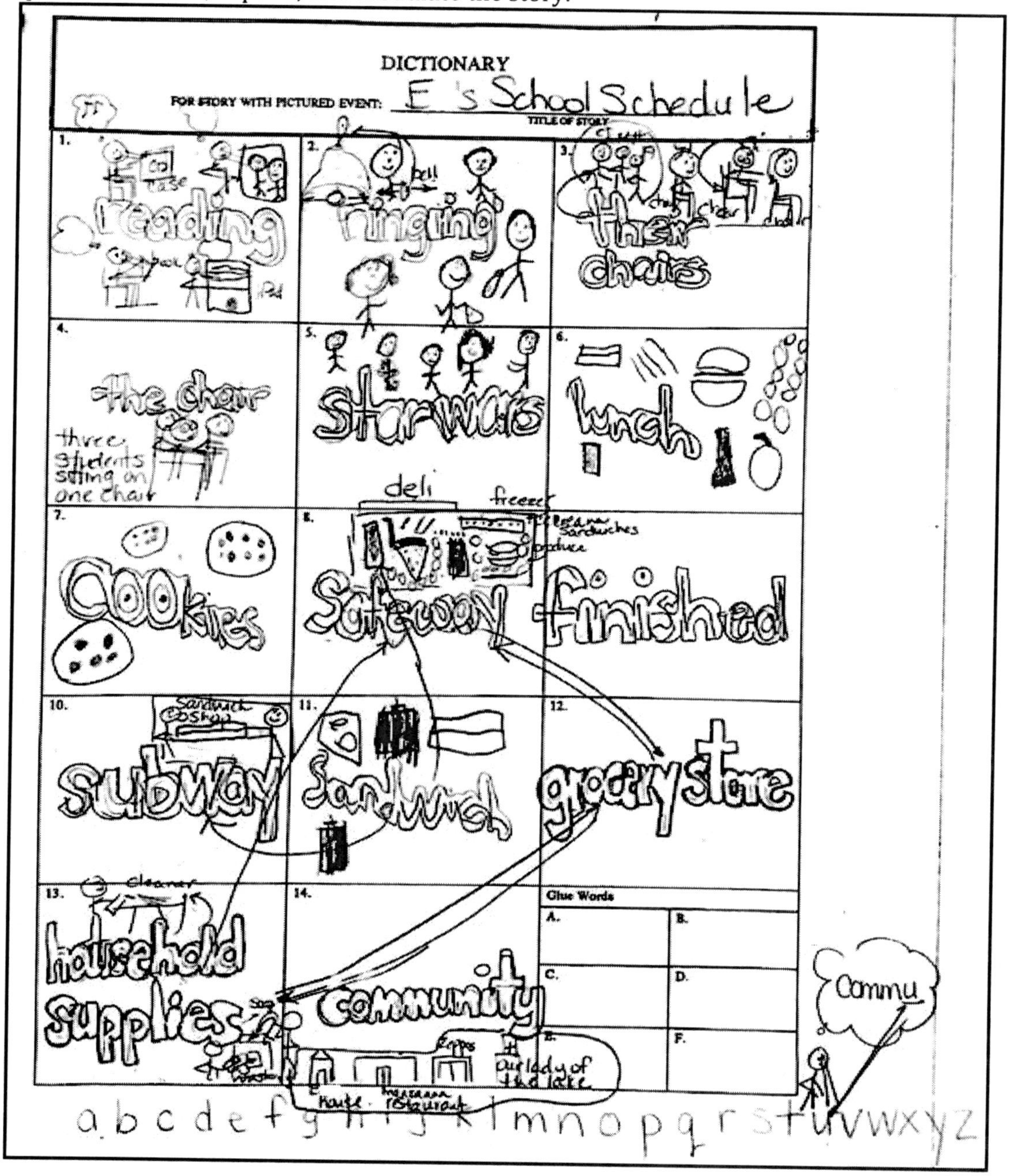

Figure 5.4: Picture Dictionary Showing Events of Typical Day
Image © 2017 M. Poulson, used with permission

To help Gerald "see" how the parts of speech functioned in language, I would draw them out, bubble the shape of the word, and provide numerous examples for each idea. For an example of drawing out the parts of speech, see Figure 5.5.

Since the start of our time together mid-year to the end of the school year, I have seen Gerald grow in his use of the words we have worked on in all of his stories and his relating picture dictionary. He has even asked to write more often and independently. We have much to work on but I am confident that such teaching strategies will build and improve his concepts in reading and writing.

Figure 5.5: Drawing Out Parts of Speech

Conclusion

Over the past year, I have taken my work with these two boys and applied it to many similar students across grade levels and disability categories. I have found that there is a fundamental shift in the way I approach each student, not only the ones whom I work with, but also those I hear about through our evaluation process. Studying Arwood's Neuro-Education theory has allowed me to view learning and behavior from a perspective that is unique from my colleagues. Now, when teachers list their concerns about a student I am immediately able to make a quick evaluation of their language levels to determine how the student may benefit from the new interventions I have learned.

Prior to learning Arwood's Neuro-Education theory I was often at a loss about how to work with the Geralds and Elios of the world. Incorporating new Viconic Language Methods has allowed me to better communicate with teachers about their students. Additionally using some of these strategies in the general education classroom has helped to support many students that may have been referred to me for more specific academic needs. It makes my job much more enjoyable to see struggling students now succeed. But most importantly, I am now able to understand why these students are able to make progress. Getting the results I have obtained has proven that these successes can be replicated with many future students as well.

Summary of Neuro-Education Methods

Neurobiologically, both of these students have atypical learning systems, meaning they were responding negatively (or not at all) to acoustic input without visual input. When the author provides multiple forms of visual input (rich language, agent-to-agent feedback, drawing, writing, semantic relationships etc.), there are multiple opportunities for neuronal pathways to access information and develop. With more layering over time these pathways will form additional connections resulting in a network of neurons with a vast number of access points (Baars & Gage, 2010). These networks are evidence of the concepts acquired through the layering of information and the feedback given by the author. When working within their visual systems both students are able to access the information and therefore are able to build upon layers of input. These layers literally allow the brain to function at higher levels. Before they had received input that matched their visual learning systems, both boys may have only been accessing their mid-brain regions with low-levels of input at best. Now however, with more meaningful input, information is working its way up into the pre-frontal cortex, a brain region necessary for higher order critical thinking (Anderson, 2010). When the author was able to access their learning systems through visual input, both students exhibited fewer behaviors that indicated atypical development.

From a cognitive psychology standpoint, Elio's behavior was consistent with his autism spectrum label. He had difficulty transferring rule or behavior concepts and applying them to multiple contexts, resulting in "inflexible" and "meltdown" behaviors. By cartooning the idea the teacher wished to convey, such as walking in line, he was able to clearly see what was expected of him. When his mental picture became clear, he was able to understand what was happening in his environment. When Elio understands what's happening, he is no longer anxious or confused and is able to then follow directions and behave in a more pro-social way. Gerald benefits from developing agency through drawing and writing about agent-action-object relationships, and by getting close feedback from another agent. Both students show major improvements in behavior and responsiveness when their learning systems are accessed.

The study of language function makes all of these gains possible; which is why it is so critical for the author to learn Arwood's model of Neuro-Education. By assessing the language levels of Elio and Gerald the author was able to determine the appropriate level of concept development to begin instruction. Meeting students at their individual developmental level reduces blowups and behavior that indicates learning is too challenging. By adding rich language to Elio's pictures through writing and drawing, Elio will now be able to cognitively access those pictures with the language the author used to tag them. Gerald also benefitted greatly from drawing and writing. By working with event-based pictures, picture dictionaries and tagging these concepts with language, Gerald will develop whole language function and improve his cognition. Gerald's verbal skills improved as a result of his improved cognition. Over time, both Elio and Gerald's conceptual acquisition will deepen, resulting in more of the brain being used and more flexibility to apply these concepts in more contexts.

Unit 3: Case Studies: How Neuroeducation Remediation Can Address Literacy, Behavioral, and Mental Health Challenges

Preface

All adults who work with children should understand the educational theories that guide and inform the practices they use with their pupils. For example, what is the educational *rationale* for using fill-in-the-blank worksheets with students? What psychological *principles* guide the use of rewards and punishments as an effort to control student behavior? And, how do we as teachers *substantiate* the notion that a child has truly internalized the information we hope to impart to them?

Out on the front lines of education in the United States, in schools and in homes, the answers to these questions are often missing. How can this be the case? After all, many instructors go through teacher preparation programs where the study of educational theory is expected. Yet, it is the experience of this author, and many of the authors presented in this anthology, that their initial training to become a teacher focused most heavily on *what* to do with students, and spent little time uncovering *why* these methods were used. In other words, the educators collected in this anthology graduated college with a full tool belt of tricks and strategies; but, these strategies were often recommended without an accompanying ideology to support their usage. As a result, once the educators got into the field, they rarely had a backup plan for what to do if these tools failed.

It is for this reason that the majority of the authors collected here continued to seek answers to the vexing challenges their students presented, long after they had graduated from their original teacher certification courses. In addition, these same authors express their enthusiasm for finding neuroeducation precisely because it is a field of study that explores deeply *why* students do what they do, and *how* their brains can be jump-started to begin learning again. These are the questions that hold the power to sustain life-long learning in both teacher and student.

Unit 3 presents four case studies where the use of neuroeducation methods in classroom settings produced marked growth in learning, pro-social behavior, and higher order thinking. These four authors have all peeled back the layers of what goes into effective teaching and have explored why the viconic language strategies of neuroeducation find success where other tools have failed in the past. The authors have studied first-hand research about how the brain learns, how the mind operates, and how language represents the underlying cognition of all humans. In a synthesis of these three ideas, these authors have triangulated their focus into the multifaceted Arwood's Neuro-Education Model to understand a comprehensive view of how to best promote learning in all students.

This unit presents a few concepts that might be confusing for a person new to this subject area. To best prepare the reader, these ideas are briefly explained below:

Synergy of the brain – Much of the past 100 years of brain science, from the initial vantage point of psychology to the theories of neuroscientists today, has attempted to classify the brain using a medical model of analysis (Greenberg, 2013). This means that as scientists begin to discover more and more brain unique regions, the natural assumption is that, like the parts of the human body, each area of the brain must be in charge of a specific function. This has led to myths that still pervade today's thinking, such as language being handled by Broca's/Wernicke's areas, or the amygdala being in charge of emotions. This default to the Western psychology's medical model has led many researchers over time to believe that the mind is a collection of individual building blocks in the brain (Fodor, 1983).

These brain regions, however, do not operate in isolation, but rather in concert with each other. Though we do not yet know exactly how, each brain region is dependent on every other region to filter and process the electrochemical signals that we call *thinking*. This interdependence between regions, this spread of information from one corner of the brain to the other corner, is called *synergy*. Simply put, the brain operates in a synergistic manner because the whole is greater than the sum of the individual parts (Arwood, 1983, 2014; Brevoort, 2012, Gallistel & Matzel, 2013, Levine, 2000). In other words, the pieces don't always add up in a predicable manner. Therefore, we cannot understand the true function of the brain unless we look at it as a vast network of interdependent connections.

High vs. low context languages – Linguists define a language as utilizing either a "high" or "low" level of context by determining if single ideas can be communicated in a straightforward manner, or if they require a host of connecting ideas in order to make sense. The properties of low-context languages such as English allow individuals to communicate with each other from all walks of life, from different dialects, or even from entirely different countries. In this way, English is a highly portable and widespread language, and even matches the fierce individualistic nature of the countries that speak it. In a low-context language like English, a speaker can use a variety of interchangeable words to explain their ideas. Moreover, the denotation of these words is often clear to the listener, and they do not need to know the speaker well to understand what they mean.

High-context languages such as Mandarin, however, do not provide for straightforward communication. In fact, speakers of this language are constantly changing the ideas they use and the manner in which they speak, depending on who the audience is. Individuals in this language are always looking for the "hidden" contextual message that may be implied, but not expressed outright. Interestingly, American Sign Language is also considered a high-context language because individuals rely solely on the visual context of the scenario to determine part of the intended communication (Bellugi & Fischer, 1972). Individuals who sign can change their facial expressions, body posture, and orientation of their hands to reflect aspects of communication that written or spoken English would handle with words. As a result, many children who are Deaf/Hard of Hearing may struggle to translate between the high-context rules of ASL signing and the low-context nature of English. This phenomenon is explored in detail in chapters seven and nine.

Cultural neuroscientists (e.g. Kitayama & Park, 2010) are learning that the language one uses and the culture that one grows up in can shape the physical connectivity of their brain and therefore the underlying thought processes of the mind as well. Therefore, a student's brain will be wired differently depending on if they come from a high or low context macrosystem. Remember that the brain is wired based on what is put into the brain. Educators who know about this new cutting edge research can be better prepared to help children learning English as a second language, especially if that child is also learning how to adapt to the roles and customs of a society that is new to them.

Doing is not thinking – As explained in Unit 2, many Western systems of education are influenced by the tenets of behaviorism. These principles assume that if a child can imitate patterns that the adult has provided, or can provide correct answers to a multiple choice test, or can recite the rules of a school, or can be nice to fellow classmates when a teacher is watching, then these children must have "learned" the desired material. However, Arwood (2011) explains that "doing" a task is not an adequate substitute for "thinking" original thoughts about that task. The only way to truly measure if a student has acquired an idea is for them to write about it, draw about it, communicate about it, explain it, and critique it using their own language, not the words of their teacher, their textbook, or their peers.

In Unit 3, the authors give examples of their work with students struggling with conventional educational practices. They reveal how applying the tenets of Arwood's Neuro-Education Model have allowed them to enable their students to be successful in areas of study that previously eluded them. The case studies demonstrate significant educational progress as measured by improvements in learning, behavior, and higher order thinking.

Chris Merideth

Chapter 6

I See You in my Picture:
Use of Viconic Language Methods in a Behavior Classroom Setting

Dawna Spencer, M.A

This chapter is dedicated to my brother Shawn, the reason I became a teacher.
He is a fellow visual thinker who had amazing ideas, incredible creative energy,
and the kindest of hearts – all attributes beyond standard measurement.

Abstract

This chapter describes the author's experience in a behavioral classroom setting using Viconic Language Methods (VLMs), a pedagogy based on the Neuro-semantic Language Learning Theory (NsLLT) (Arwood, 2011). The author provides a brief overview of the NsLLT and a comparison of learning and teaching paradigms. The author uses VLMs in a structured behavior classroom setting and analyzes the impact these methods have had on student language development in communication and interaction with others. Results show that, after implementation of VLMs, the majority of students were able to participate socially and academically in a classroom community and successfully integrate to a general education setting. 60% of participating students made a full transition into the general education classroom and remained there. 82% of participating students either fully participated in the general education classroom or partially participated in the general education classroom at the end of a five-year period. Using Viconic Language Methods that take into consideration individual learning systems, how a learner neurobiologically processes input, and facilitating conceptual and language development within the context of the classroom community have shown to enhance student growth academically and socially. Student growth was recognized in the classroom, within the school community, by parents of the children involved in the program, and by administration. Learners enjoyed the process of learning, and saw themselves as learners, part of the classroom community, and part of the greater school community.

About the Author

Dawna Spencer is an award-winning teacher who works with special education students who are diagnosed with social-emotional and behavioral disorders, learning disabilities, autism, and oppositional defiance. Dawna has been studying visual language teaching strategies for numerous years, and most recently graduated with a Post-Master's Degree in neuroeducation studies from the University of Portland. She has seen tremendous success using Neuro-Education methodology to promote pro-social community among her students and has received recognition for her accomplishments from fellow educators, parents, and district administrators.

Background

Upon first being introduced to Viconic Language Methods (VLMs) based on the Neuro-semantic Language Learning Theory (NsLLT) (Arwood, 2011), the author experienced a huge shift in understanding as an educator as to how learning can be defined. The NsLLT, which provides a pivotal cornerstone of Arwood's Neuro-Education Model, contrasts a *learning paradigm*, which is learner centered, with a *teaching paradigm*, which is teaching centered. The former can be described as how children process, conceptualize, and develop cognition at a neurobiological level, where the child's concepts are represented in their language. The latter can be thought of as the information a teacher disseminates to students and expects back as an indicator of acquisition; or rather, the products the child produces as a representation of what they "know."

At the start of the author's higher educational experience, two major questions came in to focus. One question regarded language acquisition for students learning English as a second language. In particular, the author wanted to know: By what means do we acquire language and how does it become conceptualized for use? The other question was related to the process of concept acquisition. In terms of working with struggling learners receiving special education services, this author wanted to know the underlying brain science that represents the concepts that a student has actually learned. Specifically, how does the brain apply what it knows in order to think critically? What does the mind's conceptualization for use look like from a neurobiological perspective, especially in consideration of atypical learners that don't fit into the current education paradigm?

The author unconsciously came into the higher education experience with a Western psychology and behaviorist influence that is accepted in most institutions as the default learning paradigm. From the neurobiological perspectives of most Western psychology and behaviorist viewpoints, there is an input-output model, or a two-tier paradigm of learning where learning is defined as what and/or how well the student can reproduce what the teacher has given them. The Neuro-semantic Language Learning Theory, however, proposes a new four-tier model of learning that will be explained throughout this chapter.

Introduction

Academic learning is often explicit: Professors point out the things that need to be learned, and students try their best to memorize them (Baars & Gage, 2010). This influence underlies the currently accepted models in teaching and education as a whole within our auditory culture of English. Some examples of default input-output models include a heavy emphasis on structured and scripted curriculum that teachers are told to follow with fidelity. Our culture uses an auditory language, meaning that we primarily communicate using oral speech and written words. Moreover, we often present ideas out of context, such as asking students to memorize spelling and math patterns, and then build from these patterns in a stair-step model. Students cannot possibly master first grade standards, for example, if they haven't finished kindergarten.

In addition, our culture believes that reading and writing can only be taught using sound-based, auditory instruction. Therefore, it is from these sets of beliefs that we teach. According to Arwood, Kaakinen and Wynne (2002), "English symbols are made up of spoken sounds (acoustics) and seen letters (visuals or auditory concepts (sound + sight)). Any language that uses a change in the sound patterns of letters to change meaning is an auditory language."

Auditory languages use words to convey language meaning. "English, as an auditory language, is considered a 'low context' language. The speakers assume that the underlying meaning of words convey any context" (Arwood, Brown, & Robb, 2005, p. 21). Our culture may indeed be auditory, but according to research done over a span of 45 years by Dr. Ellyn Arwood, an overwhelming majority of learners think in visual properties. Arwood (2011) writes:

> In today's English speaking cultures, about 10-15 percent of the speakers are able to use auditory thinking to match the auditory language they use for education and for the workplace. The other 85-90 percent of the population thinks in visual properties that are relational, high context based and spatial, rather than a temporal nature, even though their language is English, an auditory language (p. 87).

All learners are unique, having individual learning systems functioning both neurobiologically - how the brain functions at a cellular level, and neurosemantically - how one creates meaning from the world around us. "Concepts represent the way the learner's brain is 'wired' neurologically, independent of external patterns of teaching. The neurobiological system determines the way a learner conceptualizes" (Arwood & Brown, 2001, p. 10). Within the learning system, auditory concepts "overlap past spoken ideas with present visual and spoken ideas" (Arwood & Brown, 2001 p. 4). Spoken ideas represent the acoustic patterns; visual input represents visual patterns. Together, these ultimately result in auditory language (acoustic + visual = auditory).

Visual concepts, however, require multiple layers of visual input, such as combining drawings and writings. Unlike auditory concepts, visual concepts "overlap past visual experiences with present visual ideas" (Arwood & Brown, 2001 p. 4). When visual patterns overlap, this ultimately results in visual language (visual + visual = visual concept). Moreover, visual and auditory learners use their brains differently, and therefore conceptualize differently. Arwood, Brown, and Robb (2005) write:

> Both visual and auditory thinkers can use visual and acoustic patterns for regurgitation but learning new concepts occurs in the way the learning system meta-linguistically functions to form language. A visual thinker uses visual-motor graphics for acquiring meaning. An auditory thinker uses his/her own voice with external visuals to create auditory concepts. (p. 26)

Since our culture is auditory in nature, there exists an underlying assumption in most teaching methods in our educational system to teach primarily to the auditory learning system and not the visual learning system. Arwood (2011) writes, "Educators and employers who speak English assume that the majority of their learners and workers think in time-based, low context, sound properties of English" (p. 91).

Learning is not Input-Output

For educators, it is important to facilitate each child's language and conceptual development. This is best achieved by utilizing the brain-based methods proposed by the NsLLT, not an input-output model where "knowledge" is represented mimicking back a pattern that is given by the teacher. This shift is important because a learner's very future in school is at stake. An input-output model is a descriptor for pattern development that does not facilitate long-term memory, higher level thinking, and cognitive flexibility. It simply seeks a desired response, usually in the form of a multiple choice question or fill-in-the-blank response. In comparison, by focusing on facilitating the thinking *process* of the student, the four-tier model of the NsLLT leads to richer conceptualization, higher level cognition, flexibility of mind, and long-term retention of concepts in the brain.

According to Arwood and Brown (2001),

> Language adds meanings to concepts. For concepts to be meaningful they must be in the form of the way the person thinks. If my thoughts are in pictures I will picture concepts. If my thoughts are in self-talk I will use self-talk for the concepts. A person's ability to learn may be assisted by using language strategies that match the person's underlying thinking or conceptual development – visual symbols or auditory symbols (p. 9).

High vs. Low-Context Languages

Visual languages follow the characteristics of "visual concepts that represent integrated visuals..." (Arwood, Kaakinen & Wynne, 2002, p. 4). Visual languages require that most of the meaning comes from the **context** and not from the words. Languages such as Mandarin Chinese, American Sign, or Hopi are relational languages, or "high-context" languages (Arwood, 2011). "In relational languages, the speakers tell stories about people, what people do, where people do what they do, how and why they do what they do as an important component to everyday life and doing business" (Arwood, 2011, p. 89). Learners with both an auditory or visual learning system benefit from this context and the use of visual language.

Arwood, Brown, and Robb (2005) write, "...the speakers talk about the context. The context includes elements of 'who, what, where, when, why and how.' The context refers to all of the non-verbal and verbal meaning collected from everything surrounding the words" (p. 21). Visual language is by definition a high-context language because every drawing, every depicted idea, and every movement of the hand or mouth is connected to each other. If a visual image is taken completely out of context, it then ceases to have contextual meaning. In other words, when a visual depiction loses its visual properties, it becomes auditory.

English and other auditory languages, such as Spanish, French, and German, are "low-context" languages because they are sound based, highly portable languages where words can be used in isolation (Arwood, 2011). In an auditory culture, for example, we may use a single word *appreciate* to mean a countless number of things. I could *appreciate* the kind act a friend does for me, but I could also *appreciate* a piece of art. My stock portfolio could *appreciate* over time if Wall Street is having a good year. I could *appreciate* someone sharing a point of view that I am diametrically opposed to. And so on.

When we attempt to teach an idea like *appreciate*, we often do so completely out of context, such as asking students to memorize a definition, and then choose that same definition on a multiple choice test. But how does a visual learner make a picture in their head of a formal concept like *appreciate* based off of a single definition? Students whose brains process sound or take ideas off the written page effectively will be able to pick up on the multiple uses of the word by listening to it used in various kinds of conversations or sentences. Visual thinkers who don't use sound well, will struggle to see on their own the endless combinations that can be made when concepts are unpacked in different contexts.

This begs an important question: if the majority of learners have visual learning systems and the majority of people "think" in contextual, spatial, relational, and visual thoughts (Arwood, 2011) would it not be important to teach in the way the majority of learners learn best?

As this author gained a conceptual understanding of Arwood's Neuro-Education theory, there was a realization that she herself had a visual learning system. The actual "learning system," whether visual or auditory, provides the basis for the learner to acquire new ideas and

100

concepts and not the external features of instruction in relation to the learner's acquisition of ideas and concepts (Arwood, 1991). Arwood and Brown (2001) describe this process as, "A person's ability to learn may be assisted by using strategies that match a person's underlying thinking or conceptual development – visual or auditory systems."

The author started using Viconic Language Methods in her undergraduate studies. She had already developed many coping strategies in the past to be successful in school, such as spending more time studying (working harder), and retaking notes in an attempt to translate auditory information. The author found that using visual language strategies, where auditory input was translated to visual spatial, contextual, and relational meaning (such as drawing out notes in context), was much easier and less time consuming because it matched how the author conceptualized.

The Synergy of the Brain

The Neuro-semantic Language Learning Theory represents a "whole to part" perspective and advocates for facilitating language development by presenting it in context. "Language" here means more than just oral speech or written text. Language can also be made "visual" by adding in such components as connecting drawing to writing, writing to shapes, and shapes to movement. Most importantly, all of these connections inter-relate to create knowledge and understanding that is greater than the sum of the individual parts (Arwood, 2011).

These methods are in stark contrast to the focus on the Western psychology / behaviorism paradigm where knowledge is build "part to whole," or in isolation. From the NsLLT perspective, the language that one uses represents the level of neurobiological connectivity in one's brain. The higher the use of language, the higher the level of thinking and brain connectivity will be (Arwood, 2011).

Therefore, from a teacher's perspective, the more *assignment of meaning* one does "in-context" in order to develop language, the more neurobiological connections one's pupils will make at the cellular level in their brains. *Assignment of meaning* refers to using visual language to "tag" or mark something as important. For example, if a child misspells a word, a teacher may either correct them using auditory methods of sounds to letters or, a teacher could use Viconic Language Methods such as drawing the concept out using multiple representations, write down multiple ideas to go with each drawing, and tie all of these together using arrows and other pictographs to represent connectivity between thoughts. In sum, assigning meaning using auditory methods (oral speech, etc.) alone will not form concepts for visual thinkers (Arwood, 2011).

Using instructional methods that are meaningful can also be reflected in brain chemistry. The function of the language one uses will drive the structure of brain connectivity at the neurobiological level. Put another way, function (neurosemanticity or conceptual development and language) drives structure (neurobiology at the cellular level). Moreover, the interplay between brain structure and function is *synergistic*, meaning it is constantly changing through interaction (Arwood, 2011; Brevoort, 2012). Neuro-Education theory proposes that the whole of the combined interaction of neurobiology and neurosemanticity is greater than the individual structures of the brain or of language (Arwood, 2011). In other words, the mind cannot be carved up into pieces because no regions of the brain work independently from each other (Anderson, 2010). This idea stands in stark contrast to much of the last 50 years of thought and research in psychology and neuroscience.

How Does the Brain "Learn?"

How is it, actually, that humans learn new information? This is such a simple question, and yet people working in the educational profession rarely ask it. Studying the brain informs us of a great number of truisms about learning. From a neurobiological and neurosemantic perspectives according to the NsLLT (Arwood, 2011), we take in sensory input (e.g. visual and acoustic features) through our sensory receptors. Our distance receptors - the eyes and the ears - take in raw data from the world around us (e.g. light, movement, sound). This raw data must be in the form of meaningful input to the learner's neurobiological system utilizing the all or none principle (or threshold of electrochemical reactions that trigger the cell to fire), where, given meaningful input, cells fire or, given non-meaningful input, cells do not fire. Figure 6.1 shows an illustration created by this author to provide a visual example of the neurobiological process of learning.

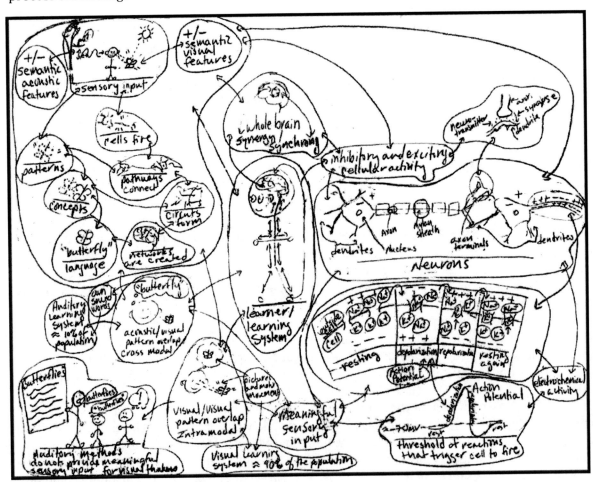

Figure 6.1: Conceptual Flow-Chart of Brain-Based Learning

As shown in the drawing, raw data from sensory input moves through the peripheral and central nervous system through inhibitory and excitory cellular activity creating action potentials. As this input overlaps, the raw electrochemical signals create patterns, or, "the cellular structures are recognizing patterns of past and present input" (Arwood, 2011, p. 45). Electrochemical changes at a cellular level take place that include action potentials (the act of a neuron firing). When input (eyes + ears) leads to neurons firing, this is typically called information moving "upstream," meaning into higher order brain regions such as the pre-frontal cortex (Baars & Gage, 2010).

However, information can also flow "downstream" from the higher order brain regions back down to other areas known to process visual and auditory language, such as Wernicke's and Broca's areas (Baars & Gage, 2010). This downstream process is, in essence, the brain giving feedback to itself. In fact, the brain is wired so that approximately six times as much information travels downstream in the form of feedback, for every amount of upstream data (Baars & Gage, 2010). This multitude of feedback is referred to as "cascading," in that downstream information travels together much like a waterfall. Indeed, the brain is designed for refining itself.

Forming concepts requires both upstream and downstream channels in the brain to work *synergistically*. When layered, cascading effects of neuronal connections/networks in the brain form concepts, "the overlap of visual data or the overlap of acoustic visual data develop concepts" (Arwood, 2011, p. 53).

> The visual and auditory structures overlap in terms of integration of acoustic input at the same time at the cellular level to the brain, the cortical pathways represent complex connectivity patterns that are critical, not only for processing sound but also for integrating information to other regions in the brain (Baars & Gage, 2010, p. 204).

Lastly, when action potential (upstream) and cascading cellular networks (downstream) concepts are employed for use at a higher level of thinking, then layered concepts that form language can be utilized. Circuits and pathways are formed in the grey matter (less efficient areas) moving into white matter (more efficient areas) with pathways stimulating at the neural level to the cerebral cortex, all in a very dynamic and synergistic way where there is cellular activity at all levels. Much of this information is run up and downstream through "relay stations" in the brain such as the medial temporal lobe.

> The medial temporal lobe is a hub with wide spread connections. The MTL, including the peripheral cortex, has a very wide connectivity to visual, auditory, somatosensory, emotional, motor, memory, and executive regions. This makes the MTL an ideal place to receive, bind and distribute information for long term memory...all connections run in both directions (Baars & Gage, 2010, p. 307).

"Doing" is not "Thinking"

When humans use language, this requires the brain to utilize higher level thinking in terms of function and biological structures. Animals use their brains as well, but only at "subcortical" or lower level regions. When humans use their advanced cerebrum and cerebral cortex, they engage in higher order *thinking*. However, when sensory input stays at the pattern level, such as "drill and kill" style exercises, this involves only the sensory structures and, at most, mid-level regions of the brain. In human terms, we call this *doing*. An example of *doing* would be reciting something from rote memory, or going on "autopilot."

Doing and thinking are not the same and require a different degree of language function as well as brain structure use. For example, when spelling words are memorized to be reproduced on a spelling test, this focuses on the pattern of the word and its reproduction in the same way it was presented (sensory structures and mid-brain at most). However, if the word is used in context, in multiple ways, and relationally drawn out, then higher level meaning is assigned which activates higher level brain structures and networks (cerebrum and cerebral cortex). Drawing assigns meaning and builds language, whereas rote memorization of formal symbols is simply pattern repetition that is not held in long-term memory. The brain will dump non-meaningful information after approximately six weeks (Arwood, 2011). Such memorization is not how we know the brain to function in order to develop language, the underlying representation of our concepts, and higher level thinking.

So, in terms of learning systems and what we know about the brain neurobiologically and the brain/language synergy neurosemantically, how are we as teachers facilitating the conceptual development of our learners and demonstrating an awareness of the underlying biases in our field that we may unconsciously operate in with regards to how students learn? It seems imperative to think of teaching in terms of facilitating meaningful input for the child's learning system so that they can develop concepts and language. After all, "Children only learn how to think the way they are able to process their world" (Arwood, E.L., Ormson, K., Kaulitz C. & Brown M., 2013, June).

Understanding the neurobiology, neurosemanticity, dynamic and synergistic nature of the brain and language where function drives structure, has been profound for the author as a learner and a teacher. The Neuro-semantic Language Learning Theory (NsLLT) provided the answers to the previously mentioned questions the author was looking for, in terms of how concept and language acquisition occurs and how learning occurs neurobiologically.

Introducing Viconic Language Methods into a Spanish Classroom

Given this new understanding, the author embarked on a thesis study with a stated hypothesis that incorporating visual metalinguistic lessons (Visual/Viconic Language Methods) in a classroom with a target language of Spanish would be more effective in reaching all learners in terms of how they conceptualized when compared with a class where traditional auditory metalinguistic lessons were used. The research was conducted with 44 high school students, grades 9-12, in two first year Spanish classes.

Pre- and post-assessments using descriptive statistics and t-tests (unequal variances) at a probability of .05 as statistically significant were used. Two surveys were also included to determine the number of visual thinkers in each classroom and to gain student input about the type of instruction used. The Temporal Analysis of Propositions (TemPro) was used to analyze student language samples to determine how individual students learned new concepts and if the populations of Group A and B conceptualized in the same way.

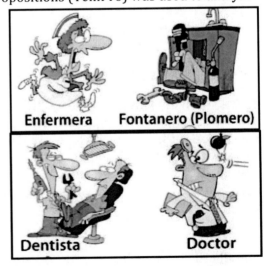

Figure 6.2 represents a sample lesson with integrated vocabulary in an auditory metalinguistic form, exemplary of traditional classroom lessons using auditory, low context thinking. In the target language, concepts are introduced in written and spoken form and written concepts are referred to through the lesson. Iconic visuals, such as pictures, in the Spanish resource book "Expresate" © (Humbach, Valesso, Chiquito, Smith, and McMinn, 2006), maps, and vocabulary from the book are used. The key vocabulary is: dentista, doctor, enfermera, fontanero (plomero).

Enfermera   **Fontanero (Plomero)**

Dentista   **Doctor**

Figure 6.2

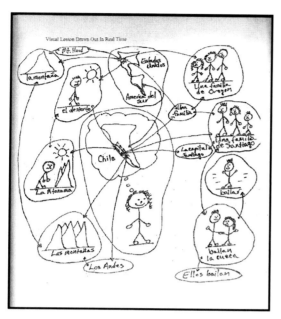

Figure 6.3

Figure 6.3 represents a sample lesson with integrated vocabulary in a visual metalinguistic form, exemplary of Viconic Language Methods using high context, visual thinking. In the target language, concepts are introduced by drawing them out in real time. The teacher uses an "I" story to introduce the concepts. Students add their ideas. The drawing is flowcharted and key vocabulary is added last. The drawing is referred to and added to throughout the lesson. The key vocabulary are: el desierto, Chile, la familia, La Atacama, Santiago, Los Andes, la cueca, bailar, la montaña.

After data was collected, one hundred percent of learners were identified as visual learners in both Spanish classes using written language samples evaluated with the TemPro (Temporal Analysis of Propositions) (Arwood, & Beggs, 1992). Pre-test to post-test learning gains showed that in the group that was taught using auditory metalinguistic lessons some learners' needs were better met than others, as some made significant gains while others made very little (Figures 6.4 & 6.5). However, in the group that was taught using visual metalinguistic lessons, the results were more uniform in terms of gains that students made, indicating that learners' needs were better met because the information was presented in a way that matched their learning system.

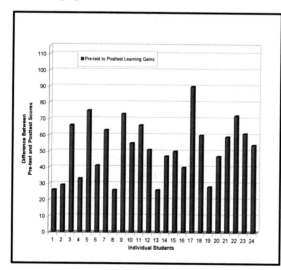

Figure 6.4: Pre-test to post-test learning gains from Group A instructed using auditory metalinguistic lessons.

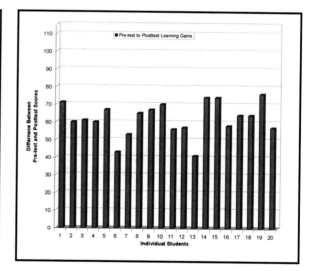

Figure 6.5: Pre-test to post-test learning gains from Group B instructed using visual metalinguistic lessons.

Visual metalinguistic lessons meet both auditory and visual learners' needs in that,

> "If visual students are presented the concepts on the board in visual language, then they actually see the pictures of the concepts and see the mental ideas simultaneously. They will not need to use only the [teacher's] spoken words but will be able to

encode their visual mental ideas into their memory without translation. The auditory student takes the spoken words by the teacher and connects them to the visual language pictures on the board. The auditory thinker is also able to follow the visual format." (Arwood, Kaakinen & Wynne, 2002, p. 11).

Conclusions from this work added to the author's understanding that in order to meet all learners' needs when teaching the author needed to use Viconic Language Methods. The author also determined that as a teacher, Viconic Language Methods worked for the author as a learner. The author continued using VLMs in several areas such as special education, Spanish as a second language, and English language development.

Utilizing Viconic Language Methods in a Behavioral Classroom Setting

For five years the author worked in a structured learning classroom with a focus on behavior (SLC-B) that included kindergarten through second grade levels. The school the author taught at was Title I in a rural area with approximately 500 students in attendance in grades K-5. During that five-year timeframe a total of 37 students (8 girls and 29 boys) went through the SLC-B program. The class size was between 11 and 14 in any given year. The SLC-B program was the only one in our district of eleven schools. The district determined through functional behavior assessments or assessment of student's needs as it related to their goals, that the students who qualified for the SLC-B program could not function in a general education classroom.

During five years, 4/37 students needed to continue on to the next level of structured setting with a focus on behavior as 3rd graders; of those four, the majority were also able to partially mainstream. Two students did need to return to the next behavioral setting after 2 years mainstreaming, as they struggled emotionally for various reasons, and the use of Viconic Language Methods were not available in their new classrooms. 9 of the 37 students did move out of district but several parents stayed in contact, and several of those students who moved either stayed mainstreaming or ended up mainstreaming. 60% of students (with the exception of some students who moved and those who were participating in the mainstream setting less than full time) made a full transition to the mainstream setting and remained there. From a global perspective of the program, 82% of students (with the exception of some students who moved) during the final year were either fully integrated into the general education classroom or were participating partially in the general education setting and making progress towards accessing general education full time at the end of five years. The remainder of the students this author continued to work with experienced growth across all goal areas that indicated readiness to either partially or fully mainstream. As students progressed, they met their goals more consistently overall, 85% or more across 7 goal category areas whereas previously they might have been operating at 20-30%.

Over the first several years the author worked to integrate Viconic Language Methods (VLMs) replacing the existing behavior system of rewards and punishers that had previously been used in that classroom. Students who may struggle with behavior benefit greatly learning new ways to communicate. After all, behavior is simply another form of communication (Arwood, 2011). These new skills equip them with the language, in terms of conceptual development, to engage in relationships with others, as opposed to not being able to see others in their picture and having negative interactions with others.

For example, if students have enough assigned meaning to the world around them and their interactions with others, they can begin to see how their interactions impact others. If a student is upset because they were accidently run into in line, instead of getting angry and hitting the other person, they could see the context of what happened if it is drawn out, thus having visual meaning assigned to it. They could begin to see others in their picture and realize it was an accident that the other person was in their space. They could use their language from the assigned meaning they derived in context to communicate verbally rather than physically.

Due to the influence of many years of Western psychology and behaviorism traditions, behavioral classrooms by nature tend to focus on teaching desired behaviors with methods where the teacher teaches the desired behavior and the student gives it back in the same way. This concept is an input-output model. Remember, however, that doing is not thinking, imitating is not necessarily learning. A student who simply imitates what the teacher expects of them will not internalize lasting change.

Contrasted with this imitation of behavior, Arwood advocates for helping a learner acquire their own meaning of the world around them. Using visual language methods builds language and facilitates conceptual growth, "[Educators can] use behavior methods to teach skills or patterns, [or] use cognitive methods to allow for opportunities to learn concepts...make choices...be the agent" (Arwood, E.L., Ormson, K., Kaulitz C. & Brown M., 2013, June).

In order to build language and increase conceptual development enhancing communication and positive relationships in the classroom community, the author and educational assistants continually used Viconic Language Methods such as drawing and writing in the classroom in order to bring the learning to all our students. Viconic language methods are unique in that they add visual language to spoken language and incorporate all developmental levels. This includes drawing concepts at a preoperational level, drawing in real time, drawing before note taking or writing, drawing on boards or papers so that the drawings can be referred later, and drawing ideas so they are relational or connected and flowcharted (Arwood, Kaakinen & Wynne, 2002).

The classroom was organized in a way that whiteboards were available on three walls so that if needed the teacher could draw on the whiteboard at any time in any location as students moved around the classroom to do their work. When using visual language strategies, all learners need to be able to see the board at all times. There was an easel on the carpet that afforded another place to draw and write. If a problem arose and we needed to assign or reassign meaning quickly and bring the drawing closer to the student, there were several small clipboards on the walls around the room with Arwood drawing templates that the team could quickly access and use.

"Yesterday, I went hiking in the woods with my dog Bella. It was a sunny spring day and I could see many flowers blooming on the forest floor. Bella was very excited to be walking in the forest, so excited that she started running in the grass and chasing butterflies. There were many butterflies flying in the air and drinking nectar from the flowers. I began thinking about a butterfly's life. How did their life begin? Did they start their lives as butterflies? Does anyone have any ideas about how a butterfly's life begins?"

Figure 6.6: "I" Story Including Oral Language Sample

Whatever the subject area, the class drew and wrote. Drawing was event-based and language was not taught in isolation, or in parts, but as a whole. The author always tried to use visual oral language (Arwood, 2011) and started drawing with "I" Stories related to any subject matter being discussed, on whiteboards using a black marker. For an example of using an "I" Story to start out a lesson, see Figure 6.6. Notice that the author puts herself in the picture so that students can see her start to form the questions that will drive the next unit of inquiry.

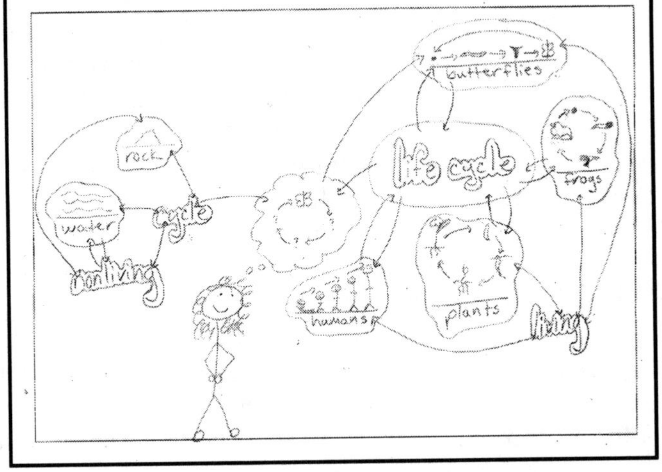

As our discussions would progress, the author would make sure to ask the most important questions that help to expand students' own thinking: "who," "what," "why," "where," and "how." These questions related to the event based story we were unfolding together. Next, the author would begin to flowchart ideas that we came up with as a class on the white board or on large pieces of white butcher paper which would be hung in the room for later reference (See Figure 6.7). Notice that all of the ideas are connected semantically using arrows. These represent on paper the meaningful connections that are occurring in the students' brains.

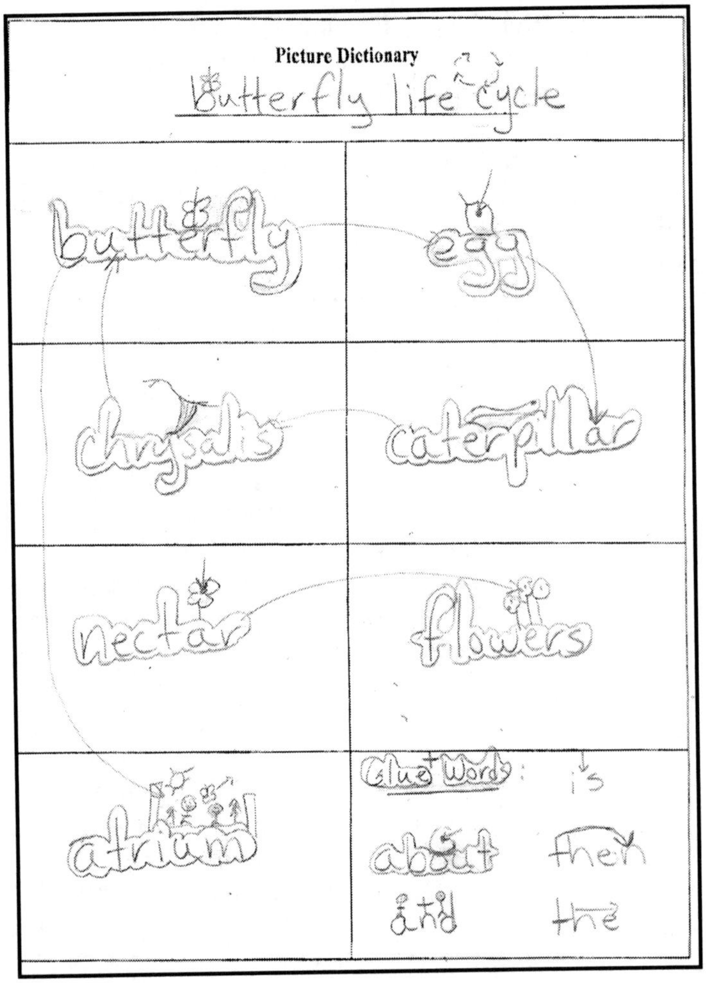

Figure 6.7: Visual Flow Chart

Students also drew their own pictures about the ideas. We also made picture dictionaries together (Figure 6.8) to be used in writing. If students needed words for their picture dictionaries we would write them on sticky notes and give them the shape of the word so that they could write it in their books and draw a pictograph attached to the word. If they needed hand-over-hand assistance to make the shape of the word we helped them with that. "What a student can do you let them do, what a student can't do you give them" (Arwood, E.L., Ormson, K., Kaulitz C. & Brown M., 2013, June). Language was taught in high context through drawing.

Figure 6.8: Picture Dictionary of Butterfly Life Cycle

One student who came to us had not participated in academics at her previous school. The previous school had focused on giving her a lot of "sensory breaks" for her "tantrums." This student had experienced a significant amount of trauma and did exhibit some extreme behaviors, understandably so. Below is a comparison of a writing sample from the fall when she first joined us with no exposure to VLMs (See Figure 6.9) and one in the spring after several months of using VLMs (See Figure 6.10). By analyzing the language she used to describe her own experiences, we are able to see evidence that her thinking increased in complexity. Figure 6.9 shows virtually no language at her disposal, indicating that she is operating at the lowest level of social development and cannot understand the world around her. In contrast, Figure 6.10 shows her starting to actually "see" the stories that people tell. This is a necessary step for her to be able to integrate successfully into a classroom.

Figure 6.9: Language Sample Pre-Intervention

Indeed, she demonstrated a tremendous amount of growth and not only had the language and concepts to completely participate in all academic activities, but had the language and concepts to participate in the classroom community quite successfully without having "tantrums." She was able to begin mainstreaming.

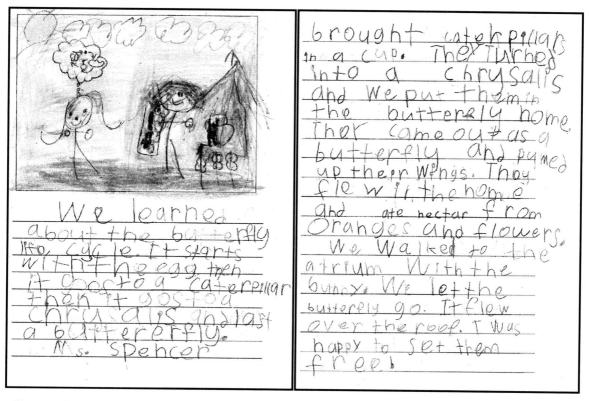

Figure 6.10: Drawing/Writing Sample After Multiple Months of Visual Language Intervention

Students' Behavior Changes When They Can "See" Themselves

The beginning of the year was always "frontloaded" with drawing out what it looks like to be a learner at school, the school environment as a whole (involving the "who," "what," "when," "where," "why," and "how"), and drawing out what it looks like to be a learner in a community of learners. Students began to see themselves as the learner (agent) participating in the community as visual language assigns meaning to what that looks like. These drawings were posted in the classroom and referred to frequently. Part of our morning routine involved drawing out an aspect of what it looked like to participate in the classroom community. The educational team drew "I" stories, incorporating visual oral language and then students drew themselves and others in the picture with teachers labeling and assigning meaning to the drawing. These "rules" were focused on translating auditory expectations of a general education classroom to a visual format in order to develop the language of expectations needed to move toward and function in a general education setting.

Some of the rules related to "keeping hands to one's self," or visually translated, "my body is in my own space, your body is in its own space, our bodies are in their own spaces in relation to where we are in the classroom, playground" (or whatever the situation may be); "listening to the teacher," or visually translated, "my body is facing the teacher and I can see her mouth move while I am making pictures in my head"; etc. Working with these goals through drawing and how students progressed on a daily basis, translated to data in terms of IEP (Individual Education Plan) goals in self-management or social skills; however, the most important data came from the in-class drawing and writing samples that represented student's underlying language and conceptual development as it progressed.

The author and the educational assistants used these Arwood drawing templates with students multiple times a day to assign meaning to what a learner looks like in a community of learners, giving multiple examples and layering concepts in multiple ways throughout the day while drawing. These drawings could go home with students so that parents could discuss what happened and further add meaning to any situation that occurred. Time was spent at student conferences and summer meet-and-greets with parents in the classroom to explain that these "draw outs" were for discussion and communication in order to build language, not for punitive use.

If a situation occurred, for example one student starting to be physically aggressive with another student (Figure 6.11), any member of the team would immediately grab a clipboard with an Arwood template, bring it close to the student, and start drawing to add meaning to the situation. As an alternative we would do a draw out with the whole class for behaviors they all needed to work on.

The learner was always drawn into the

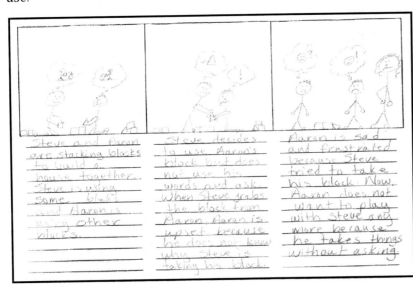

Figure 6.11: Cartoon Depicting Behavioral Choices

picture with other learners in context using multiple examples while language and meaning were assigned. It was amazing how the students began to participate with the change of sensory input while the teacher was drawing. They were watching the drawing, the motor movements of the teacher's mouth when talking, and eventually began to participate by taking over the drawing, more often than not, thereby facilitating a reassignment of meaning to the situation. Arwood explained what was happening:

> Meaning is acquired through levels of sensory input, perceptual organization and integration, and concept development. This process of acquiring meaning explains how the learning system is developed. Therefore, changes in the semantic acquisition also result in changes to the product of the learning system (Arwood, 1991, p. 36).

With all our learners, no matter what the category of disability (emotionally disturbed, learning disabled, Autistic, communication disorder, etc.) the team used VLMs throughout the day in any given situation, an opportunity to assign or reassign meaning. The NsLLT methods address all "categories of disability" and address all learners whether with a visual or auditory learning system.

> ...Learning disabled students who perform the best academically and socially are those who are diagnosed early in their education and have been offered visual ways to compensate – sometimes with the help of parents or educators and sometimes with the help of their own innovations. Even students who have developed numerous ways of compensating do not know that they have learned to use other means of learning, or know why learning takes so much time, why they don't understand what others understand, why social situations are difficult, etc. (Arwood, 1991, p. 86).

It is important to note that a structured learning center, with a focus on behavior and highly specialized instruction, would be considered a restrictive setting for addressing students with a very high level of need. The author's main goal was to facilitate language and conceptual development that would in turn positively impact students' social and academic growth and be transferable across settings so that each child accessed the mainstream setting and functioned successfully there.

A Change of Behavior is a Change in Thinking

One student, who was identified as having autism, started in our classroom by participating about 5 minutes at a time in classroom activities with peers. The student loved the "Lion King" movie and was constantly "in" the movie. The student was a great singer and would often break out into one of the main theme songs, which were wonderful, but it was a little distracting to the other students. We "drew out" with the student daily, always carrying around a pencil and piece of paper.

The student went from participating in the classroom 5 minutes a day, communicating in one word utterances, not wanting to write, and not being able to see others in her picture, to progressively participating in the full day schedule and in the classroom community using VLMs. The student now enjoys reading, writing and communicating with others and the student sees others in her picture. The student went from using one-word utterances to full and comprehensible sentences. The student now takes the lead in interacting with and helping others; she loves learning and sees herself as a learner!

This student had never been exposed to Viconic Language Methods before. By using methodology inspired by Arwood's Neuro-Education Theory, such as visual language strategies, we were able to literally rewire this child's brain. A child can only become more pro-social when they have the underlying thinking to know how to behave. Auditory and behaviorism methods of instruction rarely provide such concepts for our most struggling learners.

According to the observations of an educational assistant who was trained in the basics of VLMs to use with the student daily,

> "Using Viconic Language Methods and working with the student over a period of 3 years, she started out with a few simple words and eventually grew to using full sentences. I was able to watch her grow both in her language, skills and academics. She is now a thriving 3rd grader full of words. It was such a beautiful thing to be a part of. " (A. Dragoo, personal communication, October 10, 2013)

Another example was a student who struggled very much with physical aggression and communicating his needs. Using Viconic Language Methods helped the student to grow, conceptualize, see others in his picture, and be able to engage in positive relationships with others. This student went on to read, write, and participate in all academic activities spending time in the general education classes. As he developed language the student began to use his words instead of exhibiting physical anger; aggressive behavior decreased as conceptual development and language increased. The student saw himself as a learner and a participating member of the school community.

According to the educational assistant trained in the basics of VLMs who worked with the student when he first started, "He could not write, he could not read, but he started feeling empowered because he could communicate his needs through drawing it out." (J. Gleason, personal communication, October 7, 2013)

As the success stories kept coming, this author knew she was on to something powerful. Another student who had limited experience in the school setting started out with us participating about 5 minutes at a time in the classroom activities and with his peers. The student was very much in his own world of "Thomas the Train". The student was very meticulous and very talented in how he set up his train tracks. Some other teachers even commented on how advanced he must be. However, remember, doing the same repetitive activity over and over again does not represent fluid thinking; these are merely patterns, and use only the lowest levels of the brain.

In the beginning, the student was not able to see other kids in his picture and only interacted minimally with others. Again, we drew out with him daily, carrying around a pencil and paper with Arwood templates. The student went from limited participation in the classroom and with others to participating in the full day schedule and interacting with others throughout his day. The student now enjoys reading, writing and all other academic subjects. The student can communicate his needs to others and interacts in a positive way with others in his classroom community. The student sees himself as the learner.

According to an educational assistant who worked in the classroom and was trained in using the basics of using VLMS daily,

> "One student we have been working with for two years has improved greatly. Using Viconic Language Methods on a consistent basis, his language has grown and he is able to

communicate his needs better. With this, his academics and
behavior grew and improved. (R. Ferris, personal
communication, October 7, 2013)

Many of our learners had prior negative experiences in school and when they started in our classroom they often had a tremendous amount of anxiety around school or academic tasks. It is important to note that 100% of our students over the 5 year period of teaching the structured learning center and using VLMS's made significant academic growth (in all subject areas), as well as behavioral, self-management and social growth from when they first came to the classroom. This was directly connected with using Viconic Language Methods daily to facilitate conceptual growth represented in the student's language. This growth was reported in IEP goals, district assessments and reports cards. One student went from having several meltdowns a day when he first came, reading at a DRA II (Direct Reading Assessment II) level 4, and barely participating in academic tasks, to a year and a quarter later, reading at a DRA II level 28, participating in all academic tasks (most at grade level) and then mainstreaming in the general education setting. The student is now fully mainstreamed and a contributing member to his classroom community.

When given the opportunity to have meaningful input presented that matches their neurobiological learning system, students thrive. This author has seen this in her own teaching experiences. There is a broader societal impact to providing meaningful input presented to match neurobiological learning systems in any field. As concepts and language develop so do the learners' ability to communicate thoughtfully with others in a relational way.

Inter-Professional Collaboration

In the author's classroom the staff of educational assistants were very engaged and actively involved with supporting the students and functioned as part of a team in a classroom community. It was a very positive environment that reflected community and was student-centered. Those educational assistants who were exposed to and trained in the basics of using Viconic Language Methods were also very engaged in the process and noticed student success. One educator stated, "Using Viconic Language Methods I have seen students grow leaps and bounds in their language skills. They are better able to communicate their needs. Frustration levels decrease immensely as communication increases" (A. Dragoo, personal communication, October 10, 2013)

Another staff person commented, "All of our students have benefited from using Viconic Language Methods. Language builds, communication grows, and behavior improves. Their language seems to progress so much faster throughout the year with this method. With a better understanding of language, behavior improves, which helps kids mainstream." (R. Ferris, personal communication, October 7, 2013)

We also had a very engaged principal who has observed the use of VLMs. She became interested in using VLMs and has some templates in her office where she draws out with kids who come to her office and are struggling behaviorally. She noted,

"I see Viconic Language as a useful tool for any elementary age
student in any setting. All students at the elementary level are
developing language skills and this approach provides the visual
support to language development. I have used a 3 part chart with
students when problem solving and have found it highly
effective." (K. Brooks, personal communication, October 15,
2013)

At the district level the TOSA (teacher on special assignment) representing Student Services, although not trained in VLMs, mentioned her observations speaking from a global perspective and detailed involvement with our class for two years,

> "I saw Viconic Language Methods help students develop language creating a bigger repertoire of pro-social strategies in communicating with others and building relationships. I was able to observe the majority of the kids were able to move from a more restrictive setting into the general population and remain there" (L. Marquardt, personal communication, October 10, 2013)

Teachers, specialists, and educational assistants in the district inquired about VLM resources, and parents inquired about using the resources at home. The feedback from parents was that students experienced tremendous growth, enjoyed coming to school, and saw themselves as learners and as part of the school community. One parent commented,

> "Our daughter came to us from the state foster system with a history of abuse and neglect. She has symptoms of Reactive Attachment and Post-traumatic Stress Disorders and was constantly in a highly reactive state. She had participated in Play Therapy and Rhythm and Music Therapy, as well as Therapeutic preschool for two years, but still had frequent meltdowns and, at times, got physically aggressive. Time outs and punishment meant nothing to her. Her kindergarten placement was a special education behavior learning classroom, which utilized Viconic Language Methods. When she had a conflict, her teachers would help her "draw it out," which taught her insight and problem solving skills as well as the language and confidence to verbalize her feelings. She would bring the draw-outs home, which allowed us to see what occurred and discuss the resolution with her, and in turn, communicate with her teachers. Talking through her drawings helped us better understand and anticipate her triggers, which in turn reduced her reactive behaviors. She no longer needed outbursts to communicate, and meltdowns disappeared. Visual language and a very dedicated group of educators gave our daughter the skills she needed to mainstream before the end of the year, and now, two years later, she is thriving in mainstream classes. I am incredibly thankful for the gift visual language has given my family and highly recommend it. (B. Bennett, personal communication, October 21, 2013)

Challenges

Some challenges to implementing VLMs in the classroom and promoting collaboration have to do with continuing education, time for training, and overcoming the underlying auditory assumptions that pervade our current educational system. This author has personally been studying and working with VLMs for several years and will continue to learn about the NsLLT in the future. District and school-wide training on VLMs and NsLLT would be beneficial for all teachers and learners. When students transition to the general education classroom it is difficult if the teacher does not use VLMs and teach in the way the learner learns. The majority of classrooms at most schools do not use VLMs. A lack of understanding of the process and underlying theory in implementing VLMs with regards to language, learning, and neurobiology where language drives structure, can render minimal results if not implemented with this training and understanding. It is very easy for auditory assumptions and biases to seep in, as that is the dominant cultural paradigm today. Training and exposure are important because many times a fundamental understanding of the why and how (why we are doing the draw outs and how that is connected to learning systems) is misstated or misunderstood without having time to work with the theory behind the method.

Moreover, the idea of a student having a visual learning system can be confused with other previous ideas such as having "learning styles," which are merely preferences. Additionally, many teachers think they are using visual methods when they use isolated picture cue icons. However, these do not include the learner, are iconic and not viconic, and do not support conceptual growth through the developmental levels of language. In this author's experience, the institution itself is product based, by virtue of underlying auditory and behaviorist assumptions, therefore the allocation for time to focus on the "process" of learning from a neurobiological perspective tends to be limited for teachers and learners both.

Community and the Growth of Learners

The use of VLMs contributes to classroom communities. The learners see themselves as the agents, see others in their picture and communicate and interact with adults and peers within the community, "Language improves through cognitive stages of development therefore increasing the way the students use language to communicate thoughtfully about themselves as well as others" (Arwood & Young, 2000, p. 317).

Using brain-based visual language strategies has also brought this author accolades. For example, the author and team member were recognized in the district for student success and exceptional teaching (Excellence in Education Award), people requested to work in the classroom, and parents requested that their child be placed in the classroom. The team was wonderful, caring, and eager to learn in order to facilitate children's learning. Collaboration existed between personnel, administrators, and the greater school community. In all, this author found success because she included the primary conduit for language development: visual language strategies.

Conclusion

The Neuro-semantic Language Learning Theory and the use of Viconic Language Methods takes into consideration the neurobiological system of the learner and therefore makes the learner the focus in a respectful way, cultivating higher order thinking and relationships. The NsLLT has wide reaching ramifications in every field in which Western psychology or behaviorism has had an influence.

In addition, the study of neuroeducation provides a comprehensive view of how students actually learn from a neurobiological as well as language perspective. As a result, many scholars (e.g. Brevoort, 2012) advocate for the inclusion in teacher preparation programs of at least one course that focuses on the study of the brain and how it relates to education. The interrelated studies of cognitive psychology, neuroscience, and language provide an overview that highlights the importance of a Neuro-Education perspective with its foundation in the NsLLT in comparison to the current paradigm and influence of a Western psychology/behaviorist perspective that exists in our auditory culture. The paradigm shift from product (an input-output model) to process (a layered model including interrelated neurosemantic and neurobiological relationships) and from teaching to learning is integral to the success of student's conceptual development. This creates an incredibly positive classroom community where students are enjoying the process of learning because they are being taught in the way their systems are neurobiologically wired to learn.

Summary of Neuro-Education Methods

From the examples provided in this chapter, it is clear that the Viconic Language Methods (VLMs) make it possible for a large variety of students to thrive. This chapter provides evidence for the efficacy of Neuro-Education methodology from general population language scores, to special need students school work, anecdotal evidence, and intervention outcomes. This summary will explain why these strategies work through the lens of neuroscience, cognitive psychology, and language.

From a neuroscience lens, using visual language methods is effective at raising conceptual understanding because nearly all learners utilize a visual learning system to develop concepts. Auditory learners use an overlap of acoustic and visual patterns to form concepts, while visual learners access multiple visual patterns to form concepts. This means that all people utilize the visual system to learn new concepts. For a visual learner, a concept that is acquired can be accessed by an acoustic tag, but the formation occurs only through layering visual patterns. This explains how some students can still succeed in a typical classroom with auditory cultural assumptions despite being visual learners. They have the advantage of having already acquired the concepts.

From a cognitive psychology lens, Viconic Language Methods support pro-social behavior by supporting the agency of the learner. In a traditional classroom with an auditory cultural bias the learner is objectified. The student receives the teachers' input, and produces the appropriate output. If they are not capable of this exchange, then there must be something wrong with them. The VLMs support the agency of the learner by recognizing his or her own unique experiences and perceptions as valid. The student begins to see himself or herself as an agent, and by extension is capable of seeing others as agents as well.

From the example of the young girl in Figures 6.9 & 6.10, it is possible to see how the VLMs support language development. As mentioned earlier, students develop the concepts that they can then tag with words. One component of the auditory cultural bias of traditional education is that teachers introduce the word with its definition in an attempt to teach the word. We learn concepts that we name with words, not the other way around. Words without concepts are stored in short term memory and dumped, while concepts that are tagged are stored in semantic long-term memory. The VLMs supports language development by raising conceptual understanding.

As the author of this chapter has demonstrated, the VLMs are effective strategies that are supported by neuroscience, cognitive psychology, and language. They harness the incredible innate learning capacity of the human brain, support the child as an agent in their interactions with teachers and other students, and develop their natural ability at conceptual understanding.

Chapter 7

Thinking with the Space of Shape: Visual Language Instruction for Deaf/Hard of Hearing Populations

Carole Kaulitz, M.Ed., CCC-SLP

Abstract

The purpose of this chapter is to provide the background behind making an educational shift in practice from emphasis on products to an emphasis on learning processes for a Deaf/Hard of Hearing student. The chapter will demonstrate how the focus of this student's programming was placed on language function across subjects in order to shift the educational focus from working on parts to facilitating the student's learning as a whole. According to Dr. Arwood's teaching, learning is a neurobiological process and learning to think is a process of acquiring language through the Neuro-semantic Language Learning Theory (NsLLT). Therefore, helping a student learn to use language also helps the student increase the student's level of thinking. Part of that process is the acquisition of language. Through the introduction of Neuro-semantic Language Learning Theory (NsLLT) as a brain-based learning model, language will be defined from both a developmental perspective as well as from learning or functional perspectives as a tool for increasing academic and social development for the learner.

About the Author

Carole Kaulitz has been a speech-language pathologist at a residential School for the Deaf at different times since 1989 and has been responsible for Speech-Language services for Deaf/Hard of Hearing students of all ages, grades, and cognitive levels as well as those students who were Deaf/Hard of Hearing with co-occurring conditions such as autism spectrum disorders, multiple disabilities, and social thinking challenges. Although she recently resigned her position, she continues to work in private practice, consulting with families, group homes, and education systems as a specialist with a focus on visual thinking strategies for individuals impacted with autism spectrum disorders, individuals who are Deaf/Hard of Hearing, and those individuals with multiple disabilities. The following case study highlights one of her students during her tenure at the residential school.

Background

Pragmaticism Methodology was developed by a philosopher named Charles S. Pierce in the 1800's who believed that "the whole is greater than the parts." He called this philosophy Pragmaticism. Dr. Ellyn Arwood applied this philosophy to education and developed a methodology in the 1980's before the field of neuroscience was available to validate Peirce's or Dr. Arwood's research. She called it Pragmaticism Methodology and has worked diligently over the years expanding her understanding of how we use our thinking of 'whole to part' learning to gain meaning academically, socially, and behaviorally. Today, neuroscience supports the philosophy that Peirce put forward in the 1800's and Arwood applied as Pragmaticism Methodology in the 1980's.

This author first heard Dr. Arwood present information about Pragmaticism Methodology almost three decades ago at a conference for school-based Speech and Language Pathologists held in Vancouver, WA. Dr. Arwood provided Peirce's theory for how learning occurs neuro-semantically and how students learn from 'whole to part'. Over the years, as Dr. Arwood further developed her Neuro-semantic Language Learning Theory (NsLLT), with an emphasis on how learning shifts current educational focus from teaching to learning, this author continued to learn and refine her thinking as well as her own professional philosophies and methodologies. She realized that the NsLLT impacted her and others in ways that continue to have far-reaching consequences for the field of education by attempting to change the current paradigm of teaching from one of a deficit model to one of a model based on learning strengths. Dr. Arwood's methodologies are solidly based on the most current neuroscience and brain research, and she disseminates this information with the knowledge that changing any paradigm can be an uncomfortable process at times.

This author has had the distinct opportunity to be mentored by Dr. Arwood for many years and to co-author three books with her. The books are based on Dr. Arwood's teachings about language, learning, and behavior and have been distributed throughout the United States, Canada, and the United Kingdom to positive reviews.

Introduction

Most professionals understand that individuals who are Deaf/Hard of Hearing think with a visual meta-cognition based on learning processes; but, most educational programs for Deaf/Hard of Hearing students utilize auditory methods to teach students to imitate, copy, repeat, practice, transfer, and test even when they support the use of American Sign Language as a primary mode of instruction. It is this author's belief that these auditory methods utilize an educational approach that is not brain friendly for the majority of Deaf/Hard of Hearing students. This chapter will provide information on how one Deaf/Hard of Hearing student's academic and residential program was changed to include his thinking processes. Numerous examples will be provided for how using the student's language function for improving his thinking or cognition and social development was accomplished.

Byron: A Case for Neuro-Education Methodology

Byron is a twelve-year-old young man who has been diagnosed with severe to profound bi-lateral hearing loss and autism spectrum disorder (ASD). He has been enrolled in an academic and residential program for students who are Deaf/Hard of Hearing since preschool, although the issue of ASD was not diagnosed until elementary school and was not addressed in his school program until 2 years ago. He often exhibits unexpected behaviors that have included aggression, hitting, kicking, and spitting. He also toe walks (a sign of a student not being developmentally "grounded"), has tactile and sensory issues, and has very focused topics of interest. Over the years, Byron has struggled with delays in language development and communication over and above those commonly associated with hearing loss.

Although Byron does use aspects of American Sign Language to communicate, he is perceived as 'deceptively expressive' because he can express more than he truly understands. This leads the adults in his life to guess, assume, and infer what he is expressing. For example, Byron has a repetitive use of known phrases that we call 'borrowed language'. He 'borrows' language from people around him, TV shows, movies, and video games and at times, he seems to take on the personalities and characteristics of his teachers, taking control of the classroom and "helping his peers" without being asked. He is also allowed to change his classroom schedule because "he is expressing his preferences" and is not expected to follow his schedule if he does not want to.

This author was asked to set up a new classroom program for Byron as well as monitor the residential program where Byron currently resides on the school campus. In addition to a new classroom program, this author was also asked to provide an in-service/workshop, along with the school psychologist, to all staff that work with Byron to prepare Byron for returning to school after a period of absence due to non-compliant and violent behaviors that the school did not feel they could address at the time.

The classroom teacher, the classroom aide, as well as the residential staff were new to the school and have had limited experience working with students who have co-occurring conditions such as ASD, CP, ADHD, LD, and various syndromes over and above hearing loss.

Previous staff had done their best over the years to provide effective programming for Byron. However, their intervention approach has been based on a philosophy that teaches skills in isolation and reinforcing good behavior with rewards and bad behavior with punishment. Staff had not previously been trained in Neuro-semantic Learning Theory (NsLLT) which looks at how an individual uses thinking language to get his/her needs met academically, behaviorally, and/or socially, or on how to teach students to think using Viconic Language Methods (VLMs).

Because, it is the belief of many professionals, including Dr. Arwood with the NsLLT that all behavior is a form of communication and Byron has been communicating for years how he actually learns and thinks through his behavior, we also believe that changing the teaching paradigm from teaching skills out of context and in isolation to learning how to think in relationship to others will result in Byron changing his behavior and improving his learning based on how he uses thinking for meaning.

The following in-service was developed to provide staff with a different theory of learning than what is currently in practice throughout the US, as well as examples of visual thinking strategies to help Byron change his behavior and improve his learning based on how he uses thinking for meaning.

Uncovering Presupposed Beliefs about Bryon

We began with a sampling of Byron's behavioral characteristics as recorded on behavior reports throughout his school years from his school staff, residential staff, and peers to examine our participants' beliefs about this student. Some adults who work with Byron had written the following statements:

> "Byron appears to acknowledge people and at other times does not acknowledge/ignores people."

> "He can appear perfectly 'normal' but at other times appear very withdrawn and/or 'odd'."

"Byron is unruly and/or spoiled and *just has* a behavior problem."

"Byron is without feelings and emotions."

"He makes progress so that means that he doesn't have autism."

"He smiles at you so Byron can't be Autistic."

"Children with autism do not have eye contact and are not social."

"Byron has eye contact when he wants to have eye contact."

"Children with autism do not participate in physical affection."

"Byron loves to hug and be hugged."

"Byron is very manipulative."

"Byron could sign clearly if he wanted to."

"Children with autism do not notice others and don't pick up cues from peers/adults, but Byron is able to copy every move I make."

"When Byron does not respond to a question/direction to which he has shown a previous correct response, he is being stubborn/non-compliant/obnoxious."

"He knows what he is doing."

"Underneath all of the difficult behaviors, Byron is really a normal child."

This lead to a discussion about sensory processing and how Byron has significant differences in the way he self-regulates.

Sensory Processing and Self-Regulation Differences

Oral stimulation (I.e., food textures, hot and cold sensitivities), olfactory (smell sensitivity), and proprioceptive input appear to be issues for Byron. Byron has also shown that he is sensitive to soft touch and prefers a more course or firm touch. In the past, he has had no way to let others know of these preferences except by his behavior, and thus he has acted out. When he acts out, the adults around him respond in a negative way and give negative consequences without understanding what Byron is thinking about when he reacts to something sensory or how his body is feeling.

For example, according to the adults who work with him, Byron runs away and doesn't stop until he runs into somebody or something in an attempt to avoid doing what he is being asked to do. From a developmental perspective, this is called "falling through space" because Byron is not grounded in the world around him. In reality, Bryon's actions express a need for movement to help him process information about the world.

In another example, Byron has shown that he is sensitive to visual input; e.g.: rapid signing/ASL. This has been interpreted, as Byron purposely does not want to watch others who try to communicate with him. Instead, although Byron has a need to process information through his motor system, he is more than likely overwhelmed by too much movement so he may need to block out visuals in the environment. In other words, in both examples, his brain has not yet acquired the level of language needed to separate the foreground from background visuals and movement, so slowing his body down within his environment and having a consistent eye gaze with others is difficult to maintain, if not impossible for him to accomplish. Overall, it is felt that Byron has sensory processing difficulties and difficulty with self-regulation because he does not yet have the language that names his thinking to understand who he is in relation to how his body feels and moves, how things he sees affect how he moves, and/or how to self-regulate his behavior in relationship to others so he can include them in his mental pictures.

Cognitive and Learning Differences

Typically, individuals with Hearing Loss/ASD have trouble with changes and transitions. Byron is no exception. Byron has a need for sameness/consistency. Individuals with Hearing Loss/ASD can come across as obsessive or compulsive as they tend to act on what they see in their heads. Adults interpret Byron's tendency to act compulsively as negative, purposeful non-compliant behavior instead of just actions he is not conscious about because he is only acting on what he sees in his head at the time.

Individuals with Hearing Loss/ASD have difficulty generalizing; doing the same task in different settings. Byron has difficulty generalizing tasks that are similar but not exactly the same, such as following the rules for not interrupting in his Life Skills classroom and applying those same rules to his mainstream classrooms, or following the rules about not bringing toys and games from home to the cottages, then bringing items from the cottages that he is not supposed to have at school. The above concepts greatly impact the way that Byron functions in his academic, residential, home, and community settings.

Like many people with Hearing Loss/ASD, Byron focuses on details and is unable to see the whole, or how things fit together. He has difficulty organizing his thoughts in a coherent way, integrating information, extracting meaning, and distinguishing among relevant details. He has many differences in how he learns compared to his peers with only Hearing Loss. Generally individuals with Hearing Loss/ASD, because their eyes process information much better than their ears, are typically strong visual thinkers and have more difficulty processing language through only auditory means or by one modality only (e.g.: ASL only, spoken language only). Individuals with Hearing Loss/ASD have difficulty organizing their thoughts, doing tasks, and processing information given to them through one modality (e.g. only ASL/sign, only written, or only role-played).

Differences in Pro-Social Thinking

Typically, individuals with Hearing Loss/ASD struggle with the complexities and nuances of social interaction and have difficulty socializing and sustaining relationships. Byron has difficulty with social relationships. It is not that Byron does not relate, he relates in a different way. Byron often relates better to adults, because adults typically are more predictable and flexible to meet his needs. It is not that Byron doesn't want to make friends, often times he doesn't know how to interact with others in appropriate ways. For example, Bryon will insult his peers and/or go into teaching mode and correct what they are doing. He also does not have a good understanding of reciprocal conversation skills so his peers have difficulty following and maintaining a conversation with him especially if the peers want to talk about a subject that Byron has no interest in discussing

The complex set of skills necessary for making friends needs to be formally taught through multiple modalities, over a variety of settings and situation so that the concept can be acquired in terms of how Byron thinks about others. Byron has great difficulty understanding someone else's perspective, which is one of the most complex aspects of social interaction and one that is the hardest concept to master for individuals with Hearing Loss/ASD.

Communication Differences

Although Byron's ASL skills are emerging as measured by formal and informal assessments (Kendall Conversational Proficiency Scales, language sample), his communication is often not clear enough for a conversation partner to understand without guessing, inferring, or assuming what he is trying to communicate. In other words, adults and peers fill in what Byron has expressed with their own language in order to have what he is saying make sense. Because adults must "gloss," or fill in their own interpretation of what Byron means to communicate (Arwood, 2011), he cannot act socially without constant adult assistance. This not only impacts his communication, but also his ability to be social, and even learn new material on his own. Byron has a preoperational interpretation (Piaget, 1952) of what is said to him so he is very literal and may respond in a literal way.

Understanding Byron's Behaviors

As was stated earlier, we believe that behaviors demonstrated by Byron, **_are a form of communication_**. His behaviors, such as aggression, hitting, kicking, and spitting are characteristic of many children significantly impacted with ASD and are symptoms of the difficulty he has in understanding how he thinks in relationship to others. Functional Behavior Assessments, Behavior Intervention Plans, and family reports have been the most common way that staff and family have used to discover the purpose of Byron's behavior and previous education programs have been set up with reward systems to extinguish unwanted behavior. It is important to note that these methods are inspired by the tenets of behaviorism, and are the de-facto approach to working with behavior disorders in schools today. But until now, how Byron thinks and learns to behave has not been addressed, so his behavior has not seen lasting change.

One of the most controversial strategies for our staff to use when working with students like Byron is drawing. It was interesting to note that with a show of hands more than 60% of the participants in our staff meeting to discuss Viconic Language Methods were reluctant and/or hesitant to draw. This opened up an honest discussion about why we draw and what to draw. Since drawing is a very controversial topic with our staff, we started by showing a slide that demonstrates how stick

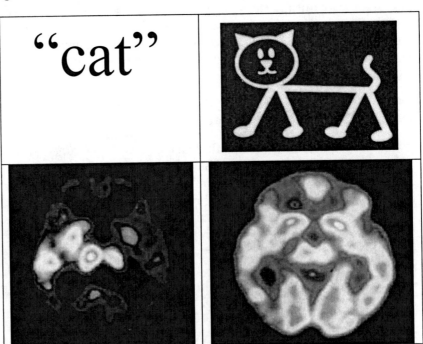

Figure 7.1: PET scan from Mayo Foundation for Medical Education and Research shows a brain when it hears the word "cat" and a brain seeing a drawing of a cat. The areas that are lit up mean that the brain is "turned on" ready to process and understand what is being said more easily and faster.

figure visuals benefit *all* of us. The slides in Figure 7.1 from the Mayo Foundation for Medical Education and Research demonstrate that humans are more receptive to stick figure images than we are to words alone, so spoken language alone is not enough for individuals with Hearing Loss/ASD to understand and process. The most effective way for an individual with Hearing Loss/ASD to learn is through a multi-modal approach such as incorporating spoken, written, and drawn information. Providing spoken language alone, sign language alone, or visual images alone are not enough to make learning more meaningful.

Because staff had been hesitant to draw, we thought that with information about the most current neuroscience research they would feel more confident, and along with multiple ways to represent ideas such as signing, writing, hand-over-hand support, fingerspelling, shaping/bubbling ideas, they could teach concepts to Byron through the use of drawing as a strategy and help him to build stronger retrieval cues. Staff agreed that they all want Byron to be more engaged in learning, and as a result were willing to add drawing to our list of strategies. However, we emphasized that we *must* always pair drawings with language to make learning happen and to grow neural pathways in the brain. Writing represents the pattern; drawing represents the underlying concept(s). Taken together, these will form visual language that the brain can process to make meaning (Arwood, 2011).

Fortunately, the most current research in neuroscience supports why stick figure drawings are easier for the brain to process than other more symbolic/iconic types of pictures (Arwood, 2011) and combined with a variety of other strategies can represent thinking and result in long-term learning. Providing ASL, spoken language, or visual images alone is not enough to make long-term learning happen because the student will not have enough overlapping modalities to form sufficient intraneuronal connections and thus will not build a sufficient level of conceptual development.

Figure 7.2: A drawing completed by the student with hand-over-hand assistance.

We wanted staff to use drawing to show Byron what he looks like and what he is supposed to be thinking about to engage in pro-social behavior, so we planned to introduce some language strategies as replacements for his physically aggressive behavior. But before the staff could know what to draw, we wanted them to practice changing their language to reflect their own thinking. So we developed a handout specific to Byron that went to his educational, residential, home, and community settings so that everyone could practice changing their language to meet Byron's needs in a variety of settings and situations. Staff and family could choose phrases from these examples in real time and as events warranted.

Here are a variety of drawings that were used with Byron. Some were presented using hand-over-hand at the beginning of intervention using NsLLT, and some are Byron's own independent drawings as he gained more thinking language through the process of learning.

Figure 7.3: A visual schedule to orient the student as they progress throughout their school day.

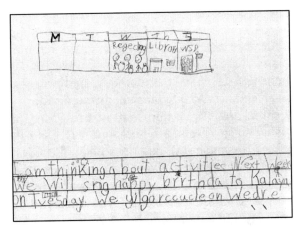

Figure 7.4: A student drawing visualizing the events of the week.

Figure 7.5: An event-based picture showing the semantic relationships between agents, actions, and objects.

Figure 7.6: A drawing completed by the student with hand-over-hand assistance.

Cartooning an Event Changes the Behavior

The following are some examples of replacement language that one could use to help address concerns about Byron's communication. Replacement language instruction can best be provided through *cartooning events* before known/foreseeable challenges and after Byron is calm and ready to process. It is recommended to teach replacement language by giving Byron the ASL for phases he should use when confused, frustrated, mad, upset, and in need of help. For a student such as Bryon, we want him to use language rather than behavior, even though the consequences will remain the same. We need to choose a different example of replacement language each time depending on what is going on and/or make up other things to express as we go. Byron will need the following ideas to be translated into ASL concepts for him to fully understand as English is not his primary language.

When Byron throws himself on the floor, bites, scratches, pinches, spits, runs away, or says things like, "I don't care!" "I hate _____!" or "That's stupid!" or "_____ called me names!" (or other blaming language), or repeats the same phrase over and over again, etc. we can use this key phrase: "Those words/signs don't tell me what you really need, (or what you

124

really mean, or what you really want to know)". You can sign/point to these ideas here." The following ideas would be drawn out in a communication book.

"I'm sad".

"I'm mad."

"I need help."

"I'm not finished."

"I need a break."

"I need more information about _____."

"I'm confused."

"I don't know what you mean."

"I don't understand what you are saying."

"I don't have anything to do."

"I don't know how to do _____."

"I can't do _____ right now because my pictures are stuck in my head."

"What am I doing after breakfast today?

"Where are we going today?"

"Why are we going to _____today?"

"What will we do at _____today?"

"What will we buy at _____ today?"

"How long will we be at _____?"

"I don't know what is happening next."

"What am I doing next?"

"What are you doing?"

"Why do you want me to do_____?"

"Why are you (list whatever the Byron can see us doing i.e. writing, walking fast, saying something, cooking)...?"

(Be careful not to actually address what Byron said exactly or respond to his words by defending yourself or him.)

In addition to teaching replacement language using the communication book,, we taught staff to be careful how to praise Byron and say "Thank you for getting dressed so fast this morning," or "I appreciate that you were ready to leave the cottage with me at 8:00," or "Thank you for giving me your finished homework so I can see it," or "Thank you for picking up your clothes and putting them away in the laundry hamper," etc. instead of "Good or nice job, high five, nice cleaning, good sitting, etc.". Many language intervention programs recommend limiting the amount of words adults use as to "not overly confuse" the learner, but by looking at the way the brain acquires new information, we see that the opposite needs to happen – a student struggling with language will need all phrases used to be specific to that context so they do not have to infer meaning (Arwood, 2011). That way, Byron won't have to guess what he is being praised for. Remember, "Thank you" language as well as using the words "because" and "so" or "so that" are the most powerful words in the English language.

Here are some more key phrases to use with Byron that help provide pictures in his head and promote his learning:

"Your body is telling me that you don't know what you are supposed to do (or how to do ____, or how you're supposed to look) right now. You can sign (or you can move your body this way...) and get what you need."

"Your face and your body are telling me that you are upset about something. You can sign...

"I'm angry about (reading, math, recess, something that happened at home, etc.)"

"I'm mad about (sad about...confused about... etc.)"

"I don't want to do _____ because I don't know how."

"My picture is stuck and I don't know what to do."

"I need help to move my body."

"I need help to understand what I need to do"

"I need to be left alone for 2 minutes (set a time), so I can think about my pictures which will help me calm my body down"

"I need a break so that I can change the pictures in my head."

After going over the examples of things to sign when Byron acted out, there was time given to the participants to practice drawing out examples of things to sign and to discuss what they would sign and draw if Byron acted out based on the following scenarios:

Scenario: Byron was up late the night before and did not have enough sleep. Byron does not want to get out of bed. What have we done? What should we do?

Scenario: Byron is playing the Wii and refuses to give up his turn when asked by peer/SLC. What have we done? What should we do?

Scenario: It is snack time and Byron has decided he will run the snack time activity and wants to take the place of the adult and/or help other classmates. What have we done? What should we do?

Scenario: Even though it is time for reading instruction according to his visual schedule, Byron decides he does not want to read and would rather play a Smartboard game. What have we done? What should we do?

Visual Language Learning Strategies for Byron

The Neuro-Education based language learning strategies discussed in this chapter were developed by Dr. Ellyn Arwood, Mabel Brown, and this author to give examples of multi-modal ways of giving students information in ways that their brain can process ideas as a whole instead of separating ideas into parts. This idea, of teaching the whole rather than the parts, may sound counterintuitive to some readers as the aforementioned theory of behaviorism advocates for a reductionist viewpoint that breaks down tasks into small additive steps. Indeed, most teaching methods try to break learning down to individual units. In this classroom, this is called "chunking" assignments or "scripting" learning. However, it is important to distinguish that this philosophy breaks apart the process of learning from the adult's perspective and not from the point of view of the child. The child will need to see full ideas in the appropriate context so that the process of visual neurobiological learning can take place.

For our intervention, the strategies we used were individualized to meet Byron's needs after multiple observations, therapy data, and informal drawn/written interviews with Byron. Each of the strategies listed was discussed at the workshop and all participants had an opportunity to practice each strategy to be sure everyone was on the same page about how to work Byron in multiple settings and situations. These visual language strategies are listed below:

1. Since Byron processes information visually and through his motor system (movement), it will be important that new information or information that he is confused about is presented in some sort of visual representation. This could be in the form of cartoon strips, drawings, full English written sentences, hand-over-hand support for writing, contextual social narratives, flowcharts, etc. Visual thinkers may also require movement to access more parts of their brain, such as the motor strip. This is an additional visual layer of input. Once this has been inputted, the brain will start to make meaningful connections between all of these layers (shape + movement)

2. In spite of his Hearing Loss/ASD, Byron has a lot of signs he can put together so adults in his environment may feel that he is in full control of what he is communicating. We might say that he is 'deceptively expressive'. His parents and staff most likely tend to respond to what they see him sign and may need to consider what it is that Byron is being asked to do at the time he uses a strange sign combination and/or makes inappropriate vocalizations. Family/teachers might consider 'reframing' language for Byron and could say something like, "Thank you for raising your hand to ask for help, with your hand raised I knew to come and help you'. "It looks like you don't know what to do or how to do ____. You can say, "I don't know what to do," or "I need help". In addition, attention needs to be paid to whether or not Byron's signs match what he is doing or being asked to do and will need to reframe what he has said for him e.g.: "Those words don't tell me what you really need. You can say_____."

3. It may help Byron to express his wants and needs to have a communication book available to him in the form of stick figure drawings, printed full English sentences, and/or pictographs in every area of the home/classroom as well as one to take along when he is outside in the community so that Byron will have more choices of ways to communicate with adults and peers.

   Right now his family and staff is anticipating his needs and he doesn't have to communicate appropriately to get his wants and needs met. The communication book should have pages for requesting, protesting, and social phrases/greetings that Byron can use to communicate with adults and peers in the general education setting and out in the community. The pictures would need to have full English captions on them, i.e. "I don't know what to do," or "I need help," as opposed to just "help," so that he can learn what English looks like in print and can communicate in whole ideas. This may help reduce the inappropriate signs/vocalizations on his worst days.

4. Byron needs more processing time to translate his use of head pictures into signed and written words (e.g. conversations, standardized or content area tests as he gets older, assignments, homework, etc.). If people 'jump in' before Byron has time to fully process what is signed to him, without additional visual cues such as drawn and/or written information, he may not respond in a way that is typically expected of him and may become agitated and non-cooperative. It will be important for Byron to learn to let people know that he needs more processing time. Teaching Byron some key phrases or cues such as, "I'm thinking," or putting up a finger to show people that he has seen them and is thinking of a response will show that he is using the time to process and is not ignoring them.

5. It was observed that Byron does not look at people all the time when they are signing to him and this is interpreted by his family and school staff as he is purposely ignoring them. Another idea may be that Byron has not yet learned how to use his eyes to watch what people are saying on their hands and hasn't learned to use the movement of the people's hands and mouths as additional information to process into mental pictures. Due to the severity of his Hearing Loss/ASD, it may help Byron understand the full picture of what people are saying and see what is said if he learns conceptually accurate American Sign Language rather than Signed English code. In other words, Byron may need to be taught the semiotics, or the purpose, for looking in the direction of the person who is signing.

   Byron may not be able to learn how to speech-read in context in order to form pictures in his head i.e. 'listening with his eyes'. However, if he has to rely on only ASL instead of being able to 'see' ideas through multiple modalities, there is a chance that he will not be able to do what is being asked of him in a way that is expected. Using conceptually accurate American Sign Language rather than Signed English code for support will also help Byron 'see what is being said' and will add another multi-modal layer.

6. When communicating with Byron, it will be important to make sure he has good visual contact with the speaker, and that he has an unobstructed view of the speaker's face and mouth so he can see their facial expressions, which are an integral part of ASL. For example, the speaker should not have untrimmed facial hair, should not put things in his/her mouth that may detract from what he/she is expressing while communicating with Byron, and/or should not turn away from Byron until the intended message is completed. The movement of the mouth also creates shapes that the brain can process as meaningful. This is often overlooked, even in hearing populations.

7. Byron needs consistent strategies to help him to visually organize his day. A visual schedule/ calendar has been used in the school program to help Byron stay on task, although because the schedule was not composed to meet Byron's visual learning needs, he struggled to use it independently. Currently, formal line drawings/symbols representing events of the day are placed with Velcro backing vertically on a strip to form his schedule. As Byron finishes an event, he has been asked to take the picture off the schedule and put it in a finished envelope so that the pictures disappear off of his schedule.

Instead, staff members might consider using stick figure drawings to depict all of the events happening during his day. These would be displayed using two Velcro strips horizontally, one below the other, so that Byron can put pictures of events he has completed on the second strip and staff can refer to them throughout the day as events are finished. Byron might also need a list or cartoon strip much like a 'drop down' menu showing him all the steps that it takes to complete an activity, an assignment, or his homework on time.

8. It will be very important to introduce new vocabulary to Byron in multiple modalities such as ASL, drawing, written English, so he can get multiple pictures in his head of language concepts and their meanings. Because of the way he processes information for thinking and learning, Byron cannot easily change his picture of a meaning of a word/idea and may respond inappropriately and/or not recognize words/ideas out of context. In addition, focusing more on the structures of English out of context, ex. English grammar such as 'pronouns' 'parts of speech, 'and/or 'wh' questions, instead of the function of English for communication and meaning, may not result in Byron having the ability to use the vocabulary he is learning appropriately in a variety of settings and situations.

9. Byron needs to be able to visually scan pages of written or drawn information before signing them word for word 'out loud' in order to take as many ideas off of the page as possible and change them into pictures in his head. When Byron signs word for word, he may be losing his head pictures and is simply signing the words without necessarily comprehending them (word calling). This is analogous to the process of reading out loud in English – many students focus all of their mental energy to sounding out the words correctly and neglect to understand what it is that they are communicating. "Word calling," as this is called in English or ASL, does not allow Byron to fully comprehend and process the ideas that he reads. He can learn to be able to see ideas (read) in a book by translating them into a video or movie in his head for use in cartooning, listing, or flowcharting academic content (e.g. history, science, etc.). This will capitalize on Byron's visual motor learning system.

10. Math appears to be a subject with which Byron's staff has stated that he has less difficulty, perhaps because of his ability to picture some numbers and work out problems in his head. However, he may have trouble slowing down his thought processes long enough to show the process on paper. He should be encouraged to draw story problems on paper in picture form so he can see them, rather than just memorizing a procedure or a rule only in sign. This will help him slow down his mental processes and allow him to put the process down on paper easier and more accurately. In addition, general math can be very rule-based and can also be very visual, but there is a tremendous amount of language needed to process many concepts in higher math and as long as Byron is able to see how math relates to other content areas and can form pictures of the concepts in his head he will have more success with math.

11. Spelling words by using his acoustic system for phonics/visual phonics (sounds and letters) will not work for Byron in the same way it might work for a typical learner, so emphasis should be on what words 'look like' as opposed to what they 'sound like'. It is highly probable that Byron has no letters in his head, and so for new words and concepts that he has to spell, he must visualize the words in picture/shape form and "spell" off of what he sees in his head. If he cannot "see" the words or concepts, he cannot spell them, which may explain why writing is difficult and he has difficulty

spelling words that are abstract and have no picture for him. Byron does not need to know his 'sounds and letters' in order to access print for meaning and can become a fluent reader by learning the whole shapes of ideas instead of isolated phonemes which have no meaning to him.

12. It appears that Byron does not yet have a clear picture of what it means to be a student and what school age children look like when they are in school. This is information that can be drawn and written about so that Byron can see what it looks like to be a student in relationship to others around him. He may also need more language information about what he can say to adults and students socially instead of yelling at them or striking out at them. This is information that could be drawn and/or written in a social narrative form.

13. As per staff and family reports, Byron appears to have some difficulty transitioning from one activity to another during his school day and during activities at home and in the community at times. This may be because he uses time differently than a typical learner uses time, meaning that he sees his day as a series of events. If one or more of those events changes and Byron does not have a full picture of the events, there is a good chance he may be upset in some way (e.g.: acting out, or not doing what's expected of him, being off task, etc.) A cartooned visual schedule with transition times drawn in should help Byron see what he will look like going through his day so he won't have to guess and he will be able to picture what his body needs to look like doing an activity.

14. Staff and family members might consider changing the way they are using their language to praise Byron. For example, instead of saying, "Good job," "Good boy," or "Good work," they could say, "Wow, you finished all 10 of your spelling words," or "Thank you for cleaning up your bedroom when I asked you to." That way, Byron will not have to guess about what he is being praised for and will more likely repeat a task successfully. It will also be important to give Byron information about why he is being asked to do things in a certain way. Using 'because' and 'so that' language will help Byron fully understand what he is supposed to do.

15. Byron needs to learn how to provide more information to a listener in conversations, so that the intent of his message is clear. For example, when Byron asks questions, he needs to be given answers in a variety of ways so he will generalize what is said to similar situations and will stop making the same errors over and over. Writing and drawing ideas on paper can also be extremely helpful in explaining social situations and clarifying opinions, and beliefs.

16. Byron's severe to profound hearing loss and moderate to severe ASD significantly affect his ability to fully understand people in his environment and he has adopted inappropriate behaviors and saying, "No," "I can't," and "I don't want to" because he does not have a fully developed language base to understand why he is being expected to behave in a certain way and comply with adults wishes.

The adults in Byron's environment need to be very careful not to assume what Byron is meaning by his behavior, or give Byron mixed messages about what he needs to do because he takes information very literally and may not be able to modify or generalize what he does to fit similar (but not exactly the same) situations. This is why drawn, written, role played, as well as conceptually correct signed information will help clarify situations for Byron so he will be better able to respond in a way that is expected of him. It is also important to remember that when

Byron is asked to do something in question form such as "Do you want to do your spelling now?" then family and staff needs to be prepared to accept his answer. For example, staff could say, "It's time to put your things away and start your spelling now" and not offer it as a choice if it truly is not a choice.

17. Placement of books or papers in relation to Byron's midline and in relation to his own body can make a big difference in what he does and how he does it. It may help Byron to move his writing paper to above his eye level on the side that he writes with so he can see what he is writing in relationship to the four quadrants of spatial planes. Byron may also benefit from using a slant board to get information to him at eye level so he won't have to tip his desk or sit on his knees to access written material. Providing material at appropriate eye level lowers the cognitive load, making it easier for him to access the knowledge (Arwood, 2011).

18. Byron appears to be somewhat slowed down by the labor involved in handwriting. He was observed writing his name and his schedule on paper confusing capitals and small letters and reversing letters in words. Hand-over-hand support is a way for Byron to learn the motor patterns for the shapes of the words he is being asked to write and will make what he is trying to do error free. In addition, teaching Byron how to access a computer for typing will be a very helpful tool for him in addition to writing because the computer allows him to see an exact copy of what is put into the computer at eye level and can speed up the process of writing. In addition, the letters are formed the same way that they are seen in book form which gives Byron a consistent 'picture' of what words look like. Spell check and thesaurus programs are also helpful computer programs for people with visual-motor learning systems like Byron's.

19. It might be beneficial for Byron to have a variety of sensory activities that are used throughout his day as a way to calm his neurological learning system and help him learn how to self-regulate sensory information. This will be important to continue especially before Byron is asked to do an activity that will stress his system.

Additional Visual Support Strategies

Providing drawn and written portable visual schedule/wall visuals should be available for Byron in all environments. Byron needs to know what kind of work, how much work, where he puts his work when finished, what he does next, all of which can be drawn and written about. Picture sequence strips showing steps of a task from start to finish and what Byron should be thinking about when he goes through each activity needs to be provided. Figure 7.7 shows an example of how Byron can orient himself to a visual schedule.

It is important to take a moment to reflect that many neurotypical learners will acquire all of the above concepts relatively effortlessly by harnessing their brain's ability to connect sight with sound to follow typical developmental milestones. Individuals with atypical brains such as Byron cannot formulate these concepts in such traditional manners and will need consistent viconic language instruction to increase his socio-cognitive development.

Cross-deptartment communication log/data will be important so that everyone is on the same page about what is working and what may not be working with Byron. As the primary SLP, this author is available to tweak strategies to give more information to Byron and staff as needed.

Remember that using descriptive positive praise with Byron is helpful and recognize, describe, and celebrate when Byron makes appropriate choices and uses replacement language.

It is important to rephrase what Byron does to deserve praise, such as "Thank you for taking a small amount of mayo so that others eating will have some too."

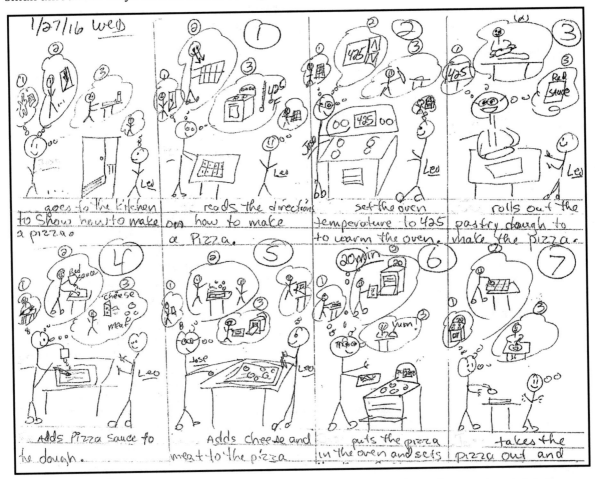

Figure 7.7: A visual schedule showing a series of numbered events that the student must complete in order to make a pizza.

No matter what is put in place, Byron may still be noncompliant for known or unknown reasons. It is recommended not to worry about "why" he has escalated or is noncompliant. Step back, breathe, and follow the prescribed multi-modal approaches you have learned in this workshop to help Byron de-escalate. For example, "If Byron signs "My turn, not finished." Sign and write, "Thank you for telling me. Your time is up (point to visual timer), so please give the remote to _____." or "Thank you for handing me the remote and for giving _____ his turn. Your turn will be next, so let's wait.

Conclusion

In summary, after the workshop/in-service, the staff working with Byron became more aware that language intervention for Byron is about teaching him strategies to improve his ability to think about himself in relationship to others in his environment, so providing what happens when a behavior occurs through drawing cartoons provides him with true choices of thought for behavior, social interactions, and academics.

Too often, Byron has used inappropriate/acting out behaviors to help make meaning out of the world around him. We feel we owe it to him to begin to understand how he is using behavior to communicate across a variety of environments and with a variety of communication partners. We asked staff and family to think about how we could all change our instruction to reflect Byron's learning system and reduce the need for acting out behaviors. Byron's program is still a work in progress, but even on week one with his team on board, data showed that Byron not only responded to our interventions, he began to make changes in how he thinks. Instances of aggressive, acting out behaviors went from over 200 instances in a week to less than 50. We will continue to monitor and change our language based on what Byron needs as he improves his ability to pro-socially think. We believe that Byron has the potential to be a productive, independent citizen when the right supports are put into place for him and we look forward to watching him progress and realize his own capabilities through the visual thinking language learning strategies of Neuro-semantic Language Learning Theory.

Summary of Neuro-Education Methods

The author found success working with Bryon, an individual who is Deaf/Hard of Hearing with ASD, because she introduced Bryon to brain-based Viconic Language Methods for the first time in his schooling career. As with many Deaf/Hard of Hearing individuals, Byron had previously been taught using methods and techniques borrowed from suppositions about how all individuals learn. For example, teachers were trying to use auditory methods of connecting sounds to letters by fingerspelling letter by letter (Visual Phonics) in order to teach reading. Needless to say, they were not effective.

From a neuroscience perspective, the fingers are great for movement, and therefore can excel at sign language. In fact, numerous renowned scientists (e.g.: Merzenich) have spent their careers proving how human's ability to use their hands for increased dexterity over other species allowed us to evolve at a much greater rate than other animals. However, the fingers cannot process sound – only the ears can do this. So why were educators attempting to put sound on Byron's fingers, an impossible task?

Additionally, teachers were using very short, signed phrases to try to "control" Byron's behavior such as "stop that" or "enough!" However, these short phrases are not enough language to form pictures in Bryon's head of what he is supposed to do. From a cognitive psychology perspective, educators were effectively reducing Bryon to a series of undesirable behaviors. This only served to objectify him, not teach him how to be pro-social and fit in.

Lastly, being born Deaf/Hard of Hearing, Byron should have a rich visual mind's eye – if he were born neuro-typical, that is. The fact that Byron was not able to naturally use many of the strategies that Deaf/Hard of Hearing students use to thrive suggests that his brain was born with issues that impede connectivity. Using Viconic Language Methods may have been the first time that Byron could learn in a less stressful manner; that is, in a way that didn't overload his system. Increasing the amount of visual language he could acquire allowed his brain to start functioning more efficiently, leading to less anxiety, fewer meltdowns, and increased problem-solving.

Chapter 8

Increase Language, Decrease Anxiety

Chris Merideth, M.Ed.

Abstract

Anxiety, as it is regarded in American society, has diverse origins and equally numerous ramifications upon personal well-being. Students and young children are among the large number of Americans who identify as anxious. It is the responsibility of the educator, however, to determine the most effective methods for teaching each individual in the manner in which they learn best, often taking into account cognitive stress, temperament, and anxiety. This chapter describes the process of a special education teacher thoroughly assessing the behavior, psychology, and language function of a student experiencing severe stress, and documents the progress of implementing visual language strategies to reduce anxiety in the classroom. These strategies incorporate theories of learning contained within the fields of neuroscience, cognitive psychology, and language. Student growth in the areas of socio-cognitive development, pro-social behavior, and language function are tracked over a year's time to demonstrate effective remediation of psychopathology. Student and educator drawing and writing samples are included to illustrate examples of pedagogy teachers can use in practice, as well as provide chronological evidence of students improving their own mental health over time.

About the Author

Chris Merideth is a former special education teacher who now instructs teacher candidates at the University of Portland. Chris has over ten years of experience working in education teaching English as a second language and special needs students in grades K-12. He is passionate about helping future teachers develop strategies that will include students with exceptionalities in inclusive classroom settings. Since receiving his Post-Master's degree in neuroeducation, Chris has presented his research at conferences in Oregon, Texas, Louisiana, Hawaii, and Alberta, Canada. Chris is the co-author and developmental editor of this anthology.

The Neurobiology and Psychology of Anxiety

Anxiety is often described as a brain disorder, a mental illness, or both depending on the theoretical background of the researcher making the claim. Neuroscientists point to irregularities in neurotransmitter function in the brain as a cause of stress and doctors may recommend drugs to mitigate (Baars & Gage, 2010), where psychologists opt to explore one's mental history and untangle unresolved conflicts buried deep in one's unconscious mind (Anderson, 2010). Because of these disparate approaches to studying mental health, our society struggles to define anxiety as a formal concept. Though it cannot be seen directly (as opposed to plaque buildup in our arteries), we nevertheless classify anxiety using a default medical model of observing and analyzing one's behavior in order to look for possible biological or mental causes/correlations.

Neuroscientists often look first to the brain for clues about causes of behavior. Their research has shown us that anxiety neurologically vitiates neuronal development by causing our brain to over-respond to stress over time (Lupien, 2009). A certain amount of stress during our developing years is normal and expected. This natural process typically leads to healthy, regulated neural pathways that connect the parts of our brain together in functional ways. However, adding high levels of stress to our neurobiological system (especially at an early age) effectively forces our brain to re-allocate neurotransmitter resources to deal with the increased brain activity caused by such stress.

As mentioned, a temporary increase in biological stress to the system can indeed have positive effects. For example, athletes who want to perform at their peak may push their body in practice to extreme measures in order to find where their physical limit is. Then, in actual competition these athletes can pull "back from the edge" because they now have more awareness about how far they can exert themselves before they risk doing damage.

In contrast, researchers who study children who have been abused or neglected, or who simply do not know how to socially engage with the world around them, notice that the children often experience chronic stress. When scientists study the chemicals that their bodies produce, they see heightened levels of stress that lasts for long periods of time. If the child is not able to calm themselves and return to homeostasis, they run a severe risk of developing an anxiety disorder; meaning, they experience unnatural levels of stress in their system upon experiencing events that many would find routine.

If such high levels of stress continue throughout brain development in childhood, our body involuntarily starts sending high amounts of glucocorticoids, or "GCs" (a neurotransmitter that responds to stress) to receptors all throughout the brain. By our sympathetic nervous system responding in such an elevated manner (think: fight or flight) we are unwittingly training our brain to respond to stress with more healing GCs more often (Lupien, 2009). This excessive re-routing of the neural pathways from healthy functionality to that of overworking neurotransmitters can have long-reaching effects that may lead to behavior associated with a clinical anxiety disorder later in life. Since our brain controls our behavior, we can only expect a profoundly imbalanced brain to eventually lead to behaviors associated with mental illness.

Turning to the field of cognitive psychology allows one to view how the mind processes and copes with anxiety. Though psychologists may acknowledge that brain chemistry plays a role in the development of anxiety, their discipline instead focuses primarily on uncovering and analyzing deep-seeded emotional conflict and stressors in order to help regain a sense of mental equilibrium (Coleman & Webber, 2002). The theory behind this approach attempts to heal the mind by understanding and coming to peace with psychic struggles. This approach has demonstrated moderate success over the past century – ongoing research indicates that many patients who undergo Psychotherapy or Cognitive Behavioral Therapy report an overall improvement in physical, emotional, and psychological health after alleviating mental suffering (Anderson, 2010).

Including Language Function in the Study of Anxiety

Scientists, academics, and other professionals engaged in the societal paradigm dominated by Western Psychological thinking tend to specialize in a relatively narrow field of study. For example, if a parent brings a child exhibiting disturbed behavior (hitting others/self, cutting, severe anxiety, etc.) to their primary care doctor, that professional is apt to refer the family to a child psychologist for cognitive testing or to a neuroscientist for imaging of the brain.

These two professionals may be experts in their own fields, but not communicate findings, methodology, or theory with each other. Moreover, rarely in our current psycho-educational model do professionals pause to assess how a student uses their own acquired mental language to function in the world around them (Arwood, 2014).

According to Arwood (2014), keeping these clinical approaches separate in practice, as well as ignoring the role that one's internal language plays in both brain and behavioral development neglects to paint a full picture of the student's strengths, nor does it accurately portray how that patient compares developmentally to other neurotypical peers their own age. It is only by including a comprehensive analysis of how the student uses language to function in the areas of literacy – reading, writing, speaking, thinking, listening, viewing, and calculating, that we may see where their socio-cognitive growth falls on the spectrum of development encapsulated in the Neuro-semantic Language Learning Theory.

Therefore, to best understand the effect anxiety has on an individual's mind, brain, and being, we cannot neglect to incorporate our third discipline – that of language function – into our study of one's socio-cognitive abilities. The amount and quality of language function one has acquired mediates both their brain and mental operations (Arwood, 2014). Studying this deep structure of language informs us how an individual will respond metacognitively to the impact of anxiety to their own psyche (Arwood, 2014).

Accordingly, anxiety remains a prime topic to explore with the lens of neuroeducation - or the intersection between the fields of neuroscience, language, and psychology - because it requires an understanding of theory from all three disciplines in order to determine how one's socio-cognitive function becomes impaired and how language remediation can best serve to alleviate this mental suffering. To provide enough depth of observation in these three areas of research, a single individual will be explored in the form of a case study.

"Jaime" – A Case Study Exploring the Remediation of Anxiety

Jaime is an 11th grade female who is kind, inquisitive, and a strict rule follower. She qualifies for special education services under the autism and emotionally disturbed categories. Jaime attends all general education classes, but for numerous years relied heavily on aide support in order to navigate the academic expectations and social culture of school. Documented through self-reporting and family acknowledgment, Jaime struggled severely with anxiety for her entire childhood and early adolescence. Case files report that for years it was commonplace for Jaime to become "triggered" by a long list of fears, phobias, and social situations, evidenced by rapidly shifting from a calm mood to a highly anxious and panicked state. These responses continued to the time this author first began working with Jamie.

In her case, becoming "triggered" may result in varying types of behavior depending upon the context, but typically involves stiffening her body and shortening her breath, or lying on the floor shaking, or pacing around the room, or yelling at adults in the vicinity. Upon careful study, many triggers could be traced back to a recognizable stimulus. At other times, Jaime appeared to become triggered by nothing external in particular but rather by what she would describe as the "disturbing" nature of her own thoughts.

Until this author began working with Jaime, previous attempts at her rehabilitation have focused primarily on pharmacological and psychotherapeutic approaches to reduce anxiety. Jaime has been prescribed a significant dosage of anti-anxiety medication for the past five years, but neither she, nor her family, nor her psychiatrist have reported a significant qualitative effect of the medication in reducing episodes triggered by anxiety.

Concurrent to this biomedical intervention, Jaime has regularly participated in school-based counseling. The goals of this therapeutic approach have been defined as "alleviating" Jaime's anxiety by offering (or demanding) that she take part in stress-reducing activities such as taking a break, journaling, or pacing around the school track. These efforts can only be categorized as short-term solutions at best because they neglect to investigate the root causes of Jaime's anxiety, address underlying thought disorders, or explore how Jaime responds to stress metacognitively.

In other words, these previous therapeutic approaches neglected to consider how Jaime's language functions to address her own anxieties when they arise. As Jaime's special education teacher, part of this author's job is to help coordinate therapeutic approaches between professionals in the aforementioned fields of neuroscience and psychology, but in order to obtain a deeper metacognitive understanding of the thought processes behind Jaime's anxiety, a thorough language sample needs to be obtained. Because language names our thinking (Arwood, 2014), we as educational practitioners should be able to take a language sample from Jaime that mirrors her own mental understanding (or lack of understanding) of her cognitive processes during times of stress.

This author noticed that Jamie would often become most anxious at school when she felt she could not keep up with the academic material of a class, or when she felt she could not understand why a peer had interacted with her in the way they had. Jamie would often approach this author and spend great lengths of time asking his interpretation of what other people might be thinking of her and would carefully analyze social situations from a multitude of angles while trying to decide what to do.

Because of this behavior, this author suspected that Jamie might indeed think with a visual learning system, meaning she sees pictures and movies in her head about the world around her. In addition, Jamie exhibited behavior that lead this author to believe that she was attempting to reduce the perceived turmoil of the world around her using whatever methods she could. For example, when her teachers would lecture, Jamie would attempt to write down their notes verbatim so that she could go over the words later. Arwood, (2011), informs us that visual learners who may not know how their own cognition systems work might exhibit peculiar coping mechanisms. For these reasons, this author began to suspect that Jamie might benefit from learning about her own brain and how she could use her natural strengths to reduce the stress she feels from participating in the world. The following steps document this author's journey along this path of attempted discovery.

Baseline Writing Sample

A pre-intervention, baseline writing sample needs to be obtained to assess how a student naturally uses language to describe his or her own experiences of anxiety. Accordingly, this author began asking Jamie about her own understanding of her thoughts. When asked in a calm moment to describe her state of mind during a panic attack, Jaime reported that her thoughts begin to "spiral" out of control, and also revealed certain paranoiac thought disorders involved with people conspiring against her (See Figure 8.1).

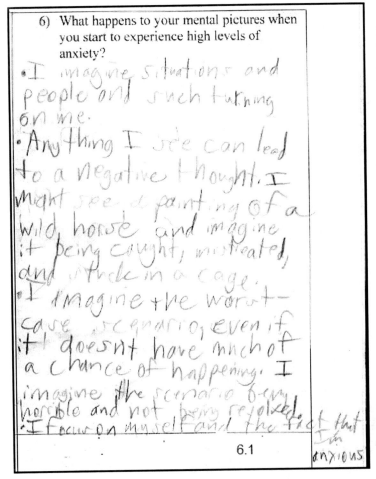

6) What happens to your mental pictures when you start to experience high levels of anxiety?

• I imagine situations and people and such turning on me.
• Anything I see can lead to a negative thought. I might see a painting of a wild horse and imagine it being caught, mistreated, and stuck in a cage.
• I imagine the worst-case scenario, even if it doesn't have much of a chance of happening. I imagine the scenario being horrible and not being resolved.
• I focus on myself and the fact that I'm anxious

6.1

Figure 8.1: Writing Sample Pre-Intervention

To many professionals from a variety of academic fields, this response may seem relatively articulate. Jamie is able to answer the question by using grammatically correct sentences, and one could argue that her depiction of a wild horse being caught and mistreated represents a symbolic metaphor for her own feelings. However, it is important to distinguish that these interpretations are offered by the adult as a way to try to understand the child's thinking. These perceptions actually represent more of the adult's mind than of Jamie's.

Instead, a semantic linguistic analysis shows that Jaime does not demonstrate a clinical understanding of why her anxiety occurs, nor does she reveal self-awareness of strategies that might be used to address negative thoughts or feelings. Importantly, when asked to write her response to the question, Jaime's answers are not specific to her own thought processes. She relies on the imagery of a wild horse being mistreated to represent formal ideas that are not concrete. Therefore, in this pre-intervention sample, Jamie demonstrates that she lacks the higher order language function processes required to think about, view, and calculate abstract concepts such as feelings.

Writing her response to the question of how Jamie processes anxiety yielded some clues to her cognition. However, this author knew he needed to dig deeper to learn about Jamie's mental pictures because these images would lead to more accurate representations of her thinking. Arwood, (2011) informs us that visual thinkers often represent their concepts via a visuospatial modality. Therefore, when working with a student struggling to communicate, it is essential that all samples of language function also include a component of drawing and a task of speaking to help determine a students' strongest method of communication (Brown, 2013).

Consequently, when asked to draw out how anxiety might affect her mental pictures, Jaime drew a picture of herself being chased by a figure wielding a knife, and a separate picture of her character unable to respond in a social situation (See Figure 8.2).

Notice that in this drawing, Jaime depicts a more specific set of mental images. In both examples, the reader does not need to interpret Jamie's language as heavily in order to decipher what she means. In addition, Jamie demonstrates more of a sense of agency by including multiple visual representations of herself. When a student demonstrates agency, or concept of self, the practitioner knows that the student is honing in more closely on their own experiences, not just borrowing phrases or ideas.

For Jaime, this drawing shows progress. However, in one of her visual depictions, anxiety is again represented by an abstract concept, just like the wild horse in the prior example. This could use some semantic refinement to personalize it to Jaime's experience. In the bottom drawing, Jaime references a specific example of feeling anxious when she is indecisive and expected to make a decision quickly. Already, Jaime shows more strength of introspection by visually representing her ideas.

Figure 8.2: Drawing Sample Pre-Intervention

Lastly, when asked to verbally describe the same process, Jaime orally shared stating that in particularly violent moments of hysteria she simply "sees red" and nothing else.

Interpreting Language Samples

By analyzing these language samples, one sees that Jaime communicates with more semantic complexity and specificity through her drawings than through her writing or speaking. Arwood (2011) explains that this is not surprising for individuals who use visual mental pictures in their heads to make meaning of the world around them. The Neuro-semantic Language Learning Theory (NsLLT) posits that approximately 95% of individuals in society think with a visual learning system - this number may be closer to 100% for individuals with disabilities. Based off of these language samples, in addition to a close study of Jamie's behavior in academic and social situations, this author concluded that Jaime did indeed think making pictures and movies in her head. The NsLLT provided a starting theory with which this author could start building a remediation plan that would target Jamie's natural learning strengths.

This author knew that any subsequent interventions to address Jaime's debilitating anxiety must focus on viconic language intervention strategies in order to see the most salient results. It should be noted that such emphasis on visual language function includes an extra modality layer (the function of language) that is not contained within many other therapies such as Psychodynamics or Psychopharmacology.

A thorough analysis of language should include not only the semantics of what is presented but also the pragmatics, or the context in which the learner is presenting their thoughts (Arwood, 2011). Arwood (2014) informs us that all of Jaime's descriptions of anxiety make sense because they illustrate the temporary cognitive paralysis that happens when visual thinkers lose their mental pictures and cannot make meaning of the world around them.

When a visual thinker's pictures go away, even partially, this stresses their neurobiological system to maximum proportions and causes their brain to respond with a wash of inhibiting neurotransmitters (Lupien, 2009). In turn, this chemical imbalance in the brain further mirrors the visual thinker's ensuing loss of language and access to their mental imagery (Anderson, 2010). This vicious cycle of debilitation is often referred to as the "stress-brain loop" because individuals often find it challenging to escape this spiral of anxiety on their own (Women's Health Network, 2013).

The fields of neuroscience, psychology, and language all provide evidence that anxiety affects the mind, brain, and the body. Therefore, when viewed as a synergistic concept that is greater than the sum of its parts (Arwood, 2014), we begin to see that anxiety manifests itself in and continuously interplays between the chemicals in one's brain, the subsequent discord of the mind, and the resulting loss of language needed to function in the world. Arwood's Neuro-Education Model as a theory informs us that we need to address all three of these neurodevelopmental issues to raise one's cognition and assign pro-social meaning to help provide healthy alternative responses to the debilitating effects of anxiety.

Behavioral Assessment

According to Arwood (2014), we cannot solve severe mental imbalance within our own mind alone, especially if stress renders our neurobiological system temporarily inoperative. Remediation, therefore, must be provided externally by visually representing the issue and exploring it with an educator (an external feedback source) at a cognitive level that matches the learner's needs in that moment. Language names our concepts (Arwood, 2014). Visual thinkers like Jaime, therefore, benefit from visual feedback in the manner in which they acquire meaning; namely, through drawing out concepts, writing a description of actions, and incorporating the two into language that will help her better understand her metacognitive functioning during times of stress.

This process looks slightly different depending upon the emotional state in which the learner approaches the educator. For example, will a student work willingly with the practitioner, or will they reject offers of remediation? It is essential to include these questions when assessing how a student functions developmentally. Therefore, in addition to assessing the learner's written, visual, and oral language, it is also imperative for the practitioner to observe the student's behavior in multiple contexts across time to see how they interact with the world around them. This will help provide a starting point for intervention so that the educator does not interact with the student using language and expectations that are too developmentally advanced that may cause the student to act out.

Since all behavior is a form of communication (Arwood, 2011), it is the job of the educator to not overburden the individual. Doing so risks causing more harm than good during intervention. An educator must interpret their pupil's actions and social cues and adapt their methodology in real-time to work off the learner's signals. To the best of their ability, an educator should customize their starting level of language therapy so that students are able to follow the tasks and feel successful while doing so (Brown, 2013). Accordingly, this author was able to compile a clinical "thick description" of Jaime in multiple school settings to compare and contrast her behavior addressing situations as they arose.

While observing Jaime, this author noticed a cycle of unhealthy behavior that regularly accompanied her stress. In moments of mental pressure, Jaime would often dig her fingernails deeply into her skin, seize up her muscles and tremble, and occasionally drop to the floor and moan. Arwood (2014) advises in the Neuro-semantic Language Learning Theory that such hysteria results from the brain attempting to seek out reliable information in an environment that no longer makes sense to the learner.

The brain never rests unless it has been severely damaged or impacted to the point of catatonia (Baars & Gage, 2010) Therefore, to stay alive, the brain must constantly seek out new information. Though the brain cannot be "overstimulated" (Arwood, 2014), it can nevertheless allocate its resources inefficiently, such as rushing blood glucose to a particular region, washing synapses in an excess of neurotransmitters, or passing along stress signals through the nervous system to decrease one's ability to inhibit verbal/physical responses (Baars & Gage, 2010).

Understandably, individuals who experience such high levels of stress throughout their body and brain will often report that they feel "out of control" of their actions. Knowing the neurobiological reasons behind their behaviors provides the educator with an extra layer of empathy for an individual that may legitimately not be able to control their actions in that moment.

For example, during Jaime's incidents of disordered behavior, her learning system becomes flooded with inhibiting neurotransmitters such as cortisol. As a result, her brain no longer functions at equilibrium, and this manifests itself in her personality with the disturbed behavior mentioned above. While experiencing such stress, Jaime's body and brain become overly taxed, and her mental functioning regresses developmentally to that of "sensorimotor" level – the most rudimentary of behavioral states typically associated with infancy. In this state, we know that Jaime is not processing sensory input, nor is her brain making new memories. Jaime is unresponsive in these moments and needs a cognitive intervention to raise her thinking in order to put mental pictures back in her head so she can see herself again as an agent interacting with the world and not merely an extension of the environment around her (Arwood, 2014).

This author also noticed in clinical observations that Jaime often became stressed when she was not able to make sense of the task being assigned to her, or she could not keep up with the course content that her teacher was orally sharing with the class. Unlike auditory thinkers, in which acoustic and visual input are integrated simultaneously in the brain to form perceptual patterns and eventually concepts, visual thinkers like Jaime require an intermediary step in which auditory information must be translated into mental pictures and sufficiently layered to form enough overlapping ideas to develop conceptual understanding (Arwood, 2011). Many neurotypical visual thinkers are able to integrate acoustic and visual input relatively automatically. However, individuals with disabilities such as Jaime always require extra overlapping visual patterns to connect existing neuronal circuits back to previously acquired information in order to build new concepts (Arwood, 2011).

For Jaime's brain, one modality is simply not enough to learn new information. Jaime is not an auditory thinker; she is a visual thinker. This has been established. But, Jaime's behavior demonstrates that in moments of stress her visual system shuts down, and she has not yet acquired strategies to help herself get back on track. In addition, the plan of action that adults had recommended for Jamie (taking a stress break) had only served to alleviate her symptoms in the short term.

The adults in Jamie's life had good intentions for their suggested therapies, but they had not yet found success in supporting her. Many psychosocial theories attempt to help individuals such as Jaime, but fall short of including all necessary components of remediation. For example, the tenets of Collaborative Problem Solving inform us that "children do well when they can," but do not go into significant neurological detail as to why Jaime's learning process has become derailed.

What we now know through brain science research (Arwood, 2014) is that Jaime's confused and often panicked behavior in class illustrates that, for her, sound alone will not form concepts. This means that if an adult attempts to use auditory methods such as "talk therapy" or verbal problem-solving, they are missing the target of her brain. If Jamie could have been able to make progress using the plethora of auditory therapy methods prescribed to her, she would have already done so.

Instead, when asked to learn any new concept for which she does not already have the mental pictures, Jaime must follow another route. In order for her to learn, Jamie must be able to visually represent the new idea through an overlap of visual layers such as drawing, writing, pointing, tracing, and semantic refining. This is because in order for her innate neurobiology to sufficiently recognize, or *inhibit*, new information to be stored into long-term memory, she must have an overlap of input that her brain can actually process (Baars & Gage, 2010; Arwood, 2011).

It is imperative that a clinical observation of behavior includes multiple school settings. This is because a student may function extremely well in one environment, yet greatly struggle in all others. Notably, many psychological assessments provided by professionals are written about a student after only one office visit. These write-ups are then used to make school-based or legal decisions. This author believes that such a limited exposure to the student does not provide enough of a neuropsychological context to fully document a spectrum of behavior in multiple settings. Notably, students that have regressed significantly may require visits to their home to provide a more complete picture of mental health.

The evidence collected during this author's numerous observations across multiple settings shows that Jaime functions primarily in the third tier of the Neuro-semantic Language Learning Theory: concrete development. A student who is "concrete" in their thinking can often follow rules in society, but cannot effectively problem solve in an impromptu manner if someone deviates from these rules. As previously mentioned, this author found much behavioral evidence to support these conclusions. The concrete level of social development is considered typical for students who are seven to eleven years of age (Piaget, 1959). This fact meant that Jamie's cognitive and social-emotional development was delayed at least three years behind her same age peers.

Because Jaime often cannot navigate complex social or cognitive stimuli on her own, she operates in the world almost exclusively by a strict adherence to rigid social rules that have been passed down to her through former teachers, parents, and books. In order to keep progressing developmentally, students like Jaime need to increase their own social thinking by viewing themselves as agents able to independently interact with the world and spontaneously resolve social conflicts as they arise.

This is not to say that, pre-intervention, Jaime did not possess any social strengths. During behavioral observations, Jaime presented some examples of strong resiliency in the face of daily debilitating struggles. For example, to cope with her anxiety, Jaime would actively welcome feedback of how to help her deal with stress. In fact, Jaime would frequently "annoy" peers and adults by the sheer amount of questions she would ask to help herself navigate decisions and behavioral cues that many individuals would process unconsciously, such as, "What should I do if a teacher appears annoyed at me," or "How do I know if someone is interested in what I have to say?" or "How do I choose which coping skill to use?"

In other words, this author found Jamie to be a highly amenable research companion because she naturally possessed a strong desire to understand why she acts the way that she does. This strength of character should not be overlooked in children. Arwood (2014) informs us that such incessant questioning, as Jamie had presented, represents the brain's search for input that is meaningful to its own neurobiological mechanics.

Visual Language Intervention – Drawing in Real-Time

Jaime's incessant questioning about her mental state and behavior demonstrates her strong desire to help herself cope with symptoms of anxiety. As previously mentioned, in moments of severe stress, Jaime admits that she cannot see herself in her mental pictures. This author knew that the best opportunity to work on language remediation would be in moments of calm, while Jaime's learning system is operating at equilibrium. While her brain is best primed for learning, Jaime will need to take in feedback in the form of drawing and relational language that shows the effect that losing one's mental pictures has upon their academic functioning. Figure 8.3 shows this author's first attempt of drawing in real-time to show Jaime what she looks like – and more importantly – what her jumbled thoughts look like to an outside observer during moments of panic.

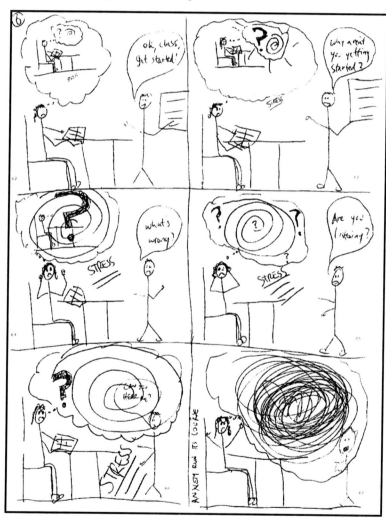

Figure 8.3: First Real-Time Drawing for Intervention

In the first box, Jaime's teacher has just orally explained directions that Jaime was not able to fully translate into visual pictures. The teacher has asked the class to "get started," but all Jaime sees in her own mental pictures is herself unable to complete the task. In the second frame, Jaime's teacher asks again for Jaime to get started on the task, at which point Jaime's thoughts begin to spiral because she feels stupid that she was not able to understand what the rest of the class had been able to, and because she feels embarrassed to ask for help on what others might interpret as an "easy question."

In box three, Jaime's anxiety has started to peak. As previously mentioned, this is the point that Jaime's teachers have told her to "take an option," meaning to take a walk, or choose another coping skill. However, by this time, Jaime's thoughts have become so jumbled so that even this small choice is too developmentally demanding for Jaime to handle. Neither Jaime nor the adults in her life had been able to understand why a simple choice to take a walk had produced such panic in Jaime. The answer was that in those moments, she was only using a portion of her mental faculties.

143

Boxes four through six show how Jaime's spiraled thoughts eventually grow so big that they take up the room and she cannot see anyone else, even those trying to help her. Drawing this out for Jaime was the first time she had been able to "see" what she looks like when experiencing a panic attack. Upon viewing this visual depiction of anxiety, Jaime asked, "Can other people see my thoughts spiraling too?"

Visually Depicting Anxiety

After completing the first drawing intervention, this author began working with Jaime for approximately two to three hours a week on drawing, writing, labeling, and communicating about a multitude of reasons that Jamie might feel anxious in school. The intervention sessions were scheduled only part of the time; the majority of the drawing and writing together occurred during more impromptu meetings, such as if Jaime had left a class upset and come back to the "home room" for guidance.

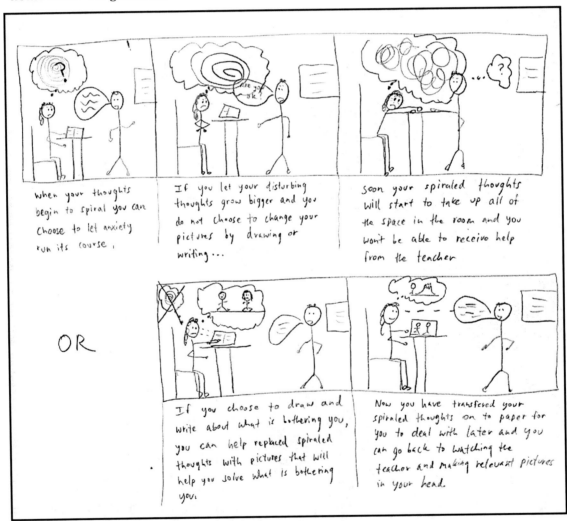

Figure 8.4: Visually Depicting Alternatives to Anxiety

At first, while Jaime would orally explain what had happened, this author would begin to draw out the scenario and write out what had happened below the drawings. Eventually, Jaime began to feel comfortable enough to orally critique the drawings and refine them to match her own mental pictures. Once teacher and student had agreed on a picture that accurately represented what had actually happened, then therapy could resume by writing or drawing healthy alternatives to processing anxiety that Jaime may not have considered. For an example of a visual depiction of alternative ways to react to stress, see Figure 8.4.

This cartoon shows two options for dealing with anxiety that Jaime could choose. In the top example, Jaime starts to feel her thoughts spiral, but then does not do anything to change her mental pictures or interrupt her stress cycle. In the bottom panels, the author has depicted an option for Jaime to draw and write on her own about what is bothering her. By doing so, Jaime can take the spiraled thoughts out of her mind and transfer them onto the page in front of her. Now, these thoughts no longer control Jaime – she is in control of them. By becoming in control of her thoughts again, Jaime can now start making pictures in her head about what the teacher is talking about, thus allowing her to follow along with the class.

The tangible exactness of using such visual language may sound strange to many educators. Of course, for an outside observer, Jaime's thoughts do not *literally* transfer from her mind to the page. However, visual thinkers such as Jaime who do not process sound (oral speech) efficiently require such literalness of communication in order to know what is expected of them. When neurotypical individuals hear the phrase, "Just put your thoughts down on paper," they know what to do. However, such an expression would be distressingly vague for Jaime. Before viconic language intervention, such a simple request could cause her to blow up. Therefore, this author knew he needed to continue to provide Jaime with rich visual language strategies that she could do (such as drawing and writing) to begin to take care of herself in moments of need. As a 15-year-old girl, Jaime should be able to soothe herself.

Because we take in information best when we have fewer numbers of stressors impairing our cognitive abilities (Anderson, 2010), a period of relative calm is also the best time for Jaime to prepare for future panic attacks by drawing herself participating in pro-social alternatives rather than relapsing to a set of neurotic behaviors. Jaime's previous behavior has demonstrated that "taking an option" can sometimes be too stressful for her, partly because she cannot yet see herself completing this task successfully. Without seizing this opportunity to interrupt previous self-destructive patterns, Jaime will not be able to see herself successfully navigating her often-nebulous world of anxiety.

This fact of neurobiology is important to consider because many therapies (i.e.: desensitization – Coleman & Webber, 2002,) and cognitive assessments (i.e.: BASC 2 – Overton, 2012) attempt to work with the learner at too high a level while they are actively experiencing anxiety. The aims of this are ultimately futile because the educator is not acknowledging the temporary cognitive impairment of the learner. In other words, asking someone like Jaime to rationally describe his or her thinking during moments of panic is a fool's errand.

If a student is having a meltdown, as it were, we as educators must instead provide many layers of pro-social external input in a 2-D visual manner (drawing and writing). This after all is the way the brain acquires sensory information (Baars & Gage, 2010). Our goal should be to help the learner begin to make meaningful neuronal connections again. If the learner has relapsed, despite previous efforts of drawing and writing, the learner will need help putting pictures back into their head to reorient themselves using language.

Figure 8.5 is an example of drawing in real-time of an attempt to insert thought bubbles back into Jaime's head once she has started to "freak out."

Figure 8.5: Drawing in Real-Time to Put Pictures Back in the Head

Helping Jaime to put mental pictures back in her head during times of severe stress allows her to access her concepts and language once again (Arwood, 2014). But remediation should not stop there. Jaime will benefit daily from drawing out and writing about various emotionally healthy ways of thinking about stress in the future to provide the metacognitive language she needs to thrive.

Results

This author worked with Jaime over the course of a year for approximately two to three hours per week while she was his student. It should be noted that Jaime experienced few, if any, panic attacks while in this author's classroom, and that the majority of her anxiety episodes occurred while in general education classes or at home. This can be contributed to the fact that when we as educators make consistent efforts to pay close attention to and work within the learning systems of our students, we can effectively "preempt" most challenges and stressors that could arise.

For example, knowing that oral instructions alone neurologically taxes a majority of students means that this author now gives two or more step directions in writing. In addition, if a student such as Jaime arrives in an agitated state wanting to orally debrief their

Figure 8.6: Jaime Drawing and Writing for her own Therapy

concerns, this author knows that he must draw out in real-time their conversation so that both parties know they are referring to the same idea.

Developmentally, students at this age are primed to emulate the behavior and strategies that they see working for others (Anderson, 2010). Consequently, this author was gladdened to see that over time, Jaime began picking up and incorporating the Viconic Language Methods that had been modeled to her. Eventually, she was able to draw and write about her problems on her own and then bring them to this author in a calm moment for a discussion. Figure 8.6 is an example of Jaime internally trying to resolve an issue by representing it externally for her and others to see.

Comparing Figure 8.6 to Jaime's initial drawing pre-intervention (Figure 8.2) shows a remarkable amount of growth on behalf of Jaime's level of language function. In the top panel, Jaime is able to depict herself as an agent who is interacting with another agent (a peer). She is able to represent the complexity of using verbal words to communicate one's sentiment, all the while secretly thinking a different idea about them. Notice that Jaime is now able to isolate single incidents that cause her anxiety, rather than describing them in abstract terms and images such as a horse or cage. This shows that Jaime has become more self-literate about what causes her stress.

Figure 8.7: Visually Working Through Stressful Situations

Figure 8.7 is also a two part example illustrating the progress Jaime has acquired in helping resolve internal conflicts on her own by visually representing incidents that cause her to feel anxious.

Jaime also improved her performance in her general education classes. Eventually, instead of trying to write down verbatim what the teacher was saying in class, Jaime started representing the material via visual notes that she could go back and add to later. An example of visual note taking is depicted in Figure 8.8.

Arwood (2011) informs us that writing the word on the page provides the pattern, while drawing a picture represents the underlying concept. When put together and overlapped

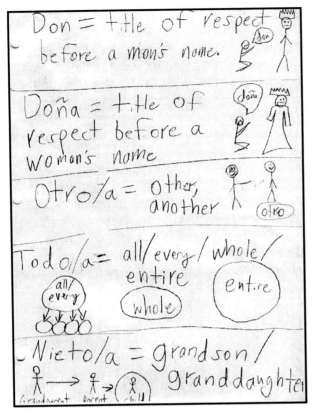

Figure 8.8: Visual Notes in Spanish Class

sufficiently using visual layers, this will form language that store into the learner's long-term memory.

Jaime progressed enough socially in one year to exit this author's "emotionally fragile classroom" and into a mainstream academic support learning center. The majority of Jaime's socio-cognitive progress maintained throughout her next academic year while in the learning center, and she experienced fewer "meltdowns" both at home and at school. Jaime attended prom on her own and graduated high school with a standard diploma.

This author had the fortune to catch up with Jaime at the time of her graduation and was contented to hear how much she has progressed developmentally. Before remediation, Jaime used to perseverate about the idea of living alone and all that this entails, such as doing laundry, going grocery shopping, cooking food, taking public transportation, looking for a job, going to college etc. Jaime is now indeed successfully living alone and doing all of these things. Most strikingly, when this author spoke to Jaime about how she was feeling about participating in these once-scary tasks, she simply shrugged and said that she was handling life one day at a time.

Visual Learners' Brains Differ in Structure and Function

Our society often asks individuals such as Jaime to solve or deal with such complex problems of the mind not by using their visual mental strengths, but by orally sharing their troubles in the hope that enough overlap of auditory explanation will connect to form new concepts. In other words, because we don't know any better, we ask children to try to solve their own problems using tools that are not intuitive for them. If we knew more about the differences between visual thinking and auditory thinking systems, we could tailor our educational interventions to have more efficient results.

In fact, not all brains are created equal, and modern researchers are just now starting to scratch the surface of how these differences manifest themselves in the mind. In one illustrative example, neuroscientists can now point to dissimilarities of physical structure in infancy to predict what types of learning challenges a child may have in the future. We now know that physical changes in the brain as a result of exercise, diet, using prescription drugs, etc. affects how the circuits and networks function. In short, any detriment to the surface structure of the brain can affect its capacity to function, as well as *inhibit* – or promote – efficient learning (Baars & Gage, 2010).

The Neuro-semantic Language Learning Theory aims to demonstrate that all visual learners struggling from mental disorders such as anxiety need to see their behavior and mental functioning reflected visually back to them so that both educator and pupil have a "shared referent" of understanding to be able to refer to and build upon (Arwood, 2011).

Research is now starting to tell us about how data in the brain is processed for neurotypical learners beginning with the eyes taking in sensory input and how this information is integrated in higher brain structures.

In typically developing brains, all input is processed *synergistically* as the result of certain regions such as the visual cortex, hypothalamus, amygdala, temporal lobe, parietal lobe, and prefrontal cortex all working together. However, if any one of these regions becomes impacted, the system as a whole does not function as efficiently. For learners such as Jaime, sight and sound simply do not integrate effortlessly. Jaime needs specific targeted visual intervention to connect these disparate sensory information streams so that they will consolidate into concepts higher up in her neuronal processing circuits.

Analysis of Visual Language Intervention

Arwood (2014) informs us that the principles of neuroscience support the need for Jaime to continue to improve her cognition and language in order for her brain to function at its healthiest level. It is critical to understand why Jaime's brain has responded to stress with a severe excess of GC hormones throughout her childhood and early adolescence. To begin with, we can determine by analyzing her neurodevelopmental history and behavior that Jaime was born with a learning system that responds to stress in what can be considered an "atypical" manner. For example, Jaime told numerous stories of having to be held down by adults throughout elementary and middle school because she would thrash and convulse her body and sometimes strike out at others during panic attacks.

How did Jaime's behavior progress to this state? Jaime's disordered conduct and overflow of motor movements indicate that in these panicked moments her brain struggles to make meaning of the world around it; including, and most importantly, the social interactions of child to adult. No child is raised in a vacuum – caregivers are continuously assigning meaning to children in social situations through the oral and body language that they use to react to an event. Interviews with Jaime's parents suggest that in infancy she was often difficult to soothe and that the features of her autism made it challenging at times to emotionally connect with her. It would be understandable for parents in such a role to react with fear, anger, or disdain as their child began to incorporate more "disturbing" behaviors into daily life. Unfortunately, such responses do not validate the child and can even cause anti-social emotional development because they neglect to nurture, protect, and support the child in moments of trauma (Arwood, 2014, Coleman & Webber, 2002).

It is important, therefore, to acknowledge that in addition to being born with an atypical learning system, the language Jaime received throughout her childhood impacted the way that she herself responded to stress. This in turn, cued her brain to reciprocate with more stress hormones. This principle is explained in the concept of the Stress-Brain Loop, where the more unfavorable language we assign to situations, the more our brain responds with stress accordingly. In turn, the more stress we experience, the worse we perform in areas of memory retention, attention, and perception (McEwen, 2007). Unwittingly, Jaime's parents (and her other caregivers) played a large role in furthering the impact of this debilitating cognitive loop on Jaime's psyche, especially in situations where Jaime presented challenging behavior.

The question then remains: How did the intervention of using drawing and writing work inside the brain to untangle Jaime's entrenched destructive mental spiral? We have established that Jaime functions with a visual learning system: she does not make enough meaning from sound alone to form concepts. Jaime herself provides evidence to support this when she talks about "zoning out" in class when the teacher is speaking, or attempting to meticulously copy down everything that the teacher is saying so she can go back and attempt to re-learn the material at a later time.

Having worked with Jaime in both special education and general education classes, this author can report that nearly all previous academic and social instruction was presented in an auditory manner. This often takes the form of teacher-directed activities such as "direct instruction" in social skills, spelling rules, oral fluency, social stories, and more. Unfortunately for Jaime, a student who could benefit from help in scaffolding pro-social development, the vast majority of this teaching pedagogy failed to meet her needs in the way she learned best: through an overlap of visual and motor sensory input, such as the aforementioned drawing and writing (Arwood, 2014).

The brain scaffolds meaning by connecting new meaningful information to existing synaptic patterns over time (Arwood, 2014). As enough of these patterns begin to overlap and connect to various parts of the brain, circuits begin to form in the brain to represent our understanding of a vast multitude of concepts. We further develop these concepts in the mind and corresponding groups of neurons in the brain through both our own metacognition and through others assigning feedback to our thoughts and actions. In neurotypical socio-cognitive development, these interconnecting circuits will begin to spread out to vast areas of the brain and form networks of meaning that we access through the function of our language (Arwood, 2014).

Unfortunately Jaime was born with a learning system that has not allowed her the opportunity to make these synaptic connections by auditory instruction alone. We know that she cannot fully integrate the acoustic and visual information presented to her through auditory methods such as social stories because her levels of anxiety remained virtually unchanged despite these auditory efforts. This in turn means that Jaime will continue struggle to inhibit sensory information unless it is given utilizing the visual language methods presented throughout this case study.

The language intervention this author used worked because he was able to provide Jaime with enough meaningful information for her to begin to interrupt and reconfigure her established Stress-Brain Loop. One might notice the parallels between this language remediation and the process of Cognitive Behavioral Therapy (CBT). Indeed, both theories aim to reassign pro-social meaning to situations and events that the learner has previously experienced in a negative manner. However, it is important to note that most CBT practitioner training does not distinguish the important difference between auditory and visual instruction. In fact, the majority of CBT involves orally working through problems (Coleman & Webber, 2002). For a student like Jaime who needs visual/motor methods of drawing and writing to make sense of the world, CBT may not provide enough meaningful layers of input for her brain to scaffold information successfully.

Following the aforementioned principles of neuroeducation and consistently responding to Jaime in a calm manner regardless of what stress level she functioned at allowed this author to build a strong therapeutic rapport with her that ultimately allowed her to trust the pedagogy being used.

Quantitative data kept from year to year marked a significant drop in panic attacks from the range of approximately twice per week to approximately once per month. This allowed Jaime to "fit in" more socially with her peers, and thus she performed at 100% of all social/emotional IEP goals. As this past school year progressed, Jaime relied less and less on adult aides, which had marginalized her in social situations. Even halfway through the school year, it was clear to the IEP team that Jaime would not need the sheltered instruction offered by the social/emotional special education class and that she would be able to meet her educational needs in a less restrictive setting. Jaime began achieving better grades by herself after learning methods of taking visual notes; this accomplishment reduced her overall phobia of asking peers and teachers for help and provided her with materials she now knew how to study.

Working with Jaime has taught this author that though anxiety cannot be seen directly, its effect on our learning systems is very real. Moreover, by drawing out and writing notes on an issue to provide an external referent, visual thinkers like Jaime are finally able to "see" these effects both on their psyche and on the world around them. In addition, drawing produces a permanent product whereas conversing is temporal and fleeting (Arwood, 2014). A visual learner needs such external referents to refer back to in order to scaffold new information with existing ideas. We cannot expect a student to learn in any other way except that in which they take in meaningful information. By understanding this fundamental principle, this author was able to accept Jaime for who she was, and not let her behaviors define her. By her own account, this author was the first teacher in many years that had been able to do so successfully.

Summary of Neuro-Education Methods

In this chapter, the author begins by emphasizing the importance of discerning and understanding how the learner processes input and at which cognitive level a learner is currently functioning. He has illustrated how the cognitive level may change depending on external and internal stressors the learner is experiencing, and therefore remediation must reflect these changes in order to be effective. By meeting Jaime at her functional level both in times of stress and in times of calm, the author was able to access her learning system through modalities that proved most effective for Jaime: drawing and writing.

Through these techniques, Jamie was able to develop her agency, lessen stress on her neurobiological system, and improve her conceptual thinking. By building her agency and "keeping herself in her pictures," Jamie is able to exhibit more pro-social behaviors and thus increase positive feedback from adults in her life as well as peers. She is able to see herself coping with stressful situations in a productive way and prevent herself from spiraling out of control. By managing this stress, she is keeping her brain equalized, preventing a flooding of stress-related neurotransmitters and a continuation of the Stress-Brain Loop. By seeing concepts through visual note-taking, visual cartooning of events and social situations, and her own drawing and writing paired with external feedback, Jaime is able to increase the meaningful input her brain receives and improve her cognitive function. As a result, Jaime experiences academic, social, and personal successes that will continue to be a source of meaningful feedback.

Chapter 9

Teaching Writing Through Seeing the Movement

Courtney Gillaspy, M.A., CCC-SLP

Abstract

The cases of two students, one who is deaf and one who is hearing able but on the autism spectrum, are explored in this chapter. As the author, a speech and language pathologist, begins to understand the underlying neural mechanisms of each child's visual-motor learning systems, she is able to use Neuro-Education based strategies that work with the students in ways that are completely new to them. For both students, the author finds notable success by using the movement of the hands during writing to provide visual layers of input to the brain. Because these two pupils are severely impacted by their disabilities, they both require the extra motor layers of hand movement, finger spelling, and mouth reading (among other strategies), in order to "see" what adults expect of them. Both students had failed previous interventions that focused on isolated tasks and sound-based instruction. In contrast, these same students were able to "jump" ahead four to six years in social cognition and language development after approximately seven months of brain-based visual language therapy.

About the Author

Courtney Gillaspy is a speech and language pathologist with over ten years' experience working with students who are Deaf/Hard of Hearing, among other special needs populations. After completing her post-master's degree in neuroeducation studies at the University of Portland, Courtney has presented her research and case studies at regional conferences and has developed professional workshops for her colleagues. She is enthusiastic about advocating for the rights of students with exceptionalities to access comprehensive courses in the least restrictive environment and for helping students learn how to fit in to their communities in a pro-social manner.

Introduction

As a speech language pathologist there is often an expectation that in order to support students, intervention needs to focus on sound production, such as connecting sounds to letters, rather than using whole language, such as unpacking the many ideas embedded in a single word concept. Even if a student struggles with both of these skills, which most students receiving communication services do, the majority of time in session is spent on the former. As a result, the efforts of the adult spent in remediation can be thought of as "weakness-based" speech language therapy: because a child has a weakness in using sound for learning, more time must be spent to catch them up to their neurotypical peers in this area.

This author experienced a wake-up call when she began to understand that language function and speech production are intertwined. What this means is that language is more than just oral speech and written words; language represents the underlying thinking of all learners (Arwood, 2011). Moreover, by working with a student to increase the complexity of their thinking, rather than trying to increase a student's vocabulary, a speech and language pathologist can elicit more profound results in that student's overall communication. When this author first began to learn about the Viconic Language Methods (VLMs) inspired by Neuro-Education Methodology (Arwood, 2011) it became clear that by improving learning and language development in more meaningful ways, more long-lasting and dynamic changes could occur within her pupils.

As a result of these discoveries, when providing weekly intervention that is limited in time, this author chooses do reading and writing within a shared context; in this case a picture of an event (See Figure 9.1 for an example). When information is embedded in context and language is considered through its function, a different kind of data set must be analyzed to look for achievement in communication. For example, using Mean Length of Utterance (MLU) measures is a common tool to measure a student's oral speech development. However, saying more words overall does not necessarily reflect a deeper understanding of ideas, nor does it mean that a student has acquired the ideas they are able to say out loud. Instead of counting grammatical structures as correct or incorrect or counting the number of words used correctly in an utterance, progress can be measured through the lens of Arwood's language development levels that will be explored throughout this chapter.

Often, educators are asked to work on isolated skills like having students copy simple sentences or copy phonemes. This assumes a great deal about how learning takes place in the brain. For example, many educators believe that the brain builds information in an additive and sequential manner. They assume that a child must learn a multitude of two-syllable words before moving on to three-syllable words, etc. In reality, learning in the brain takes place much like a spiral, where new information is constantly connecting to old information in a fluctuant manner (Arwood, 2011). A student doesn't acquire knowledge immediately; the brain must continuously refine it over time.

If the student uses their own ideas, their own writing, signing, or talking, their thinking improves because it creates connections between what is already known by the learner and new information being learned (Arwood, 2011). They are not simply doing a straight imitation of the language structures provided for them without having a change in their thinking. Since language names our thinking, we can use language to share our ideas (Arwood, 2011). If the student is imitating language structures without a deeper understanding of what they are writing, this will not deepen their concepts.

The following case study is an example of using context and layers to develop a student's own thinking and language. The author utilizes numerous Viconic Language Methods that are directly inspired by Neuro-Education methodology. A strong effort is made to overlap input into the brain in multiple ways, such as using more than one point of input i.e. a picture, writing on a picture, pointing to an idea, finger tracing an idea, writing on a picture dictionary, talking/signing, and cartooning out a story, among other strategies.

Case Study 1: Ricardo

Ricardo is a 12-year-old student in 6th grade. He has severe hearing loss, which he has experienced since birth. He uses aspects of American Sign Language (ASL), Pidgin Signed English (PSE), and gestures to communicate, but he does not use spoken language other than a few functional approximations that sound like utterances. Spoken Spanish is the primary language used by his family at home. Ricardo's main exposure to ASL has been through sign language interpreters and instructors at the Teachers of the Deaf school. His family uses gestures and one to two word signed phrases to communicate with him at home. Ricardo has used his hearing aids occasionally throughout his life. However, these devices do not bring his hearing to a level sufficient to hear many sounds of spoken language.

During most of his elementary school education he has attended school in a Deaf and Hard of Hearing program housed within a public elementary school. Students within the program receive instruction in a small group with a certified Teacher of the Deaf, as do other peers who are deaf or hard of hearing. They also participate in a general education classroom at grade level to an extent deemed appropriate by the educational team and family.

During Ricardo's 6th grade school year he spent more than half of his day in a small group with a Teacher of the Deaf. This decision was made due to his low levels of language expression, reading, and writing. Ricardo was substantially far behind the content of the regular 6th grade classroom in these areas: his reading was measured at a first grade level. However, he was able to join his sixth grade peers with an ASL interpreter for Physical Education and Computer classes.

Ricardo's Individualized Education Plan (IEP) included the goal of progressing to a second grade reading level over the course of his sixth grade year. His writing goals included writing brief personal narratives and simple sentences including noun + verb and adjective + noun + verb phrases. Notice that these writing goals focused on increasing the complexity of his language structures (grammar), not necessarily the function of how he used language to communicate.

In addition, Ricardo had self-advocacy goals and expression goals to improve his ASL. His ASL was difficult for interpreters and his teachers to understand, and he could not answer questions or share his ideas about events that occurred in the past or were going to occur in the future. This difficulty often left adults to guess, infer, and assume his intended meaning. In the study of developmental levels of language, Arwood (2011) describes this kind of expression as being highly "restricted" in functional communication. Neurotypical children do go through a phase of exhibiting restricted language function; however, this is typically outgrown by age seven at the latest, even in Deaf/Hard of Hearing students (Arwood, 2011). By studying how he communicated, and how restricted this communication actually was, the author was able to determine that Ricardo was approximately five to seven years behind his peers in his functional language expression.

Ricardo's IEP described how he could not "stick to a point," meaning he only shared a few ideas about each topic and then moved on to another. He could memorize vocabulary, but could not use that vocabulary in other settings and situations. This meant that his brain was only learning at a pattern level, and information was not reaching areas known for higher order thinking such as the prefrontal cortex (Baars & Gage, 2010). He could not sequence information in time or include a clear "who," "what," "where," "when," "why," and "how" in his ASL communication or in his written English. Therefore, it could be concluded that Ricardo was severely developmentally delayed in all areas of his life.

Motor Movement of the Hand

Since Ricardo presented as a student who moved his body and his eyes frequently in the classroom (such as standing up, walking and looking around frequently), this author decided to focus on writing as the method for supporting his reading and writing goals. Arwood (2011) informs us that Ricardo moves so frequently because this represents how he learns information best. In other words, Ricardo has what is called a "movement access" learning system: he needs to be moving *something* at all times in order for information to be acquired.

In terms of how the brain functions, writing cannot be accomplished without moving the hand. If a student can move their hand (on their own or with the assistance of an adult), this means that the motor strip of their brain is functional, *and* it can connect to other regions of the brain known to process language such as the occipital cortex, the temporal lobe, and Broca's/Wernicke's areas (Arwood, 2011). If a student requires movement in order to learn, the most efficient way to achieve this is through their hands. In fact, neuroscientists know that the hand is one of the appendages that uses the greatest amount of interconnected resources in the brain (Baars & Gage, 2010).

Writing can capitalize on the movement of his hand to create overlapping patterns that represent concepts through written language. Enough overlapping patterns of the movement of written language can then develop concepts if the patterns are meaningful to the student. A person takes in sensory information through movement. Then, the brain begins to create patterns from this movement, and connect these patterns to other brain regions known to process language. As educators, our job is to *assign meaning* to this movement. In other words, we must help the student sift through what is important to learn (such as names, faces, objects, actions, etc.), and what is simply background information that we can filter out (extraneous details such as ground, sky, walls, etc.) When the student is presented with enough overlap of meaningful patterns, then they can develop concepts. The movement of the hand creates visual shapes that can add a crucial visual layer of access for Ricardo's brain. When enough visual shapes overlap, the patterns begin to form concepts (brain circuits). Eventually, the patterns plus the concepts equals language (brain networks) (Arwood, 2011).

Event Based Pictures as Shared Referents

When the author first began working with Ricardo, he would write about his weekend, his family, etc. Ricardo could indeed write, but as previously mentioned he could not clearly communicate his ideas, so the adult was regularly guessing as to what he meant. Ricardo would become frustrated with this author because she could not see the ideas inside his head. She did not have enough information about those topics to fully scaffold his written and signed communication. Because his language was so restricted, therapy sessions with Ricardo showed little gains.

It was established that Ricardo was a visual thinker, meaning he made pictures in his head of what he wished to communicate. Moreover, *movement* was what Ricardo's brain was seeking as a way to gain information. Because of these facts, this author chose to create a *shared referent* that she and Ricardo could work off of together. The author needed some object that she and Ricardo could touch, point to, trace, write on, and draw on. Therefore, this author selected an event-based picture to place in front of both child and educator.

Having a picture present allowed for better scaffolding for Ricardo's learning because this author did not have to guess what he meant. A *shared referent* is something that two communication partners share; it can be an idea that is specified through language. Or, in this case since language expression is a deficit area for Ricardo, a picture that both could see that has a pictured event with semantic relationships (agent/action/object), (Arwood, 2011). (See Figure 9.1 for an example of an event-based picture).

Figure 9.1: Event-Based Picture
From Arwood, E. (1985). *APRICOT I kit*. Portland, OR: APRICOT, Inc. Reprinted with permission.

Rather than presenting Ricardo with a "cloze" procedure or a written prompt in order to focus on grammatical structures as a primary goal, this author used the event-based-picture as a tool for intervention. Ricardo could now draw his own ideas about what he understood from the picture and then receive refinement from this author about his ideas. This refinement could occur through both written and sign support via a translation process between American Sign Language and written English, but may also include other visual strategies.

For example, a teacher could pair an idea such as "friend" with its sign language equivalent using the hands. Then, the teacher and student could draw two friends playing with each other, draw thought bubbles coming from their heads indicating what they are thinking, point to the drawn friends and finger trace their names, finger spell the word "friend," write ideas about why the two people are friends, and even make shapes with the mouth to show what the lips do when they vocalize the word "friend." A learner who is as severely impacted as Ricardo needs all of these visual layers overlapped one after another because their brain function is *atypical* and cannot learn new information easily (Arwood, 2011).

Notice that many of these layers of instruction pair visual and motor movement together. As previously mentioned, this is how Ricardo's brain learns best – through movement access. By repeating these visual-motor movement strategies multiple times per session in order to learn the new target ideas, Ricardo can start to overlap various methods of visual language input in a way that his brain can now make meaning, forming circuits (concepts) and eventually networks (interconnections) between ideas.

Increasing Language Function Increases Literacy Skills

This author met with Ricardo and one other peer from the DHH program weekly for forty-minute sessions during the school year. Sessions were conducted both in ASL and written English. The official school-based goal of the intervention was to support the written English and reading goals that were on his IEP. However, as previously mentioned, the overarching aim of therapy sessions was to increase Ricardo's ability to use functional language to express himself at an age-appropriate level. By increasing Ricardo's language function, this would increase his higher order thinking. By increasing his higher order thinking, this would increase his capacity for *literacy*. Increasing his capacity for literacy would naturally increase his abilities in reading, writing, listening (non-verbal), speaking (non-verbal), viewing, and calculating – all aspects of increased language function (Arwood, 2011).

Intervention included group discussion (through ASL) of people in a pictured event, picture dictionary development where students would write words on their own dictionary as well as a shared group dictionary drawn on a large paper in front of the two students. For an example of a shared picture dictionary, see Figure 9.2.

Figure 9.2: Student-Created Picture Dictionary

Before regular therapy commenced Ricardo's starting baseline data was collected using an event-based picture from APRICOT I kit (Arwood, 1985). This particular image used to determine baseline scores depicted a family having a barbeque at a park and was not used as a regular intervention device during the course of the therapy so as to maintain the authenticity of the pre-post data comparison.

The author chose this event-based picture in order to determine baseline (pre-therapy) information about Ricardo's written English and ASL levels. As part of the first pre-therapy session, Ricardo was asked about other people in the past or future through ASL. The language he used was not well organized and was difficult to understand. In order to obtain baseline data that could help guide intervention, Ricardo was asked to draw a story about the events happening in Figure 9.1. He drew and wrote (See Figure 9.3) simple sentences that were not related to the event-based-picture that was presented such as, "The man is happy. The woman is happy. The girl is play. The boy is play. The boy and girl is play. The man and woman is happy." Note the use of Ricardo's correct language structures for some sentences, such as, "The man is happy." Some educators would point to this correct use of language structures as evidence of progress. However, while the grammar is correct, this is a sentence that does not relate to the picture or describe the action of the man. It appears that Ricardo wrote subject-verb-object sentences that he had practiced in other educational contexts demonstrating that he lacks connection between his thinking and language. There is no writing here that represents what he knows about the picture. He described "who" was in the picture such as mom or dad, but did not otherwise express ideas about the picture. He did not name the people in the picture to create a story and he did not have a sequence of events that occurred describing what, where, why, when, how about the picture.

Figure 9.3: Ricardo Baseline Language Sample (Pre-Intervention)

Viewing Ricardo's drawings also illustrates how he shows only minimal semantic relationships between agents (people) in the picture. For example, the stick figures are not looking at each other, and, in the final panel, there is a line that separates them both literally and figuratively. From a developmental psychology perspective, Ricardo's language shows that he lacks *agency*, or a sense of self that knows how to successfully navigate the world. Twelve-year-old neurotypical students should be able to identify, initiate and maintain meaningful relationships (Piaget, 1959). When analyzing these language samples for *function*, it is clear that Ricardo is severely restricted in language usage, as well as developmentally delayed far behind his peers.

Because he is working between two languages - written English and ASL - Ricardo's writing shows the differences between ASL and English grammatical structures such as when he used the word "play" instead of "playing." ASL does not reflect time using verb tense so Ricardo's writing of verbs does not include time-based structures (morphemes like –ing or –ed). This is not surprising, as human's ability to use time stems from the brain processing the auditory properties of spoken English (Arwood, 2011). Because they do not use the auditory portions of their brains in typical ways, individuals who are Deaf/Hard of Hearing already struggle more than hearing-able adults to internally process time (Arwood, 2011). Ricardo will need to be able to see the *passage of time* as actually *moving through space*, meaning conceptualizing time in a completely visual manner. More on this phenomenon will be explored later in this chapter.

Based on this initial language sample, and by observing the quality of his use of sign language, it was determined that Ricardo functioned at the preoperational level of learning based on the Neuro-semantic Language Learning Theory (NsLLT) (Arwood, 2011). In other

158

words, Ricardo had great difficulty communicating ideas outside of the "here and now" of his immediate environment. He struggled to conceptualize ideas that were unrelated to him, and he was unable to communicate about the world on a symbolic level comparable to his typically developing 6th grade peers. The preoperational level of language is exhibited primarily between three and seven years of age (Arwood, 2011). This fact meant that Ricardo was far below his peers in his cognition and language.

It is important to note that Ricardo's behavior was described by sign language interpreters as "lazy" and that he "fooled around a lot." These descriptions could be interpreted as a non-clinical manner of describing his restricted level of language function. However, once this author was able to refine an understanding of Ricardo's behaviors using the NsLLT, this author considered that this analysis was likely an adult interpretation of Ricardo's behavior. In other words, since Ricardo's language functions were not at the level of his peers, he appeared "immature" to adults.

Visual-Motor Intervention Strategies

Previous therapists had used many sound-based activities in hopes of providing multiple academic examples for Ricardo. These strategies included breaking apart words into small units, spelling words, and defining words out of context. However, Ricardo had not made progress using these auditory strategies. Using the principles of the NsLLT to analyze Ricardo's level of language function, this author determined that an appropriate intervention would be for adult and child to work together using event-based pictures of shared events, such as people doing actions with other people and things within the context of an event. The goal of using this shared referent together would be to add multiple visual layers of instruction to semantically connect ideas. This meant that we could write, draw, point to ideas, bubble words, finger spell, mouth words, and sign in ASL during our weekly sessions. Multiple sessions could be spent working with a single picture to allow enough time to develop and refine the connections between agents, actions, and objects in the scenes.

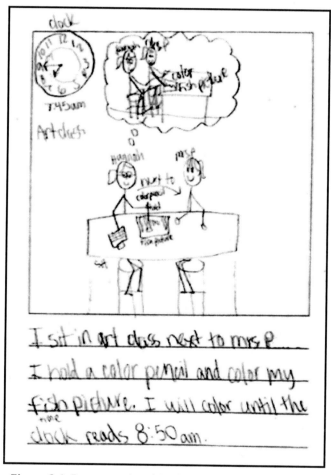

Figure 9.4: Pre-operational Student Including Others in Their Mental Pictures
Image © 2017 M. Poulson, Used with permission

Considering Ricardo's visual-motor symbolizing system, as well as his preoperational language level, the author knew that the movement of the hands would create visual points of access for Ricardo's brain. Therefore, whenever this author introduced a new idea for Ricardo, she provided a variety of visual layers while working with her hand on top of his. This was important because "movement-access" learners such as Ricardo need an overlap of points of visual-motor access so that their learning system can actually process the material. Eventually after many hand-over-hand layers, Ricardo could demonstrate that he understood an idea by using the concept in a semantically correct, spontaneous manner. Once this happened, Ricardo no longer needed hand-over-hand instruction to continue to access that concept; now, he could write and draw about the idea on his own.

A characteristic of children who function at the preoperational level of language is that they communicate about ideas primarily in relation to themselves ("me, myself, and I"). As mentioned, this is because they have not developed a sense of agency. Nevertheless, learners at this level can still think about people doing actions with other people, if it is scaffolded to them in small, meaningful doses. In other words, an adult can first draw the child on the page and wait for the child to recognize themselves as being part of the lesson. Then, once the learner has "grounded" themselves on the page, the adult can draw thought bubbles coming from that child that depict the child thinking about another person. For an example of this type of cartoon, see Figure 9.4.

Figure 9.5: Drawing and Writing About an Event-Based Picture

Notice that the intervention started at the preoperational level ("me" language, 3-7 years old) and slowly built up to concrete ("we" language, 7-11 years old) rather than beginning at higher level concepts that are more formal or symbolic. Despite great intentions, many speech and language therapists overshoot their learning target by beginning intervention at "too high" of a developmental level for the child.

Ricardo was given many event-based pictures to work with over time. To process the agents, actions, and objects of each event, this author would cartoon out each image and help Ricardo write down what was happening. Figure 9.5 shows Ricardo drawing and writing about an event while receiving help and refinement from the author. Notice that all of the agents are named, and that all of the actions (cleaning, yelling, looking, seeing, running, etc.) are all clearly labeled. In addition, the drawings match the writing – a sign that there exists a cognitive link between the two in the learner's mind (Brown, 2012). This language sample shows significant progress for Ricardo in his ability to think about others.

The event-based pictures were necessary to create a shared referent between the speech language pathologist and the student since the student had difficulty giving complete ideas about what he knew. By using a shared referent the adult could scaffold meaning for the student about the event without guessing since the picture was something we could both see and work from.

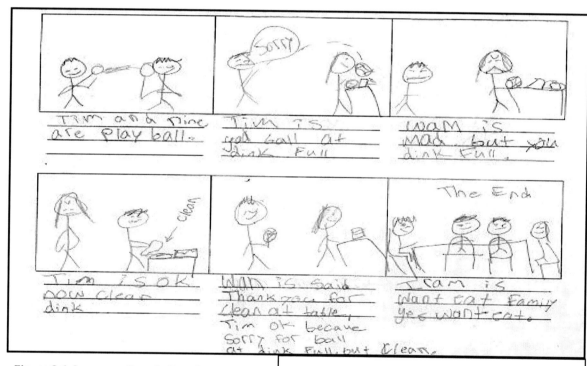

Figure 9.6: Language Sample Post-Intervention

Script reads: *"Tim and Nine are play ball. Tim is yad ball at dink full. Wam is mad. But you dink full. Tim is ok. Now clean dink. Wan is said thank you for clean at table. Tim ok becaue sorry for ball at dink full, but clean. Iram is want eat family yes want eat."*

Results of Case Study 1

In May 2012, Ricardo was given the same event-based picture from October 2011 that was used to establish his "baseline" level of language function. He was again asked to tell a story from the same picture. By this time Ricardo had received approximately six to seven months of visual-motor language intervention therapy. When Ricardo explained the picture this time, his language presented with decreased structures, but increased semantic relationships (See Figure 9.6).

Although this drawing and writing sample shows a decrease in grammatical structures, it demonstrates a significant increase in meaning and more complex semantic relationships. This sample shows great difficulty with spelling of the words and grammar: "dink" is "drink"; "Wan" appears to be a name he has given to the mother. Ricardo seems to be using sounds and letters for the written patterns of the words (spelling). When asked by the adult, Ricardo signed that he meant "accident" for the word written "yad". Unlike the first time he viewed the sample, this time his ideas relate back to the picture presented and he now begins to create a sequence of events that creates a story, something he did not do initially.

Using the NsLLT to analyze this sample, it is clear that in seven months of visual language therapy, Ricardo has developed his language function from a low preoperational level to nearly a concrete level. Evidence of this can be seen in the fact that Ricardo's drawings of people have now made them agents, meaning they have a purpose for existing in his mind and on the page. Each stick figure now has two eyes that are at least partially engaging with the other figures in the panel. In addition, the figures' faces now have a variety of expressions ranging from happy, to sad, to mad. The figures are also not separated in the panel by a line, meaning that the artist shows intentionality for placing them together.

The drawings also show a clear progress of action from the first panel to the last. In other words, they tell a story that is relatable to anyone and does not require an adult to interpret what the child might mean. In terms of developmental psychology, this means that Ricardo can now see other people in his mind's eye (Arwood, 2011). Seven months prior, Ricardo's use of language during the pre-intervention sample indicated that he was not able to do this. His behavior around adults and other children also suggested much the same. Because language and social development are closely intertwined, it is not surprising that Ricardo's social-emotional progress would increase as his level of language function advanced (Arwood, 2011).

This language sample also shows how Ricardo is using space (an aspect of a visual language such as ASL) to describe an event that progresses through time. He is writing with the structure of ASL and shows his own thinking, and not a memorized pattern. Despite using the English words "incorrectly," Ricardo is still demonstrating that he is starting to understand how actions develop. The slides move the people through time, which is a change in his writing, but they do not contain English time features, as these are auditory properties (Arwood, 2011).

In ASL, using space to represent time is called utilizing *aspect*, and is a natural part of communication within ASL. For example, individuals who sign can use temporal aspect to physically show with their hands and face how an action is being done with relationship to time. One can physically "inflict" verbs to show if an action is done regularly, continually, repeatedly, or for an extended period of time. Therefore, Ricardo's use of words that do not reflect accurate representations of time are understandable for a person who is Deaf/Hard of Hearing and should be analyzed using this frame of reference.

In the phrase "Iram is want eat family yes want eat," each individual would be set up in space and then the communicator in ASL would use role shifting (moving the body side to side to show each individual communicating). If he were signing this writing, the ASL grammar requires shifting position for each new character, with one character asking, "Iram want to eat? " then he would shift his body to show the other character saying "Yes we want to eat." In English people use "he/she said" as one way to show dialogue, but ASL sets up dialogue in space with a communicator taking on both "roles" to construct discourse (Valli, Lucas & Mulrooney, 2006).

Now that his own thinking is represented through his drawing and writing it is possible for this author to show Ricardo the matching patterns (grammatical structures) in written

162

English that match the ideas in his own head to help him refine his work. When the adult uses visual language surface structures to tag meaning, the learning is more likely to store into deep semantic memory.

It is important to note that an educator not trained in studying language function may not see a significant difference between Ricardo's language in the pre-intervention sample and in this post-intervention sample. After all, the primary focus of many speech and language pathologists is to analyze a student's use of language structures, such as spelling, grammar, syntax, etc. From this perspective, Ricardo is still writing many ideas incorrectly. Many educators might assume that this author had worked with Ricardo on adding vocabulary to his repertoire and formulating correct sentence structures, and that he needed more of this kind of remediation to continue to see progress.

However, for the purposes of this case study, it is critical to point out that this author did not work with Ricardo to build his vocabulary, nor did she work with him to fill in sentence frames or complete cloze style activities. Arwood (2011) explains that using the viconic language strategies inspired by her Neuro-Education theory focuses on increasing a student's functional communication abilities. An added benefit to increasing language function is that it increases language structures as well. It is important to note that the reverse – working on structures to increase function – is simply not supported by modern brain-science.

Neuroscience Research Confirms Results

Neuroscientific studies on "good readers" using brain imaging by Beaulieu and colleagues (2005) have found that there is significant connectivity, or communication, between all areas of the brain involved in reading. They describe three groups of fibers running from the front to the back of the brain, left to right, and up and down within the brain (Baars & Gage, 2010). These fiber tracts connect the different regions of the brain involved in reading such as the visual cortex, Broca's and Wernicke's area, the temporal lobe, etc. The more input a learner receives in the manner in which their brain can make meaning, the more these fiber tracts will become strengthened and interconnected. The old adage is the "neurons that fire together, wire together" (Baars & Gage, 2010). This exemplifies a principal of neuroscience that multiple regions of cells working together are most efficient and represent higher order thinking abilities of the mind.

Therefore it stands to reason that activities in therapy or in a classroom should be done in multiple ways across time and across curriculum for better thinking to support the brain in making connections between ideas. When the brain processes single words or sounds, information is presented at a single word level only, without context. Moreover, diverse patterns of input related to the topic are not given over time. Words are not the unit of analysis for the brain (Arwood, 2011). The brain "learns" through a complex interplay of sensory input (ears + ears or eyes + movement) leading to electrochemical impulses that eventually form neurobiological patterns and concepts.

Unless information is integrated between the parts of the brain, it will only stay in the lower regions of the brain and will not be connected in long-term semantic meaning. Retrieving single words through memory processes will not connect to other circuits in the brain, which is what had occurred during Ricardo's education so far, practice on simple sentences out of context. As educators we are often trained to simplify information so that lower-level students can "understand" what we are saying. This process of working on skills in isolation had greatly limited Ricardo's learning as exhibited by his initial writing about the barbecue picture. In fact, struggling learners actually need more language input into their brains, not less (Arwood, 2011).

Another concern of working on isolated skills such as phonemes and grammar out of context is the lack of continuation and connection between old and new learning. Remember that the brain learns in a "spiral" manner, where new information continuously connects to old information in a strengthening process. Using an event-based picture provides a natural context and shared referent for both adult and child to work from. If a topic is initiated and then ended on an adult's time frame to move on to a new unit, a child can't make connections between ideas at their own rate.

The human brain has, through time, evolved to be made up of six layers, compared to other mammal brains that do not have the neocortex, the highest part of the human brain (Baars & Gage, 2010). If the words and simple sentences are presented as a memorization technique and the child does not have language to put the patterns in context of an idea they understand, the areas of the brain that are utilized are significantly limited, and information will therefore be dumped by the brain as non-meaningful (Arwood, 2011). The more sensory information that is given in a way that Ricardo learns (visual-motor) [that begin to make patterns that can turn into concepts (circuits) that can then be connected by communicating circuits in the brain (networks)], the greater number of layers of the brain will be used (Arwood, 2011).

This relates back to the description of the fibers in a successful reader's brain communicating throughout the layers (Baars & Gage, 2010). There is not conclusive evidence that when reading is broken down into sounds or other small parts that it will help deaf readers, despite attempts to teach phonology to deaf students. An article by Piñar, et al (2011) states, "deaf reader's access to phonological representations may follow rather than precede initial word identification" (p. 693). In other words, only after a deaf adult has acquired a complete grammar in their first language (ASL), will they be able to break down this language into smaller units, such as sound-based morphemes. Arwood (2011) echoes this idea by saying that learning the "whole" of a language comes before being able to segment it into its subsequent "parts."

Visual learners, whether deaf or otherwise, will therefore learn to read more efficiently if ideas are kept whole and not broken apart. This principle provides part of the neuroscientific rationale for bubbling the shape of words to keep them as one singular idea. The brain does not learn words, but instead it acquires semantic ideas (Arwood, 2011). Breaking apart whole ideas into smaller units only hinders the 90%+ of students who think with a visual symbolizing system (Arwood, 2011).

Another article by Hoffmeister, et al (2014) explores the idea of using ASL as a first language for deaf students and then using a written language as a subsequent second language. They suggest a model for learning to read that includes mapping out print forms to the ASL meanings that have already been acquired by the child. Their work discusses that metacognitive processes are essential for reading, meaning that the act of "reading" is really connecting visual symbols to information that has already been acquired by the mind (Hoffmeister, 2014). This supports the idea that the mind does not need to break apart ideas into small parts in order to learn them, and a child does not need to break words apart in order to recognize what they mean.

Many young deaf students are not at a developmental level that allows them to meaningfully break apart the English language. This means that any efforts of reading intervention that involve teaching to the smallest unit are misguided. Examples such as attempting to teach phonemes, copying simple sentences without the background understanding, and working on vocabulary out of a greater context are all working "against the grain" of the visual learner's mind. Only after a child has reached a concrete level of language development will they be able to take apart language in a fluid manner (Arwood, 2011).

Case Study 2: Alex

Remediation for another 6th grade student on the autism spectrum also sought to use his strengths to provide an intervention that would match how he learns best. Alex is a student who only attends his regular sixth grade classroom for specials: PE and music. Otherwise, he could not be with his peers because he continued to talk to himself (make movements of his mouth) all day, repeating TV shows and movies. He was very rigid about his schedule and tended to run from the building when there was any sort of schedule change. Alex also responded with what seemed to be an overreaction when his clothing got wet from washing his hands or being outside. Even a small drop of water on his pants would cause him to take them off, often in class.

Alex had a one-on-one assistant all day and rarely initiated communication with peers unless it was an inappropriate act such as touching their hair or repeatedly saying phrases he had heard from a movie. Alex had reading and writing skills that were measured to be almost at grade level on a standardized test that measured oral reading and multiple choice types of comprehension, but did not have concepts at a developmental level to share what he was reading with others. He did not fully comprehend what he read and could not take multiple communicative turns about a topic initiated by someone else, nor could he use language to mediate his own thinking (i.e. figure out how to cope with his schedule change).

Rationale for Visual Motor Intervention

Because Alex had these major social deficits, his goals during speech and language intervention focused mainly on his social development. Social development describes the ways a person relates to other people by initiating and maintaining relationships (Arwood, 2007). In therapy sessions this author also observed many atypical behaviors from Alex such as constant mouth movement, running away from the school, and perseverating upon getting wet, causing him to take his clothing off. Since he could not modify his behavior, it stands to reason that he did not see others in his environment and could not use his language to mediate his thinking. Based on the principles of the NsLLT, this behavior indicated that he was at a high sensorimotor to low preoperational stage of development (Arwood, 2011).

Students at the sensorimotor level of social development act much like a toddler who is zero to two years old. This means that they do not recognize other humans as unique individuals in their mind's eye; instead, they just see moving objects. Moreover, children at this stage often do not see themselves in their own mental pictures, meaning that they cannot remember what they did in the past, nor can they engage in any sort of planning for the future. Remember that neurotypical students who are 11-12 years old should function at a concrete level of social development. This means that they should be able to initiate and maintain healthy relationships with others (Piaget, 1959). Because Alex could not interact at all with others, and because he spent the entirety of his day "in his own head," he was actually functioning at a social level seven to nine years behind his grade level peers.

Standardized testing appeared to show that Alex could "read," but in reality, he could merely "word call," meaning speak words out loud. He did not understand what he "read." The evidence for this was that though Alex could sound out words, he did not retain any knowledge from his "word calling." This meant that he did not use sound to guide his own thinking (Arwood, 2011). If he could actually read, Alex would at least retain a part of the content from the sentences he spoke aloud.

Since oral and reading development does not progress in an orderly upward-moving manner of learning one skill after another, Alex was a student who was reading and writing at a higher level than his spoken language. This fact indicated that the movement of writing and the saying of words that are on his mouth in the form of movement patterns would benefit him. The overlapping movements of "reading" the ideas were not sound based and he was not saying the words out loud when he was writing. This author concluded this because if he could use sound for learning he would be communicating with adults and peers much more efficiently, and would have been demonstrated in his behavior and communication.

Alex did not appear to process the sound of his own voice because he was imitating movies or songs verbatim and not changing the information for a listener into his own language. Orally, he was able to answer some basic questions by imitating oral patterns of speech such as, "I am fine. How are you?" However, in regards to anything that wasn't about the "here and now" or about his family, Alex could not answer even basic questions.

When this author started working with Alex, his IEP goals for his 6th grade year asked to use specific social programs (learning rules of social situations) or address topics in the form of role playing so he could say specific things in specific situations in order to provide him with "social interaction skills." These goals are typical of many social skills programs. By imitating adults and providing memorized, robotic answers, students can appear to be able carry on a conversation. However, Alex was not at the developmental level to fully understand the meaning of role-playing or to practice social "skills." Even a set of conversation patterns imitated by an adult, such as rules about greetings, when out of context, were too challenging for him to process. In fact, by the time this author started working with Alex, he had received many years of these types of socialization lessons and had not demonstrated any significant social growth.

Instead of having oral conversations, this author decided to approach Alex's speech and language therapy in a different manner. This author deduced that Alex's need for movement in order to access learning could be used as a strength. Providing Alex with visual-motor methods of therapy increased his overall opportunity to have meaningful social interaction. Therefore, this author decided to write back and forth dialogues with Alex on a piece of paper, rather than having oral conversations. The rationale for this strategy was based on the fact that 1) Alex was not learning through using sound, and 2) Alex was already demonstrating, with his "overflow" of movement behavior, that he learned through a visual-motor access system (Arwood, 2011).

Considering these factors, written dialogue between this speech and language pathologist and Alex was done to prepare him for events using his strength: working off the written word through his own mouth movement when he was reading the ideas shared by the adult, and through the movement of the hand of his own written responses. As previously discussed, the movement of the hand activates the motor cortex as well as interconnected pathways used to process visual language. This hand movement provides another layer of meaningful visual input that will start to form conceptual pathways of the information; however, for visual-motor learners such as Alex, sounds alone will not (Arwood, 2011).

Written Conversations as Dialogue Therapy

When this author would ask Alex a question or try to give him information from sound alone he would seldom respond. However, when information would be given to Alex in print, he would write back to form a dialogue with the adult. (For an example, see Figure 9.9). When asked by an adult, Alex at times could give some information about himself such as his concerns, specifics about his day, or his bus trip. Nonetheless, he did not use language to show he could think about others: his language was "I" heavy. By recognizing this about Alex, this author set out to provide strategies that would give him much more information about how he could navigate and interact with the world.

For example, in one session, this author learned that Alex would be going on a school trip to Outdoor School (a science oriented program in Oregon, where students spend a few days away from home). However, Alex did not know who else would be accompanying him on his trip, so this author thought he might want to be prepared for what might happen while there. The author began to write about the upcoming trip using language that was rich in high context scenarios. Context is created by using people, the actions of the people, and the objects and locations related to people in the given story or situation they are in (Arwood, 2007). Since Alex's language was not at a level to mediate his thinking, if something went wrong on his trip, like getting a drop of water on his clothing, the fear was he would respond as he typically did - by taking his pants off.

There was great concern felt by his educational team and by his parents that these behaviors would mean he would not be able to participate on the trip or they would cause Alex to be sent home or even be in an unsafe situation by running from a place that was unfamiliar. Therefore, this author wrote back and forth with Alex to attempt to problem solve so that he might plan what to do if these events were to happen. This was indeed challenging for Alex, but more successful than having oral conversations had been throughout his school career.

Seeing the "Self" in Written Ideas

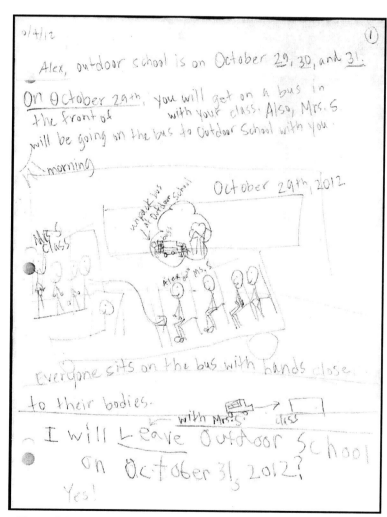

Figure 9.7: Written Dialogue as a Social Conversation

Language sessions occurred twice weekly for thirty minutes between Alex and this author as his school speech language pathologist. The sessions would prepare for an upcoming event that might be a challenge for Alex, or they would reassess an earlier challenging experience. Some examples of therapy topics would be: what Alex did with his backpack on the bus in the past and what the new expectation was; what the schedule change during testing would be like; what happened when he ran away from the school; and many other topics related to what he himself had done or would do. Note that topics in sessions started at a point of being about him, at a preoperational level. This author knew that starting at a formal level by explaining a social rule such as "making eye contact" or "being respectful" would be too developmentally challenging for Alex, and may have resulted in losing rapport with him. In addition, this author also met Alex at his level of development so that he could begin to build connections between "self" and "others."

Inherent in all of the topics discussed were various social etiquette "rules" that would come up in the context of the story we explored. We would analyze what Alex did or did not do and why. After all of the facts had been established we could describe everything we discussed as examples of "being respectful." Notice that this author intentionally started at a preoperational level ("I") before building up to a concrete level ("we"), and then ending with a formal level ("rules").

The following dialogue (See Figure 9.7) is an example of a few pages from a total of twenty-four pages of written communication between this author and the student discussing his upcoming trip to Outdoor School and preparing him for what to expect.

When this author wrote back and forth with Alex, he would overlap motor patterns (say what was on the page) in order to begin to make meaning about Outdoor School. This author wrote in real-time when Alex was in the room, and not before, so that he could watch the movement of the hand and so that we could work off any questions that would come up at the moment. The movement of the writing and drawing provided overlapping visual-motor information about what Alex could do in social situations. Writing (motor patterns) and then adding the drawn pictures (the concepts) develops higher order thinking abilities for visual-motor learners. Over time, students who struggle with social cues such as Alex can better understand the ideas about "respect" that relate directly to him. Students at a preoperational level need to see themselves and other people in their thinking (Arwood, 2011).

This author found success working with Alex by using his natural inclination for visual-motor access into his brain. In contrast to the viconic language instruction methods presented here, when a well-meaning assistant was asked to write with Alex, she wrote quite differently. Instead of writing a conversation, she provided a list of rules for Alex to follow. However, it was clear by Alex's behavior that he may or may not have understood each rule, and the rules also changed, depending on the situation.

For example, to "respect animals" means something different in different contexts – this needs to be built through written patterns that match drawn concepts for each unique situation. This author's methods of writing back and forth with Alex established a context around what could happen in social situations and gave him strategies for what he could do to naturally cope in his environment. By comparison, the aforementioned assistant did not create overlap and context about Alex in space with other people. She presented a list of rules as shown in Figure 9.8.

Needless to say, the efforts of this assistant were not well received. Rather than writing what not to do, this author wrote exactly what was expected of the students on the trip. This is presented in Figure 9.9.

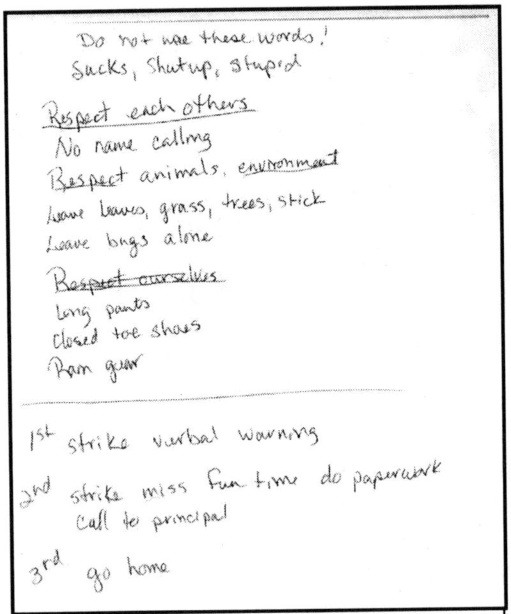

This figure shows what another adult viewed as writing that would help the student. However, it was written with less language and using very formal level concepts such as "respect" without descriptions of what that means in this situation.

Figure 9.8: Written Rules Out of Context

Results: Case Study 2

After receiving intervention therapy from this author to prepare for his trip, Alex went to Outdoor School and made it through the entire week without his mother needing to pick him up early. Alex only had one behavior difficulty when his clothing got wet. He describes how he handled this in Figure 9.10. The aide that went with him reported being surprised at how well Alex behaved and felt glad that even though he had to leave the group to get his clothes dried, he decided to change his clothing inside the cottage. In the first therapy sessions after his trip, Alex demonstrated that he knew what to do when he got wet at Outdoor School.

Notice that in this short language sample, Alex has demonstrated that he is now able to "see" in his mind's eye an accurate reflection of the past, and he has demonstrated the ability to self-regulate previous impulses in order to get his needs met in an appropriate manner. This author did not work specifically on social skills or a social story, nor did she provide a set of instructions for Alex to follow if his pants got wet. Alex did not follow a set of rules; he was able to follow the suggestions of an adult –

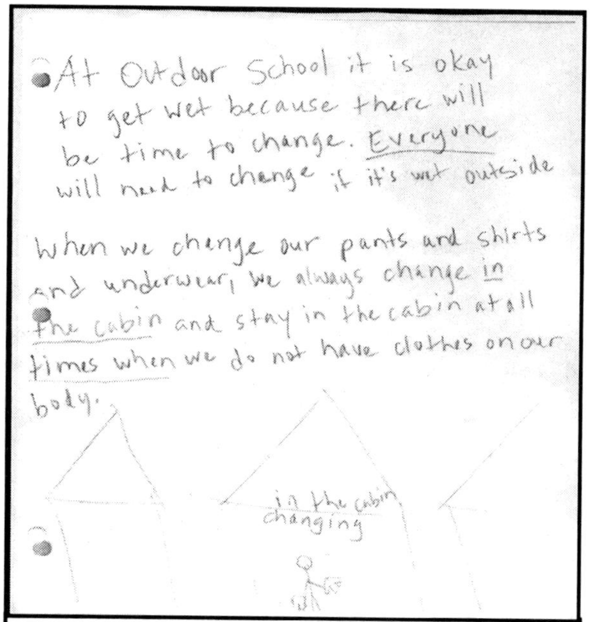

Author's Note: A modification that would have improved this approach would have been to add more "because" language to increase the cognition around why clothes stay on when you are wet so the behavior would decrease through cognitive changes in a way it cannot through writing a rule.

Figure 9.9: Social Writing Presented in Context

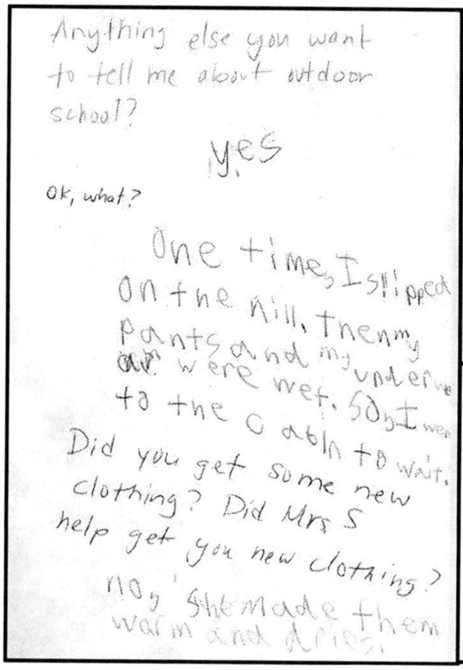

something he had rarely been able to do before intervention. The fact that Alex was able to act spontaneously in an appropriate manner while under duress shows a significant improvement in his social-emotional abilities.

This sample illustrates that Alex's level of language function has increased from high sensorimotor (zero to two years old) to high preoperational (six to seven years old) – an approximate five year jump in social-emotional development. The reader does not need to physically see or interact with Alex to determine this. Why? Because the language Alex uses represents the underlying functions of his *mind*. The language Alex

In Figure 9.10, this author asks Alex if there is anything more he wants to share about his trip to Outdoor School. He writes, "One time I slipped on the hill. Then my pants and my underwear were wet. So, I went to the cabin to wait." He is also able to respond to the author's subsequent questioning about what happened to the clothes next (they became dry).

Figure 9.10: Ricardo's Writing Improves

uses informs the reader that he is now able to "see" the past, and "see" other individuals as agents with whom he can interact to get his needs met. Alex made these gains not because the author specifically worked with Alex on these sets of skills, but rather because she helped Alex raise his overall level of cognition. By doing so, she helped him gain higher order thinking skills and become more independent.

Conclusion

Both case studies presented in this chapter focus on providing remediation for students using their natural learning strengths. The strategies documented here include providing therapy in the form of visual movement access to the brain. When an educator recognizes the potential for struggling students to learn, and when they observe a student's behavior to see *how* they learn best, they can target their intervention to become more efficient and effective. In the case of both Ricardo and Alex, writing became the primary focus of therapy since writing is a movement access to the patterns of written language to name the drawn concepts. By using the Neuro-semantic Language Learning Theory to recognize student developmental levels and watching student behavior to see how they are learning, this author could scaffold what and how this author worked with them to support their learning.

As seen in the language samples collected here, both children made marked gains in their development in the areas of language function, social cognition, higher order thinking, impulse control, patience, and civic engagement. Without a deep understanding of Neuro-Education theory – *how* and *why* students learn information – this author would have lapsed into using traditional teaching methods that are out of context and auditory in nature. By recognizing the visual-motor learning potential of these children, this author was able to affect change in students who would have otherwise continued to struggle.

Summary of Neuro-Education Methods

In the cases of Ricardo and Alex, the use of multiple layers of visual-motor input helped to increase the concept acquisition for each student. Both students were able to access their visual systems by watching the movement of the pencil, watching signs or fingerspelling, as well as the movement of the speaker's mouth during the intervention. They were able to layer additional visual input when they wrote, signed and drew their own ideas. From a cognitive psychology perspective, both students benefitted from an intervention that employed a shared referent in order to meet the students at their preoperational level of learning.

In the case of Ricardo, the use of an image depicting agents, actions and objects provided enough context for developing his concepts of the semantic relationships depicted in the drawing. Alex drew and wrote about his own personal experiences, actions that are additionally beneficial for a preoperational learner who thinks best in terms of their own experiences. From a language perspective, the use of rich "because language," helped Alex to add layers and deepen his understanding of formal-level concepts like "respect" or "social appropriateness." In Ricardo's experience, his language function improved dramatically as a result of his improved thought processes. In both interventions, each student was able to work with his strengths and abilities, as opposed to his weaknesses, which maximized the time spent on deep concept acquisition.

Unit 4: Next Steps: Using the Principles of Neuroeducation to Drive Curriculum and Programmatic Changes

Preface

The study of Mind, Brain, Education (as it is currently called in most institutions) is very new. In less than 20 years, this discipline has uncovered insights into the intersections between human anatomy and cognition, and proposed a framework for how humans learn best. Many of these principles about human thinking can help transform education by grounding instructional practice in effective scientific truisms. For example, in her review of the field of Mind, Brain, and Education science, Tokuhama-Espinosa (2011) highlights five well-established concepts of M.B.E science:

1. Human brains are each unique

2. All brains are not inherently equal in ability

3. The brain is changed by experience

4. The brain is highly plastic (amenable to change)

5. The brain connects new information to old

These five axioms about the brain culminated from pooling dozens of the most respected academics in the fields of neuroscience, psychology, and education and arriving at a collective consensus. These adages provide a foundational view of learning upon which future researchers can build new studies and propose new claims. By working together, experts in these three fields can help translate the importance of their findings to each other, and ultimately impact change upon how schools operate in the United States.

The authors of this anthology would like to acknowledge the achievements that Mind, Brain, and Education science has had upon instilling a scientific rigor into studies of the brain. Because of the efforts of the pioneers in this field, more researchers are pursuing careers exploring how to revamp educational practices, and more teachers are paying attention to how the findings of neuroscience can affect the methodology they use in the classroom. In addition, numerous academic journals and international conferences have been established to help translate research from one field in M.B.E. Science to another. Indeed, there is much to be celebrated.

And yet, at the same time, these authors would like to point out that no other model of human learning besides Arwood's *Neuro-semantic Language Learning Theory* includes the study of language function as a third academic lens through which to view primary research in neuroscience and cognitive psychology. No other model uses the study of language to triangulate findings between the mind, brain, and teaching. As a result, many M.B.E. iterations succumb to academic pitfalls when researchers from one discipline attempt to "put on the hat" of another field to explain their results.

Some of these pitfalls include relying heavily on theories of how animal brains learn (e.g. mice, primates, etc.) to explain how humans think, as well as using input-output models of cognition as a lens to interpret scientific findings. Neuroscientists, such as those at Oregon Health and Science University, (e.g. Gilbert, 2015) have spent millions of dollars to attempt to catalog every neuron of the rat brain in hopes that knowing its complete biological package will uncover truths about how connections form in humans' brains. Then, these same scientists have run these findings through an assumption of cognitive psychology that human thinking follows an input-output design, where sensory input ultimately leads to an output in thinking – after being filtered through a complex maze of hidden layers of the mind (Baars & Gage, 2010).

Perhaps not surprisingly, the field of M.B.E. Science is often left with more questions than answers to their inquiries. The authors of this anthology would like to propose that this occurs because M.B.E. neglects to include the study of language function as a third pillar to anchor the wobbly base that is left when trying to translate from neuroscience and psychology directly to education. Because of its distinct uniqueness, Arwood (2011) distinguishes the model of cognition used in this book as "Neuro-Education". Though the name change may not immediately seem significant, a careful study of the work presented by the authors in this unit will clearly differentiate otherwise.

These authors compare and contrast Arwood's model with recommendations of different brain-based educational practices made by other experts in the field (such as phonics instruction) (e.g.: Berninger & Wolf, 2009; Eden & Moats, 2002). By including language function in classroom instruction and one-on-one literacy remediation, these authors are able to find success with struggling students where previous methods had failed to promote growth. The findings are impressive; but above all, the results of their educational findings speak for themselves.

In Unit 4, the three authors explore how the use of Arwood's Neuro-Education Model may be expanded beyond a single classroom and into the culture of a school at large. Chapter 10 examines the impact that the Smarter Balanced Common Core test has upon English Language Learners and other students who struggle to read at grade level. The district of the author is under the gun to "catch up" all students to their grade-level peers in all areas of literacy. Because of this impending pressure, the author can propose Neuro-Education as a model to narrow the achievement gaps between successful and poor readers.

The author compares and contrasts the effectiveness of Arwood's Viconic Language Methods with other phonics-based programs that her district had previously implemented. The author then trains her colleagues over the course of a year in how to distinguish between identifying the surface structures of language and uncovering the underlying deep semantics contained within words. By understanding that drilling isolated phonics skills only results in short-term growth in their students, the author is able to shift her school's perspective toward promoting long-term changes in their children's brains. By including the study of language function into efforts at literacy remediation, a majority of the participating students achieve successful results.

Chapter 11 tackles the question that many school administrators wrestle with: why don't students use academic planners? The author first reveals that most planning devices require students to be fluent in auditory concepts such as organizing time. But, the vast majority of children think using visual pictures and movies in their heads. As a result, many schools require students to use organizational tools that most students do not find meaningful. The author proposes numerous visual augmentations that can be added to planners for them to become more intuitive for visual thinkers. In addition, she explores how educators can become more in tune with their students' minds by asking them to transfer their mental images onto the pages of their planners. This strategy is a pre-requisite for visual thinkers to be able to "see" themselves move through their day. More on this concept will be explored later in this preface.

In Chapter 12, the author provides a rich literature review of educational theory by comparing five different methods to teach literacy. The results of numerous primary source research studies are explored in each of the five areas. The author ultimately concludes the most effective methodology to promote literacy involves taking into account the manner in which children's brains function. The viconic language teaching methods proposed by Arwood's NsLLT match most closely with the suggestion to include brain function as a guiding principle for instruction.

This chapter also analyzes the results of a study undertaken by the author comparing the effectiveness of phonics-based instruction versus language-based visual strategies in promoting literacy among her students. The children that had been required to drill isolated language components had only demonstrated scant evidence of literacy remediation. Perhaps not surprisingly, the children in the study learned the skills of literacy more robustly when provided with the methods of neuroeducation and when given authentic opportunities to use their own natural language.

Unit 4 also includes a discussion of a few components of the American education system that may not be familiar to the reader. They are:

Scripted curriculum – As previously mentioned, the principles contained in the philosophy of behaviorism still pervade many educational practices used in today's classrooms. behaviorists believe that children exhibit evidence of learning when they can repeat back correct answers to a teacher's prompt. Additionally, they believe that the more times a child repeats an idea, the more this idea will become strengthened in the mind (Bandura, 1965; Skinner, 1953). (Notice the similarities between this practice and the aforementioned assumption that learning follows an input-output model of cognition.) The direct educational application of this theory is when a school adopts a "scripted curriculum" for every classroom teacher. Each teacher is given a page number goal to be on at the start of each day. Each page contains a script that teachers read out loud to their students to require "call and response" style interaction. In addition, the script requires teachers to use certain kinds of worksheets (often fill-in-the-blank) each day and even generates questions for future tests.

In this author's opinion, the use of scripted curriculum remains one of the largest cons that educational corporations have pulled over the American educational system. None of the practices contained in scripted curriculums (call and response, drilling skills in isolation, fill-in-the-blanks worksheets, repeating ideas over and over again, etc.) are supported by brain science. In fact, all of these tasks listed here actually *disengage* the brain and render it less effective to learn new material. Notice that tenets #3-5 above of the Mind, Brain, Education science principles directly refute the claims made by behaviorists about how the mind operates. In other words, the brain is flexible and changeable, but only learns when new information is connected to existing ideas. This can only happen when knowledge is presented in a variety of ways that allow for natural curiosity and exploration. Repeating and drilling ideas in a scripted format contradicts an overwhelming amount of brain-based evidence.

"Re-tagging" from one language to another – Linguists have argued for decades about the best manner to learn a second language (L2). Some theorists reference linguistic models and theories that outline how knowledge is transferred from one's first language (L1) to their second (L2). For example, Cummins (1986) proposes that if enough of a "common underlying proficiency" exists between a person's L1 and L2, they will be able to transfer cognitive and academic skills between the two languages. Some believe that such a transfer occurs in various stages, with students learning "basic interpersonal communication skills (BICS)," such as oral conversation, before acquiring "cognitive academic language proficiency

(CALP)," or the level of language used in grade-level classroom instruction (Cummins, 1986). Notice that the assumption contained in this theory is that different languages develop at different rates in the brain, and that the concepts in a student's L2 acquisition may lag behind their L1.

Arwood (2011), however, proposes a different theory of language development. In the NsLLT, language represents the underlying deep semantic concepts that a child has acquired in their mind. Language represents a student's thinking and unfolds at a rate that matches a student's growth in cognition. As a result, a student who is learning an L2 will acquire that language more quickly if instruction focuses not on BICS and CALP, but instead on "re-tagging" the concepts a learner already has in their brain.

The most effective way to re-tag an idea is to draw out multiple representations of that idea, and pair those drawings with the shape of the corresponding words in L1 and L2. For example, a drawn image of a ball would be paired with the shape of the English word "ball" and the shape of the Spanish word "pelota," or the shape of the Italian word "palla," etc. When we think, 95% of us pull up visual images in our heads and visual symbols (words) associated with those images. Learners who are becoming bi-lingual simply have the shapes of two symbols (words) for one underlying idea. This visual method of tagging L1 and L2 together promotes the fastest linguistic growth in both languages (Arwood, 2011).

Moving through time vs. moving through space - The ability for a person to perceive the passage of time relies on their brain being able to use its auditory processing channels to learn new concepts. As a result, many individuals with visual thinking systems struggle with time literacy. For example, this means that they cannot intuitively feel how many minutes have passed while they are engaged with an activity. Because they have difficulty estimating the passage of time, they cannot easily make plans with others or schedule out their day. As a result, these visual thinkers are regularly late to class, or they run out of time on a test, or they "flake out" on appointments with friends.

When we understand what is happening in their brains, however, we realize that these social lapses are not their fault. In order for a visual thinker (95% of the population) to be literate with time, their brain must be able to translate the acoustic properties of time to visual equivalents (Arwood, 2011). This means that their ears and auditory cortex need to be able to process the elements that make up time such as attuning to properties of sound waves. The brains of visual thinking students who struggle with time literacy will not be successful without remediation.

Successful intervention can best be achieved when an adult is able to cartoon out the entirety of a student's day and draw out how long each action takes (Brown, 2012; Kaulitz, 2016). For example, an adult could draw out all of the tasks needed for a child to get ready to go to school. Above each task, the adult could draw and write out how long each task takes: waking up and getting out of bed (2 minutes), taking a shower (15 minutes), changing clothes (4 minutes), eating breakfast (20 minutes), brushing teeth (4 minutes), packing bag (4 minutes), walking to bus stop (10 minutes). When these actions are drawn out, a visual thinker can "see" himself or herself moving through the space of their day. Now, they can "see" that their body takes up 15 "minutes" of space to take a shower, and this concept can provide an anchor to be a frame of reference for how much time (space) other activities might take up. The more actions that can be drawn out, the more frames of reference these visual thinkers will have. This will lead to more success for the brain when it needs to translate between auditory time and visual space, and vice versa (Arwood, 2011).

Unit 4 discusses the achievements of Mind, Brain, Education science as a basis for knowledge of neuroscience, cognitive psychology, and education. Then, it builds on these ideas by adding the language component as discussed in Arwood's Neuro-semantic Language Learning Theory to reveal more effective educational practices. Unit 4 also examines the limitations of animal brain research as it is applied to human thinking and learning, as well as the constraints of the current American educational system for overall human learning and specifically for visual thinkers. Lastly, the advantages of NsLLT is compared and contrasted with other status quo methods of teaching.

Chris Merideth

Chapter 10

Coaching Through the Stages of Literacy in a Title I Elementary School

Gina McClain, M.S.Ed.

Abstract

This chapter documents the efforts of an instructional coach as she begins training her colleagues how to recognize levels of language function in children and how to use Neuro-Education inspired Viconic Language Methods to best prepare these students for passing the state's Common Core summative achievement test. In this section, the author explores her district's previous efforts at teaching isolate skills of literacy such as sound-to-letter correspondence, vocabulary drills, and memorizing patterns of language. As the teachers begin to focus more on allowing their students to acquire the function of language, the students are able to catch up more quickly with their age-level peers. Practical advice is also shared about how to best use professional development training time as a school in order to maximize the desired results of learning in all children.

About the Author

Gina McClain is an instructional coach who works directly with English Language Learners and other struggling students to provide them strategies for how to improve their literacy and higher order thinking skills. Gina also trains other teachers in how to utilize Neuro-Education based Viconic Language Methods in the classroom. Gina has over fifteen years' experience working with children in grades 1-3 and is recognized in her district for her knowledge about second language acquisition strategies.

Background

I work as an Instructional Coach in a high poverty elementary school in the Willamette Valley in Oregon. We are a Title 1 school with >95% of our students economically disadvantaged which qualifies 100% of our students to receive free and reduced school meals. I have been the Instructional Coach for the past six years and before that taught 1st and 2nd grade for eight years. Our elementary school is a K-6 grade school. The average class size is 30.69 students. English Language Learners make up 46% of our student population. The percentage of students who are receiving Special Education Services is 9%. There are five different languages spoken at our school.

This chapter will explore what is missing in literacy instruction at my district, and across many schools in the United States. In particular, the instruction that our students need is a focused and integrated language approach. ELLs, but also other struggling students, need to be taught explicit academic language to be successful with the demands of the Common Core State Standards and the English Language Proficiency Standards. The only way to achieve these goals, however, is to successfully raise the level of language function among our schools' population. Our students have a huge need for successful language acquisition to make meaning and apply their learning to help close the achievement gap.

Introduction

I have stumbled upon a self-revelation: in the educational world of schooling, of which I have been a part for the past 15 years, educators have been going about teaching students in the wrong way. What exactly do I mean? During my time as a teacher, there has been a dramatic focus on program/curriculum-based instruction around teaching academic skills, especially reading. We have always had standards that we needed to teach from; in fact, our instructional focus has typically come from adopting reading curricula. We all know these curricula – they are the ones every district purchases in bulk every few years arriving wrapped in shiny plastic. Of course, with the arrival and implementation of these reading curriculums we were asked to mirror them with fidelity, prevented from deterring from the teacher's guides in the delivery of instruction.

In the field, we call such methods "scripted curriculum." The reference is easy to understand. For example, my teaching partners and I would teach the same curriculum, in the same format, from day to day, explicitly following the teacher's guide. We weren't allowed to deviate from this schedule. Where did this leave the students who couldn't keep up?

Even if the majority of the class struggled, we still had to assess. Even for students below grade level, we still had to give grade-level curriculum and intervention programs. When we thought about how to guide our instruction, it always came from the perspective of, "Which program will be the best to get our students to grade-level achievement? Which program will close that achievement gap the fastest? Which program will get students who are two years behind up to grade level by 3rd grade?" As instructional specialists entrusted by the district, it always seemed as though we were playing catch up.

I have come to realize that the solution does not come from a prefabricated curriculum. Real change for students comes when we as educators know how our students are learning and understanding the content of our instruction. According to Arwood (2011), 95% (or more) of the population thinks with a visual learning system, while the other 5% use auditory learning systems. Visual learners make connections to concepts by creating pictures in their head to remember the concepts, where auditory thinkers take information and translate it into the sound of their own voice in their head.

Learning these differences between visual and auditory thinking has opened my eyes to the fact that as an instructional coach, I need to re-evaluate the techniques, strategies and curriculum that my district uses to teach children how to acquire literacy skills. If our goal is to promote reading, writing, listening, thinking, viewing, speaking, and calculating – all the *true* qualities of literacy (Arwood, 2011), then we should be providing students with authentic opportunities to practice all of these competencies, not just teaching patterns from a box.

Now I know that if we want to promote higher order thinking, what we need to focus on is acquiring higher levels of language function in our children. Since language names our thinking (Arwood, 2011), language remains the most important factor of Neuro-Education theory in helping increase cognition. The use of language in the brain helps acquire new ideas and in the mind to name and refine concepts is extremely powerful.

In fact, many districts flock to implement "brain-based curriculum" or "brain-training" programs based off of marketing alone. Representatives from large corporations make pitches to district leaders and tout "large gains" in memory and vocabulary acquisition while using their products. The truth is, however, that there is no other substitute for the study of language function when considering how the brain operates. Language is the glue that holds all cognitive processes together. Without it, marketers are left promoting just hype.

Typically, we think of acquiring language as learning the structures of language; parts of speech, words, and sentence structure. But it is more than that. Arwood (2011) states that children can easily imitate the patterns of the structures, but this is not evidence of true learning. Instead, they must learn the underlying meanings as part of a language acquisition process that is greater than the sum of structures. Language structures plus the learning of language for thinking is the focus of acquiring language. In order to begin this paradigm shift from teaching patterns to helping students acquire literacy, we must understand the stages of how language functions for each individual learner.

Making Use of "P.D" Time

As an instructional coach I offer professional development surrounding a multitude of topics. However, professional training opportunities are only as good as the methods being presented, and more importantly, the theories used to drive these methods. During one weekend, I attended an educational workshop put on by Dr. Ellyn Arwood at the University of Portland. The information she provided ended up inspiring me to change my approach in working with the other teachers at my school.

The first step in getting educators to see how their students function linguistically is to understand the four developmental stages as explained by Arwood (2011) and Piaget (1959). Now, the teacher education programs I know of do in fact emphasize the cognitive development stages of children; but, these labels have little to no emphasis on the stages of language function for the learner. For example, a third grade student could be classified as in the "concrete" level because they exist within the seven to eleven year old age range that this entails. However, this student may not function socially or linguistically at the same developmental level of his peers.

As a quick primer, Arwood (2011) describes that language names our thinking. As students progress as learners through developmental stages of growing up, so too does their level of acquiring levels of language that allows them to think, see, calculate, make meaning of, and socialize in the world around them. Under neurotypical development, the stages of language function match with a child's social and cognitive development. However, for some learners, there exists a gap between one or more of these areas that greatly impacts a learner's ability to function in the world.

Many of these students fall behind their peers because they have not been taught in the way that their learning systems create meaning: through a visual cognition. Therefore, they are now developmentally "lagging" behind their peers. Thus, in one class, you may have students all around the same age, from the same walk of life, but all possessing vastly different levels of language, which impacts their ability to navigate the classroom and world around them.

Informing teachers of these language function stages through professional development opportunities would improve their instruction and hopefully have major benefits to their students. Since in my job I have limited time to devote to going in-depth into major language theories with fellow educators, I feel that the most beneficial impact I have in imparting this knowledge is to provide opportunities for modeling instructional techniques, teaching strategies, and giving teachers the background knowledge on why it is best practice to do these with their students. I feel it is my job to take big ideas and make them manageable and practical for implementation in our classrooms.

Structure vs. Function of Language

Pre-language: (Birth - 2 Years) • Beginning pre-language learners function in a pre-production, or silent period • Adults must interpret the intended meaning for all pre-language communication • Pre-language learners may communicate with hand gestures, eyes, and face before speech • Learners may exhibit undifferentiated vocalization before telegraphic, or two-word, verbalizing
Restricted Language (3 - 7 Years) • In restricted language function, the listener must infer meaning; consequently, conversation is not yet shared with mutual real understanding from both parties • Preoperational communicators function with spontaneous imitation • Language is restricted to communicating about basic semantic relationships (agent, action, object) of the "here and now" • Learners begin to expand: grow their language; extend: seek out semantic meaning to classify; and modulate: modify language structures to change the meanings of words
Language Function (7 – 11 Years) • At a concrete level of language function, a learner is able to give and take in a conversation in a comprehensible manner using "we" language • Learners have developed an infinite, or fully-formed, grammar • Learners begin to flourish in all areas of literacy: • Their language is flexible: they can apply their own concepts to other settings, and displaced: concepts outside of the "here and now" are studied and understood • Language is efficient: not redundant • In regards to semanticity, or conveyed meaning, concrete learners are able to speak about share referents that are not in the immediate environment
Linguistic Function (11 + Years) • Formal learners utilize symbolization, in which symbols represent ideas • Language use represents highly developed concepts in all semantic fields • Learner now acquires non-tangible concepts, including fluency with time

Table 10.1: Summary of Language Functions by Developmental Level
Figure © 2017 Arwood & Merideth

In working at an elementary school as an instructional coach, one can only hope that I would see learners essentially go through all three stages of language development as outlined in the book Language Function by Dr. Arwood (2011): prelanguage function, language function and linguistic function, and become fully literate with a linguistic language function and formal cognition. Prelanguage function is thinking that occurs about people, their objects, and their actions before a child develops a full grammar. Language function is the underlying cognitive understanding or thinking that language represents. Linguistic function is the most complex use of language to extend meaning of concepts and to expand the structures of language into formal thinking (Arwood, 2011). Table 10.1 presents a summary of how language functions for a child at the four different developmental stages.

It is crucial that when looking at our students and determining what learning needs they have, we would take into account language structure, including the forms of language (words, phrases, parts of speech, etc.), language function, the thinking of language, and how they interact. A child acquires their language in order to function in the world through the Neuro-semantic Language Learning System and becoming literate (speaking, reading, writing, thinking, viewing, listening and calculating) is greater than adding language structures (Arwood, 2011).

In my school, we have been using literacy programs and curriculum that have focused solely on the development of products, such as phonology, semantics, syntax and morphology. We have drilled and taught students the patterns and skills of language structure by learning sounds, taking those sounds and creating words, taking those words and creating grammatical sentences, while teaching vocabulary. This is a stair-step approach to learning and the brain tends to disengage because the focus is on patterns and skills, not meaning (Arwood, 2011; Mazard, et al., 2005).

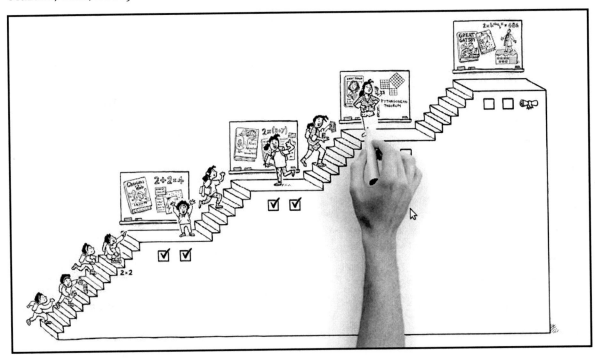

Figure 10.2: Stair-Step Model of Sequential Learning
Image © 2017 Council for Great City Schools, Used with permission

Figure 10.2 is a diagram produced by the Council for Great City Schools (2017) that advocates for educators to utilize a stair-step model when teaching the Common Core Academic Standards. In this figure, math literacy is purported to be learned through a series of incremental concepts that all build upon one another. Many educational philosophies and organizations structure their teaching methodology based off of this approach. This occurs even today despite a multitude of research that shows that the brain does not learn sequentially, but rather as in a spiral, where new information is continuously being connected to old information (Anderson, 2010; Arwood, 2011). See Figure 10.3 for an illustration of brain-based learning being modeled after a spiral diagram.

The majority of schools in the United States follow a stair-step model to educational practice (Arwood, 2011; Robb, 2016). Under this model, if a student has not met their grade level proficiency in my building, they are put into a replacement literacy curriculum. These literacy programs have focused on the structures of language and not the process of acquiring language function. As a result, we have continued to see gaps in the achievement levels of our students. With the implementation of the Common Core State Standards (CCSS), we have begun to realize that these sound-based programs will not get our students to achieve and become the literate college and career ready people needed in our society.

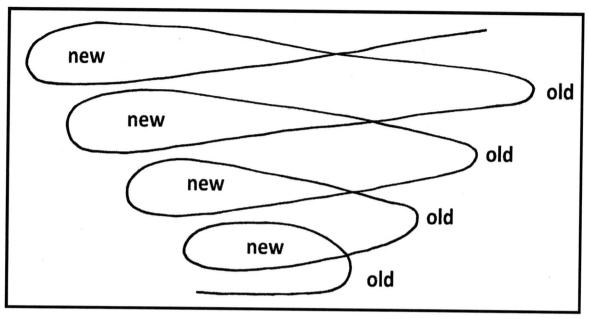

Figure 10.3: Brain-Based Learning Follows a Spiral Model
Image © 2017 APRICOT Inc., Used with permission

With the CCSS, students need not only phonics-based programs to promote literacy, but the ability to be exposed to a balanced reading program where all areas of literacy can be addressed equally. As a result of my efforts to infuse the study of language function into the curriculum, our school is slowly moving away from the emphasis on sound-based curriculums, but as a whole, we are not completely confident in how to proceed. With the Common Core Standards we still need to make sure students have the foundational skills for reading, writing, listening and speaking, but also need the pathway to access meaning and understanding of high level depths of knowledge. Somehow we need to bridge those skills together for our students in a meaningful way.

Language is the Cornerstone to Literacy

As the instructional coach at our school, I have slowly introduced these language function concepts and strategies with teachers to get them to understand that we need to view literacy as a process of language acquisition. Moreover, my goal is to convince fellow educators that increasing the level of language function for our children is the tide that lifts all boats of student achievement. What this means is that working on individual isolated skills such as sound to letter correspondence may increase a child's ability to read words on a page. But, increasing the level of language function for that same child increases their other areas of literacy: *speaking, reading, writing, thinking, viewing, listening and calculating.* If we want to see lasting changes to the minds and brains of the students at our schools, focusing on the latter provides much more bang for our buck.

As educators, we need to gain a deeper understanding of how language is acquired and use that knowledge to guide the way we instruct our students and the way we set up environments. All efforts made by adults in schools should encourage the cognitive understanding of language. Literacy is not acquired through drill and practice, memorization, repetition, and regurgitating of language structures. Instead, we need to focus on students learning concepts - the structures will be learned later through the functions of language. If we continue to focus on structural patterns, the students are just going to give back what we have put into their learning system. They will not "own" their own knowledge. If we teach concepts, then the children will learn and use language to name what they learn. We should be scaffolding, assigning language to concepts to create meaning.

The children that we get in our classrooms need to be exposed to language structures from the people around them, which in this case, would be us, the educators. We need to provide opportunities where children are immersed in a language-rich environment, where the focus is on acquiring the uses of English as a natural function of their thinking. Environments are richest for growth where teachers and students are using language constantly by modeling, explaining and referring to their thinking, through reading, writing, speaking and listening. Understanding the way language functions for learning concepts is the key in developing the literacy of our students.

New Strategies for Increased Language Function

In order to promote higher order literacy strategies among my school's student population, I have taken the foundations gleaned from Arwood's Neuro-Education Model to some teachers at my school and suggested they start implementing the strategies. I have gradually introduced some Viconic Language Methods to teachers by modeling these strategies in their classrooms with their students. Some of the strategies that I have shared and modeled are "I" Stories, picture dictionaries, and gestural signs.

In an "I" Story the teacher and/or the students begin the lesson by telling and drawing out a story about themselves. In order for students to fully access the story (in other words, see the pictures in the teacher's head), they draw out "who, what, when, where, how, and why" of the event or context. While drawing it out, the author uses language to talk about the event and then writes the language on the drawing by labeling.

The neuroeducation based rationale for starting instruction with an "I" story is that all children learn ideas first at a preoperational level; meaning, by allowing themselves to access the concept through the lens of a beginner. Many teachers, on the other hand, start their instruction at too high a level, and students get lost. For example, if a class is studying bees, many third grade teachers simply start by reading "fun facts" about a bee or watching a video about bee colonies. For many visual learners, this will not provide enough context for them to "hook into" the lesson. These kids are still trying to figure out how they relate to bees.

Instead, by having the teacher share their "I" story, and then asking the students to write their own, all students now can access the material at a low enough level. Some questions to facilitate "I" stories might include, "Have they ever seen a bee? Have they been stung by a bee? Have they seen different kinds of bees? Have they tasted bee honey?" etc. The use of "I" stories also mirrors what happens in the brain: new information needs to be connected to existing information in order for it to "stick" with the learner. Showing a video or listing of fun facts does not provide enough context for many visual learners to start their learning journey.

Picture dictionaries are a way for students to interact with language by spelling, writing, drawing, reading and speaking. Students write the shape of a correctly spelled word, read the word, bubble around the word and draw a personal visual representation of the word. The personal visual representation is a way for the students to assign meaning to the word that has meaning to the individual who draws it. Students shouldn't all draw the same thing. The drawing should be what the student visualizes when they see, hear or read that word. Figure 10.4 shows a picture dictionary that an adult has drawn out to illustrate the concepts students will need to know in an art class.

Using gestural signs is another strategy that I have shared with teachers. These are non-verbal gestures and actions that students create to show understanding of concepts. Just like with the drawing of the visual representations in the picture dictionaries, the gestures are student generated. The student creates it because it has meaning for that individual. If a student is given a word or concept, they think of the meaning and create a gesture of what that means for them.

I have also helped teachers plan units with these strategies in mind. More importantly, I have sat down with teachers and talked through the theories, so they understand how meaningful these strategies are for the students in their classrooms. I have tried to get them to realize that children go through these

Figure 10.4: Picture Dictionary for Art Class
Image © 2017 M. Poulson, Used with permission

language stages along with the cognition stages. They also have learning systems that don't match with the way we deliver our instruction. So by introducing teachers to these theories and strategies, I hope that we will start to change the way we view our students' learning and the way we deliver our instruction.

Strategies in Kindergarten

On one occasion, a kindergarten teacher came to me wanting help in teaching her students about the life cycle of a butterfly. I had shared some of these theories and strategies with this teacher and was eager to help her implement them in her lesson. The butterfly's life cycle is a formal level of information – much too challenging for six and seven year olds to be able to understand. The students in her class typically would be at a lower preoperational level of cognition (three to five years old). We needed to provide a way to teach this material in a way that the children's learning systems could access the material; in other words, so their brains could convert patterns into concepts.

To introduce the unit and to help make connections for the students, we decided to start with the "I" story strategy. This would take the formal level of information down to a preoperational level where the students could see themselves in their own pictures. Drawing out the information contained in the "I" story increases academic language, a key precursor to increasing literacy functions. The context of the picture revolves around her students and how they see themselves in their own pictures and learning. The "I" Story provides context in an event based way and the more information about who, what, where, when, how and why, the more the children learn about the context or event (Arwood, 2011).

Moreover, when doing an "I" story, be aware of the strategy of using visually rich language. This is important because the more details one puts in to the story, the easier it is for the students to create visual mental meaning. As the teacher tells the story, I would suggest they layer the language to provide students with a visual of what the idea looks like. In the past, I thought that by simply using high academic vocabulary words and explaining their meaning, the students would be exposed to higher level thinking and understand the words. What I have since learned is that I need to provide more details and explicit language for the students to "see" the picture of the word in their heads. They need the word to be developed into a concept that will have meaning to them, not just be able to use the word in a sentence. The concepts need to be formed because once a concept is formed, the brain will not get rid of it. Concepts are unique and once acquired, are specific to each student.

After modeling an "I" Story for the students, as a class they can create picture dictionaries based on the words the teacher used in her story. This would help students start to create visual layers of the words and the concepts. The teacher can then have the students draw out their own story. Then the students can tell their story, and the teacher can add the words to their pictures. She would be re-tagging their ideas. She would write the word, and then the students could add it to their picture dictionaries. As a class they can develop picture dictionaries to help do their own writing of their drawings. By using the picture dictionaries, the students can trace the word, draw the concept attached to the word and bubble the word. By doing these components of the picture dictionaries, the students are layering the visual-motor patterns of the word thus creating a concept (Arwood, 2011).

Figure 10.5 shows an example of a story created by a student after the target vocabulary words had been written in a picture dictionary and drawn out in front of the class.

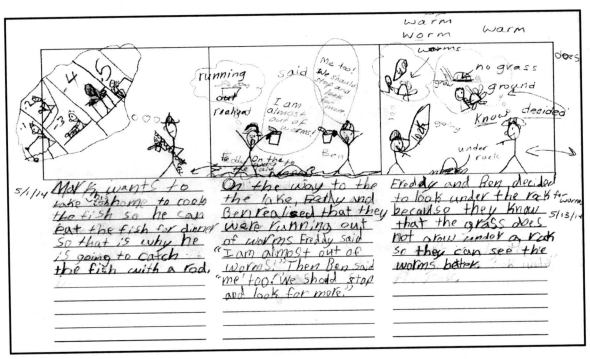

Figure 10.5: Drawing out the Events of a Story
Image © 2017 B. Robb, Used with permission

For these kindergarteners, I would type up the words for them as examples because it is important for them to be able to have the letters look the same and be in proportion to each other. The students can trace these letters, draw the pictures with the idea of the word and bubble the word. When tagging new words in their pictures, the teacher can use hand-over-hand when writing the word. This would be adding another layer to the concept of the word. Students need to see the written patterns as movements of the hand shapes to form visual-motor patterns that will become written and drawn concepts (Arwood, 2011). I also would suggest that this teacher create a word wall using the words they have created with their picture dictionaries.

Another way to add layers to the concepts of the words is by using gestural signs. So for instance, if the words are butterfly, caterpillar, egg, hatch, etc., as a class we can come up with gestural signs for the meaning of the words. This adds another layer to their visual-motor learning system. Every time they use the word, they use the sign. This will help form the concepts of the words.

After the students have written about their drawing, they can share their stories with others. By writing their stories, it provides the students with a preoperational task. When shared with others it becomes concrete to others. It is taking this task from the "me" stage to the "we" stage that truly builds language function in the brain. Since all the students are writing about the same thing, just using their own language, they all have the context of what the speaker is saying. It is a shared experience where the listener can understand the point of view of someone else and understand the concepts too.

Illustrative Case Study – Struggling Second Grader

One particular case study provides an example of how incorporating neuroeducation methodology into a classroom setting can have increased literacy success for visual language learners. A student in a second grade classroom was struggling with learning how to read. Her first grade teacher and her mother noticed her inability to retain skills required to decode words for reading, and at the end of the school year were very concerned. When she entered second grade this fall, she was immediately placed in a small reading group with a skilled paraprofessional. In typical fashion at most schools, the reading intervention focused on the phonics skills of sounding out, blending and recoding words. The paraprofessional was instructed to use reading strategies that focused on word sorts with word families, digraphs, blends, etc., pictures and text that used these word patterns in context. For the other students in this small group, these strategies were proving to be working, but not for this girl.

I conferred with our special education teacher, who had also received training in neuroeducation methodology. We met with the classroom teacher and paraprofessional and together we came up with a plan to use "I" stories as a way for her to connect her learning and make meaning through language. Using the background knowledge that the student had learned in her classroom from a unit on ants, the paraprofessional used an "I" story about walking to school and seeing ants. We needed to focus on present tense verbs such as walk and see. The paraprofessional wrote her "I" story with pictures, labeling the pictures and writing the story in simple language. She repeated this process and added in a visual vocabulary. They took five words from the story, wrote them, bubbled them and drew pictures to represent the meaning for the girl. After they repeated that process several times, the girl wrote her own "I" Story. This was very successful. She drew a picture, labeled it and wrote her story that represented the picture. The words were all spelled correctly. Her teacher did notice that the ideas she acquired via the "I" Story had crossed over in to her other writing and she could see improvement in her work.

This was one small example of how the use of language helped this girl with an area she was struggling in. Now, this girl has a long way to go in her journey of acquiring language, reading, and the other skills of literacy. She definitely saw visual patterns in her learning and these strategies of bubbling the vocabulary words, writing these words in context and repeating these patterns have helped her create meaning. These are small steps in making meaning for her, and will need to be continued for her to be successful. Her teacher has incorporated the use of visual vocabulary for her entire class. For every unit they are learning, she uses this strategy for the vocabulary words that are necessary for creating meaning for the students. We will continue our efforts of language acquisition for this student in hopes that we will continue to see gains in her learning.

Visual Strategies in a Second Language

Part of my job as an instructional specialist involves working with children who are learning English as a second language (ELLs). Our school population currently averages around 500 students. According to the 2012-2013 school year our school demographics were 65% Hispanic, 28% White, 2% Multi-Racial, 2% American Indian/Alaska Native, 1% Asian, 1% Native Hawaiian/Pacific Islander and <1% Black/Native American. When I started at this school 14 years ago the demographics were the opposite with about 65% White and 30% Hispanic and only about 50% economically disadvantaged. With this shift in population, also comes a shift in the learning needs of our students and the way we approach our instruction. Our English Language Learners need language instruction that supports the receptive, productive and, interactive language modalities. Along with the academic language, our ELL population also needs support with the functions of the English language.

If teachers are aware of the differences between auditory and visual learning systems, language function stages and the stages of cognitive development of their students, then hopefully we can start changing our instructional practices to create more meaning and conceptualized learning for our students. Focusing on the acquisition of language through concepts and patterns, one would hope that a child would develop an intact first language. For many students in our schools today, they are learning a second language. In my school, many students have Spanish as their first language and are acquiring a second language, which is English.

If a student has an intact first language, then the learner has already acquired the underlying semantic concepts, but is just trying to find the patterns of the new language. The visual learner, who is learning a new language, needs to use language to name what they learn. They need things to be re-tagged, or named in the second language. They already know it in their native language, now they need the language patterns of the second language.

Research suggests that re-tagging a second language using the first language as a basis shows great success. The "Jim Cummins" position of common underlying proficiencies is the belief that a second language and the primary language have a shared foundation, in that once something is learned in the primary language it has formed a basis for learning in any language (Diaz-Rico, 2010). For example, in the kindergarten classroom, once a student learns the life cycle in their primary language, the concept is the same in any language. They don't need to learn the concept of a life cycle; they just need to learn the content specific words in the new language.

This makes the idea of transferring ideas and concepts to the second language possible if these concepts have been learned in the first language. With the understanding of common underlying proficiencies, teachers need to be aware that although an ELL may appear to be fluently speaking English they may be lacking the necessary knowledge for understanding and comprehending in a second language. As teachers we need to provide academic language support so that ELLs can have the opportunity to catch up to the academic language level of their monolingual peers. Students who learn English as a second language typically acquire oral language proficiency (BICS) in two or three years' time, while academic language (CALP) may require between five and seven years or up to ten years to acquire (A. Brice & R. Brice, 2009).

It seems that if we focus on teaching all students using language function, then they have a better chance at achieving academic language proficiency in both languages. An instructional program for bilingual students where language growth is vital would emphasize growth in cognitive skills, academic topics, and critical language skills (A. Brice & R. Brice, 2009). This statement again would require the need to focus instruction of language function over sound-based instruction. The need for the brain to learn patterns to form concepts, no matter what language you are learning, would be the foundation for acquiring any language.

For many of the students in my school, they are from Spanish speaking families but are learning both English and Spanish at the same time. They are emerging bilinguals and may not necessarily be higher in one over the other. Their level of proficiency in their first language is possibly the same as their level of proficiency in their second language. Again, this calls for instruction to be focused on using language function as a means for acquiring language and literacy skills. The students need to be able to make meaning and form concepts that are unique to them.

If we just give students the structures of language, again they are just repeating back what they took in. If we give them access to cognitive and visual language appropriate instruction, then the acquisition will come through layering, scaffolding, visually rich language, appropriate strategies and visual-motor patterning instruction to fit their learning systems. In either language, we need to teach students the way they acquire concepts. We need to pay attention to their learning systems and develop higher order cognition all the while scaffolding the language function stages so we can get learners to the formal linguistic level.

Conclusion

As I continue in this journey, of helping teachers recognize the importance of helping students acquire language, I will continue reinforcing these strategies and skills in their classrooms. One of the strengths of these strategies is their ability to be grafted onto existing lessons and units with ease. As a school we are using a lot of the GLAD (Guided Language Acquisition Design) strategies to help our ELL's gain linguistic fluency to facilitate success. It is clear to me that while these strategies are extremely beneficial, it is necessary to incorporate other strategies as well. For example, it is simple to add visual vocabulary to GLAD strategies to build conceptual meaning. We can incorporate total physical response alongside gestural signs to create personally relevant meaning. We can take the strategies we use from day to day, incorporate even more language strategies to make effective instructional routines and pathways to understanding for our students.

I will continue to provide background knowledge to my fellow educators and stress the importance of understanding the stages of language function and how this affects our students' learning. By incorporating these language acquisition strategies into our instruction, students will derive substantial academic benefit. Beyond scholastic achievement, students' ability to comprehend a higher level of knowledge will both enrich and encourage further understanding of all aspects of their world. As educators, it is our goal for students to independently utilize language in thinking critically and problem-solving. To guide our students on this journey it is imperative that we not only scaffold their learning, but also be intentional in our instruction of the language necessary to grant linguistic proficiency in both the classroom, and the world. .

Summary of Neuro-Education Methods

From the lens of neuroscience, layering instructional methods is a critical component of conceptual development. As neurons make connections with other neurons, those connections form recognizable patterns. As those connections network with other connections of neurons, the patterns become conceptual networks in the brain. Every overlapping experience adds breadth and depth to the cortical network in the brain.

Through a cognitive psychology lens, we understand that students' cognitive development occurs in stages. From preoperational (I, me, mine), to concrete operational (logic & rules), and formal (abstract concepts), students perceptions of the world evolve.

Understanding where students are in their cognitive development allows teachers to more effectively support learning.

The language lens reveals that language names our thinking. For the majority of students who possess a visual learning system, their language uses mental images to form concepts. Teachers can use rich language that helps the student to "see" the concept in a variety of overlapping ways. By using viconic language strategies and layering concepts, teachers can support students' conceptual understanding and raise their cognitive level of thinking. This author utilized all three of these fields of knowledge in order to provide neuroeducation methodology to her students and other teachers. As a result, she was able to find success helping English Language Learners and native speakers acquire refined literacy skills.

Chapter 11

Seeing How to Organize:
Why Students Don't Use Planners in Middle School

Loretta Walsh, M.Ed., CCC-SLP

Abstract

Many of today's students find it challenging to complete homework on time, turn in their assignments on time, as well as come prepared for class. In response to these struggles, parents and educators attempt to teach their students to use planners. However, many of these same students reject the use of planners because they have not bought into their effectiveness in organizing their lives. The results of a two-year study with a group of sixth grade students, conducted by a speech-language pathologist and special education teacher, showed that students needed more than evidence-based instruction to use a planner. Students need a certain level of cognition and function of language in order to independently use a planner to track their own assignments. This chapter describes how an educator can use assessments to evaluate language function levels, and how these results can be interpreted through the lens of neuroeducation. In addition, the author provides multiple examples of how a school could implement the use of planners to achieve long-lasting usage among students.

About the Author

Loretta Walsh has worked in the public school setting as a speech-language pathologist for over 30 years. She was introduced to Dr. Ellyn Arwood and the Neuro-semantic Language Learning Theory (NsLLT) early in her career. Over the course of her profession, Ms. Walsh has applied the principles and practices of this theory to students on her caseload, and incorporated them into the classroom setting while co-teaching with general and special education teachers. Utilizing the NsLLT, she served as a consultant to a variety of educational professionals including teachers, counselors, school psychologists, nurses and administrators. Ms. Walsh considers the NsLLT to be the foundation and substance of the work she does with students, professionals and families alike.

Introduction

Faced with a caseload of middle school students who were struggling with planning and organization, this author attended a neuroeducation workshop put on by Dr. Ellyn Arwood that focused on innovative teaching methods using visual language strategies. During the workshop, a topic of discussion by the participants arose: "Why don't kids use their planners?" A follow-up conversation between this author and her principal led the author to the idea of developing a series of lessons to teach middle school students how to use a planner using visual language teaching methods.

When students reach middle school, parents and teachers expect that they should be able to use a school planner to write down assignments, complete their homework on time, and submit homework on time. But even in middle school, many parent/teacher conference discussions center on the lack organizational skills and the difficulty with on time homework completion. From the adult's perspective, the expectations are clear – the student should use the planner in the manner in which they have been instructed. So, why aren't middle schoolers successfully planning tasks and using organizational skills to be prepared to participate in class and complete assignments on time?

A typical parent/teacher response is that students are "lazy" or "unmotivated." Many believe there are other issues involved, but are at a loss to identify those issues. Sometimes, the deficiency in organization and follow-through is excused as a "lack of brain maturation." After all, the prefrontal cortex region, which is required for planning and execution, is still developing in the adolescent brain (Jernigan et al., 1991; Reyna et al., 2012; Sowell et al., 2003). But these same students have no problem planning what they will do after school with friends or how to get to an after-school job on time. These examples show that adolescents can indeed plan when the goals are meaningful to them.

After collaborating with Dr. Arwood, a university professor who performs research in the areas of thinking and learning, the author began to develop a series of lessons. She created a unit to be co-taught with a colleague in special education, Julie Schile. The students receiving this instruction were ten 6th graders, selected because their teachers identified them as needing assistance with organizational skills. All students in the group received general education programming. Three students received no special education service; four students received learning support and speech-language services; two students received only learning support services; and one student received only speech-language services. The group met for thirty minutes, three times a week. What follows is an overview of the visual language curriculum designed to help increase the students' cognition in the area of time management, as well as the outcome of the project and some insights into the question, "Why don't students use their planners?"

Methods

In developing the series of lessons, the intent from the outset was to make the organizational, time-based lessons "user friendly" so that any educator could pick up the lessons as a curriculum supplement and incorporate them into existing curriculum and learning strategies. Each lesson followed the same format of identifying the lesson objective, providing a desired student outcome, listing instructional procedures, and suggesting materials needed. There was no specific timeline indicated for completing each lesson, however each lesson was designed to build upon the previous lesson. The lessons were intended to help students learn how to measure time, use a planner for tracking both time and assignments, and be successful in turning in assignments on time. To accompany the curriculum, a customized planner was created for students to use. The planner was arranged to facilitate ease of use, with sufficient space for writing in assignments, and with a place to record activities in a combination of month, day, and time-of-day occurrences. Setting up the planner in this manner allowed for cross-referencing activities in triplicate, so the student could see the days and months as a series of pictured-event sets (Arwood, 2001). For an example, see Figure 11.1.

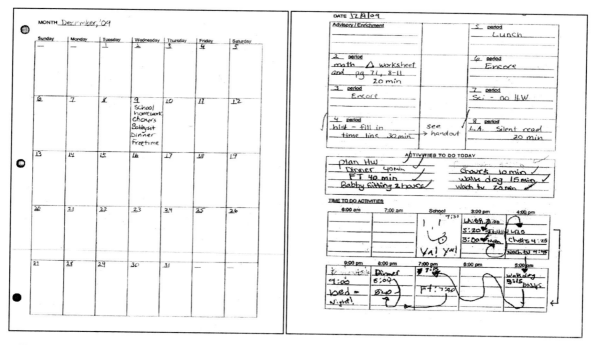

Figure 11.1: Cross-referencing activities on monthly & daily pages

Before using their own planners, students were given opportunities to schedule activities in practice planner pages. On the daily page, they were encouraged to check off tasks after they wrote them in the time section to ensure that all activities were scheduled with a time to do them. Additionally, students used arrows in the time-of-day section to show when an activity began and ended, to provide a visual representation of how much time it took to complete the task.

The instructions for each lesson were presented in a manner that would help students understand the "how" and "why" to use a planner. That understanding would be the key to the students' conceptualization of the task and would aid to increase their developmental cognition (Arwood, 2011). In turn, it would foster the likelihood of students using the planner independently.

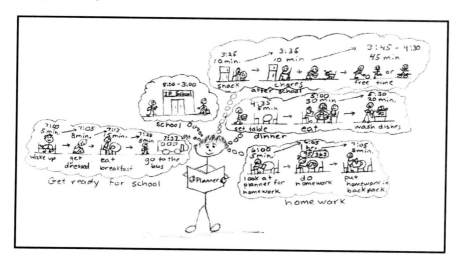

Figure 11.2: A single planner entry consisting of multiple events

The goal of the lessons was to keep the students' learning as the focus, irrespective of the range of academic levels within the group. With that in mind, the educators presented lessons visually, using real-time drawings on large sheets of butcher paper, showing lesson content and a drawn representation of

191

what students looked like as they worked on the various tasks of the lesson. The following example illustrates the idea that some single entries written into a planner are made up of multiple events. This lesson emphasizes that each event's total time allotment needed to be considered when scheduling it into the planner (See Figure 11.2).

Students were also asked to draw their ideas, or "take picture notes" during the lesson to facilitate their understanding. Using this visual language strategy of picture notes (See Figure 11.3) helped the students attend to the presented material and gave them an opportunity to add new information to what they already knew about planners. This scaffolding approach of visually representing new information as it relates to the students' previous information followed the principle of the neuro-semantic learning system: we acquire new meaning only as we are able to attach it to information we already possess (Arwood, 2011).

Figure 11.3: A student's visual notes showing the student thinking about the planner entry

Butcher paper was used, rather than the classroom white board, for two reasons: (1) if a lesson was not completed on a given day, the visual information was saved and did not need to be redrawn the next day; and (2) the ideas on the saved butcher paper could be referred to in later lessons, if needed (See Figure 11.4).

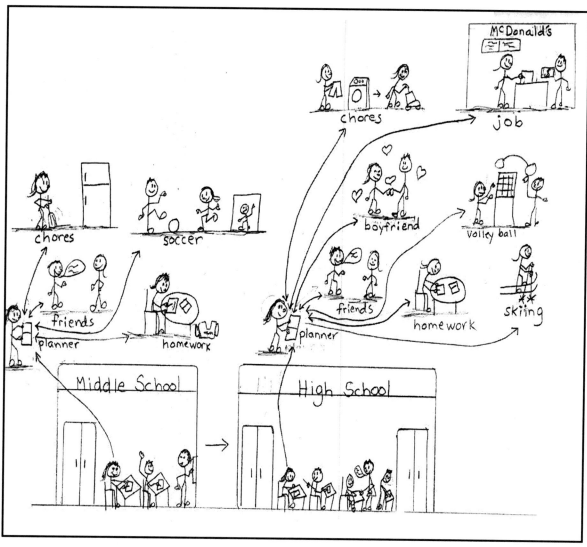

Figure 11.4: Lesson content drawn on butcher paper using visual language (Activities that require planning often increase as students advance from middle school to high school)

Notice that in Figure 11.4, the author has visually represented, on a single paper, the kind of information that some visual thinkers struggle to picture in their minds. The author has drawn all of the events that happen in a child's life to illustrate how these events can be depicted on paper (i.e. in a planner), rather than just stored as a mental checklist. When adults ask students to write in their planners using words only, visual learners struggle because they need to be able to "see" the different tasks in their mind before they can organize them in any logical order. That is why this author always asks students to draw out the items they need to arrange in chronological order before writing them down.

This same idea can be utilized with a child when drawing out the events that occur during a typical school day. Many visual learners who have not acquired organizational strategies forget which days of the week they have certain classes or what times those classes start and end. In addition, these students often forget to take notes in class, collect assignments that a teacher passes out, and bring all of their supplies to school. Figure 11.5 shows a cartoon visual language strategy that can be used to help the student visualize themselves progressing through a typical day. The adult can draw out a school day and label the times that events occur, the people that the child will interact with, the expectations of each class, and what the child should be thinking about when they are in that environment.

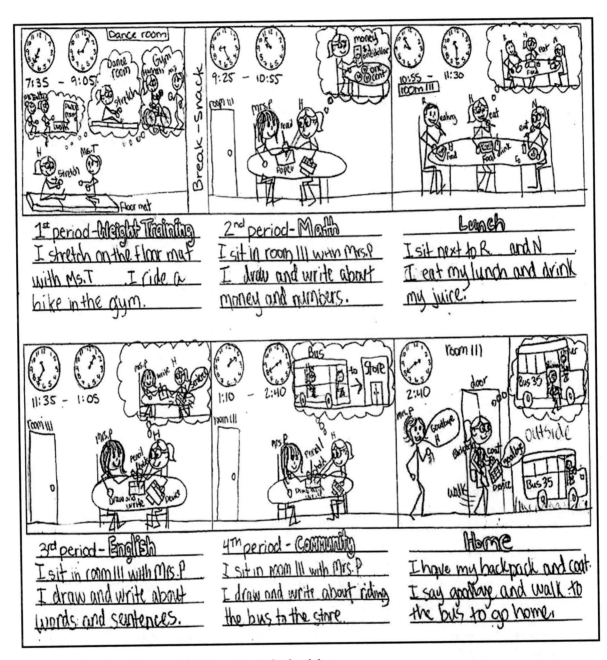

Figure 11.5: Visual cartoon depicting a typical school day
Image © 2017 M. Poulson, Used with permission

Adult vs. Child Understanding of Planners

On the surface, using a daily planner seems like a relatively simple task. From an adult perspective, all one needs to do is get some type of paper or electronic planner, write down what needs to be accomplished and when, and then follow through by looking at the planner regularly and checking off tasks when completed. But adults often forget about all of the interconnected concepts they had to master to effectively use a planner; chief among them is the concept of time.

Many students who struggle with organizational skills do not understand the measurement of time as it relates to planning events. The internal property of time is part of the auditory language processing system. Inherent in the sound wave itself is the raw sensory data that our brain needs in order to understand different measurements of time. For example, when English is spoken orally, it is composed of three main acoustic features: volume (how loud), pitch (how high/low the frequency), and duration (how long each word sounds, and the spaces between words). Figure 11.6 shows a diagram of a sound wave illustrating these components.

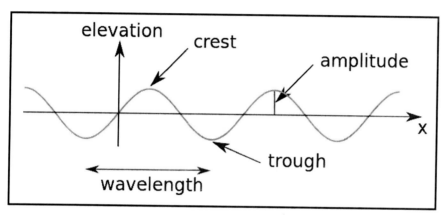

In this image, the *wavelength* represents the total distance from one crest to the next or one trough to the next. It is the distance of each wavelength, as well as the space between the end of one sound wave and the next that from the raw sensory data that our ears and brain will eventually conceptualize as differences in time.

Figure 11.6: Diagram of sound wave
Image © 2017 L. Kraaiennest, Creative Commons

When a child is born with a neurotypical hearing system, this actually means that their ears can process sound and that the auditory pathways in their brain successfully integrate with other brain regions well enough to pass on information through these channels. In fact, many children who are born as visual thinkers can still use their auditory pathways because these channels eventually connect with visual pathways, which can then process the bulk of the information in a way that makes sense to them (Arwood, 2011).

However, many visual thinkers are born with auditory pathways that have not fully integrated with visual pathways to be of significant use for acquiring new information in the brain (Arwood, 2011). These students often lag behind their peers in terms of academic achievement, social competency, and organization. Because many teachers assume that all children can successfully take meaning from auditory instruction, they neglect to provide these children with alternative methods of organizing information. This author hopes that the visual organizing methods presented in this chapter can be used by educators to reach this often-neglected population of learners.

Representing Time as Taking Up Space

How the brain processes sounds impacts how a person is able to use auditory concepts to prioritize and organize multiple events internally. Individuals who process information through the visual language system do not have an internal literacy of time. In order for them to understand time measurement, it helps to represent time visually when planning the events of their day (Arwood, 2011).

Because of this, the first few lessons in the experiment outlined in this chapter were developed to help students recognize that estimating how much time an activity takes to complete may be different from the actual time of completion. The remaining lessons covered: (1) visualizing themselves as part of their planning process when filling out their planner; and (2) understanding why using a planner in middle school can lead to success in adult life (See Table 11.1).

As students draw and visualize themselves doing a task, it becomes easier for them to complete it, because this provides a context that gives the task meaning. Similarly, information, tasks and events of the present can be visually mapped out in a planner. This allows provides a context to which students can attach meaning to a job or duty they will need to do in the future.

Results of Organizational Lessons

What students know	*What students understand*	*What students do*
Lesson: Activities take time to complete	The estimated time may differ from the actual time it takes to complete an activity	Students estimate the time needed to complete activities before recording the actual time it takes to complete them
Lesson: Steps to filling out a planner	Activities must have 3 cross-referent spaces in the planner in order to view the day as a set of pictured events	Selecting a sample day, students fill in the planner using the monthly calendar space, the school day activity space, and time of activities space
Lesson: Future success depends on using a planner	Using a planner to see days as a set of pictured events in the present is necessary to visualize the future	Students draw their life activities backwards, from adulthood goals to their present activities

Table 11.1: Examples of three different lessons

There are several factors the author and Schile considered when determining the criteria to assess the successful use of a planner. Once the students met the requirements of using the planner, they would "graduate" and move to an "enrichment" class. This was a school-wide program to enhance reading, writing and math skills that ran concurrently with the planner class. In order to graduate and move to the enrichment class, a student had to: (1) write his/her activities on the monthly calendar, on the daily page, and in the time-of-day section for the current day and the following day; and (2) have no more than two missing or incomplete assignments each week, for three weeks in a row. Data collected during the first week of the planner class in October showed an average of four missing or incomplete assignments per student.

The time required for students to meet the graduation requirements varied. The amount or type of educational programming students received did not appear to be a determining factor in the rate at which they completed the requirements. For example, one of the three students who graduated in February received learning support and speech-language services, while one student who received only general education did not meet the requirements by the end of the school year (See Table 11.2).

Comparing assignment completion from the onset of the planner class until the end of the school year, nine of ten students showed improvement ranging from 2% to 59%. One student showed a 5% decline in assignment completion. (See Table 11.3)

Month	General education only	General Education and Learning Support	General Education and Speech-language	General Education, Learning Support and Speech-language
February	Student #2		Student #1	Student #9
April		Student #4 Student #8		Student #5
June	Student #3			
Did not meet criteria	Student #7			Student #6 Student #10

Table 11.2: Time students needed to complete graduation requirements listed by their educational programming

After students had graduated and moved to an enrichment class, the author continued to track their use of planners for the remainder of the school year to determine their level of independent compliance. Of the seven students, the percentage of days they used the planner as taught ranged from 40% to 100%. In the fall of the two subsequent years, Walsh interviewed the students who had been in her planner class to follow-up on their planner use. Of the remaining nine students (one had moved), none used it daily and some did not use the planner at all.

Student #1	20% improvement
Student #2	16% improvement
Student #3	30% improvement
Student #4	8% improvement
Student #5	26% improvement
Student #6	59% improvement
Student #7	26% improvement
Student #8	5% decline
Student #9	2% improvement
Student #10	36% improvement

Table 11.3: 3rd trimester improvement in assignment completion as compared to 1st trimester of the school year

Discussion of Results

Faced with the unexpected outcome of this experiment, one might ask, "Why didn't the students continue using their planners?" During the time the students participated in the planner class, they were actively engaged in the lessons and they learned how and why to use a planner. Because understanding the concept of time is a cognitive task that develops with age and experience, perhaps the students did not develop the necessary level of thinking about the concept of time during their involvement in the planner curriculum.

To address this question, the author consulted with Dr. Arwood who commented that the curriculum did not provide the variety and frequency of events needed to increase the students' developmental cognition. It taught the skill of filling out a planner, but left the students with little understanding of why a planner would benefit them and others in their life. Students' ability to independently utilize a planner may not be determined by exposing them to a curriculum that teaches its use. Instead, the underlying determining factor may be the students' developmental cognition (preoperational, concrete) and language function (pre-language, language) (Piaget, 1952 and Arwood, 2011).

In other words, students will only use educational tools that are useful to them. This author had provided the students with an educational device that was more intuitive for their visual thinking needs, and tried to convince the students of the potential benefits of using them daily. However, some of the benefits of using planners, such as turning in homework on time and raising one's grades, may not actually be goals of the students themselves. They may not have seen the importance or relevance of such tasks. Perhaps it would have been more effective to let the students to discover on their own how the planners could benefit their lives. Students filling out devices that were created for them provides learning only at a pattern level, despite how well-constructed the devices are. In order for these organizational patterns to be turned into concepts that the students can apply to tasks, they must have several opportunities to scaffold learning over time, and thus raise their own level of cognition (Arwood, 2011).

Assessment of Language Function

More information was needed to develop the next course of action after receiving the initial results. With input from Arwood, the author decided to look more closely at the students' levels of developmental cognition and language functioning. To do this, she met with each student and collected a verbal language sample by asking the student "What do you do on a typical day?" This is a formalized method of sampling students' levels of language function (TemPro; Arwood & Beggs, 1989).

For example, if a student can reply using language that reflects a typical beginning, middle, and end to an average day, it means they can "see" themselves participating in a multitude of events and organize these events chronologically. Students will often use words like "first," "second," "next," "while," "lastly," etc., which indicate their ability to successfully visually move through time. However, many visual thinkers who struggle with organizational thinking do not list daily events in a logical order, but instead provide an unorganized set of situations that do not appear to be connected in a coherent manner (Arwood, 2011).

Each student in the study completed the TemPro language assessment and Dr. Arwood assisted the author in analyzing the samples. The data revealed eight students were using language that represented thinking comparable to a three to seven year old child, even though their ages were actually between eleven and thirteen. These results showed that all but one of the students in the study functioned at a developmental level that was approximately six to eight years behind their neurotypical peers. Students at this age should be at a "concrete" in their thinking, which means they should be able to think about others in relationship to themselves (Piaget, 1952). However, these students actually functioned at a preoperational level, focusing solely on "me, myself, and I" and not seeing other people in their mental pictures.

Preoperational thinking centers on ideas related only to the student. There was just one student who demonstrated a level of thinking that corresponded to their age group, based on their rule-governed, concrete use of ideas. Given the age range of middle school students, typically 11 to 14, they should be moving from the concrete to the formal (age 11 to adult) level of cognitive development. For examples of how the TemPro language function assessments were analyzed see Table 11.4.

By analyzing the language that students used, this author was able to determine that all of the participants struggled with their ability to function in organizational thinking. As students reach the concrete level of development and move toward the formal level, they should begin to understand the need and the process of managing multiple and concurrent events in their life, separate from what others tell them to do. With that understanding, use of a planner could be easily assimilated into a student's life, because they would be at the conceptual level needed to understand its benefits. Children who think only about themselves cannot explain ideas that are outside of their own experience. They use three- to seven-year-old language, which is indicative of preoperational thinking. At the preoperational level of language functioning, multi-tasking and planner use would not be understood or incorporated. This could explain why the students did not fully buy into the use of planners. They only thought of themselves and did not see the relationship to other events in their lives; the semantic purpose of using a planner had not yet been acquired.

Student #1 (12 years)	
Utterance in Response to Probe: *"What do you do on a typical day?"*	Well, I get up and I go to school, come home, eat food, do my chores and then watch TV and sometimes I take a nap and then get up and play and get ready for bed. Wake up and start all over.
Developmental Level	Preoperational; speaks in terms of here-and-now displacement; no temporal markers
Expectation for Chronological Age	Describe activities beyond here-and-now using a variety of temporal markers
Language Level	Pre-language

Student #2 (12 years)	
Utterance in Response to Probe: *"What do you do on a typical day?"*	I don't know—when I get home, you mean? PROMPT: Whatever you think a typical day is for you. Like, what kind of day—like Monday or a weekend day? It doesn't matter? PROMPT: Just choose a typical day. On a school day I-after school I, uhm, on Tuesday and Thursday I go to volley ball and then, uhm, I go home, do my chores, then my homework and then I have to watch my baby brother until my mom gets home and then take care of my puppy and then go outside and exercise and stuff like that.
Developmental Level	Preoperational; did not demonstrate an understanding of "typical day"; use of non-specific referents
Expectation for Chronological Age	Understand the temporal concept and describe a "typical day" using specific referents
Language Level	Pre-language

Student #7 (12 years)	
Utterance in Response to Probe: *"What do you do on a typical day?"*	On a normal day I, uhm, usually I would go to—I would eat breakfast and then I might do –I would probably leave at 2:20, maybe 2:25 but because I might be late because I have to –I have to eat with my brothers so sometimes we play a little bit.
Developmental Level	Preoperational; not semantically accurate; ideas are not relationally or temporally connected
Expectation for Chronological Age	Utterances are accurately stated so listener does not need to interpret the intent or meaning
Language Level	Pre-language

Student #10 (13 years)	
Utterance in Response to Probe: *"What do you do on a typical day?"*	A typical day for me is going to school, or course; I have to. Uhm, yesterday I did basketball intramurals which I forgot about until I got home. So, uhm . . .and pretty soon I'm going to be heading into basketball season. And that's pretty much it. Oh yeah, and homework.
Developmental Level	Concrete; response addressed the prompt, although activity examples of "typical day" were limited
Expectation for Chronological Age	Talk about a variety of activities of a typical day demonstrating flexibility in language function
Language Level	Pre-language

Table 11.4: Students' levels of developmental cognition and language functioning

With the findings that the majority of the students in the planner class were at the preoperational level of thinking, it would be tempting to conclude that this makes sense because most of the students received some kind of special education service. However, a person's cognitive ability does not necessarily have a 1:1 correlation to their level of functioning. For example, a student may be seen as being "bright" by others but "not working up to capacity," because they don't meet the educational and/or social expectations for their age. Conversely, a student or individual with an identified cognitive disability may have had sufficient, meaningful social and cognitive input to allow them to live and work independently, beyond the level of initial expectations.

Next Steps for Visual Organization

As the data for this study clearly showed, learning how to fill out and use a planner did not result in the middle school students adopting it for themselves in the long-term, even when visual language strategies were used to scaffold lessons. Follow up assessments indicate that independent use of a planner may correlate to an individual's level of cognitive development and their corresponding level of language function. If a student's developmental level is preoperational (age 3-7 years), the child does not possess the expanded language functions, such as displacement, semanticity, flexibility, and productivity that allow the student to think about and plan for future events. Preoperational students cannot *displace* themselves in order to consider what needs to be done beyond the *time* of here-and-now. Their language does not yet have the depth of meaning, or *semanticity*, to help them understand how a variety of events can overlap and impact them, nor how their actions can affect others. This lack of *semanticity* also limits a student's *flexibility* to organize activities, which leads to a significant reduction in their *productivity* (Arwood, 2011). All of these elements of *expanded language function* need to be present for students to independently use the planner as a tool.

Understanding the connection between the students' cognitive development and their language function enabled the instructors to modify the curriculum to include more opportunities for the students to use their language as part of the thinking and planning process. Including multiple ways for students to draw, write, and talk about themselves doing a variety of meaningful activities provided the overlap needed to increase their language function. This allowed them to effectively manage their educational and social lives using a planner.

Possible next steps to promote this higher order thinking could include more individual one-on-one drawing and writing sessions, with the goal of getting students to translate the pictures in their heads to paper, as a shared referent for the educator to see. During these individual drawing and writing sessions, a student should receive help in refining their thinking about time and how much "space" events take up during their day. These sessions could also provide many opportunities to layer understanding about the relationship between moving through time and moving through space during the day.

In addition, students can also get together to share their drawings and writings with each other, allowing them to layer between preoperational thinking (all about themselves) and concrete (considering the ideas of another person). This may also allow them to learn strategies from each other that they had not previously considered. These possible next steps for intervention would help scaffold towards the goal of increasing connections in the brain between old and new information, which is ultimately the most effective way to learn new concepts (Arwood, 2011).

The students in this study did not adopt the usage of planners because their level of cognition about the tasks was not at the appropriate level. It is important that students are thinking at a higher level in order to accomplish multiple cognitive tasks. The teaching of assignment calendar skills alone did not increase the students' level of cognition or the function of their language because it did not provide enough depth on the concepts. Students also need to understand how a planner will help them complete multiple tasks and be present at multiple events throughout the day, week, and month. However, understanding this multiplicity is not enough for students to effectively use planners independently. This can only be achieved when the student understands how their life impacts others with whom they live, work, and play.

Conclusion

Attending school, doing homework, taking care of chores at home, participating in extra-curricular and family events are just a few of the activities in the life of the typical middle school youth. At this age, it is expected that students become more independent in the planning for and carrying out these activities. A planner can be an effective tool to assist in this process, but based on the results of this study, students need to have language development at a concrete level in order to support the higher cognitive activities needed for planning and organizing. The planner curriculum should focus on increasing the language function of the student as an integral part of the use of planners. To facilitate this, it may have been beneficial to include more drawing and writing about how the student's activities impacts others in their life. Providing multiple opportunities for students to see their actions impact others may help them move from the preoperational to the concrete level of cognition.

The challenge for educators is to help students increase their language function and cognitive ability by teaching them to think at a higher level as they do their planning. The primary lesson from this study is that, while teaching students tasks that require help to aid their thinking, educators also need to attend to the development of language, which is the mediator of cognition. This may allow the students to incorporate the use of a planner as part of the natural progression of their cognitive development.

Summary of Neuro-Education Methods

From a neuroscience lens, time itself is an auditory concept. The auditory system, unlike the visual system, processes input over time. The auditory system must decode acoustic input, which comes into the ear over a period of time. This difference between the auditory and visual learning system is a direct result of the differences between light and sound. The large majority of students in schools, especially those requiring special services use an overlapping visual/visual or visual/movement system for learning concepts. For them, learning time-based concepts presents a challenge.

From a cognitive psychology perspective, the formal level of thinking required to successfully use a daily planner is not yet developed in students who operate at a concrete or preoperational level. Preoperational students can only conceive of things that they have seen, heard, or touched. Students operating at the concrete level can extend those experiences to include rules and social expectations.

From a language perspective, students who operate at concrete or preoperational levels lack the expanded language function (displacement) necessary to visualize themselves in a picture that they are not able to see or touch (the future). A full adult grammar is required to gain access to expanded language functions like displacement.

As this study shows, a middle schooler's use of a planner is not based on motivation, cooperation or a desire to please. Rather, it is only as consistent and effective as their developmental cognition and language functioning level allows.

Chapter 12

The Case Against Phonics in Preschool Instruction

Brigette Mahoney, M.Ed.

Abstract

In this chapter, the author presents a review of literature that explores five common modalities for teaching literacy: oral language development; written language development; speech and language delays; strategies for autism spectrum disorder (ASD); and neuroscience and visual learning. The evidence from primary source research studies is explored in each strand to determine which body of work presents the most consistent results. The author concludes that the Viconic Language Methods inspired by Arwood's Neuro-Education methodology are best supported by a wide variety of scientific findings to teach literacy remediation skills. Next, the author completes a six week study using these viconic language strategies to help her Pre-K students attempt to catch up to grade level standards in reading, writing, speaking, listening, viewing, thinking, and calculating – the seven areas of cognition most impacted by literacy skills (Arwood, 2011). The author contrasts the effectiveness of these viconic language strategies with the failures of previous phonics-based instruction that did not promote growth in her students.

About the Author

Brigette Mahoney is a preschool teacher who specializes in reading and literacy remediation. Brigette enjoys focusing her efforts on helping this young and often overlooked population. As part of her master's thesis in education studies, Brigette familiarized herself with the most pertinent areas of research in her field. After being introduced to Arwood's Neuro-Education Model, she conducted a wide-ranging review of dozens of studies in other fields to determine whether to validate or dispute the theoretical claims inherent in this model. Her review of literature found many inquiries that confirmed the tenets shared in this anthology. Brigette continues to fine-tune her own research skills as a practitioner and hopes to share more of her findings in future publications.

Background

Nationally, there is a heightened emphasis on the importance of preschool. Common Core standards have been implemented across the country putting an increased pressure on teachers, especially those in the primary grades who have the task of helping students learn appropriate social skills and academics. Because of the incredible challenges the kindergarten teacher faces, added pressure to make children "school-ready" has been passed down to preschools and pre-kindergarten programs. Many districts have begun assessing their students on the first day of kindergarten to determine reading readiness. Some parochial schools even have a screening system that measures reading and math ability along with school readiness skills, like being able to follow directions and sit still.

Most preschool and kindergarten programs focus on direct instruction of phonics, letters, and sounds. In fact, numerous leaders (e.g. Berninger & Wolf, 2009; Eden & Moats, 2002) within the field of reading literacy advocate for all elementary school children to receive a significant increase in the amount of time spent studying sound-to-letter correspondence. In the field of Education it is widely accepted and believed that this skill is an absolute requirement for children to learn how to read successfully. The thought is that by learning these tools students will be able to tackle unknown words by sounding them out. The accepted idea about reading fluency is that many children lag behind their peers in reading skills because they have not sufficiently practiced these sound-to-letter correspondences (Ehri & Wilce 1985).

The ability to sound words out and therefore read out loud fluently is indeed a useful skill that children need to know how to do in society. However, what many reading specialists neglect to understand is that the act of comprehension and, more importantly, the process of how language functions for that student, are in fact absent from this process of oral reading fluency. By focusing on sounds and letters and neglecting to address the underlying deep semantic structure of how the human brain uses language to name our thinking, we are setting up our students to continue to lag behind their peers who can already read fluently (Arwood, 2011). When readers struggle in our culture, we assume they are deficient. And, because our current educational practices tend to focus solely on one way of teaching reading (phonics), we assume that struggling children simply need more time using these methods in order to catch up to their peers.

Put another way, when a student's brain does not intuitively understand the science of phonics, they are given remediation. Usually intervention consists of increased time in teaching letter and sound knowledge out of context. Why? Because this is the only way the majority of adults in our culture believe learning to read is possible. If a student has been given more individual time using phonics, but they are still not successful, they are labeled as being behind their peers, sometimes diagnosed with a learning disability, and may often have social insecurities as a result.

This chapter will argue that an entirely different method of teaching reading can have more success for those students who have struggled in the past. Considerable evidence, such as Dr. Arwood's Neuro-semantic Language Learning Theory (NsLLT), exists that certain kinds of students can improve their understanding of what they read by being taught with visual strategies. Those with speech and language disabilities show improvements using conversation with a visual component, such as writing down and drawing out ideas. In addition, students who speak different languages show improvement in English when they are shown pictures with associated words, as they are able to connect their first language with English, and actually have more understanding for the concept than their peers who have not been shown pictures.

In the example of viconic language strategies that will be explored in this chapter, Arwood (2011), Arwood & Kaulitz (2007), and Arwood & Young (2000) advocate for teaching every child to read using the principles gleaned from the study of neuroeducation. This exciting new field of study provides abundant evidence that children who struggle to read do so because the instructional methods do not match their natural way of thinking by using visual aids, such as making pictures and movies in their heads. Neuro-Education theory provides a blueprint for how visual thinkers can be taught to read without using any of the sound-based auditory methods that have failed to help them in the past. In particular, this chapter will explore how to teach reading using a plethora of Viconic Language Methods, such as picture dictionaries, hand-over-hand instruction, cartooning, and using semantically rich "because" language.

Introduction

Based on nearly 45 years of research in the fields of reading, communication, and language studies, Dr. Ellyn Arwood (2011) has proposed that approximately 95% of individuals in our society think with a visual symbolizing system. This means that these children and adults alike learn new information best by making pictures in their mind's eye of what they are studying. The brains of *some* visual thinkers can process sound sufficiently to create pictures from the words being used. However, for visual thinkers, this process is always a translation that occurs in their minds, and may not happen automatically (Arwood, 2011).

While some children are able to make the switch from auditory stimuli to visual processes independently, most students, especially those with disabilities, cannot. Indeed, most of the aforementioned research from Arwood has been with students with disabilities. Arwood has used her decades of research in language to inspire many of the methods (such as viconic language strategies) proposed by Neuro-Education theory. These methods have demonstrated great success with elementary aged children; but few practitioners have implemented these strategies with students who were as young as Pre-K. Because this area of research had not been extensively explored, this author sought to determine whether the viconic language strategies inspired by Neuro-Education theory could impact the reading readiness and language ability of Pre-K learners to a sufficient extent.

This author aimed to determine whether using viconic language strategies as the primary method of reading instruction could improve the students' oral language and reading abilities. In her instruction this author would not be working on sound-to-letter correspondence or other auditory skills. This meant that she would not focus on the traditional methods of reading instruction that experts have claimed are necessary for success. If the oral and reading abilities did improve in her students, without her specifically working on them it would mean that learning to read can actually be taught using a combination of visual language instructional methods, and does not require phonics-based instruction.

Of the students in this author's Pre-K classroom, none have diagnosed reading disabilities, though one does have a diagnosed speech disorder. A review of the literature was first conducted to focus on the research that exists on the implementation and theory of visual strategies to increase language and literacy ability in multiple contexts. Research about reading literacy sought to explore the common themes that emerged in the literature: (1) oral language development; (2) written language development; (3) speech and language delays; (4) strategies for autism spectrum disorder (ASD); and (5) neuroscience and visual learning. A brief summary of each strand is presented here to provide a background of established status quo theories currently accepted in the field of reading studies.

Review of Literature

1) *Oral Language Development*

Oral language, sometimes called *expressive and receptive language,* is a well-established predictor of reading ability, according to many researchers. Vocabulary in primary grades is associated with later reading skills (Muter, Hulme, Snowling, & Stevensen, 2004). Vocabulary in early childhood (usually meaning preschool through kindergarten) is currently one of the best long-term predictors of literacy development that can be measured (Gerde & Powell, 2009). A longitudinal study found that vocabulary development in preschool predicted kindergarten and fourth grade reading comprehension and word recognition (Dicksinson & Porche, 2011). Another study found oral language and comprehension parallels between fourth and seventh grades (Dickinson, McCabe, Anastasopoulos, Peisner-Feinberg, & Poe, 2003). A student's development of oral language has an impact on their developing literacy skills, learning, emotional and social development, and life achievement overall (Leyden, Stackhouse, Szczerbinski, 2011). The importance of vocabulary development cannot be understated. There is an expectation that preschool and kindergarten teachers focus on letters and phonics, partly because this is the only method that many educators are aware of. There is much research that supports this strategy. For example, Ehri and Wilce (1985) debate which is more important: visual or phonetic processing. Ultimately they decide phonics is essential, concluding that word recognition is the result of a phonics basis.

However, it should be noted that many of these educators define "visual processing" differently than Dr. Arwood, the author of Neuro-Education theory. For example, many researchers do not distinguish between the semantic complexities of different kinds of visuals, nor do they describe the difference between thinking in a visual manner versus an auditory manner. Because these differences are not included in the questions these researchers ask, it is impossible for these researchers to make conclusions that reflect an understanding of the Neuro-Education theory presented here.

Often researchers advocate for a balanced approach between visual and auditory methods, seeing the merits in both approaches (Vellutino, Tunmer, Jaccard, & Chen, 2007; Muter, Hulme, Snowling, & Stevensen, 2004; Lonigan, Allan, & Lerner, 2011). It is well documented that the development of children's vocabulary plays a role in at least bringing about emergence of phonological awareness, though there is some disagreement about whether oral language skills continue to interact with decoding once phonetic skills have been gained, or whether oral language skills provide the foundation for phonics and then phonics takes over (Dickinson, McCabe, Anastasopoulos, Peisner-Feinberg & Poe, 2003).

Some studies fall outside of these accepted paradigms. There is strong support that suggests, contrary to popular belief, the development of language creates a foundation for phonics and not the other way around. Often children do not have the vocabulary background to be able to support phonics, but phonics is seen as essential and drilled in isolation of any other methodology. For example, Goodman (1967) suggests that drilling phonetic skills actually impedes language learning, and thus, reading ability. This view takes the approach that phonics represents the surface structures of language, while the underlying concepts represent the deeper semantic nature of how humans use language to communicate.

Kindergarten and first grade curricula typically stress letters and sounds, but Lonigan, Allan, and Lerner (2011) found that those who are poor readers by the end of first grade almost never acquire average level reading skills by the end of elementary school. They also found that entering kindergarteners who were not given a strong vocabulary basis were not as inclined to "crack the alphabetic code" (that is, to understand that letters represent sounds which can be put together into words). In contrast, Lundberg (1994) showed that Scandinavian children who had been given rich language backgrounds but had not been taught phonics by age seven could perform well on phonics tests. This provides further evidence that the study of phonics is not a required component in order for students to learn how to read for comprehension.

It is clear to this author that there exists a large body of research about effective strategies to promote reading using auditory methods. However, many of these studies produce contradictory results, which is not surprising to this author because, according to Arwood, only 5-15% of students think using an auditory system. Because we use teaching methods that only match the way that a small percentage of students learn, it is understandable that these methods would be called into question for effectiveness.

In addition, there is little to no research that advocates for using Viconic Language Methods as the primary strategies to promote reading, other than the numerous books written by Dr. Ellyn Arwood and her collaborators. Therefore, while the majority of researchers in the area of reading development advocate for a strong emphasis on phonics and sound-to-letter correspondence as necessary to learning how to read, these authors have not yet been exposed to the alternative methods explored in this chapter. As a result, their findings should be considered as merely one side to a possible multi-part view of literacy.

2) *Written Language Development*

Exposure to print is also an important reading readiness component that involves language. Pairing pictures with written words has been shown to foster print awareness and beginning reading skills in children with autism (Meadan, Ostrosky, Triplett, Michna, & Fettig, 2011). Furthermore, students who are immersed in print rich environments are more prepared in print concept awareness, reading readiness, and word reading than students who practiced isolated words and letters, though not as well prepared as students who had a combined form of instruction (Reutzel, Oda, & Moore 1989).

Although in picture book reading, the students more often pay attention to the pictures, when teachers do point out print or aspects of print, students pay attention to it. Otherwise, non-reading children do not spend a lot of time in storybook reading looking at print compared to looking at pictures. Students internalize information about print and begin to make generalizations about it (Zucker, Jusce, & Piasta 2009).

The evidence collected by these research studies suggests that oral fluency skills only play a role in a student's ability to read out loud, not in their underlying ability to comprehend what they are reading. The students who were exposed to print rich environments at least received the visual layer of being able to see the shapes that words make and match these shapes to their corresponding pictures. If the researchers were following Neuro-Education methods, however, further instruction in visual literacy could have included bubbling the words, drawing out the ideas, tracing the words, pointing to the words, and including these words in picture dictionaries (Arwood, 2011). These extra visual layers are specific to Neuro-Education methodology and were not included in any studies found in the review of literature.

3) *Speech and Language Delays*

There is some research in the field of speech and language pathology that promotes the use of visual supports in helping those with special needs learn to read and communicate better. The components of literacy (reading, writing, calculating, viewing, speaking, and listening) are important for all students to learn, but are crucial for those with disabilities. Over time, some of these children might become unable to function in school without considerable intervention. Literacy rich environments are critical for helping children with language disorders build reading, writing, speaking, and listening skills (Watson, Layton, & Pierce 1994). Wellington & Stackhouse (2011) found that students with speech and language delays benefited from visual strategies such as signing, pictures, symbols, and written words. The more fully their classroom implemented the visual supports, the better success the students had.

The Wellington and Stackhouse (2011) study highlights the movement from a pull-out model to a push-in model for speech pathologists. The hope is that the teachers can collaborate with the speech pathologists to shift from a structural approach in teaching speech and language to a functional approach (Ukrainetz & Blomquist 2002). One study found that when speech pathologists pushed in to create a language-rich program with the classroom teacher, the students (whether diagnosed with a disability or not) performed significantly better on measures of understanding vocabulary, cognitive-linguistic concepts, writing, and spelling. The speech pathologists added listening and writing centers, involved children in authentic literacy events, engaged in problem-solving discussions, promoted discussion of ideas, expanded critical thinking, and created student-led written schedules (Farber & Klein, 1999).

The actions of the researchers to include students who had previously struggled into an inclusive environment with their peers follow the best practices that many in the field of cognitive psychology advocate for (Anderson, 2010). That is, students who are included socially have been shown to more quickly catch up with their peers in literacy skills (Arwood & Young, 2000). Using the methods that Ukrainetz & Blomquist promoted allowed students who had been marginalized to access general education classes. By providing them with a language-rich program that included authentic teaching events to promote literacy (rather than drilling isolated skills), these researchers achieved more profound gains in all areas of social-emotional cognition.

In another case where speech and language pathology concepts were applied to an entire school, similar results were achieved. For example, one school adopted a school-wide approach to language. With additional training, teachers saw the benefits of providing language-rich opportunities to everyone, regardless of whether or not they had a disability. The visual methods they implemented were: objects labeled with pictures, visual schedules, and bringing discussion to the forefront of each of their lessons. The staff also reported fringe benefits such as networking with other staff members, seeing the children excited about the lessons, becoming aware of discrepancies in their own lessons, and seeing children engage and learn language just from their environment.

The success of these programs confirm what Smith and Goodman (2008) have found: that language taught in context and students interacting with informed and informative peers or adults prepares pre-readers for reading to a greater degree than telling children how to read and write using scripted, phonics-based programs. Furthermore, each of these tasks can be thought of as promoting visual thinking in that many involve taking on another's perspective, "seeing them in your picture" (Arwood, 2011; Arwood & Kaulitz, 2007; Arwood & Young, 2000), or seeing oneself as one relates to the community at large. These contextual strategies have indeed found success in helping adults remediate speech and language delays in children.

4) Autism Spectrum Disorder

The area that has received perhaps the most attention for use of visual supports is autism spectrum disorder (ASD). Arwood (2007) has found success with children with ASD using a variety of visual strategies such as cartooning, picture dictionaries, bubbling unfamiliar words, and creating flowcharts (interactive graphic organizers). Dettmer, Simpson, Mysles & Ganz (2000) found that since young children with ASD have problems understanding material presented in auditory ways, visual schedules help to make sense of their days, help them to organize themselves, and lessen their anxiety throughout the day. Meadan, Ostrosky, Triplett, Michna & Fettig (2011) found that using photographs, line drawings, and words paired with visual representations (similar to Arwood's picture dictionaries) aided young children with ASD in conceptualizing new information. They were also successful in implementing rule reminder cards – drawings of children behaving properly in the event that a student was not behaving as expected.

These studies found success because they provided students who had autism with instructional methods that matched the manner in which they think. For example, Arwood (2011) estimates that approximately 95% of learners think in mental pictures/movies. These students do best when the language that is used with them paints a picture in their mind's eye. Figure 12.1 shows an example of one of Arwood's Viconic Language Methods: cartooning expectations for a student who has a job working in a school-run coffee shop [Joe's Boathouse]. Notice that the adult has drawn the student successfully completing all of the required tasks and has included thought bubbles that show what the student should be thinking about as he proceeds through his responsibilities. In addition, all of the objects that the student will need are labeled so that he can recognize them in real life. Lastly, the writing that the adult uses to describe the events closely matches what is depicted. Doing so allows visual thinkers, such as those with ASD, to establish a mental connection between written directions and their visual counterparts in real life.

Despite the knowledge that children with ASD who struggle with social concepts need a plethora of rich language in order to understand what is asked of them, many therapies such as Applied Behavioral Analysis use extremely short commands with children such as "touch swing," "point to dog," "don't pull hair," etc. These commands do not provide enough rich visual language (such as explaining *why* the commands are important); therefore, they set visual thinkers up for failure because they cannot "see" themselves completing what is expected of them. Further Neuro-Education methods to address these issues will be explored later in this chapter.

Figure 12.1: Cartoon Visually Depicting Job Expectations
Image © 2017 M. Poulson, Used with permission

5)   *Neuroscience and Visual Learning*

There is brain research that suggests that visual supports in the classroom may work well for all children, though the applied research on this is sparse. Frey and Fisher's research (2010) into reading and the brain says that the occipital lobe, which is used for object recognition, is also used to recognize words. It attaches to Brocca's and Wernicke's areas, which are the hubs for speech production and reception, respectively. Neural pathways that have

208

already been formed, such as making connections between the shape and meaning of words, are used in reading tasks. The authors suggest that student engagement may be improved with oral and written language to allow children to explore sounds, sights, and meanings of words. Instructing in ways that reinforce connections and visualization make new concepts easier to acquire, learn, and recall which will also benefit the learner. Of the sensory inputs that are available to a learner without a diagnosed disability, Frey and Fisher say visuals are the best single tool to use in learning anything. Pictures consistently trump text or oral presentations and are more likely to be retrieved. They suggest pairing text with pictures.

To present a word as a picture, Arwood and Kaulitz (2007) suggest outlining (bubbling) the word. This way the word can later be recalled as a picture rather than using phonics to recall the word. Goodman (1967) postulated this when he said there is a misconception that graphic input (words) are recorded in the brain as phonological input and decoded bit by bit. Notice here that this misconception appears to provide a rationale for breaking apart words from whole ideas (shapes) into sounds and letters. In other words, we think that the brain acquires a whole idea, and then separates it into small pieces to reconstruct later. However, little to no research supports this idea; and, Arwood (2011) advocates for the opposite interpretation. When students were given words (ideas) as single bubbled shapes, the students were more likely to retain these patterns because the words were visual, not auditory, in nature.

Figure 12.2 shows how the edges of an idea (word) can be bubbled to form a singular shape. In addition, students and adults can add their own graphic interpretations (drawings) onto this shape to provide a visual referent to the idea. By overlapping visual + visual layers (bubbling, shaping, drawing), the brain will retain this image as a visual pattern (Arwood, 2011). Notice that by utilizing this method, no two shapes in the English language will look exactly the same. By drawing out their mental pictures, the artist has created a rich visual context for their idea. Visual thinkers benefit from the use of high-context, relational language, as this is more likely to enter long-term, semantic memory than vocabulary that is presented out of context, such as memorizing definitions (Arwood, 2011; Robb, 2016; Lam, 2016).

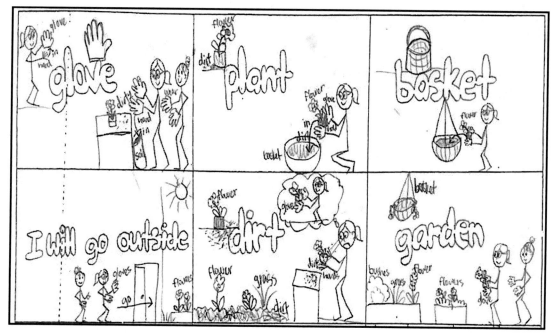

Figure 12.2: Bubbling Shapes of Ideas (Words) and Including Visual Referents
Image © 2017 M. Poulson, Used with permission

Goodman believes that the more language a person has acquired to begin with, the easier it will be to integrate that graphic input into a concept that can later be recalled. Notice, however, that Arwood argues for visual input using shapes of words because this matches the visual metacognition system hypothesized in approximately 95% of neurotypical learners and 100% of students with disabilities. Muter, Hume, Snowling, & Stevensen (2004) agree that word recognition is predicted by underlying language skills.

Other research regarding the brain shows that reading stories activates visual and motor representations in the brain (Speer, Reynolds, Swallow, & Zacks, 2009). This supports theories of language comprehension that a reader's representations of situations are constructed from sensory and motor representations (movies in the head). Brain scans showed that readers understand a story by simulating the events in the story via pictures in their heads and refining and accommodating the simulation when features of the world within the story change. A teacher can ask questions, and use the pictures in picture books as props bringing about deeper semantic meaning (e.g. What is she doing in this picture? Why do you think she is wearing a coat inside?). These studies provide ancillary support to the visual language strategies proposed by Arwood (2011) in this chapter.

Challenges in Implementing Visual Language Teaching in the Classroom

The previous review of literature exposed numerous holes in the presupposition that the teaching of phonics is necessary for students to become better readers. It also provided numerous primary source research studies that indicate that children acquire information best when it is presented using a variety of visual language methods. However, because there exists a strong bias in our educational culture to use auditory methods of instruction (possibly due to a lack of awareness of alternatives), many teachers remain skeptical that such alternatives could indeed be effective. The argument goes, "If I haven't heard about the methods, how indeed can they be so effective?"

There is truth to this sentiment. Nevertheless, teachers are the ones with the most control of the way information is presented in their classroom. Some of the research on visual supports points to teachers not feeling confident in using visual strategies instructionally (Wellington & Stackhouse, 2011). Some teachers understand the merit of visual strategies, but feel they do not have time, or are not able to have a separate instructional method for certain students in addition to meeting the usual classroom demands (Alant, 2003). For visual support to be effective in any educational setting, the professionals need to understand why and how to use visual supports, and that use of such supports allows them to measure the child's learning in a more representative way than other assessments do (Alant, 2003).

Moreover, the assessments that we use in modern U.S. education also reflect a bias to test how well students do completing auditory tasks. For example in a typically developing child it becomes cumbersome to write down every word the child has memorized by the time they are three years old. Therefore, many assessments (Woodcock Johnson, KTEA II, etc.) test for oral vocabulary fluency, such as being able to pronounce words out loud. This method, however, may not reflect a child's visual strengths.

In contrast, the Peabody Picture Vocabulary Test-III, Expressive Vocabulary Test, and Receptive One-Word Picture Vocabulary Test are norm-referenced tests developed to assess young children's language and vocabulary in a representative fashion. However, Ukrainetz and Blomquist (2002) found that when the standardized tests were compared to language samples, there was very little reliability between the four tests. This could mean that none of the tests truly assessed the child's vocabulary, but it is more likely that the standardized tests were not representative of the child's thought processes or language ability, as language samples take the child's own language in a context familiar to them. Any time a standardized reading assessment is used, this is a potential area of concern.

If the purpose of the test is to qualify a child for special education services in an area related to language (i.e. autism spectrum disorder, speech and language, or reading), using a language sample may give more accurate results than a standardized test for an individual child. If the purpose of the test is to inform teaching practice, Cohen (2003) recommends asking the students how they prefer to learn and giving personality tests to find the best test to use. While this may take pressure off the teacher to determine which student learns in which way, personality tests have flaws, and children often are not aware of how they learn best, especially if they have not been trained in metacognition. Arwood (2011) proposes using alternative methods to assess students for how they use language to function in the world, such as gathering a natural language sample and analyzing it for developmental levels. More on this assessment method will be explored later in this chapter.

Creating opportunities for students to think about their learning enables them to think creatively, advance language ability, and become self-reflective. Mandated curriculum creates a classroom environment where there is no time for questions from the child, for imagination, or for creative thought (Soundy & Qiu, 2006). If supported, children can bring their individual way of thinking to the reading process, instilling a positive sense of self-esteem, as they create their own learning (Smith & Goodman, 2008). Reading is a process of the brain; when encountering an unfamiliar word or idea, the reader confirms, rejects, or refines the input based on his or her understanding of the rest of the passage (Goodman, 1967). Johnson-Glenberg (2000) found that being exposed to, visualizing and drawing or writing a picture or text from memory improved metacognition and a poor decoder's comprehension. Metacognition relies on a child's ability to think about how they think, and a discussion within the classroom about each person's metacognition promotes the idea that everyone thinks differently. The way to best do this is by giving them opportunities to contribute to themselves and to the classroom community (Arwood & Young, 2000), and teaching in ways that are compatible with how the learner best learns (Arwood, 2012).

Visual Language Research Study

As acknowledged during the review of literature, this author discovered that few primary source studies exist that utilize a wide variety of visual language methods to teach reading. As a result, this author set out to study whether using the Viconic Language Methods inspired by Neuro-Education theory could more effectively teach the skills of literacy than auditory methods such as teaching sound-to-letter correspondence and teaching isolated vocabulary definitions. Success of the study would be measured by collecting natural language samples of the participating children and analyzing the language developmental level they used to function in their school setting.

This author's Pre-K class is part of a private preschool and daycare in an urban area. The school is connected to a K-8, and many of the graduates of the Pre-K continue their schooling there, though they need to apply and be accepted to do so. The test group in this study was made up of 27 four- and five-year-old students, all of whom are in the Pre-K class. The children are present at the school anywhere from four hours to eleven hours. The majority of their time is spent in educational play: building, creating art, playing pretend, exploring with science materials, and playing board games. Besides rule reminders, most of the person-to-person interaction occurs between the students, not between the students and teachers. Teachers will sometimes pull small groups for formative assessments. Between play times, students are read to and then discuss topics relevant to the area of study, typically in a whole group setting. These teaching periods occur throughout the day and, combined, last for less than two hours.

Most of the children have been a part of the preschool and daycare for several years. The classes the students take during the two years prior to coming to this author's classroom focus primarily on teaching letter recognition, sounds, and rhymes in an effort to promote literacy skills. Despite two years of daily instruction using these methods, many students fail to demonstrate their knowledge of letters and sounds when unguided by a teacher or adult. This means that by the time the students in the study arrive in Pre-K, they can imitate the sound patterns that adults provide them, but they cannot apply these patterns in spontaneous communication. Because they cannot intuitively use sound-based rules to read new words, it is clear that they have not acquired the underlying semantic concepts attached to these skills.

This author has a co-teacher, and she will sometimes talk about letters and sounds, but usually in an indirect way. Her area of focus with the children is math. This author's area of focus with the children is literacy. As opposed to the methods of the previous two years where the students were drilled on reading "skills," this author provides opportunities for the children to acquire knowledge on their own terms. The children are read to, asked questions about the stories, asked questions to activate prior knowledge, and speak to one another about their ideas.

Evaluating Students with Auditory Assessments

There is an assessment tool in the school that purports to measure reading readiness for three to five year olds, called Ready to Read! (Whitehurst & Lonigan, 2010). In December, this author's students were taken to a quiet room in the school and asked the questions on this exam. It is a norm-referenced test that has the child point to one of four possible answers to a question. The questions vary in difficulty and in the skill they assess. The questions test print concepts: letter and sound knowledge ("point to the picture that shows the letter f," "point to the picture that shows the letter that makes a 'buh' sound"), print and book knowledge ("point to the word that is written best," "point to the picture that shows the back of the book"), and word-segmenting knowledge ("point to the picture that shows what you get when you put sea and shell together"). For sample questions, see Figure 12.3:

Figure 12.3: Ready to Read! Assessment Device
© 2017 Pearson. Images used for educational purposes

There are twenty-five questions, and the number a student correctly answers corresponds to a step score of one through four with four being the best. Each question is weighted the same, with a total possible score of twenty-five. These are then calculated, taking into account the child's age, and given a judgment of above average, average, or below average.

These results are used to inform teachers of any areas that are a concern for the class as a whole, and used in conferences with parents to tell them what they could work on at home to promote reading readiness.

Notice that all of the sample questions provided by Ready to Read! utilize auditory methods for examination. Two of the questions directly measure a student's ability to discriminate sound features. The other two questions are presented without any accompanying context (drills in isolation). The very nature of these questions assumes that all students can take meaning from ideas that are presented without an accompanying semantic framework. For example, the child is asked, "Point to the word that is written best." This is a highly subjective task for a five year old to complete. What does "best" actually mean to the child? Does it mean written "correctly?" Does it mean written using the correct shape? Many visual thinkers would struggle to complete questions presented without more explanation.

The assumption of this test is that knowing words and parts of words promotes reading readiness, and thus reading success. However, the research in the literature review above would clearly refute these assumptions. This author set out to determine if Viconic Language Methods could best promote the teaching of literacy. Using the district-provided assessment tool Ready to Read! would shed very little light on this inquiry. Nevertheless, because all students were required to take it, the results will be included in this study.

Visual Language Assessment Device

Because of the limitations of the district provided evaluation device, another assessment tool, the Arwood Neuro-semantic Language Learning Pre-Language Assessment Protocol (ANSPA) was also used to assess the children's language (Arwood, 2012). The evaluations using the ANSPA took place over the course of a month, between January and February. The children were pulled aside from their structured play and taken to a quiet place in the room to take part in the study.

The children were asked to tell about an event-based picture. An event-based picture has several people doing different things, all in relation to one another. After the children's' verbal responses were recorded and written down, all of the learners were determined to be verbal, production level, pre-language thinkers. This means they are able to think about people, what they are doing, and why they are doing it, but have not yet developed fully grammatical abilities. This is normal for children who are between three and seven years old.

After this part of the study, ten questions were asked about each child's language. They were the following (Arwood, 2012, p. 187):

1. Does the child address others and expect others to respond? This assesses the function of the child (agent) in relationship to others (relational function).

2. Are the child's utterances appropriate for the context? This assesses the function of whether the child's language refers to the topic (referential function).

3. Does the child use the utterances to share the meaning of the context? This assesses the child's shared-referent function (shared function).

4. Does the child use consistent age-appropriate forms? This assesses the child's ability to use different forms for different meanings (productivity function).

5. Does the listener have to interpret the child's intent or specific meaning? This assesses the child's ability to develop a variety of meanings (semanticity function)

213

6. Does the child talk about the "here and now?" This assesses how well the child can talk about ideas that the child cannot see or touch (displacement function).

7. Does the child talk about a variety of different topics? This assesses the child's ability to use a variety of different types of utterances (flexibility function).

8. Are the child's utterances semantically accurate in meaning? This assesses another aspect of how well the child is acquiring concepts (semanticity function).

9. Are the child's utterances succinct in meaning? This assesses how well the child can use the English language to mean exactly what is intended (efficiency function).

10. Does the listener understand the speaker's meaning without having to take on more than a "shared" level of understanding? This assesses whether or not the language functions in a concrete way (understanding that others are interpreting your words).

For each language sample, each child's words were evaluated in the ten domains, and given a score of 0 for no consistent demonstration of the language ability or 1 for consistent demonstration of the language ability. The ten questions were totaled, giving each student a score between zero and ten. This assessment, along with the reading readiness assessment, was tabulated at the end of the study as evidence of their learning gains. The language post-assessment was taken in April, and the reading readiness test taken in May.

Whole Group Visual Language Instruction

To increase language literacy using a visual approach, this author implemented several strategies inspired by Neuro-Education theory. This author taught in a whole group using more visual strategies that the students were required to complete after whole group instruction. Since some students were at school daily and some were not, rather than having each student complete one assignment per week, this author had each student complete one assignment for each day they were present. This occurred over the course of six weeks and was comprised of two themes: transportation and the ocean. There was some overlap between the themes, so instruction was not disjointed. That is, one of the weeks was spent speaking of transportation in or on the ocean.

The visual language strategies implemented included "I Stories to You Stories," picture dictionaries, event-based pictures, cartooning, and flowcharts (Arwood, 2012). In using "I Stories," the teacher tells a story that happened to her, which others can identify with. For example, in studying polar bears, a teacher could tell how she saw a polar bear at the zoo and assume others have seen the polar bear too, or use a story of her slipping on the ice to start a conversation of why polar bears don't slip on the ice. After this, the students draw and write of a time something happened to them with ice. Because the Pre-K students are not fully able to write, early in the study their pictures were labeled by a teacher, written with hand-over-hand (the teacher holding her hand on top of the student's hand as they write together so the motion and hand movement is felt). They then read back the words and talked about the picture. For the purpose of this study, the author dubbed this process a "You Story."

The strategy of using event-based pictures practices what was given for the pre-assessment. In the informal version, the children are taught to identify important aspects of a picture and speak of it. They are asked "who, what, when, where, and why" questions about the pictures to promote deeper understanding. The chosen event based pictures were related to the theme of study.

After the children are asked to orally share what they see in the event-based-picture, they are then asked to draw out a series of events that may have happened before, during, and after the picture before them. Cartooning takes a chain of events and strings them out one by one. Its implementation at this age is like a "You Story" in that the children are responsible for the drawing and the teacher labels their picture and writes their words with them.

Figure 12.4 shows a one-panel cartoon created by a student that provides a starting place for them to continue their "You Story." After the students have created 1-3 panels, an adult can come back and help them semantically refine their drawings and writing. Doing so provides a back and forth *deixis,* meaning communication that is mutual and shared between two contributors.

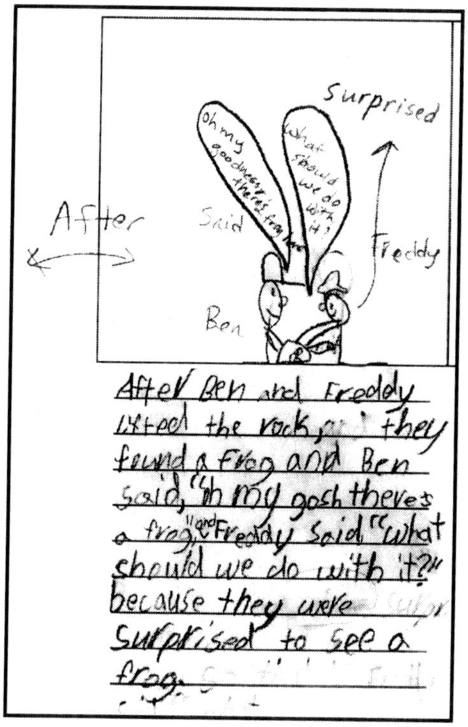

Continuing with the example of the author's polar bear "I" Story and asking the students to continue with a "You Story," this author shared what she knew about how polar bears catch their prey – a polar bear's hunt for food would have one picture of the polar bear in her den thinking of a seal. The next frame would show her walking to the ocean. The next frame would show her jumping into the water followed by a frame showing her floating on top of the water. Finally, she would see her prey and bring it to the surface to eat. This line of pictures helps the children to see that several events lead up to a final result, and the series of events cannot just be described as "she eats." It expands their language to extend the story.

Graphic organizers and diagrams were also used to classify and sort new information. A typical graphic organizer mainly uses words. The graphic organizers in this study were done with pictures hand drawn to represent ideas, with words labeling the categories and pictures. After this author created a class graphic organizer she helped the others create their own, using pictures.

Figure 12.4: One Panel "You Story" Created by Student
Image © 2017 B. Robb, Used with permission

The diagrams had full vehicles or animals drawn and labeled, using plenty of "because language" (Arwood 2001). For example, a teacher not implementing visual strategies might say "On the polar bear, this is the head, this is the foot, this is the claw, etc." Using a language-rich strategy this author would say, "This is the polar bear. Its head [while drawing the head] has its eyes [while drawing the eyes], which help it to see in the water and through the snow. Here is the mouth [while drawing the mouth], which has sharp pointy teeth inside to help it bite into its food, like seals, otters, and fish." Already the children have heard more words by using these visual methods than they would in a non-visual approach and are able to synthesize them into their own knowledge when they do the activity in small groups. There they create their own drawing, writing, and spoken explanation.

The aforementioned research of neuroscience supports the teacher's use of visual-motor strategies such as hand-over-hand instruction, and drawing out ideas in real-time while new vocabulary words are introduced. Using the hand provides an extra layer of visual movement that the motor strip of the brain can pick up (Baars & Gage, 2010). For typically developed brains, these motor movement signals can be spread and connected to other areas of the brain that typically process visual language, such as the occipital cortex. The more visual connections about a concept a child makes in their brain, the deeper their understanding of that concept will become (Arwood, 2011). Because of this deepening of bio-electrical signals, students have a greater chance of this concept sticking in semantic memory. Notice that none of the auditory instructional methods that these students had received during their previous two years had employed these viconic language strategies.

Results

Individual results from the language assessment and reading readiness test were entered into Excel documents to show if there was a statistically significant difference between the two tests as a result of the intervention. A paired t-test with a statistically significant difference (where $p < .05$) would indicate that visual strategies do positively impact reading readiness. A t-test that is not statistically significant would indicate that the group's reading readiness, as a whole, was not positively impacted by the use of visual strategies.

To be sure that each assessment was measuring similarly, this author then ran a test for correlation. This was important because the Ready to Read! test assessed reading skills, while the Arwood assessment tested language skills. Although much of the research from the literature review supports the acquiring of language as a predictor of reading ability, Ready to Read! tests phonics and letter knowledge and has no verbal language component. Similarly, the Arwood assessment tests language ability and has no phonics or letter knowledge component. Strong correlation would show that the reading readiness test could be correlated to language development. A weak correlation would show that the reading readiness test does not in fact predict language development, which the literature shows to be important in long-term reading achievement.

A total of 27 students were involved in the visual strategies intervention between testing periods. Of the 27 students, 26 took the Ready to Read! assessment. All 27 students partook in the ANSPA (Arwood, 2012).

Table 1 shows the group sizes, means, and standard deviations for each assessment, before and after the intervention. There was a statistically significant difference ($p < .01$) between the students' Ready to Read! pretest and posttest results. There was also a statistically significant difference ($p < .001$) between the students' ANSPA pretest and posttest results. That is, the students showed significant gains in learning with visual instruction in both the reading readiness test and the language test.

	Ready to Read! $N = 26$		ANSPA $N = 27$	
Test iteration	Mean	*SD*	Mean	*SD*
Pretest	22.27	3.24	4.15**	1.63
Posttest	23.42*	1.77	6.89**	2.06
*$p < .01$. **$p < .001$.				

Table 12.1: Pretest and Posttest Mean and Standard Deviation for Ready to Read! and Arwood Neuro-semantic Language Learning Pre-Language Assessment Protocol (ANSPA)

The two assessments were also tested for correlation. Using a Pearson indicator, there was not a statistically significant correlation (.164) between the Ready to Read! test and the ANSPA. This means the two assessments do not measure in like manner. Although they both measure pre-reading ability, they do so in different ways. They each test different aspects of pre-reading literacy. That is, the Ready to Read! tests individualized skills without meaning, and the ANSPA tests meaning without individualized skills.

Furthermore, the scoring of each test is different. The Ready to Read! score is based on each answer being either right or wrong. The assumption here is that letter and sound knowledge transfers to reading ability (for an overall goal of decoding). The ANSPA looks at the whole and deciphers the whole conversation, and how knowledge is being acquired and displayed through the test taker's own language. The assumption here is that language is representative of thought, and that meaning making transfers to making meaning in reading (for an overall goal of comprehension). For there to be a correlation that is not statistically significant, then, is not surprising.

There was a statistically significant difference between the students' Ready to Read! scores before and after visual intervention. This test is only visual in that it uses pictures. The pictures are not related to one another, and do not promote language. Teaching to master this assessment would not promote learning through language, but through skill acquisition. Still, the visual strategies the students applied helped to promote a statistically significant difference in mean scores before and after the intervention.

There was also a statistically significant difference between the students' ANSPA scores before and after intervention. This shows that their language did, in fact, improve as a result of the language-intense intervention. This result validates the belief of many of the researchers in the literature that visual strategies promote language growth.

There was not a statistically significant correlation between the Ready to Read! and the ANSPA. This shows that they are measuring different things. Still, the visual intervention had positive impacts on both tests, so teaching with more visuals promoted reading readiness in terms of letter knowledge and language.

Discussion of Results

The purpose of this study was to determine whether visual strategies impact reading readiness and language ability in a class of Pre-K learners. As discussed in the results section, visual strategies positively impacted reading readiness and language ability, as measured by the two assessments. Part of the concern at the onset of this study was whether visual strategies would promote reading and language learning for *all* students, since only one student had a diagnosed disorder – a speech impairment. The results indicate that as a whole, these students, most of whom do not have a diagnosed disorder, made gains in reading readiness and language ability due to the visual strategies.

The literature indicates some conflict over whether phonics provides the basis for reading (bottom up) or whether language provides the basis for later phonemic instruction (top down). From the author's study, no real conclusions can be made in regards to this, except to say that using a language intensive approach improved both language and phonics ability. Therefore, from this study, the importance of language cannot be understated. In particular, these results show that providing students opportunities to practice using their natural language in context-rich environments increased their overall ability to think, to be literate, and to problem-solve. Arwood (2011) would interpret these results by positing that language names our thinking. A student who increases their level of language function, therefore, increases their ability to think and interact with the world in a significant way.

It is unlikely that a phonics intensive program would have yielded improved language ability, as the students need to hear language and engage in conversation to improve. Teaching letters and sounds simply does not promote language ability. Teaching phonics only works on a small subset of the whole of language; it merely scratches the surface patterns of language. However visual instructional methods carve out the deep semantic structure of language. The results of this study show that the latter methods are clearly more effective at promoting literacy.

Much of the study involved immersing the students in print. Every time they watched this author draw and write, they were expected to draw and write. This follows what the literature says about the importance of being exposed to print, in order to be familiar with and ready for reading. The literature spoke mostly of students being familiar with print, especially in picture books. The students were more than familiar with print with the implementation of visual instruction because they were expected, as a part of most of the lessons, to write on, or tag, their pictures. Because the printed words were called to their attention, and the more exposed a student is to written language the better reader they are, these students were set up for success.

It should be noted, however, that this author made no attempts to break up the printed words into smaller units such as vowels, consonants, or syllables. The rationale for this was that visual learners learn new ideas (words) by memorizing their unique shapes and associating other visual images with these shapes. Arwood (2011) informs that writing words provides the patterns, while drawing out the semantic ideas represents the concepts. Taken together, visual patterns plus visual concepts will equal visual language.

Because the Ready to Read! assessment was so straightforward and narrow in its approach; this author does not believe that she could have improved these data. The assessment is norm-referenced and research-based, according to its packaging. The ANSPA has an advantage in that it allows for authentic assessment of students' language. There is no doubt that the test was valid: with the ten domains within language, this author felt confident that she was measuring language growth, and that all of the categories were important aspects of language. However, it was difficult to know whether the scoring for the assessment was reliable. That is, this author calculated the scores according to her knowledge of the subject. However, it cannot be known whether another scorer would score them differently.

Conclusion

From the results of this study, further research may be conducted. To this author's knowledge, her classroom is in the minority for classrooms whose literacy program is strongly visual and strongly language-driven. If more of this type of study is done in different populations, more evidence will be amassed, which will point to the success of language intensive literacy programs. More studies will put a stop to teachers saying that "It worked in one classroom, but it will not work in mine."

One aspect that would be interesting to study would be the long-lasting effects of the language instruction. This study was conducted over six weeks, and in that time the students' level of functional language grew. The students continued using better conversational language than they had been using before the intervention. It is unclear whether this is a result of their maturation or an extended benefit of the language intensive instruction.

This author's class benefited from the use of visual strategies but once they are in kindergarten and above they will most likely focus on letters and sounds, and receive auditory teaching. A concern is that the growth seen in the span of this intervention will not be long-term.

This author will continue to use visual strategies, and continue to push her students to expand their own language. She believes that language-building strategies are not limited to reading readiness, and could be applied across populations. It remains to be seen how visual strategies will impact the students in years to come, but this author remains hopeful that the next years will provide her with added evidence that this study's results were not isolated, and can be applied to a larger population.

Summary of Neuro-Education Methods

By using a variety of strategies, students received multiple layers of information. From a cognitive psychology perspective, the use of "I" Stories, and close one-on-one interaction helped to develop these young learners' sense of agency. In terms of language development, tagging or naming ideas helps to build contextual relationships between language concepts. The depth of language acquisition, as a result of the students drawing and writing with the teacher's feedback, is evident in the Ready To Read! assessment results.

Neurobiologically, these numerous layers of input help the brain to form multiple neuronal associations from multiple access points. These networks of neurons are stored in long-term memory and provide more potential access points for future information. It is not surprising that behavioral products (such as phonics skills) improved as a result of visual methods in such a short period of time. This relatively fast progress is an indicator that the concepts gained during this intervention will be long lasting.

Chapter 13

Conclusion: What is Next for the Field of Neuroeducation?

Ellyn Lucas Arwood, Ed.D., CCC-SLP
Chris Merideth, M.Ed.

Acknowledging Operational Biases in Research

The translation of brain-based scientific research into educational practice is a new and exciting area of study that is capable of transforming the way in which our society views the acquisition of learning and higher order thinking in children. As such, the authors compiled here are some of the first in the country to formally apply the theories contained in Arwood's Neuro-Education Model into a teaching methodology in order to study its efficacy to help students who have previously struggled in school. The results these practitioners have achieved provide a starting point for these methods to someday be included as viable *evidence-based practices* in the national discussion on educational reform. Before this can happen, however, more educators must document their findings in academic journals and in national conferences to spread awareness of their research and establish a predictive validity to the brain-based methods chronicled here. And, perhaps even more importantly, more conversations must take place between educators and administrators, and more time must be allotted to provide professional development training for pedagogy that is supported by scientific research. Only by continuing to share positive success stories in formal and informal settings will more educators be exposed to the kind of paradigm shift these authors have experienced in their teaching practice.

Though the model of Neuro-Education used in this book is multifaceted and far-reaching in its potential to impact change, its theories still only represent a relatively small portion of the field of mind-brain science. Readers who are curious about the vast capabilities of the body to impact the brain, the brain to impact the mind, and the mind to impact the body can continue their studies by consulting Tokuhama-Espinosa's influential book *Mind, Brain, and Education Science* (2011). In this work, the author expands the scope of M.B.E. Science to include studies on the impact that health, exercise, diet, sleep, genetics, diseases, disorders, and many more factors have on the mind-brain connection, and how learning can be affected by the "whole" of a child. Curious readers can also seek out primary research articles in respected academic journals in the fields of neuroscience, cognitive psychology, language, and education, or can read summaries of these fields in M.B.E. journals that are more accessible to the layperson.

Moving forward, these authors believe that the study of neuroeducation has much work to do in continuing to re-frame the conventional wisdom in the United States of how it is that children learn best, and how we implement scientific research and interpret it for educational practice. In particular, these authors would like to stress the notion that the quality of research being conducted in any field is only as good as the questions being asked by the researchers.

In practice, this means that researchers bring with them to the laboratory a rich breadth of knowledge and experience in their field; but, this background also includes biases about how they will interpret their findings and how these findings might be applicable to humans. Granted, it is of course true that every person on earth operates with inherent biases about the world – this factor is an unavoidable bi-product of human thinking. However, whether or not these biases are examined when a scientist is proposing a research question remains one of the most underexplored and potentially problematic aspects of contemporary academia. The metaphor shared in the introduction of this book of the fish being unaware of the water they are swimming in is also apropos here: if a scientist does not acknowledge the theoretical background they bring with them to conduct their studies, they may let pre-existing notions cloud and shape the interpretations of their results. If the operational biases a scientist employs are either not known or not shared with the reader, then this can call into question the validity of the scientists' methods and the interpretation of the results as they are applied to humankind.

Accounting for Human Metacognition

It is currently impossible using existing technology to look inside the mind. We cannot see the pictures one stores in their mental imagery, nor can we hear the sound of their own voice in their head. Though this is such a simple truism, it is often completely ignored in the planning stages when studies are created. To illustrate this point, let's take the sample experiment *Body Mass Correlates Inversely with Inhibitory Control in Response to Food among Adolescent Girls: An fMRI Study,* in which participants are asked to view pictures of food on a computer screen and then click a button in response (Batterink et. al., 2010). While the participants are responding to images, neuroscientists and cognitive psychologists can use fMRI machines to study how the brain allocates glucose (energy) to certain regions and can even track the flow of electrochemicals through the cortex and into vast networks of connected fiber tracts in the brain (Göetzmann & Schwegler, 2010, etc.). As these scientists watch the brain use its resources to operate, they can ask the study participants to orally self-report what they are thinking about or can ask them to express their preferences by clicking a button for a yes or no response (a task called "go/no-go").

In this example experiment, the authors wanted to study the relationship between obesity and impulsivity. At the time the article was published, the authors acknowledged that previous neuroscientific studies had demonstrated positive correlations between the amount of calories a person consumes and their subsequent increase in impulsive behavior (as measured by both behavioral self-report and performance on neuropsychological tests). In other words, previous studies had hypothesized that some people gained more weight because of over-activation in areas of the brain thought to foster impulsive thoughts. One might think that this acknowledgment would count as revealing an operational bias upon entering into future experiments, but that is not the case. To keep our fish metaphor alive, the scientists have simply identified that they are swimming in a different location in the same body of water that is the field of neuroscience; they have not identified the water they are swimming in. More on this will be explored in a moment.

Moving forward, these authors claimed that *their* study would be unique from past experiments because it would measure whether a higher body mass index (BMI) negatively correlated with activation of brain regions known to be used in *inhibitory* control, such as the parietal areas, frontal lobe regions, superior frontal gyrus, medial prefrontal cortex (PFC), dorsolateral/ventrolateral PFC, orbitofrontal cortex, and dorsal amygdala. Put another way, they wanted to study whether the brains of individuals with a higher BMI were also negatively affected in areas known to promote inhibition of impulsive behavior.

The goal of experiments like these is to study only one factor at a time and to not include sensory input that might distract human participants from their task at hand. As such, the respondents were shown only images of either vegetables or desserts on a computer screen and asked to press a button when an image of a vegetable appeared and withhold a response for an image of a dessert. In addition, participants were asked not to eat or drink for four to six hours before each imaging session, presumably to develop a natural state of hunger. The researchers hypothesized that it would be more challenging for individuals with a high BMI to inhibit responses to desired foods than it would be for individuals with a lower BMI. To test this idea, the scientists calculated the correlation between reaction time, rate of commission errors, and BMI. After implementing a series of methods much too complicated to be explained here, they indeed concluded that BMI was negatively correlated to activation in many of the areas of the brain related to inhibition that they had suspected.

On the surface, this experiment appears relatively straightforward and the interpretations of the results seem plausible: the brains of individuals who have a higher BMI are more susceptible to impulses to consume unhealthy food. And, like countless other investigations in the fields of neuroscience and cognitive psychology, this study follows strict scientific protocol and therefore meets the rigor of credibility in the eyes of fellow scholars. As such, it won out against many similar experiments to be published in the highly respected journal *NeuroImage*. However, let's examine some of the unexplored limitations and biases of this experiment and consider how these factors hinder the application of similar scientific findings to the study of human consciousness.

First and foremost, the tasks used in these experiments are often not representative of what it is like to live in real life. For example, the computer simulation used to depict food does not simulate all of the senses of being in contact with real food such as smell or texture. Moreover, pushing a button on a computer is not the same thing as eating – or more importantly avoiding – fattening foods in real life. We may indeed get a neurobiological response to a simulated craving, such as our body releasing chemicals and neurotransmitters when our mind thinks of junk food; but, there is no detrimental impact to our body when we push a button on a computer, versus actually eating a piece of cake. To conflate these two processes would be an over simplification of the human digestive system (Miller, 2011).

Relatedly, a computer simulation of food elicits different metacognitive processes than actually reaching for and eating that food. Sensory perception studies in cognitive neuroscience demonstrate that there are significantly more metacognitive processes happening in the mind when someone is eating in real life, such as a positive association between past memories and emotions, a consideration of the contextual environment of eating (with family at a dinner table, etc.), past food trauma, or issues of addiction (Cooper et. al., 2008). These processes are actually concepts unique to each person's own learning and mediated by the language assigned to those concepts. These factors, along with other elements such as how much sleep a person has had or whether or not they have had a bad day, have all been shown to influence whether someone will indulge their impulses or inhibit them. This evidence brings up the important point that one's metacognition cannot be controlled for in experiments; meaning, it effectively cannot be separated out from one's response to a single stimulus (the picture on the screen). In other words, our metacognition is always present inside our mind; but, it is often not accounted for in studies because it is impossible to isolate. And, though the metacognition cannot be separated from the brain, the brain is affected by one's metacognition.

Remember that the default model of thinking held by many neuroscientists and psychologists is that what inputs into the mind leads directly to output (Arwood, 2011). This assumption fits nicely with the design of the computer simulation experiment and countless others like it. If cognition can in fact be traced from sensory input (image) directly to behavioral output (go/no go), then the researchers can confidently believe their results have significance to the operations of the human mind. In fact, they can establish enough examples of correlation between input and output variables to deem their findings as *statistically significant*, meaning more than just a series of coincidences. Because the two-tier, input-output learning paradigm fits hand in glove with the input-output design of most experiments in neuroscience and psychology, it should come as little surprise that few researchers acknowledge it as an invisible hand that guides their thinking and interpretation of results. To do so would be for the fish to acknowledge the water it is swimming in.

If human thinking actually follows the four-tiered model that has been proposed by Arwood's Neuro-semantic Language Learning Theory, then the findings of most scientific research about cognition have neglected to acknowledge and account for the third and fourth tiers: concepts and language. Or, evidence may in fact be found in the brain of these third and fourth tiers (circuits and networks), but not thought of as processes mediated by language (Iturria-Medina et al, 2008). In other words, scientists see circuits and networks form but may not know how they relate to language function. Most importantly, because these tiers of higher order thinking cannot be controlled for in the experiments, they are regularly set aside and ignored. In other words, because it is not possible to see into the mind's eye with current technology, the workings of the mind (metacognition) are not factored into go/no-go type experiments. Paradoxically, by neglecting to include the influence of metacognition on the results one receives, one may not be studying the true workings of mind at all.

The authors of this anthology would be remiss not to mention again that the language we use to function in the world represents the underlying processes of our thinking (Arwood, 2011). Language, such as the pictures/movies we have in our heads, the sound of our own voice in our mind, and the stored mental characteristics of orienting ourselves in time and space is, in fact, our metacognition. Few if any studies (aside from those inspired by Arwood) account for the influence of such linguistic metacognition on the outcomes or behavior of the participants. If language names our thinking, then these authors believe that language should not be excluded from any study that attempts to make sense of how the human mind operates or how the human brain functions. Moreover, analyzing just how complex human behavior can be can illuminate the unpredictable and often irrational nature of our species. Rarely do humans act so methodically that a definitive pattern of their thinking can be deduced by finding a correlation between their actions.

Expert Recommendations for Future Research

It appears that the human mind and brain operate in a fundamentally different manner when confronted with a real-life scenario versus a computer simulation of that event. So, how much academic credence should be given to the results of psychological experiments obtained under circumstances that only approximate the mind's capacity to function in real life? Do these experiments accurately represent how the human mind makes sense of the world around it? These authors would like to caution against the tendency of many researchers to overextend the significance of such experimental results obtained under extremely limiting circumstances to hypotheses about how humans operate in real life. In addition, by not acknowledging the role of language to name our metacognitive processes, future researchers will continue to analyze only approximations of human thinking and not the actual by-products themselves (such as linguistic artifacts). Doing so will continue to miss the target of how the brain actually functions.

Despite this cautious viewpoint, the march of research will continue in neuroscience and psychology. Therefore, in addition to the recommendations for changes in future research made by the authors of this book, Tokuhama-Espinosa (2011) documents an effort made by Patricia Wolfe (2006) to judge the quality of scientific research studies based on a series of critical questions about the work. These questions are designed to determine the credibility of the scientific process being used and the operating principles guiding that process. Most importantly, these recommendations help question a study's applicability and relevance to educational settings. These questions are listed here (Tokuhama-Espinosa, 2011, p. 99):

- How many subjects were in the study?

- What were the ages and characteristics of the subjects?

- Was there a control group of subjects who were matched with the subjects in the experimental group?

- What was the methodology used for the study?

- Are there similar studies that have produced contradictory findings?

Tokuhama-Espinosa also notes that the Organisation For Economic Co-Operation and Development (OECD) released a book compiled by individuals from 30 different countries entitled *Understanding the Brain: Towards a New Learning Science* (2002). These experts included three extra considerations to provide a critical eye to examine research (Tokuhama-Espinosa, 2011, p. 100):

- What was the original study and its primary purpose? (That is, are the results being interpreted in the right context?)

- Is this a single study or a series of studies? (That is, are the findings in context?)

- Did the study have a learning outcome? (That is, was an application in a real classroom setting part of the study?)

It is this last point of consideration in particular to which the authors of this book would like to bring extra attention. As previously stated, the use of animals such as rats and chimpanzees in experiments that aim to hypothesize about human cognition reveals extreme limitations. Firstly, the brain of a human and the brain of an animal differ in many profound ways, such as density of neurons in the cerebrum, myelination of nerve cells, simultaneous connectivity of multiple regions to form circuits and networks of fiber tracts, and inclusion or exclusion of the prefrontal cortex (a region widely acknowledged to be involved in higher order thinking processes) (Anderson, 2010; Baars & Gage, 2010; Bechara et. al., 2004). These differences, among countless others, exist between humans and animals because the need for the human brain to *function* in increasingly complex ways has altered its evolutionary *structure* (DeWaal, 2008; Gibson, 1979). In other words, the human brain has experienced millions of years of evolution to maximize executive functioning, linguistic competence, and problem-solving abilities. Animal brains, however, have not evolved in this way. These differences result in differences of human function, specifically the ability to change one's niche or viability, the ability to use language for higher order thinking, the ability to symbolize ideas that are not structurally in the present (e.g. ancient civilizations, outer space, sympathy), and the ability to change thinking in order to move out of homeostasis into other dimensions of living.

Secondly, as previously stated, simulations of human learning are not viable substitutes for actual learning opportunities. After all, the mind is continuously updating, refining, and changing itself in real-time faster than any computer model of artificial intelligence (Anderson, 2010; Arwood, 2011). Therefore, why settle for conjectures of what might be happening in the minds of the students we wish to help, when we could instead sample that student's use of natural, spontaneous language in order to determine how they function in the world? If our goal as educators is to study how our children learn best and increase their level of thinking, what better way is there to do this than to have them engage in real-life educational scenarios? Information gleaned about the brain (such as fMRI and ECG results) and the mind (such as analysis of behavior) is certainly more valuable and applicable to the study of human consciousness when it is gathered during tasks that use the whole of a person's thinking.

Where Do We Go From Here?

With neuroeducation in its infancy, many pitfalls of advancing this discipline have come to light as new information about the way humans actually learn are being uncovered. Within the input-output paradigm, the direct translation of research into practice has developed a pedagogy that does not match the current literature presented in this book. The authors in this anthology have provided many examples for how they have used their knowledge about the brain, mind, and language to make changes in their classrooms and/or with individuals. Such changes result in a paradigm shift. This educational paradigm shift can be summarized in the table below.

Western Psychology Current Paradigm	Arwood's NsLLT Paradigm
Teaching emphasis	Learning emphasis
Developmental products	Acquisition processes (neurobiological as well as socio-cognitive)
Mind studies of introspection and observation	Brain studies of how the learning affects the development
Model, imitate, copy, practice, transfer, generalize	Opportunity for multiple representations of ideas through literacy (reading, writing, thinking, viewing, listening, speaking, calculating)
Parts to whole (development)	Whole to parts (relationships)
Reward for associative and then habituated learning	Refine learner's thinking for higher order learning
Bell-shaped curve research (statistics on data collection)	Authentic assessment of self-evident changes of learners
Input-output	Scaffold of learning across neuro-semantic acquisition

Table 13.1: A Neuro-semantic Paradigm Shift

As the reader might see in Table 13.1, there is quite a difference between an educational approach that utilizes the teaching emphasis of the current paradigm and an educational approach that utilizes the NsLLT as a foundation. Within each of these paradigms are methods aligned with the philosophical emphasis (teaching vs. learning), the expected outcomes (products vs. processes), the focus of the literature (cognitive psychology vs. NsLLT, which is at the intersection of neuroscience, cognitive psychology, and language function), and the research model (developmental bell-shaped statistical data collection vs. authentic assessment of language function through the literacy of reading, writing, thinking, viewing, listening, speaking, and calculating). The methods for the Western cognitive psychology paradigm come from the introspection of an adult (reductionism was discussed earlier in the anthology) and the observation of children's outcomes as tested against what other children the same age would developmentally be expected to demonstrate. This adult introspection results in an input that is modeled for the learner's expected output to be the same. These responses to the adult's input are externally rewarded to increase the likelihood of the same responses occurring again and again. Such repetition or practice results in habituated patterns of the associated responses.

However, the input-output model is limited to these associated and then habituated types of learning. Conceptual learning or higher order thinking through a variety of literacy processes cannot be habituated. Therefore, the methods must be different. The reader might want to reflect back across the chapters to think about the various methods these authors utilized: cartooning, writing with shapes (not sounds), assigning meaning with rich language, utilizing picture dictionaries, etc. All of these methods have a neuroscience, cognitive psychology, and language component to substantiate their usage in the classroom.

For example, cartooning using a black pencil lead on white paper is two-dimensional, which is what the brain processes. Only with language do we see in the third dimension. The back lines are edges easily processed (neuroscience) against the white background. These edges overlap as patterns to form shapes (neuroscience) that record in the occipital cortex as circuits of meaning within the visual system. Such shapes (a type of visual concept) create the basis to write the patterns (written words) so that the concepts (shapes) are connected to the patterns (written words). When concepts are connected to patterns for expression, the learner is able to use patterns of language to represent thinking (language literature). The language represents thinking in natural form or language function. When a learner is able to use language to read, write, draw, calculate, then the learner is able to assign meaning (cognitive psychology about social learning) in a way that results in semantic memory (language and neuroscience). Furthermore, the cartoons ground the learner in a frame in the same direction so that the cognitive load (psychology) is reduced for easier learning. The learner is in each frame also reducing the cognitive load since conceptual learning begins at the level of the learner.

Furthermore, there are over 50 Viconic Language Methods that have been used to align the NsLLT with the way that lessons are planned for individuals and classrooms of learners. Cartooning is only one of the many methods used to help learners think, refine their thinking through scaffolding of material (semantic features), and be able to think at a higher level for higher language function. The ultimate outcome with the paradigm shift is to help learners think at a higher level though more success with literacy that is mediated by language function.

Conclusion

The authors of this anthology hope that the reader has been able to find some tools and ideas for starting the journey of shifting paradigms. Our hope is that you will be inspired to become a consumer of information about the vast topic of neuroeducation. Each year, individuals with similar interests gather at numerous national and international conferences to both share their research and also to learn about unique ways that people might interpret new scientific evidence. As new brain imaging technology emerges, it allows researchers to analyze new regions of the brain and develop more sophisticated models of how these regions might interconnect. But, the brain is a vastly complex organ, and scientists are still just scratching the surface of how knowledge becomes encoded and how the mind uses this knowledge to function.

Studying neuroeducation allows educators a seat at the table to share how certain research findings may or may not be practical when applied to a classroom setting. In addition, when educators know the science behind why certain methods work well and others do not, they can become empowered to push for changes in curriculum, pedagogy, and teacher preparation that match these findings. Reading primary research studies in neuroscience and psychology can be daunting, but numerous resources exist that attempt to translate these complex ideas into information that is palatable for the layperson. As new proposed teaching methods emerge, remember that a method is only as valuable as the underlying theory of learning that supports its usage. Our hope is that this book has provided you with a model that allows you to switch your focus from a teacher-centered practice to one that looks at pedagogy from the perspective of the learner.

Glossary

Acoustic features – pitch, loudness, and duration/time, which the ear receives as sensory input

Acoustic patterns – patterns from the ears; these patterns do not include or represent meaningful ideas

Agent – someone who does something with someone or something; part of a basic semantic relationship that develops across ages and stages of learning processes

Alphabetic – the property of English that refers to the use of changing the sounds of the spoken language into written letters

Anti-social behavior – the way a child moves away from initiating and maintaining healthy relationships toward more aggressive, societally unacceptable behaviors

Arwood's Neuro-Education Model – a theoretical model proposed by Dr. Ellyn Arwood of how learning takes place in the brain and how the mind uses knowledge to make meaning of the world; Arwood's Neuro-Education Model uses the disciplines of neuroscience, cognitive psychology, and language to triangulate scientific literature and translate these findings into educational practice

Assign meaning – the act of interpreting behavior through actions, verbal comments, and nonverbal responses

Auditory – a type of processing where the visual input from the eyes is connected simultaneously with the input from the ears; auditory concepts mean that a person is able to take the sounds of other people's language and integrate at the same time with what the person is able to see to form mental concepts that are in the thinker's own sound-based language

Auditory languages – refers to those types of language that assume the listeners and speakers are able to understand the sound-based unit, the spoken word, from integrating both sound and sight simultaneously; English is an auditory language and case use multidirectional processing for the development of time concepts

Autism spectrum disorders (ASD) – a term that encompasses autism and similar disorders as listed in the DSM-IV. ASD includes autism, Asperger Syndrome, PDD-NOS, childhood disintegrative disorder, and Rett's Syndrome

Because language – the use of connecting ideas so that complete propositions are created; for example, "She is rolling up the window *because* she wants to be sure that you are safe from rocks that might fly up from the wheels of the other cars and hit you in the face."

Behavior – made up of a series of recognizable movements or acts to which someone assigns meaning (e.g., the child's arm moves toward an adult who interprets the behavior as hitting)

Behavior disorders – a term used to describe behavior that is socially unacceptable to multiple people who observe the behavior occurring across multiple settings, across time, and to the determent of others or the person engaging in the behavior

Behaviorism – a theory based on B. F. Skinner's approach to learning behavior through a system of rewards and punishers

Boundaries – refer to the limit of individuals within a culture, family, or group in terms of what is personal and what is the norm

Bubbling – a procedure whereby the configuration of a word is shaped so that the learner is able to see how the idea creates a visual pattern

Calculating – a literacy function that uses both patterns and concepts for solving numeracy problems

Cerebrum – the part of the brain responsible for body sensation, muscle movement, and thinking; divided into the right and left hemispheres

Classical conditioning – refers to behavior that is paired with a natural consequence such as the smell of food paired with salivating

Cognition – the physiological organization of sensation into the basic thought patterns; or how we think

Cognitive development – refers to the stages of thinking that children pass through sequentially; sensori-motor, preoperational, operational, and formal

Communication – the conveyance of an intended message through language and speech that acts to alter a listener's or receiver's attitudes, beliefs, or behaviors

Concept – the idea or thought that comes from developing an overlap of sensory perceptual patterns (e.g., a person, place, or thing are basic concepts whereas government and respect are more complex concepts)

Context – People (agents) share actions with each other and their objects in a recognizable place, which creates a story or event (See also **event**)

Critical thinking – the ability to make choices of reasonableness that reflect the pro-social development of a society; to share those choices with others to problem solve through mediation of thought from multiple perspectives

Cross-modal – the use of multiple inputs to develop meaning in language such as the eyes provide meaning from what is seen while the ears provide meaning to what is heard; language symbolization requires some form of cross-modal development whether from within the same sensory system such as light and movement with the eyes or from two different senses

Decoding – the ability to decipher patterns into meaningful clusters; could be acoustic patterns as in the sounds of words or could be visual patterns as in the shapes of ideas

Deep structure (of language) – the underlying semantic meaning of a language; contrasted against the *surface structure* of language, which is the observable grammar of a language

Differential weight hypothesis – a neuroscientific hypothesis that states that sensory input competes for resources in the brain, and that the input that is most meaningful to the brain will be more easily integrated into existing neuronal pathways

Discrete trial training – a method of teaching new skills consisting of a series of distinct repeated lessons or trials taught one-to-one through manipulation of antecedent and consequences, to include direct instruction (specific stimuli elicit specific or target responses), prompting (stimuli or cues are used to define target responses), and reinforcing, followed with attention to intervals

Displacement – A language principle that refers to how far away an idea is from its physical referent (For example, the term "dog" refers to an animal that can be touched so there is little distance between the animal and the language term "dog" used to name the animal. But, the expression "dog days of summer" refers to how hot the day is, not a dog. This expression shows a lot of displacement since the listener cannot touch or even see to what the speaker is referring.)

Event – when people (agents) interact (actions) in a shared activity, they create a story or event

Flexibility – the ability to think about others and, therefore, have more choices and opportunities to behave in a variety of ways; linguistic flexibility refers to the ability to understand ideas from many different perspectives

Frontal lobe – the anterior division of each cerebral hemisphere responsible for executive functioning, problem-solving, and long-range planning

Function of language – the cognitive way language represents thinking, problem-solving, and planning according to cultural and social norms

Functional connectivity – the organizing principle of the brain that semantic information that is related in meaning will neurobiologically wire together in close geographic proximity (in corresponding brain structures)

Gestural signs – gestural sign language connecting two relationships of meaning (e.g., pointing)

Grounding – point of reference in relationship to the ground (e.g., when a child puts his/her body against any of the people or objects within that space to become part of the space, thereby gaining a feeling of comfort)

Hand-over-hand (HoH) – the educator or parent using his or her hand on top of a learner's hand to help him learn the shape of the patterns of moving the hand to do an activity of daily living such as eating or brushing teeth or for patterns related to academic tasks such as writing

High context – lots of information provided about a certain situation to avoid the listener having to guess, infer, and/ or assume

Inhibition – the recognition of incoming stimuli or neurological messages as old messages so that there is more opportunity for new information to be acted on; neurological inhibition occurs as cells either have already fired or are prevented from firing because of neurotransmitter activity; observers see inhibition as a change in behavior that shows that the input is recognized as meaningful

Integrate (integration) – the neurobiological ability to overlap sensory patterns to form concepts

Language – a set of arbitrary symbols that communicate conventional and shared meaning among two or more people

Layers of learning – occur as a result of complex neurological integration and inhibition of sensory input that forms patterns creating interconnected circuits of neurosemantic meaning

Learning – A process that is defined differently. Some believe that learning is a two-tier model of input and output where output is imitated, copied, memorized, and produced. Others view learning as a series of layers of acquiring meaning at four tiers or levels as the result of a neurobiological set of processes that result in the acquisition of neurosemantic concepts represented by language, referred to as the neurosemantic language learning theory (Arwood, 2011).

Learning styles – preferences for learning that may be a result of specific training or education and may not be the same as the neurobiological learning system's way of learning new concepts

Linguistic relativity – an idea proposed by various linguists (e.g. Hickman) that the language one uses determines one's thinking

Literacy – the language functions and structures of reading, writing, thinking, listening, speaking, viewing, and calculating; the process by which language acquisition is used for these activities

Marginalized – being left out of the flow of information, activities, or decision-making

Metacognition – the language used to think about thinking

Mind, Brain, Education Science (MBE) – a parallel discipline to Neuro-Education that aims to use neuroscience and psychology to inform educational practice; MBE does not include the study of language as a translational lens to interpret scientific research

Neuro-atypical learner – a person whose development does not follow predicted outcomes; whose socio-cognitive learning (functions) is different than expected

Neurobiological – the knowledge of how cells interact based on their biological nature

Neuronal circuits – several connections of cell clusters of nuclei occur to form concepts

Neuro-semantic Language Learning Theory – consists of four levels of meaningful (semantic feature) acquisition: sensory input, perceptual patterns, concepts, and language. Each of these levels parallels neurobiological function

Neuro-typical learner – person whose development does follow predicted outcomes; whose socio-cognitive learning (functions) is similar to what is expected

Occipital lobe – the posterior lobe of each cerebral hemisphere, which contains the visual areas

Ontogeny – the development or course of development of an individual organism or the history of the beginning as well as course of development of a language or any other human artifact

Operant conditioning – includes a set of methods that stem from the philosophy of behaviorism; pairing a desired need with a desired behavior; that is, a behavior occurs and something either positive or negative happens (For example, a child throws food from a high chair and the parent says *"no"*)

Overlapping – refers to the way that multiple sets of neurons and circuits of neurons interconnect to form more complex behavior

Parietal lobe – a part of the brain that deals with the reception of sensory information from opposite sides of the body; it has a role in calculation, reading, writing, and language

Patterns – sets of sensory input that form recognizable input (e.g., seeing the squiggles of "John" on a page but not knowing what the squiggles say)

Perceptual patterns – the organization of sensory-received stimuli into usable features; that is, sounds, tastes, touch, smells, and sights all integrate as sets of perceptual patterns that overlap into concepts

Phonemes – acoustic patterns in a language that correspond to a set of similar speech sounds; one of the smallest units of speech that distinguish one word or utterance from another

Phonics – a method of teaching beginners to read and pronounce words by learning the sound patterns of letters, letter groups, and especially syllables

Pragmaticism – term coined in the 1800s by Charles S. Pierce; means that the "whole is greater than the parts"

Pragmaticism methodology – a termed coined by Dr. Ellyn Arwood; based on the principles established by Charles S. Pierce. Refers to working with the whole learning process, not just the child's products

Productivity – the ability to use language in a variety of ways to communicate complex ideas

Reading fluency – an educational method of assessing reading speed by calling out the individual words in a paragraph or story

Receptors – anything that receives; as in the human organs that receive sensory input; eyes, ears, nose, mouth, and skin

Reductionism – refers to breaking down a skill or task into its parts and then teaching the parts with the expectation that the parts will equal the whole

Relational languages – those languages that contextually use a culture where the relationships among people, their actions, objects and locations are more important than the meaning of words

Reinforcement – increases the likelihood of a targeted behavior occurring again

Restricted language – refers to limited linguistic function of language; typically, restricted language function occurs in children up to seven years old or in pidgin language; restricted language utilizes limited grammatical complexity as well as limited meaning of concepts

Re-tagging – the act of a learner assigning meaning to the individual marker of specific lexicon of their target language by using an understanding of that marker drawn from their native language

Rewards – refers to tangible and non-tangible items that are paired with a targeted behavior based on the assumption that they will increase the likelihood of a behavior occurring in the future

Rich language – consists of ideas that are expanded in structure, extended to include multiple meanings, and modulated in grammar to address the constituent of who, what, where, when, why, and how questions

Schema – a semantic network of the mind that represents an understanding of a multifaceted concept; for example, the idea of "mammal" may be broken down into smaller units of meaning such as "has vertebra," "is an animal," etc.

Scripted curriculum – a curriculum where the teacher is required to follow a script when teaching; this includes questions asked to students and both formal and informal assessments

Semantic relationship – the connection between basic concepts such as agents or people and their actions or objects that may be expressed verbally or nonverbally (For example, a child looks at Mom and then points to the toys indicating a semantic or meaningful relationship between Mom and the toys, and Mom says, "I will pick up the toys")

Semanticity- The ability to acquire depth of meaning in concepts. The depth of meaning occurs through adding layers of meaning

Semiotics – the study of signs and symbols, especially as elements of language, which also includes the value of the signs and symbols

Sensory input – information from the skin, eyes, ears, and motor system

Shared referent – two or more people are able to understand the meaning of an idea through common context or agents, their actions, and their objects within an event

Social – learning to be "social" refers to using appropriate behaviors to initiate and maintain healthy relationships with self and others. This is based on being able to use the typical environmental input for becoming an agent

Social competence – refers to the ability to initiate and maintain healthy positive (pro-social) relationships

Social development – refers to the various levels of conceptual learning and is about how to initiate and maintain healthy relationships with others; the child's ability to fit into a variety of settings, to understand others' perspectives, and to initiate and maintain healthy relationships are all part of socializing (social development stems from the acquisition of meaning about being an agent so as to develop the "self' or concept of "who"); social concepts are learned over time through the use of thinking with language

Social skills – the acquisition of patterns of behavior, but without the underlying conceptual meaning of those skills; skills are acquired through imitation, practice, and reward

Stimulus – an action or condition that causes or provokes a response

Synchrony – the ability of different capacities of the brain to work efficiently together; for example, when information processing in the brain is cross-modulated (eyes + ears)

Synergy – the interaction of two or more agents or forces so that their combined effect is greater than the sum of their individual parts

Task analysis – taking a complex behavior such as reading apart into its smaller units such as letters and sounds

Temporal lobe – a part of the brain that deals with hearing, listening, language, and some memory storage

Time – a property of English represented by a variety of temporal words as well as by the structure of the language and the use of specific ways to assign meaning to referents (use of functors); time is multidirectional in that time can go through a speaker or a speaker can go through time resulting in properties of time allowing for multi-tasking in a culture; time-based languages use temporal properties

Viconic Language Methods (VLMs) – the use of what is known about visual languages imposed upon auditory English so as to help a visual thinker translate visual cognition into auditory English

Viewing – how a person sees others based on his own thinking or past learning about who the person is

Visual features – light and movement as perceived through the visual sensory system

Visual languages – those languages that use field-sensitive contexts for specifying the relationship among people, their actions, objects, and locations, such as Mandarin and Hopi

Visual patterns – vision provides sensory input in light and movement. These light and movement features form patterns from the points of light and edges or shapes of movement also known as visual patterns

Visual thinking – the use of a visual meta-cognition; utilizes the same properties as a relational of visual language

Visual perception – the way a learner organizes sensory input from the eyes in the brain

Words – the unit of English analysis typically consisting of consonant-vowel-consonant combinations; alphabetic in nature; word-based languages like English do not consider the context important in understanding the meaning of a word

Index

References

Adolphs, R. (2009). The social brain: neural basis of social knowledge. *Annual Review of Psychology, 60*, 693-716.

Adrenal fatigue and stress. (2013, October 20). . Retrieved from http://www.womenshealthnetwork.com/adrenal-fatigue-and-stress/the-link-between-stress-and-forgetfulness.aspx

Alant, A. (2003). A developmental approach towards teacher training: A contradiction in terms. In: S. Van Tetzchner & N. Grove (Eds.) *Augmentative and alternative communication: Developmental issues.* London: Whurr, 336-356.

Anderson, J. R. (2010). *Cognitive psychology and its implications* (7th ed.). New York: Worth Publishers.

Arwood, E. L. (1980). *Semantic and pragmatic language disorders : assessment and remediation.* Rockville, Md.: Aspen Systems Corp.

Arwood, E. L. (1983). *Pragmaticism: theory and application.* Rockville, Md.: Aspen.

Arwood, E.L. (1985). *APRICOT I kit.* Portland, OR: APRICOT Inc.

Arwood, E. L. (1991). *Semantic and pragmatic language disorders* (2nd ed.). Gaithersburg, Md.: Aspen Publishers.

Arwood, E. L. (2011). *Language function: an introduction to pragmatic assessment and intervention for higher order thinking and better literacy.* London; Philadelphia: Jessica Kingsley Publishers.

Arwood, E.L. (2014). *Ed 587: Neurobiological aspects of learning.* Neuroeducator Certificate, University of Portland.

Arwood, E.L., & Beggs, M. (1989). *Temporal Analysis of the Propositions (TAPS).* [Test] Portland, OR: APRICOT, Inc.

Arwood, E. L., & Beggs M. (1992). *Temporal analysis of propositions (TemPro).*

Arwood, E.L., & Brown, M. (1999). *A guide to cartooning and flowcharting.* Portland, OR: APRICOT Inc.

Arwood, E.L., & Brown, M. (2001). *A Guide to Visual Strategies for Young Adults.* Portland, OR: APRICOT, Inc.

Arwood, E. L., Brown, M. M., & Kaulitz, C. (2015). *Pro-social language: a way to think about behavior.* Tigard, OR: APRICOT, Inc.

Arwood, E. L., Brown, M. M., & Robb B. (2005). *Make it a visual classroom: I'm in your picture.* Portland, OR: Apricot, Inc.

Arwood, E. L., Kaakinen, J., & Wynne A. L. (2002). *Nurse educators: Using visual language "Learning to see."* Portland, OR: Apricot, Inc.

Arwood, E., & Kaakinen, J. (2008). Visual teaching in an auditory world [DVD]. *Advanced academy for teaching and learning.* Corvallis, OR: Center for Teaching and Learning. Oregon State University.

Arwood, E. L., & Kaulitz, C. (2007). *Learning with a visual brain in an auditory world: visual language strategies for individuals with autism spectrum disorders* (1st edition.). Shawnee Mission, Kan.: APC.

Arwood, E. & Kaulitz, C. (2014). *Why children don't learn words.* Poster submitted for ASHA 2014.

Arwood, E. L., & Kaulitz, C., & Brown, M. M. (2009). *Visual thinking strategies for individuals with autism spectrum disorders: the language of pictures.* Shawnee Mission, Kan.: APC.

Arwood, E.L., Ormson, K., Kaulitz C. & Brown M. (2013, June). Language: Neuro- Auditory Processing of Meaning. *Language function: an introduction to pragmatic assessment and intervention for higher level thinking and better literacy.* Lecture conducted from University of Portland. Portland, OR.

Arwood, E.L., & Unruh, I. (2000). *Event-based learning handbook: A guide to improve student learning.* Portland, OR: Apricot, Inc.

Arwood, E. L., & Young, E. (2000). *The language of respect: the right of each student to participate in an environment of communicative thoughtfulness* (Pbk. ed.). LaVergne, Tenn.: Lightning Print.

Baars, B. J., & Gage, N. M. (2010). Cognition, Brain, and Consciousness: Elsevier BV.

Bandura. A (1965). Behavioral modification through modeling procedures. In L. Ullman & L. Krassner (Eds.) *Case studies in behavior modification* (244-267). New York: Holt, Rinehart & Winston.

Bargh, J. A., & Morsella, E. (2008). The Unconscious Mind. *Perspectives on Psychological Science, 3*(1), 73-79. doi: 10.1111/j.1745-6916.2008.00064.x

Bassett, D. S., Wymbs, N. F., Porter, M. A., Mucha, P. J., Carlson, J. M., & Grafton, S. T. (2011). Dynamic reconfiguration of human brain networks during learning. *Proceedings of the National Academy of Sciences, 108*(18), 7641-7646. doi: 10.1073/pnas.1018985108

Batterink, L., Yokum, S., & Stice, E. (2010). Body mass correlates inversely with inhibitory control in response to food among adolescent girls: an fMRI study. *Neuroimage, 52*(4), 1696-1703. doi: 10.1016/j.neuroimage.2010.05.059

Beaulieu, C., Plewes, C., Paulson, L. A., Roy, D., Snook, L., Concha, L., & Phillips, L. (2005). Imaging brain connectivity in children with diverse reading ability. *Neuroimage, 25*(4), 1266-1271. doi: http://dx.doi.org/10.1016/j.neuroimage.2004.12.053

238

Bechara, A., Damasio, A. R., Damasio, H., & Anderson, S. W. (1994). Insensitivity to future consequences following damage to human prefrontal cortex. *Cognition, 50*(1-3), 7-15. doi: 10.1016/0010-0277(94)90018-3

Bellugi, U., & Fischer, S. (1972). A comparison of sign language and spoken language. *Cognition, 1*(2-3), 173-200. doi: 10.1016/0010-0277(72)90018-2

Blakemore, S.-J., Winston, J., & Frith, U. (2004). Social cognitive neuroscience: where are we heading? *Trends in Cognitive Sciences, 8*(5), 216-222. doi: 10.1016/j.tics.2004.03.012

Blakeslee, S. (2003). How does the brain work? *New York Times.*

Blockberger, S. (2004). Augmentative and alternative communication: developmental issues. London: Whurr Pub. Ltd., 2003. ISBN: 1 86156 331 0. *Journal of Child Language, 31*(3), 745-747. doi: 10.1017/s0305000904226678

Bookheimer, S. (2002). Functional MRI of Language: New Approaches to Understanding the Cortical Organization of Semantic Processing. *Annual Review of Neuroscience, 25*(1), 151-188. doi: 10.1146/annurev.neuro.25.112701.142946

Bookheimer, S. (2004). Overview on learning and memory: Insights from functional brain imaging. *Learning Brain Expo Conference Proceedings.* San Diego, CA: Brain Store.

Brevoort, D. (2012). A guide to neuroeducation for teachers. *1.*

Brice, A.J. & Brice, R.C. (2009) *Language development: Monolingual and bilingual acquisition.* Upper Saddle River, NJ: Pearson.

Brown, M. (2012, 11 15). [Lecture]. Learning, language, and behavior., University of Portland

Brown, M. (2013). Visual cognition strategies. ED 503 - Language and Communication. Lecture, University of Portland

Bruner, J. S. (1975). The ontogenesis of speech acts. *Journal of Child Language, 2*(01). doi: 10.1017/s0305000900000866

Bruner, J. S. (2006). *In search of pedagogy : the selected works of Jerome Bruner, 1957-1978.* New York: Routledge.

Butler, M.C. (2005). *Snow Friends.* Intercourse, PA: Good Books.

Cacioppo, John T.; Berntson, Gary G.(1992). Social psychological contributions to the decade of the brain: Doctrine of multilevel analysis. *American Psychologist, 47*(8), Aug 1992, 1019-1028.

Campbell, R. (2008). The processing of audio-visual speech: empirical and neural bases. *Philosophical Transactions of the Royal Society B: Biological Sciences, 363*(1493), 1001-1010. doi: 10.1098/rstb.2007.2155

Carew, T. J., & Magsamen, S. H. (2010). Neuroscience and Education: An Ideal Partnership for Producing Evidence-Based Solutions to Guide 21st Century Learning. *Neuron, 67*(5), 685-688. doi: 10.1016/j.neuron.2010.08.028

Carroll, J. B. (1964). *Language and thought.* Englewood Cliffs, N.J.,: Prentice-Hall.

Chomsky, N. (1968). *Language and mind.* New York,: Harcourt.

Chomsky, N. (1972). *Studies on semantics in generative grammar.* The Hague,: Mouton.

Chomsky, N. (2013). *Janua linguarum series minor: Studies on semantics in generative grammar.* Tubingen, DEU: Walter de Gruyter. Retrieved from http://www.ebrary.com

Clarke, A., & Tyler, L. K. (2014). Object-Specific Semantic Coding in Human Perirhinal Cortex. *Journal of Neuroscience, 34*(14), 4766-4775. doi: 10.1523/jneurosci.2828-13.2014

Clark, H. H. (1977). *Psychology and language : an introduction to psycholinguistics.* New York: Harcourt Brace Jovanovich.

Cohen, A. D. (2003). The learner's side of foreign language learning: Where do styles, strategies, and tasks meet?. *International Review of Applied Linguistics in Language Teaching, 41*(4), 279-281.

Coleman, M. & Webber, J. (2002). *Emotional and behavioral disorders: Theory and Practice.* (4th ed.). Boston: Allyn & Bacon.

Cooper, M., Todd, G., & Wells, A. (2008). *Treating bulimia nervosa and binge eating: An integrated metacognitive and cognitive therapy manual.* Routledge.

Cooper, J. D., & Kiger, N. D. (2006). *Literacy : helping children construct meaning* (6th ed.). Boston: Houghton Mifflin Co.

Cummins, J., & Swain, M. (1986). *Bilingualism in education : aspects of theory, research, and practice.* London ; New York: Longman.

Curzan, A. (2014). 20 words that once meant something very different. *We Humans.*

Damasio, A. (2003). Mental self: The person within. *Nature, 423*(6937), 227-227. doi: 10.1038/423227a

Damasio, A. R., & Geschwind, N. (1984). The Neural Basis of Language. *Annual Review of Neuroscience, 7*(1), 127-147. doi: 10.1146/annurev.ne.07.030184.001015

de Waal, F. B. M. (2008). Putting the Altruism Back into Altruism: The Evolution of Empathy. *Annual Review of Psychology, 59*(1), 279-300. doi: 10.1146/annurev.psych.59.103006.093625

Dehaene, S., Piazza, M., Pinel, P., & Cohen, L. (2003). Three parietal circuits for number processing. *Cognitive Neuropsychology, 20*(3-6), 487-506. doi: 10.1080/02643290244000239

Dettmer, S., Simpson, R. L., Myles, B. S., & Ganz, J. B. (2000). The Use of Visual Supports to Facilitate Transitions of Students with Autism. *Focus on Autism and Other Developmental Disabilities, 15*(3), 163-169. doi: 10.1177/108835760001500307

Dewey, J. (1910). *How we think.* Boston,: D.C. Heath & Co.

Diaz-Rico, L.T., & Weed, K.Z. (2010). *The crosscultural, language, and academic development handbook.* Boston: Pearson Education.

Dickinson, D. K., McCabe, A., Anastasopoulos, L., Peisner-Feinberg, E. S., & Poe, M. D. (2003). The comprehensive language approach to early literacy: The interrelationships among vocabulary, phonological sensitivity, and print knowledge among preschool-aged children. *Journal of Educational Psychology, 95*(3), 465-481. doi: 10.1037/0022-0663.95.3.465

Dickinson, D. K., & Porche, M. V. (2011). Relation Between Language Experiences in Preschool Classrooms and Children's Kindergarten and Fourth-Grade Language and Reading Abilities. *Child Development, 82*(3), 870-886. doi: 10.1111/j.1467-8624.2011.01576.x

Dickinson, D. K., & Tabors, P. O. (2003). Fostering language and literacy in classrooms and homes. *Young Children, 57*(2), 4-12.

Doidge, N. (2007). *The brain that changes itself : stories of personal triumph from the frontiers of brain science.* New York: Viking.

Dore, J. (1975). Holophrases, speech acts and language universals. *Journal of Child Language, 2*(01). doi: 10.1017/s0305000900000878

Dore, J., & McDermott, R. P. (1982). Linguistic Indeterminacy and Social Context in Utterance Interpretation. *Language, 58*(2), 374. doi: 10.2307/414103

Eagleman, D. (Writer). (2015). The Brain With David Eagleman: PBS.

Eden, G. F., & Moats, L. (2002). The role of neuroscience in the remediation of students with dyslexia. *Nature Reviews Neuroscience, 5*(Supp), 1080-1084. doi: 10.1038/nn946

Ehri, L. C., & Wilce, L. S. (1985). Movement into Reading: Is the First Stage of Printed Word Learning Visual or Phonetic? *Reading Research Quarterly, 20*(2), 163. doi: 10.2307/747753

Eysenck, Michael W. 2000, Psychology: A Student's Handbook Taylor & Francis, p. 24

Farber, J. G., & Klein, E. R. (1999). Classroom-Based Assessment of a Collaborative Intervention Program With Kindergarten and First-Grade Students. *Language Speech and Hearing Services in Schools, 30*(1), 83. doi: 10.1044/0161-1461.3001.83

Fischer, K. W. (2009). Mind, Brain, and Education: Building a Scientific Groundwork for Learning and Teaching. *Mind, Brain, and Education, 3*(1), 3-16. doi: 10.1111/j.1751-228x.2008.01048.x

Fischer, K. W., Daniel, D. B., Immordino-Yang, M. H., Stern, E., Battro, A., & Koizumi, H. (2007). Why Mind, Brain, and Education? Why Now? *Mind, Brain, and Education, 1*(1), 1-2. doi: 10.1111/j.1751-228x.2007.00006.x

Fischer, K. W., Goswami, U., & Geake, J. (2010). The Future of Educational Neuroscience. *Mind, Brain, and Education, 4*(2), 68-80. doi: 10.1111/j.1751-228x.2010.01086.x

Fischer, S. R. (1999). *A History of Language.* Reaktion Books. Pp. 26-28. ISBN-1-86189-080-X

Fodor JA. 1983 The modularity of mind. Cambridge, MA: MIT Press

Forster, P. (2011). *Peirce and the threat of nominalism.* Cambridge ; New York: Cambridge University Press.

Foster, C. (2013). Resisting reductionism in mathematics pedagogy. *Curriculum Journal, 24*(4), 563-585. doi: 10.1080/09585176.2013.828630

Freeman, J. B., Rule, N. O., & Ambady, N. (2009). The cultural neuroscience of person perception *Progress in Brain Research* (pp. 191-201): Elsevier BV.

Frey, N., & Fisher, D. (2010). Reading and the Brain: What Early Childhood Educators Need to Know. *Early Childhood Education Journal, 38*(2), 103-110. doi: 10.1007/s10643-010-0387-z

Frith, C. D. (2007). The social brain? *Philosophical Transactions of the Royal Society B: Biological Sciences, 362*(1480), 671-678. doi: 10.1098/rstb.2006.2003

Frith, U., & Frith, C. D. (2003). Development and neurophysiology of mentalizing. *Philosophical Transactions of the Royal Society B: Biological Sciences, 358*(1431), 459-473. doi: 10.1098/rstb.2002.1218

Fuster, J. M., Bodner, M., & Kroger, J. K. (2000). Cross-modal and cross-temporal association in neurons of frontal cortex. *Nature, 405*(6784), 347-351.

Gainotti, G., Ciaraffa, F., Silveri, M. C., & Marra, C. (2009). Mental representation of normal subjects about the sources of knowledge in different semantic categories and unique entities. *Neuropsychology, 23*(6), 803-812. doi: 10.1037/a0016352

Gallese, V. (2003). The manifold nature of interpersonal relations: the quest for a common mechanism. *Philosophical Transactions of the Royal Society B: Biological Sciences, 358*(1431), 517-528. doi: 10.1098/rstb.2002.1234

Gallese, V., & Lakoff, G. (2005). The Brain's concepts: the role of the Sensory-motor system in conceptual knowledge. *Cognitive Neuropsychology, 22*(3-4), 455-479. doi: 10.1080/02643290442000310

Gallistel, C. R., & Matzel, L. D. (2013). The Neuroscience of Learning: Beyond the Hebbian Synapse. *Annual Review of Psychology, 64*(1), 169-200. doi: 10.1146/annurev-psych-113011-143807

Gardner, R., Cihon, T. M., Morrison, D., & Paul, P. (2013). Implementing Visual Phonics With Hearing Kindergarteners At Risk for Reading Failure. *Preventing School Failure: Alternative Education for Children and Youth, 57*(1), 30-42. doi: 10.1080/1045988x.2011.654365

Geake, J. (2004). How children's brains think: Not left or right but both together. *Education 3-13, 32*(3), 65-72. doi: 10.1080/03004270485200351

Ghazanfar, A., & Schroeder, C. (2006). Is neocortex essentially multisensory? *Trends in Cognitive Sciences, 10*(6), 278-285. doi: 10.1016/j.tics.2006.04.008

Gibson, J. J. (2014). *The ecological approach to visual perception: classic edition*: Psychology Press.

Gilbert, T. (2015, July 17). *Advancing Neuroscience with Allen Institute Resources.* Lecture presented at OHSU Neurofutures in Oregon, Portland.

Goetzmann, L., & Schwegler, K. (2010). On the formation of figurative representations: An integrative psychoanalytic-neurobiological framework. *Bulletin of the Menninger Clinic, 74*(3), 187-205. doi: 10.1521/bumc.2010.74.3.187

Goodman, K. S. (1967). Reading: A psycholinguistic guessing game. *Journal of the Reading Specialist, 6*(4), 126-135. doi: 10.1080/19388076709556976

Goswami, U. (2006). Neuroscience and education: from research to practice? *Nature Reviews Neuroscience, 7*(5), 406-413. doi: 10.1038/nrn1907

Grandin, T. & Panek, R. (2013). *The Autistic Brain: Thinking Across the Spectrum.* New York, NY: Houghton Mifflin Harcourt.

Greenberg, G. (2013). *The book of woe : the DSM and the unmaking of psychiatry.*

Green-Mitchell, A. (2016). An Investigation of Language Acquisition as an Antecedent to Pro-Social Development for Secondary Students at Risk for Behavior Disorders. *University of Portland - Pilot Scholars.*

Grezes, J., & Decety, J. (2000). Functional anatomy of execution, mental simulation, observation, and verb generation of actions: A meta-analysis. *Human Brain Mapping, 12*(1), 1-19. doi: 10.1002/1097-0193(200101)12:1<1::aid-hbm10>3.0.co;2-v

Gross, J., Hayne, H., & Drury, T. (2009). Drawing facilitates children's reports of factual and narrative information: implications for educational contexts. *Applied Cognitive Psychology, 23*(7), 953-971. doi: 10.1002/acp.1518

Halliday, M. A. K. (1977). *Learning how to mean : explorations in the development of language.* New York: Elsevier.

Hargreaves, I. S., Pexman, P. M., Johnson, J. C., & Zdrazilova, L. (2012). Richer concepts are better remembered: number of features effects in free recall. *Frontiers in Human Neuroscience, 6.* doi: 10.3389/fnhum.2012.00073

Hebb, D. O. (1949). *The organization of behavior: A neuropsychological approach*: John Wiley & Sons.

Hickmann, M. (2000). Linguistic relativity and linguistic determinism: some new directions. *Linguistics, 38*(2). doi: 10.1515/ling.38.2.409

Hoffmeister, R. J., & Caldwell-Harris, C. L. (2014). Acquiring English as a second language via print: The task for deaf children. *Cognition, 132*(2), 229-242. doi: 10.1016/j.cognition.2014.03.014

Humbach, N., Valesco, S.M., Chiquito, A.B., Smith, S. & McMinn, J. (2006). *Teacher's Edition Holt Spanish I: ¡Exprésate!* Austin, Texas: Holt, Rinehart & Winston.

Insel, T. (2013). *Mental Disorders as Brain Disorders*: Thomas Insel at TEDxCaltech USA: TEDx.

Iturria-Medina, Y., Sotero, R. C., Canales-Rodríguez, E. J., Alemán-Gómez, Y., & Melie-García, L. (2008). Studying the human brain anatomical network via diffusion-weighted MRI and Graph Theory. *Neuroimage, 40*(3), 1064-1076. doi: 10.1016/j.neuroimage.2007.10.060

Jernigan, T. L., Trauner, D. A., Hesselink, J. R., & Tallal, P. A. (1991). Maturation of human cerebrum observed during adolescence. *Brain, 114*(5), 2037-2049. doi: 10.1093/brain/114.5.2037

Jobrack, B. (2011). *Tyranny of the textbook: An insider exposes how educational materials undermine reforms*: Rowman & Littlefield Publishers.

Johnson-Glenberg, M. C. (2000). Training reading comprehension in adequate decoders/poor comprehenders: Verbal versus visual strategies. *Journal of Educational Psychology, 92*(4), 772-782. doi: 10.1037//0022-0663.92.4.772

Kaulitz, C. (2016). *Learn to "See" How to Fit-in: Pro-Social Strategies to Decrease and/or Prevent Mental Health Issues*. New Orleans, LA: Autism Society.

Kiefer, M., & Pulvermüller, F. (2012). Conceptual representations in mind and brain: Theoretical developments, current evidence and future directions. *Cortex, 48*(7), 805-825. doi: 10.1016/j.cortex.2011.04.006

Kitayama, S., & Park, J. (2010). Cultural neuroscience of the self: understanding the social grounding of the brain. *Social cognitive and affective neuroscience, 5*(2-3), 111-129.

Klemen, J., & Chambers, C. D. (2012). Current perspectives and methods in studying neural mechanisms of multisensory interactions. *Neuroscience & Biobehavioral Reviews, 36*(1), 111-133. doi: 10.1016/j.neubiorev.2011.04.015

Kosslyn, S. M. (1994). *Image and brain : the resolution of the imagery debate*. Cambridge, Mass.: MIT Press.

Lakoff, G. (1969). On generative semantics. In Danny Steinberg & Leon Jakobovits (eds.), *Semantics – An interdisciplinary reader in philosophy, linguistics, anthropology and psychology*. London: Cambridge University Press.

Lenneberg, E. H. (1962). The relationship of language to the formation of concepts. *Synthese, 14*(2-3), 103-109. doi: 10.1007/bf00881988

Levine, M. (2000). *A mind at a time.* New York: Simon & Schuster.

Leyden, J., Stackhouse, J., & Szczerbinski, M. (2011). Implementing a whole school approach to support speech, language and communication: Perceptions of key staff. *Child Language Teaching and Therapy, 27*(2), 203-222. doi: 10.1177/0265659011398375

Linden, D. E. J. (2007). The Working Memory Networks of the Human Brain. *The Neuroscientist, 13*(3), 257-267. doi: 10.1177/1073858406298480

Lonigan, C. J., Allan, N. P., & Lerner, M. D. (2011). Assessment of preschool early literacy skills: Linking children's educational needs with empirically supported instructional activities. *Psychology in the Schools, 48*(5), 488-501. doi: 10.1002/pits.20569

Lupien, S. J., McEwen, B. S., Gunnar, M. R., & Heim, C. (2009). Effects of stress throughout the lifespan on the brain, behaviour and cognition. *Nature Reviews Neuroscience, 10*(6), 434-445. doi: 10.1038/nrn2639

Mascolo, M., & Fischer, K. (2003). Beyond the nature-nurture divide in development and evolution. *PsycCRITIQUES, 48*(6). doi: 10.1037/000995

Mash, E., & Wolfe, D. (2012). *Abnormal child psychology*: Cengage Learning.

Matson, J. L., Turygin, N. C., Beighley, J., Rieske, R., Tureck, K., & Matson, M. L. (2012). Applied behavior analysis in Autism Spectrum Disorders: Recent developments, strengths, and pitfalls. *Research in Autism Spectrum Disorders, 6*(1), 144-150. doi: 10.1016/j.rasd.2011.03.014

Mazard, A., Laou, L., Joliot, M., & Mellet, E. (2005). Neural impact of the semantic content of visual mental images and visual percepts. *Cognitive Brain Research, 24*(3), 423-435. doi: 10.1016/j.cogbrainres.2005.02.018

McCawley, J. D. (1976). *Grammar and meaning : papers on syntactic and semantic topics* (Corr. ed.). New York: Academic Press.

McEwen, B. S. (2007). Physiology and Neurobiology of Stress and Adaptation: Central Role of the Brain. *Physiological Reviews, 87*(3), 873-904. doi: 10.1152/physrev.00041.2006

McRae, K., & Cree, G. S. (2002). Factors underlying category-specific semantic deficits. *Category-specificity in brain and mind*, 211-249.

Mead, G. H. (1934). *Mind, self and society* (Vol. 111): Chicago University of Chicago Press.

Meadan, H., Ostrosky, M. M., Triplett, B., Michna, A., & Fettig, A. (2011). Using Visual Supports with Young Children with Autism Spectrum Disorder. *TEACHING Exceptional Children, 43*(6), 28-35. doi: 10.1177/004005991104300603

Merrell, F. (2001). Charles Sanders Peirce's concept of the sign. In P. Cobley(Eds.), *The Routledge Companion to semiotics and linguistics*(pp. 28-39). London: Routledge.

Miller, G. (2011). Sweet Here, Salty There: Evidence for a Taste Map in the Mammalian Brain. *Science, 333*(6047), 1213-1213. doi: 10.1126/science.333.6047.1213

Muter, V., Hulme, C., Snowling, M. J., & Stevenson, J. (2004). Phonemes, Rimes, Vocabulary, and Grammatical Skills as Foundations of Early Reading Development: Evidence From a Longitudinal Study. *Developmental Psychology, 40*(5), 665-681. doi: 10.1037/0012-1649.40.5.665

Organisation for Economic Co-Operation and Development. (2002). *Understanding the brain: Towards a new learning science.* Paris: OECD.

Overton, T. (2012). *Assessing learners with special needs : an applied approach* (Seventh ed.). Upper Saddle River, New Jersey: Pearson Education.

Pallis, C. (1983). Whole-brain death reconsidered--physiological facts and philosophy. *Journal of Medical Ethics, 9*(1), 32-37. doi: 10.1136/jme.9.1.32

Peirce, C. S. (1878). How to make our ideas clear.

Peirce, C. S. (1902). Logic as semiotic: The theory of signs.

Peirce, C. S., & Moore, E. C. (1972). *Charles S. Peirce: the essential writings.* New York,: Harper & Row.

Phillips, R. D., Gorton, R. L., Pinciotti, P., & Sachdev, A. (2010). Promising Findings on Preschoolers' Emergent Literacy and School Readiness In Arts-integrated Early Childhood Settings. *Early Childhood Education Journal, 38*(2), 111-122. doi: 10.1007/s10643-010-0397-x

Piaget, J. (1952). (translated by M. Cook). *The origins of intelligence in children.* New York, NY: International Universities Press Inc.

Piaget, J. (1959). *The language and thought of the child* (3d ed.). New York,: Humanities Press.

Piaget, J. (1970). *Science of education and the psychology of the child.* New York,: Orion Press.

Piñar, P., Dussias, P. E., & Morford, J. P. (2011). Deaf Readers as Bilinguals: An Examination of Deaf Readers' Print Comprehension in Light of Current Advances in Bilingualism and Second Language Processing. *Language and Linguistics Compass, 5*(10), 691-704. doi: 10.1111/j.1749-818x.2011.00307.x

Pinker, S. (1995). *The language instinct: The new science of language and mind* (Vol. 7529): Penguin UK.

Poeppel, D., Emmorey, K., Hickok, G., & Pylkkanen, L. (2012). Towards a New Neurobiology of Language. *Journal of Neuroscience, 32*(41), 14125-14131. doi: 10.1523/jneurosci.3244-12.2012

Poldrack, R. A., Wagner, A. D., Prull, M. W., Desmond, J. E., Glover, G. H., & Gabrieli, J. D. E. (1999). Functional Specialization for Semantic and Phonological Processing in the Left Inferior Prefrontal Cortex. *Neuroimage, 10*(1), 15-35. doi: 10.1006/nimg.1999.0441

Posner, M. I., & Rothbart, M. K. (2001). Brain Development, Ontogenetic Neurobiology of *International Encyclopedia of the Social & Behavioral Sciences* (pp. 1332-1338): Elsevier BV.

Potter, M. C. (2012). Conceptual Short Term Memory in Perception and Thought. *Frontiers in Psychology, 3*. doi: 10.3389/fpsyg.2012.00113

Poulson, M. (2016, 10 15). [Lecture]. Functional Assessment: Curriculum and Instruction for Diverse Learners., University of Portland

Pulvermuller, F. (2003). *The Neuroscience of Language*: Cambridge University Press (CUP).

Pulvermüller, F. (2005). Opinion: Brain mechanisms linking language and action. *Nature Reviews Neuroscience, 6*(7), 576-582. doi: 10.1038/nrn1706

Pulvermüller, F. (2010). Brain embodiment of syntax and grammar: Discrete combinatorial mechanisms spelt out in neuronal circuits. *Brain and Language, 112*(3), 167-179. doi: 10.1016/j.bandl.2009.08.002

Pulvermüller, F. (2012). Meaning and the brain: The neurosemantics of referential, interactive, and combinatorial knowledge. *Journal of Neurolinguistics, 25*(5), 423-459. doi: 10.1016/j.jneuroling.2011.03.004

Pulvermüller, F. (2013). How neurons make meaning: brain mechanisms for embodied and abstract-symbolic semantics. *Trends in Cognitive Sciences, 17*(9), 458-470. doi: 10.1016/j.tics.2013.06.004

Pulvermüller, F. (2013). Semantic embodiment, disembodiment or misembodiment? In search of meaning in modules and neuron circuits. *Brain and Language, 127*(1), 86-103. doi: 10.1016/j.bandl.2013.05.015

Pulvermüller, F., Shtyrov, Y., Ilmoniemi, R. J., & Marslen-Wilson, W. D. (2006). Tracking speech comprehension in space and time. *Neuroimage, 31*(3), 1297-1305. doi: 10.1016/j.neuroimage.2006.01.030

Quillian, M.R. (1966). *Semantic Memory*. Cambridge, MA: Bolt, Beranak and Newman.

Reutzel, D. R., Oda, L., & Moore, B. (1989). Developing print awareness: The effect of three instructional approaches on kindergarteners' print awareness, reading readiness, and word reading. *Journal of Literacy Research, 21*(3), 197-217. doi: 10.1080/10862968909547673

Robb, B. (2016). *A Paradigm Shift in Classroom Learning Practices to Propose Methods Aligned with a Neuroeducation Conceptual Framework.* (ED.D.), University of Portland, Pilot Scholars.

Sadato, N. (1996, July). Breakthroughs. *Discover,* 27-28.

Sage, J. (2010). *Mind, Brain, and Consciousness.* : CreateSpace Independent Publishing Platform.

Saussure, F. d. (1959). *Course in general linguistics*. New York,: Philosophical Library.

Skinner, B. F. (1953). *Science and human behavior.* New York,: Macmillan.

Smilkstein, R. (2003). *We're born to learn : using the brain's natural learning process to create today's curriculum.* Thousand Oaks, Calif.: Corwin Press.

Smith, F., & Goodman, K. S. (2008). "On the psycholinguistic method of teaching reading" revisited. *Language Arts, 86*(1), 61-65.

Soundy, C. S., & Qiu, Y. (2006). Portraits of Picture Power: American and Chinese Children Explore Literacy through the Visual Arts. *Childhood Education, 83*(2), 68-74. doi: 10.1080/00094056.2007.10522883

Sowell, E. R., Peterson, B. S., Thompson, P. M., Welcome, S. E., Henkenius, A. L., & Toga, A. W. (2003). Mapping cortical change across the human life span. *Nature Neuroscience, 6*(3), 309-315. doi: 10.1038/nn1008

Speer, N. K., Reynolds, J. R., Swallow, K. M., & Zacks, J. M. (2009). Reading Stories Activates Neural Representations of Visual and Motor Experiences. *Psychological Science, 20*(8), 989-999. doi: 10.1111/j.1467-9280.2009.02397.x

Squire, L. R. (1987). *Memory and brain.* New York: Oxford University Press.

Stevenson, R. A., VanDerKlok, R. M., Pisoni, D. B., & James, T. W. (2011). Discrete neural substrates underlie complementary audiovisual speech integration processes. *Neuroimage, 55*(3), 1339-1345. doi: 10.1016/j.neuroimage.2010.12.063

Tallal, P., Merzenich, M., Miller, S., & Jenkins, W. (1998). Language learning impairment: Integrating research and remediation. *Scandinavian Journal of Psychology, 39*(3), 197-199. doi: 10.1111/1467-9450.393079

Tokuhama-Espinosa, T. Dissertation at Capella University 2008. UMI Microform: 3310716 ProQuest, Ann Arbor, Michigan. *(The Scientifically Substantiated Art of Teaching: A Study In The Development Of Standards In The New Academic Field Of Neuroeducation)*

Tokuhama-Espinosa, T. (2010). *The New Science of Teaching and Learning: Using the Best of Mind, Brain, and Education Science in the Classroom.* Teachers College Press. NY.

Tokuhama-Espinosa, T. (2011). *Mind, brain, and education science: A comprehensive guide to the new brain-based teaching*: WW Norton & Company.

Tranel, D., Logan, C. G., Frank, R. J., & Damasio, A. R. (1997). Explaining category-related effects in the retrieval of conceptual and lexical knowledge for concrete entities: operationalization and analysis of factors. *Neuropsychologia, 35*(10), 1329-1339. doi: 10.1016/s0028-3932(97)00086-9

Ukrainetz, T. A., & Blomquist, C. (2002). The criterion validity of four vocabulary tests compared with a language sample. *Child Language Teaching and Therapy, 18*(1), 59-78. doi: 10.1191/0265659002ct227oa

Valli, C., Lucas, C., & Mulrooney, K. J. (2006).*Linguistics of american sign language, an introduction.* (4th ed.). Washington DC: Gallaudet University Press.

Varma, S., McCandliss, B. D., & Schwartz, D. L. (2008). Scientific and Pragmatic Challenges for Bridging Education and Neuroscience. *Educational Researcher, 37*(3), 140-152. doi: 10.3102/0013189x08317687

Vellutino, F. R., Tunmer, W. E., Jaccard, J. J., & Chen, R. (2007). Components of Reading Ability: Multivariate Evidence for a Convergent Skills Model of Reading Development. *Scientific Studies of Reading, 11*(1), 3-32. doi: 10.1207/s1532799xssr1101_2

Vygotsky, L. S. (1962). *Thought and language.* Cambridge, M.I.T. Press, Massachusetts Institute of Technology.

Wallman, J. (1992). *Aping language.* Cambridge ; New York: Cambridge University Press.

Wang, A. Y., & Thomas, M. H. (1992). The Effect of Imagery-Based Mnemonics on the Long-Term Retention of Chinese Characters. *Language Learning, 42*(3), 359-376. doi: 10.1111/j.1467-1770.1992.tb01340.x

Warrington, E. K., & Shallice, T. (1984). Category specific semantic impairments. *Brain, 107*(3), 829-853. doi: 10.1093/brain/107.3.829

Watson, L. R., Layton, T. L., Pierce, P. L., & Abraham, L. M. (1994). Enhancing Emerging Literacy in a Language Preschool. *Language Speech and Hearing Services in Schools, 25*(3), 136. doi: 10.1044/0161-1461.2503.136

Wellington, W., & Stackhouse, J. (2011). Using visual support for language and learning in children with SLCN: A training programme for teachers and teaching assistants. *Child Language Teaching and Therapy, 27*(2), 183-201. doi: 10.1177/0265659011398282

Wellman, H. M. (2014). *Making minds : how theory of mind develops.*

Whitehurst, G.J. & Lonigan, (2010). *Get ready to read! Revised.* PsychCorp, Pearson: San Antonio, TX.

Willsher, K. (2015, July 21). The French Scrabble champion who doesn't speak French. *The Guardian.* Retrieved from https://www.theguardian.com/lifeandstyle/2015/jul/21/new-french-scrabble-champion-nigel-richards-doesnt-speak-french

Winner, M. G. (2007). *Thinking about you, thinking about me* (2nd ed.). San Jose, CA: Think Social Publishing Inc.

Wolf, M., O'Rourke, A. G., Gidney, C., Lovett, M., Cirino, P., & Morris, R. (2002). The second deficit: An investigation of phonological and naming-speed deficits in developmental dyslexia. *Reading and Writing, 15*(1/2), 43-72. doi: 10.1023/a:1013816320290

Wolfe, P. (2006). Brain-compatible learning: Fad or foundation? Neuroscience points to better strategies for educators, but sorting out claims on brain-based programs is essential. *School administrator, 63*(11), 10-16.

Woollams, A. M. (2012). Apples are not the only fruit: the effects of concept typicality on semantic representation in the anterior temporal lobe. *Frontiers in Human Neuroscience, 6*. doi: 10.3389/fnhum.2012.00085

Xiang-Lam, C. (2016). *Investigating Semantic Alignment in Character Learning of Chinese as a Foreign Language: The Use and Effect of the Imagery Based Encoding Strategy.* (ED.D.), University of Portland, Pilot Scholars.

Yap, M. J., Pexman, P. M., Wellsby, M., Hargreaves, I. S., & Huff, M. J. (2012). An Abundance of Riches: Cross-Task Comparisons of Semantic Richness Effects in Visual Word Recognition. *Frontiers in Human Neuroscience, 6*. doi: 10.3389/fnhum.2012.00072

Yee, E., Chrysikou, E. G., & Thompson-Schill, S. L. (2014). Semantic memory. In K. N. Ochsner, S. M. Kosslyn, K. N. Ochsner, S. M. Kosslyn (Eds.), *The Oxford handbook of cognitive neuroscience, Vol. 1: Core topics* (pp. 353-374). New York, NY, US: Oxford University Press.

Zimmer, C. (2014, February). Secrets of the Brain. *National Geographic.* doi: http://ngm.nationalgeographic.com/2014/02/brain/zimmer-text

Zucker, T. A., Justice, L. M., & Piasta, S. B. (2009). Prekindergarten Teachers' Verbal References to Print During Classroom-Based, Large-Group Shared Reading. *Language Speech and Hearing Services in Schools, 40*(4), 376. doi: 10.1044/0161-1461(2009/08-0059)

CPSIA information can be obtained
at www.ICGtesting.com
Printed in the USA
FFOW01n2212070517
35367FF